DANTE'S
Commedia

THEOLOGY AS POETRY

THE WILLIAM AND KATHERINE DEVERS SERIES IN DANTE STUDIES

Theodore J. Cachey, Jr., and Christian Moevs, editors
Simone Marchesi, associate editor | Ilaria Marchesi, assistant editor

---

VOLUME 10
Petrarch and Dante: Anti-Dantism, Metaphysics, Tradition
edited by Zygmunt G. Barański and Theodore J. Cachey, Jr.

VOLUME 9
The Ancient Flame: Dante and the Poets
Winthrop Wetherbee

VOLUME 8
Accounting for Dante: Urban Readers and Writers in Late Medieval Italy
Justin Steinberg

VOLUME 7
Experiencing the Afterlife: Soul and Body in Dante and Medieval Culture
Manuele Gragnolati

VOLUME 6
Understanding Dante
John A. Scott

VOLUME 5
Dante and the Grammar of the Nursing Body
Gary P. Cestaro

VOLUME 4
The Fiore *and the* Detto d'Amore: *A Late 13th-Century Italian Translation of the* Roman de la Rose, *attributable to Dante*
Translated, with introduction and notes,
by Santa Casciani and Christopher Kleinhenz

VOLUME 3
The Design in the Wax: The Structure of the Divine Comedy *and Its Meaning*
Marc Cogan

VOLUME 2
The Fiore *in Context: Dante, France, Tuscany*
edited by Zygmunt G. Barański and Patrick Boyde

VOLUME 1
Dante Now: Current Trends in Dante Studies
edited by Theodore J. Cachey, Jr.

DANTE'S
Commedia

THEOLOGY AS POETRY

edited by
VITTORIO MONTEMAGGI
and
MATTHEW TREHERNE

University of Notre Dame Press
Notre Dame, Indiana

University of Notre Dame Press
Notre Dame, Indiana 46556
www.undpress.nd.edu

All Rights Reserved

Copyright © 2010 by University of Notre Dame
Published in the United States of America

Library of Congress Cataloging-in-Publication Data

Dante's Commedia : theology as poetry /
Vittorio Montemaggi and Matthew Treherne, editors.
p. cm. — (The William and Katherine Devers series in Dante studies)
Includes bibliographical references and index.
ISBN-13: 978-0-268-03519-8 (pbk. : alk. paper)
ISBN-10: 0-268-03519-9 (pbk. : alk. paper)
1. Dante Alighieri, 1265–1321. Divina commedia.
2. Dante Alighieri, 1265–1321—Religion. 3. Theology in literature.
I. Montemaggi, Vittorio. II. Treherne, Matthew.
PQ4416.D39 2010
851'.1—dc22

2009053254

∞ *The paper in this book meets the guidelines for permanence and durability of the Committee on Production Guidelines for Book Longevity of the Council on Library Resources*

CONTENTS

About the William and Katherine Devers Series   vii
Acknowledgments   ix
Abbreviations, Editions, and Translations   xi

Introduction: Dante, Poetry, Theology   1
Vittorio Montemaggi and Matthew Treherne

1
Polemics of Praise: Theology as Text, Narrative, and Rhetoric in Dante's *Commedia*   14
Robin Kirkpatrick

2
All Smiles: Poetry and Theology in Dante's *Commedia*   36
Peter S. Hawkins

3
In Unknowability as Love: The Theology of Dante's *Commedia*   60
Vittorio Montemaggi

4
The Poetry and Poetics of the Creation   95
Piero Boitani

5
Liturgical Personhood: Creation, Penitence, and Praise in the *Commedia*   131
Matthew Treherne

6
Dante's *Commedia* and the Body of Christ   161
Oliver Davies

7
Dante's Davidic Journey: From Sinner to God's Scribe   180
Theresa Federici

8
Caritas and Ecclesiology in Dante's Heaven of the Sun   210
Paola Nasti

9
Neoplatonic Metaphysics and Imagination in Dante's *Commedia*   245
Douglas Hedley

10
"Il punto che mi vinse": Incarnation, Revelation, and Self-Knowledge in Dante's *Commedia*   267
Christian Moevs

11
How to Do Things with Words: Poetry as Sacrament in Dante's *Commedia*   286
Denys Turner

AFTERWORDS

Dante, Conversation, and Homecoming   308
John Took

Dante as Inspiration for Twenty-First-Century Theology   318
David F. Ford

Bibliography   329
Notes on Contributors   356
Index of Names and Subjects   358
Index of Passages from Dante's Works   380
Index of Scriptural Passages   387

ABOUT THE WILLIAM
AND KATHERINE DEVERS
SERIES IN DANTE STUDIES

The William and Katherine Devers Program in Dante Studies at the University of Notre Dame supports rare book acquisitions in the university's John A. Zahm Dante collections, funds an annual visiting professorship in Dante studies, and supports electronic and print publication of scholarly research in the field. In collaboration with the Medieval Institute at the university, the Devers program has initiated a series dedicated to the publication of the most significant current scholarship in the field of Dante Studies.

In keeping with the spirit that inspired the creation of the Devers program, the series takes Dante as a focal point that draws together the many disciplines and lines of inquiry that constitute a cultural tradition without fixed boundaries. Accordingly, the series hopes to illuminate Dante's position at the center of contemporary critical debates in the humanities by reflecting both the highest quality of scholarly achievement and the greatest diversity of critical perspectives.

The series publishes works on Dante from a wide variety of disciplinary viewpoints and in diverse scholarly genres, including critical studies, commentaries, editions, translations, and conference proceedings of exceptional importance. The series is supervised by an international advisory board composed of distinguished Dante scholars and is published regularly by the University of Notre Dame Press. The Dolphin and Anchor device that appears on publications of the Devers series was used by the great humanist, grammarian, editor, and typographer Aldus Manutius (1449–1515), in whose 1502 edition of Dante (second issue) and all subsequent editions it appeared. The device illustrates the ancient proverb Festina lente, "Hurry up slowly."

Theodore J. Cachey, Jr., and Christian Moevs, *editors*

Advisory Board

Albert Russell Ascoli, Berkeley
Zygmunt G. Barański, Cambridge
Teodolinda Barolini, Columbia
Piero Boitani, Rome
Patrick Boyde, Cambridge
Alison Cornish, Michigan
Christopher Kleinhenz, Wisconsin
Giuseppe Mazzotta, Yale
Lino Pertile, Harvard
† Michelangelo Picone, Zurich
John A. Scott, Western Australia
† Tibor Wlassics, Virginia

ACKNOWLEDGMENTS

We express our sincere gratitude to the friends, colleagues, and institutions who in different ways have supported *Dante's "Commedia": Theology as Poetry*.

In particular, we acknowledge the generous financial support received from the Burney Fund of the Faculty of Divinity and from the Department of Italian of the University of Cambridge for the conference on which the present volume is based. We are intensely grateful to the Faculty of Divinity and the Department of Italian for their continued support throughout the project as a whole. We are likewise grateful to Robinson College, Cambridge—especially the Warden, David Yates, Mary Fuller and the conference office, and the College staff—for providing a congenial environment for the project's initial stages and for the conference. Special thanks are also due to Gillian Burrows, Ravit Capauner, Carlo Cogliati, Dee, Rosalind Paul, and Alessia Ronchetti for their invaluable help in the organization and running of the conference,

Vital impetus for the present volume was provided both by the papers presented at the conference and by the formal and informal conversations that took place throughout the conference. We are immensely grateful to all those who took part and who contributed to the creation of an illuminating setting for discussion. We also give warm thanks to Theodore J. Cachey Jr., Christian Moevs, and the William and Katherine Devers Program in Dante Studies at the University of Notre Dame for accepting this volume in the Devers Series in Dante Studies; and to Barbara Hanrahan and the staff at the University of Notre Dame Press for their generous and professional support throughout the publication process.

Preparation of this volume would not have been possible without the support of Churchill College, Cambridge, the Department of Italian, University of Leeds, or the College of Arts and Letters and the Department of Romance Languages and Literatures, University of Notre Dame, nor without the advice of Zygmunt Barański, Claire Honess, Alan O'Leary, and Janet Martin Soskice. It would also not have been possible without the kindness and patience of Florencia Cano and Victoria Treherne.

Our greatest debt is owed to Robin Kirkpatrick and Denys Turner. Their friendship and guidance have been unfailing throughout this project, and they continue to provide constant insight and inspiration.

Vittorio Montemaggi and Matthew Treherne

ABBREVIATIONS, EDITIONS, AND TRANSLATIONS

Shortened citations are used throughout the volume. The following abbreviations are used in the notes and text:

CCCM	*Corpus Christianorum, Continuatio Medievalis*
CCSL	*Corpus Christianorum, Series Latina*
Conv.	*Convivio*
CSEL	*Corpus Scriptorum Ecclesiasticorum Latinorum*
Dve	*De vulgari eloquentia*
EC	*Epistola a Cangrande*
ED	*Enciclopedia dantesca*
Inf.	*Inferno*
Mon.	*Monarchia*
Par.	*Paradiso*
PL	*Patrologia cursus completus . . . Series Latina*
Purg.	*Purgatorio*
ST	*Summa Theologiae*
Vn	*Vita nuova*

For citations from Dante's works, the following editions as listed in the bibliography have been used:

Commedia, ed. Petrocchi, 2nd ed.
Convivio, ed. Ageno
De vulgari eloquentia, ed. Mengaldo
Monarchia, ed. and tr. Shaw
Vita nuova, ed. De Robertis

Each contributor has chosen a preferred translation of the *Commedia*; references are given in the notes to each essay. Translations of Dante's other works are taken from the following versions:

[Convivio] Banquet, tr. Ryan
De vulgari eloquentia, ed. and tr. Botterill
Epistola a Cangrande, tr. Toynbee
Monarchia, ed. and tr. Shaw

Unless otherwise noted, translations from primary sources are taken from the English editions listed in the bibliography. Translations from secondary sources are the editors' unless otherwise stated.

Biblical references are taken from the Vulgate (*Biblia Sacra*). Most English translations follow Douay Rheims.

In citing from Aquinas's *Summa Theologiae*, the abbreviation form is used whereby "*ST* IaIIae.3.8.ad2" refers to *Prima Secundae*, question 3, article 8, reply to second objection.

Introduction
Dante, Poetry, Theology

VITTORIO MONTEMAGGI &
MATTHEW TREHERNE

Dante's "Commedia": Theology as Poetry has its origins in an international conference of the same title, held in Robinson College, Cambridge, on December 12–14, 2003. The aim of the conference was to bring together theologians and Dante scholars to address two related questions suggested by our title. First, what are the theological implications of Dante's poetic narrative? Second, what light do theological considerations throw on Dante's poem as a literary text? We invited contributors to the conference to offer readings of the *Commedia* that either examine Dante's poem as a theological enterprise or explore the intersection in Dante's poem between theological and literary concerns.

When we set about organizing the conference, we were driven by a sense that theologians and *dantisti* had much to offer each other, and that opportunities for dialogue were much needed. We felt, on the one hand, that theological modes of inquiry could cast new light on Dante's text; and, on the other, that a close and detailed engagement with Dante's poetic voice might significantly enrich theological reflection. This sense of the potential value of dialogue between Dante studies and theology was confirmed by the conference, not only in the papers delivered but also in the formal and informal conversations that took place over the course of the conference; and, indeed, by the ways in which the papers originally presented and discussed have developed into the essays gathered in this volume.

The title of this volume makes the claim that theology is fully integrated with poetry in the *Commedia*. However, the notion of Dante's "theology as poetry," which the essays collected here variously explore, requires introduction. Most immediately, it is important to remind ourselves that for many of Dante's readers—from the Middle Ages to the present—the idea of an intersection between theology and poetry in the *Commedia* has not been uncontroversial.[1] In the context of modern Dante scholarship, for example, the frequently cited distinction by Benedetto Croce between *poesia* and *non-poesia* in the *Commedia*—as though the "nonpoetic" elements, including the theological, were an add-on, and an undesirable one at that, to the true lyrical and dramatic work of poetry—suggests a differentiation between form and content, between poetry and theology.[2] More recent scholarship, however, has worked to remove such dichotomies. Critics as different as Erich Auerbach and Charles Singleton, in the mid-twentieth century, have provided an important foundation in moving beyond the tendency to denigrate the theological in Dante's *Commedia*.[3] Further vital possibilities have been opened up by the seminal works of other twentieth-century critics working in different traditions, such as Bruno Nardi, Étienne Gilson, and Kenelm Foster.[4] Successive works of scholarship have shown, first, that Dante's theology is intellectually dynamic and in many ways highly original; and, second, that the theological and the poetic are inextricably intertwined in his work.

The study of theological aspects of the *Commedia* continues to develop in richly varied ways. One of the clearest indications of this is in the wide range of theological sources and affinities which are being identified in Dante's text (although Dante's direct knowledge of individual texts is often difficult to prove). For example, Thomas Aquinas—once seen as the primary theological influence over the poet—now tends to be viewed as a vital but not necessarily dominant part of Dante's intellectual formation.[5] This is partly due to an increasing recognition of the poet's engagement with broader Aristotelian strands in medieval thought.[6] At the same time, scholarship continues to demonstrate the centrality of Christian Neoplatonism, and the importance of Franciscan as well as Dominican currents for Dante's thought.[7] In searching for sources and affinities, moreover, scholars have turned their attention not only to the content but also to the narrative and poetic form of Dante's theological discourse. It has been suggested, for example, that the *Commedia* can be read in relation to Augustinian frameworks of conversion and confession, or to the rhetorical and intellectual structures of medieval contemplative traditions.[8] Most importantly, however, these various strands of scholarship suggest that Dante's poem does not simply accumulate elements of different theological traditions, but offers an original conception of the possible active and constructive relationships between them. As perhaps best emblematized by the cantos of the Heaven of the Sun, Dante does not treat theological traditions and positions as static or isolated: he makes them dance.

Recent scholarship also continues to enrich our understanding of Dante's use of his most important theological source: the Bible.[9] Indeed, the status intended by Dante for the *Commedia* relative to scripture has represented one of the thorniest questions for readers of his poem. A distinction apparently made in the *Convivio* (the text that survives to us is, however, fragmentary) between the "allegory of the poets" and the "allegory of the theologians" suggests that, whereas scripture both contains allegorical meaning and is literally true, poetry can only signify allegorical meanings through fiction.[10] The problem for readers of Dante is that the *Commedia* is packed with claims for its own literal veracity. It appears to demand, in short, to be read through the same interpretive modes usually reserved for scripture: as both historically true and as containing allegorical, typological truths—a claim also explicitly made for the poem in a letter famously purporting to be written by Dante.[11] At the same time, however, the poem contains elements which seem to be self-consciously fictional. This apparent tension, long debated in Dante scholarship, continues to attract critical attention.[12] The question of the importance of the Bible for Dante has also been revitalized by studies paying attention to the complex ways in which scripture was read in the Middle Ages and the impact these might have had on Dante's work.[13]

Other fruitful possibilities reside in the recognition that Dante's theology can be understood not only in relation to theological and scriptural texts, but also in relation to the Word of God as it was seen to inform embodied experience and religious practice. An example of this is the increasing attention to Dante's representation in the *Commedia* of liturgy, whereby biblical passages and other religious texts are enacted and encountered through meaningful performance.[14] Another example is the attention currently being paid to the theological aspects of Dante's presentation of human embodiment. Scholars have shown that in the *Commedia*, theological reflection on questions such as the Incarnation, Transfiguration, and Resurrection is not carried out in purely speculative terms but is intimately linked in multiple ways with lived experience.[15] A further important development is the exploration of the varied theological implications of the interpretive, ethical, and affective dynamic of the reader's relationship to the poem.[16]

The relationship between Dante's *Commedia* and its readers is also the focus of a prominent strand of scholarship that seeks to expose the textual strategies by which Dante constructs authority for his own work.[17] Such discussions are rarely cast in ways that explicitly point to the theological implications of these strategies. This mode of criticism, however, need not be seen as contradicting the study of the theology of Dante's text: a heightened awareness of the author's poetic and narrative techniques can only enrich our understanding of the intersection between his poetics and theology. As some recent assessments of Dante's work suggest, a full understanding of the theology of the *Commedia* ought to embrace, rather than deny, the means by which the text is carefully constructed as narrative and poetry.[18] Indeed, the recognition of the integration of poetic practice and theological thought in the *Commedia* is central to the notion, suggested by the title of this volume, of Dante's "theology as poetry." Dante's theology is not what underlies his narrative poem, nor what is contained within it: it is instead fully integrated with its poetic and narrative texture.

Such an understanding of the notion of "theology as poetry" clearly has implications for debates beyond the concerns of Dante scholarship, for example in literary criticism and theory and in intellectual and cultural history. Indeed, the question of the relationship between poetic and theological concerns provides a valuable context for thinking about any dialogue between Dante studies and theology. This is not to suggest that this question need be the only aspect of such a dialogue. While detailed engagement with the *Commedia* does not often find a place in theological studies, much in contemporary theology could both illuminate and be illuminated by reflection on Dante's poem. Alongside discussions on the relationship between religion and literature,[19] one could think, for instance, of debates in contemporary theology on the relationship between

God and world, between faith and reason, and between theology and ethical theory;[20] or of debates on the nature of theology itself, on "mystical" theology, on liturgy, and on theological anthropology.[21] All of these debates have profound resonances with concerns in Dante's works.

Integrally related to all these fields of theological inquiry, and in many senses linking them together, is the specific question of the nature of theological language. What is it that human beings do when they speak about God? How does the way in which they conceive of such speech reflect and affect their understanding of the relationship between God and human beings? And how does all this, in turn, bear upon their understanding of the manner in which human beings use language more generally, in relating both to each other and to the world of which they are part? Concerns such as these are at the heart of reflection on what it might mean to read, and indeed do, theology as poetry. As such, they provide a valuable perspective from which to approach analysis of the theological nature of Dante's poem.

Furthermore, in recent years there has been a growing interest in the nature of theological language as understood specifically in and through medieval texts and thought.[22] Central to that interest are the ideas that medieval reflection on theological language reveals a particular understanding of the relationship between God, the world, and human beings; and that, in the light of this understanding, we may recognize the full value of the wide range of forms that theological language can take. This conception of the relationship between God, the world, and human beings is importantly characterized—not only in Christian but also in Jewish and Islamic traditions—by the fundamental notion that all that is, depends on God: the world is freely and lovingly created *ex nihilo* by a God who is not part of existence but who is the mystery in which all that exists originates, participates, and finds its goodness and meaning.

From this perspective, full comprehension of God lies beyond the grasp of human intellect and language, since the origin of all that is lies "beyond" being itself. To think otherwise would be to misunderstand the relationship between creature and Creator, between existence and the ground of existence. At the same time, human beings are seen as being made in the image and likeness of God, as free, intellectual creatures, whose very being is grounded by a direct and personal relationship with God and has its final end in perfect union with divine being itself. In the light of this intimate relationship between divine and human existence, human beings are seen as being able to speak theologically in a meaningful and truthful way.

The question of the ways in which human beings can speak meaningfully and truthfully about God was, of course, extensively and variously debated in the Middle Ages. That said, there is a recognizable overall shape to medieval reasoning on the dynamics of theological language. For thinkers as different in theological temperament as Augustine, the Pseudo-Dionysius, Gregory the Great, Bernard, Bonaventure, and Aquinas, it was fundamental that no matter what else one said about particular aspects of divine being, if one was not referring to the mystery at the ground of all existence, which brings everything into being out of nothing and sustains it; and if one was not referring to the truth and love in the image of which we are made, and in which lies the beginning and end of our being; then, one was simply not referring to God.

This understanding, which Dante shared, led medieval theologians frequently to reflect on the nature of theological language and on the measure and manner in which one might meaningfully speak of God. Such reflection appears in a variety of contexts, including sermons, commentaries on scripture, guides to contemplation, and theoretical treatises. And it took many forms: from consideration of the relationship between scriptural and all other religious language, to specific analysis of the names used by human beings to refer to God; from systematic discussions of the relationship between metaphysics and theology, to meditations on awareness of the pride that almost inevitably accompanies any attempt to speak about God. Common to all such reflection, however, and to medieval theology generally, is a strong sense that one's idea of God and of the relationship between God, the world, and human beings might be expressed not only in what one says but also in the way one says it. Given the all-encompassing, uncircumscribable nature of God, meaningful speech about God must always do more than attempt simply to contain factual or propositional truths: it must also convey, through the manner in which it is articulated, something of the truth and wonder of one's relationship with the mystery in which all truths reside.

Theologians continue to find this particular aspect of medieval thought fruitful for contemporary debates. One of the reasons is that it suggests ways of illuminating the relationship between theology and poetry. For example, one of the ways in which reflection on the nature of theological language developed in the Middle Ages was in the elaboration of particular notions of metaphor and analogy; and these notions are seen by some contemporary theologians as offering philosophical and theological insights into the nature of poetry. David Burrell, for instance, taking Aquinas as a starting point, suggests that the idea that all beings exist by virtue of participating in divine being might lead, through notions of analogy and metaphor, to reflection on poetry's theological value. As he puts it, if we think of God "as that One whose essence is identified with its very 'to-be' [*esse*],"

> creation becomes that act whereby the One whose essence is to-be makes everything else to-be by participating in being. *Participation* remains a metaphor, so this cannot serve as an explanation in any ordinary sense. . . . For this One is indeed "beyond being" as we know beings. So our relation to this One who speaks the universe—"God says 'be' and it is"—cannot be on a par with our relation to any other thing. . . . Since God cannot be "other" in the sense in which other things are other, and God remains the very source of anything's being, anything's to-be is at once a participation in the very being of God and "more intimate to things than anything else" [*Summa Theologiae* I.8.i] . . . the unique character of the *relation* called "creation" . . . demands that we learn how to think the creator *not* as an item in the universe, but as its One free creator! That mode of thinking . . . will also demand that we appreciate how to employ language analogously. For this reason, a foray into metaphysics will require poetic sensibility as well, since all analogous speech—whether used of divinity or used to evaluate human situations, as in ethical discourse—will invariably display a touch of metaphor. So we are brought . . . to the threshold of poetry and art as we attempt to attune our minds and hearts to the wonder of creation.[23]

Not all medieval authors, of course, would have unambiguously accepted the value of poetry as a legitimate mode of theological expression. It is probably fair to say that, with the exception made for the poetry of scripture, most medieval theologians would have been skeptical about the idea that poetry might be as theologically valuable as other forms of discourse. This mistrust of poetry is frequently explicitly voiced in terms of the same kind of distinction that Dante appears to have made in the *Convivio* between scriptural and nonscriptural allegory. As our earlier comments on medieval views on theological language suggest, however, this mistrust was not necessarily accompanied by skepticism about the value of reflecting on, and foregrounding as theologically significant, linguistic and rhetorical form. And this, from our contemporary perspective, might be taken as an invitation to bring literary and poetic questions to the heart of theological reflection. In this context, the *Commedia* has particular significance. For, as the essays in this volume illustrate, it is firmly rooted in the medieval tradition of reflection on the nature of theological language, and at the same time presents us with an unprecedented piece of sustained poetic experimentation, which appears to attempt to move beyond traditional theological assessments of the status and value of poetry. Understood in this way, Dante's might be seen as one of the most original theological voices of the Middle Ages.

The essays in this volume provide a wide spectrum of possibilities for reflecting on the significance of that voice. In the first essay, Robin Kirkpatrick proposes that the theological value of Dante's *Commedia* lies in the narrative and poetic forms it offers for the activity of theology, more than in any specific theological doctrine it might present. He suggests, moreover, that theological questions and modes of inquiry ought to play a vital role in literary critical approaches to the *Commedia*. The essay argues that the richness of Dante's understanding of poetry, theology, and human personhood is most fully revealed by close readings of the *Commedia* that recognize the interdependency of literary and theological concerns. The question of the theological value of the narrative dynamics of the *Commedia* is also at the heart of the second essay, in which Peter S. Hawkins reflects on the relationship between theology and poetry through a detailed analysis of Dante's presentation of the smile. The essay relates the narrative dynamics of Dante's use of the smile both to Dante's construction of his own theological authority in the *Commedia* and to the presence and development of representation of the smile in the artistic context of Dante's day. Hawkins proposes that the smile might be seen as Dante's distinctive way of revealing theological resources unique to poetry, and as Dante's most original contribution to the Christian theological tradition. Also addressing the question of how the narrative poetry of the *Commedia* might be read as theology, Vittorio Montemaggi argues that the poetics of the text is grounded in a theological understanding of the nature of language. The essay proposes that, on the basis of Dante's theology of language as presented in the *Purgatorio* and the *Paradiso*, the *Commedia* is shaped by an interplay of affirmative and apophatic modes of discourse, and that through such an interplay, language ultimately reveals itself to coincide with love. As a way of testing and refining these ideas, the essay offers a close reading of the theological significance of the figures of Ulysses and Ugolino.

With Piero Boitani's essay, the volume's exploration of the theological dimensions of Dante's poetry turns to the specific question of the doctrine of creation. The essay first focuses on the theological significance of the metaphoric texture of the *Purgatorio*'s two discussions of the creation of the human soul, and then analyzes Dante's metaphysical and theological account in the *Paradiso* of the creation of the universe. By showing how, in both cases, Dante's conception of creation is linked to his poetic practice, Boitani presents a new evaluation of the *Commedia* as a uniquely rich and resonant moment in Western culture. Dante's conception of creation is related in the following essay, by Matthew Treherne, to the liturgical performance presented in the *Commedia*. Drawing inspiration from contemporary theorists of liturgy, Treherne argues that in the *Commedia*, Dante presents liturgy in ways that relate it to personhood. By examining the changes from a penitential to a doxological mode, Treherne suggests that liturgical performance is, for Dante, bound up with a recovery of a proper understanding of the relationship between God and the world—a relationship which Dante presents, through a striking pattern of allusions and references, as sacramental. Consideration of the relationship between God and the world is also central to the next contribution, in which Oliver Davies argues that Dante's presentation of materiality and human embodiment should be understood in the light of the doctrine of the Ascension; and that this recognition, in turn, ought to be at the heart of any attempt to read the *Commedia* as both theology and literature. Davies proposes that such reflection can lead us to a richer appreciation both of the way in which language, body, and world are for Dante inextricably linked, and to an enhanced sense of the bearing this might have on one's understanding of how to read and engage with medieval texts. On this basis, the essay argues, reading Dante's *Commedia* as both literature and theology can enhance our sense of the importance of doctrines that tend to be neglected in modern systematic theology, as well as of the particularly significant contribution of Dante's poeticization of those doctrines to the work of the modern theologian.

In the next two essays, the volume focuses on a detailed consideration of the relationships of Dante's poetry to the theological and religious tradition, with a particular focus on scriptural exegesis. Theresa Federici's essay examines the significance of the figure of King David for the *Commedia*, specifically in connection with the strategies through which Dante gives authority to his authorial voice. Through a close reading of the references in the *Commedia* to Psalm 50 and Psalm 9, Federici details the ways in which David is presented in the poem in the dual role of penitent sinner and psalmist and relates this presentation to medieval biblical exegesis and conceptions of penitence. In the light of this analysis, the essay proposes, the figure of David appears as the primary model for Dante's self-presentation, first as a penitent human being and then as a theological poet. Also focusing on medieval biblical exegesis, the essay by Paola Nasti analyzes Dante's ecclesiology, and especially the way in which it finds poetic expression in the *Paradiso*. Nasti reads the *Commedia* in close comparison with traditional theological discussions of the Church and charity, thereby revealing the originality of Dante's ecclesiological symbolism, and emphasizes especially the way Dante reshapes the image of the Bride from the Song of Songs in *Paradiso* 10–14. Dante, Nasti argues, thus offers a text that, specifically in its poetic texture, both remains firmly rooted in the theology of its day and opens up highly innovative theological perspectives.

The following contribution, by Douglas Hedley, brings the focus of the volume to the metaphysical aspects of Dante's theological poetry, by offering detailed reflection on the theological value and implications of some of the central Neoplatonic aspects of the *Commedia*, especially the question of divine immanence. This reflection is primarily addressed to the ways in which Romantic thinkers found in Dante a source of theological inspiration. In turn, Hedley suggests, this opens up fruitful ways for Dante's narrative poetry to contribute to contemporary thought on the imagination. Also concentrating on Dante's metaphysics, Christian Moevs analyzes the repeated references in the *Commedia* to the image and notion of the "punto" [point], revealing its full literary, philosophical, and theological potential. By relating the *punto* to Dante's presentation in the *Commedia* of the nature of truth and knowledge, Moevs's essay offers a fresh account of Dante's idea of the incarnational union between God, the cosmos, and human beings. On this basis, Moevs suggests that in Dante's view the act of reading the *Commedia* can itself, if properly undertaken, actively participate in the dynamics of that union. With a continued focus on the incarnational aspects of Dante's thought, the final essay of the volume, by Denys Turner, considers Dante's understanding of language alongside Aquinas's and Eckhart's notions of the limits of theological expression. By locating the *Commedia* in the context of specific medieval reflections on the nature of language about God, Turner reveals that Dante's poetics are governed by engagement with fundamental questions of theological grammar. Thus, in its very nature as poetry, the *Commedia* is profoundly theological.

The essays gathered in this volume, then, suggest the rich variety of ways in which the question of theology as poetry might be explored in and through the *Commedia*. By bringing a variety of methodological perspectives to this question, and by drawing on the intellectual resources of both theology and Dante scholarship, they demonstrate the fruitfulness of the encounter between these disciplines. Some of the implications are assessed in the two afterwords with which the collection ends. In the first, John Took reflects on the conversation between Dante studies and theology in terms of a need for readings of the *Commedia* that pay serious attention to questions concerning the nature of human existence. In the second, David F. Ford reflects on the possibilities of learning from Dante something about what it means to do theology, and outlines seven ways in which reflection on Dante's *Commedia* can contribute to the work of the modern theologian.

Our hope is that *Dante's "Commedia": Theology as Poetry* will provide an impetus for renewed attention to the intersection of theological and literary concerns in Dante's poem. For not only does this volume make the claim that the *Commedia* presents us with "theology as poetry"; but, taken as a whole, it also suggests that the theological and literary significance of this claim is far-reaching.

Notes

1. The bibliography on Dante and theology is vast, dating back to the earliest commentaries on the *Commedia*; to provide references to every scholarly intervention in the debate would be far beyond the scope of an introduction such as this. The references in this introduction are intended to be indicative of particular lines of thought and suggest starting points for further reading, rather than being comprehensive. We have, where possible, given references to works

accessible in English. For useful general overviews, see Foster, "Teologia"; Iannucci, "Theology"; Ryan, "The Theology of Dante"; A. N. Williams, "The Theology of the *Comedy*." Curtius's chapter, entitled "Poetry and Theology," in his *European Literature*, 214–27, is a classic statement of the relationship between poetry and theology in Dante as seen in the Trecento. See also Lansing, *Dante and Theology* (vol. 4 of *The Critical Complex*).

2. Croce, *La poesia di Dante*.

3. Auerbach, "Figura" and "St Francis"; Singleton, *Dante's "Commedia"* and *Journey to Beatrice*.

4. Nardi, *Dante e la cultura medievale* and *Nel mondo di Dante*; E. Gilson, *Dante and Philosophy* and *Dante et Béatrice*; Foster, *The Two Dantes*.

5. Foster, "Dante and St Thomas" and "Tommaso d'Aquino"; Mastrobuono, *Dante's Journey*.

6. Barański, "l'iter ideologico"; Boyde, *Dante Philomythes and Philosopher*; S. Gilson, *Medieval Optics*; Moevs, *Metaphysics of Dante's "Comedy"*.

7. Barański, "Dante's Signs"; Havely, *Dante and the Franciscans*; Mazzotta, *Dante's Vision*; Moevs, *Metaphysics of Dante's "Comedy"*.

8. Botterill, *Dante and the Mystical Tradition*; Freccero, *Dante*; Pertile, "A Desire of Paradise."

9. Barblan, *Dante e la Bibbia*; Hawkins, *Dante's Testaments*.

10. *Conv.* 2.1.

11. *EC*.

12. Auerbach, "Figura"; Barański, "La lezione esegetica"; Charity, *Events and Their Afterlife*; Hollander, *Allegory in Dante's "Comedy"*; Moevs, *Metaphysics of Dante's "Comedy,"* 169–85; Nardi, "Dante profeta"; Scott, "Dante's Allegory"; Singleton, *Dante's "Commedia."*

13. Barański, "Dante's Biblical Linguistics"; Nasti, *Favole d'amore*; Pertile, *La puttana e il gigante*.

14. Armour, *Door of Purgatory*; Barnes, "Vestiges of the Liturgy"; Martinez, "Poetics of Advent Liturgies."

15. Cestaro, *Dante and the Grammar of the Nursing Body*; Davies, "World and Body"; Gragnolati, *Experiencing the Afterlife*; Jacoff, "Our Bodies, Our Selves"; Took, "Dante's Incarnationalism."

16. Franke, *Dante's Interpretive Journey*; Lombardi, *Syntax of Desire*; Moevs, *Metaphysics of Dante's "Comedy"*; Raffa, *Divine Dialectic*.

17. Ascoli, *Dante*; Barolini, *Undivine Comedy*.

18. Boitani, *The Tragic and the Sublime*; Kirkpatrick, *Dante's "Paradiso"*; Mazzotta, *Dante, Poet of the Desert*.

19. See, for example, Boyle, "The Idea of Christian Poetry" and *Sacred and Secular Scriptures*; Brown, *Discipleship and Imagination*; Hart, *Trespass of the Sign*; Quash, *Theology and the Drama of History*; Venard, *Littérature et théologie* and *La langue de l'ineffable*; Ward, *Theology and Contemporary Critical Theory*; R. Williams, *Grace and Necessity*.

20. See, for instance, Burrell, *Knowing the Unknowable God* and *Faith and Freedom*; O. Davies, *The Creativity of God* and *Theology of Compassion*; Hauerwas, *Community of Character*; Lash, *Holiness, Speech and Silence*; MacIntyre, *Three Rival Versions of Moral Enquiry*; McCabe, *God Matters*; Milbank, *Theology and Social Theory* and *Word Made Strange*; Moevs, *Metaphysics of Dante's "Comedy"*; Soskice, *Metaphor and Religious Language*; Turner, *Faith, Reason and the Existence of God*; R. Williams, *On Christian Theology*.

21. See, for example, Coakley, *Religion and the Body*; O. Davies and Turner, *Silence and the Word*; Ford, *Self and Salvation* and *Christian Wisdom*; Hedley, *Living Forms of the Imagination*; F. Kerr, *Immortal Longings*; Lash, *The Beginning and the End of 'Religion'*; McIntosh, *Mystical Theology*; Pattison, *The End of Theology*; Pickstock, *After Writing*; Sells, *Mystical Languages of Unsaying*; Soskice, *The Kindness of God*; Turner, *Eros and Allegory* and *The Darkness of God*; A. N. Williams, *The Divine Sense*.

22. See in particular the works by Burrell, Moevs, Pickstock, Sells, Soskice, and Turner listed above.

23. Burrell, *Faith and Freedom*, xvi, xx–xxi.

I

Polemics of Praise
Theology as Text, Narrative,
and Rhetoric in Dante's *Commedia*

ROBIN KIRKPATRICK

POETRY, PROPOSITIONS, PERSONS

The conference from which this essay proceeds demonstrated a wide variety of ways in which theologians and literary critics may collaborate. Dante's *Commedia* provided a natural focus for and encouragement to such collaboration. At the same time, the debate unsettled any easy assumptions about the relationship between theological and literary discussion. As quickly became apparent, it could not proceed fruitfully in an atmosphere of pious confidence, as if there were some such thing as "poetry," apart from specific texts and specific authors, betraying a religious dimension; or as if there were some such thing as "theology," in some equally generic way free from metaphor or simile in its deliverances. The specific matters. And this is as true of the *Commedia*—for all its apparently universal aspirations—as of any other text. Dante is a poet. But he is his own kind of poet. He is not Henry Vaughan, nor John Donne, nor even a born-again Bob Dylan. Not only did Dante write a long time ago, he also brought—in theory as well as practice—a passionately self-conscious interest to bear upon poetic and indeed linguistic tradition, seeking, in an unmistakably experimental spirit, to redefine the received idea of poetic art and even, perhaps, of language itself. One of the reasons why Dante was so beloved of twentieth-century modernists is that they recognized how far we had strayed in the Renaissance, Enlightenment, and Romantic phases of our cultural history from a full understanding of his example. And indeed Dante's poem will deny us, at every point, any preconceived or lately conceived notion as to what poetry essentially is.

In part, then, the purpose of the present essay is to insist upon the detail of Dante's text, and (in outline at least) upon the often polemical theory that is instantiated in that text. But this aim is also associated here with a specific—though very radical—question: Is it possible to make valid statements about the Divinity in terms of human language and human logic? At first, it might seem that the very title of this volume of essays—*Dante's "Commedia": Theology as Poetry*—already implies a response. Does such a title not assume that, whatever the validity of logical propositions may be, a poetic text—the *Commedia*, that is—may exemplify a language of religious discourse different from, but no less valid than, the language of ratiocination? But then, by reputation, the *Commedia* might be thought to take an especially confident view of how propositions and poetry can be reconciled—and this impression seems to gather strength in the perspective of Dante's Scholastic inheritance.

These initial considerations lead to a range of questions concerning the conception of the human person and the peculiar status that poets might be supposed to claim as prophets or scribes of the divine—and, indeed, the even more peculiar status of professional scholars, who fill their works, days, and bibliographies with well-judged deliverances and propositions about the workings of revelation. Poetry, propositions, persons: this alliterative mnemonic calls for theoretical nuance. If, in Dante's phrase, the poet grows "macro" (*Par.* 25.3) [gaunt] in the service of heavenly and earthly truth, then what is his "person" if not an epicenter of self-denial? And if that is what our poet tells us about persons, what right have we—as his commentators—to grow fat on the textual proceeds? To put it another way: Is there any form of professional procedure—in theology or in literary criticism—in which we might willingly abandon the securities of second-order discourse—ever judicious, ever neutral—in favor of those dangerous waters of first-order discourse, where the heady confession of ignorance is as likely to be revealing as our learned footnotes?

As the second part of my essay's title suggests, I wish to propose that both poetry and theology are better realized in a detailed engagement with texts and historical situations than in any pursuit of vision or theoretical system. On this view, close reading, or practical criticism, seems a very Dantean way to truth. And pursuing this view also allows me to insinuate the words that Dante attributes to Thomas Aquinas in *Paradiso* 13:

> E questo ti sia sempre piombo a' piedi,
> per farti mover lento com' uom lasso
> e al sì e al no che tu non vedi:
>   ché quelli è tra li stolti bene a basso,
> che sanza distinzione afferma e nega
> ne l'un così come ne l'altro passo;
>   perch' elli 'ncontra che più volte piega
> l'oppinïon corrente in falsa parte,
> e poi l'affetto l'intelletto lega.
>
> (112–20)

[And let this be a lead weight on your feet, / so that you move as slow as if worn out / to any "yes" or "no" unclear to you. / For no fool is as low as one / who taking either of these steps will fail / affirming or denying in distinction. / So often when our judgement rushes on, / it happens that we veer in false directions / and then emotions bind the intellect.]

These are words that deserve to stand as an epigraph to any volume of essays, let alone the present one. In the preceding cantos, Aquinas offers a fairly comprehensive picture of the workings of the created universe but does so, surprisingly, to explain a single phrase uttered in *Paradiso* 10— "non surse il secondo" (114) [no second ever rose]—in which we find encapsulated the equally surprising proposition that King Solomon was the wisest of all natural-born human beings. Aquinas then concludes with these lines, which, so far from emphasizing the competence of logical analysis, insist upon an extreme caution and even a pedestrian attention to the use of words (13.112–14). Discrimination and linguistic tact are, it seems, for Dante at least, the core of the example that he took from Aquinas. Is not this tantamount to viewing the theologian Aquinas as a literary critic?

Returning briefly to the three enticing *P*s—poetry, persons, propositions—there is little doubt that Dante's approach to issues such as these adds to their implication. Take, first, the question of what we think poetry to be; or, more precisely, what we think is the relation between poetic utterance and theological understanding or religious practice. A familiar answer will evoke the notion of epiphany to suggest that artistic utterance can momentarily present us with a world transfigured, either by recording those moments when the lighting-effects of eternity seem to break through our temporal gloom, or even, in some cases, by sheer brilliance of form, causing an effect of unanticipated splendor. Or else poetry and the arts are described as somehow "sacramental" in character, where the notion of the sacramental is understood along the same conceptual lines as that of the epiphanic just outlined above, and without taking into account the theological complexity any discussion of the sacramental requires. In whichever version, the chosen example is likely to be Gerard Manley Hopkins: "The world is charged with the grandeur of God. / It will flame out, like shining from shook foil."[1] Yet it is not self-evident that these expectations comprehensively define the possibilities of what poetry can do for the religious mind. It is not clear that they even do justice to Hopkins. And as for Dante, the thrust of my argument in this essay is that they will not do at all.

Epiphanies, "Plod," and Time

Our talk of epiphanies can easily invite us to a sort of visionary enthusiasm. Yet, whether *pro* or *con* such usage, there is a need for caution here. This is especially important when notions of the epiphanic are evoked through reference to the "sacramental." For it seems to me important—for literary critical as well as devotional reasons—that references to the sacramental should be associated conceptually with the notion of sacerdotal involvement. Priesthood is uniquely and indissolubly tied to the unknown and the unknowable—that Otherness on which all known and knowable existences depend. And whenever Dante refers with horror to the Church as the Whore of Babylon—which is to say, frequently—he demonstrates how dependent he saw himself to be upon the actions of true priesthood—true, beyond all the dreadful things he *did* know about the Church and its priests.

There is indeed a point at which priests and poets may have something in common: the interest they share in time. Priests are trained in a gamut of temporal possibilities, from the pastoral ebb and flow of life and death, to the surges of tradition, to the delicate rhythms of the liturgical year; and are thus qualified to attempt those elite syncopations in which the sacraments reconfigure our normal lumber. Poets in their own, more limited way—in metrical sensitivity—have at least an analogous function in their experiments and performances in time. Poets may of course imagine transcendence. But poems, especially if they happen to be narrative poems, are self-evidently written along a line obedient to the sentences that human beings speak and understand. So my first polemic is directed against the uses and abuses that the word "epiphany" has suffered on the lips of literary critics when it is deployed, more or less loosely, to suggest that lyric poetry in particular may open for us a bright window on the eternal or convince us that we human beings are, after all, in Seamus Heaney's phrase, "seeing things"—not merely *things* but things that can *see* and see things *anew*.[2]

Now, I do not deny that lyric poetry can stretch us to new lucidities. So, too, an Olympic high-board diver can expand our perceptions of muscle control and the sheen of air and water. Yet there are reasons—some of them theoretical, some of them specifically Dantean—to wonder whether the incandescent swoop of lyrical vision may sometimes be a camera-trick, or, less skeptically, whether such moments are all that poetry can encompass. Theoretically—and therefore, of course, in current circumstances *skeptically*—we have been urged by the modern Sorbonne to wonder whether words can ever deliver any vision at all. Words are not windows but rather reflective surfaces, subtly giving back—precisely because of the darkness beyond—the vestigial tracings of our own features and gestures. I shall argue later that Dante, who is not only a theorist but also a great comic writer, understands very well that, as human beings, we live most truly when we live on a comically small scale, within the limits of our human lineaments. It is also true, however, that Dante—in theory as well as in practice—has very little truck with unqualified lyricism. After all, in writing the *Commedia* he consciously abandons, once and for all, his earlier lyric practice and embraces the example of Virgil: he writes an epic narrative, an account of a journey articulated according to an interest in sequence rather than interruptions to that sequence. Immediately, this involves an alteration in his representation of time. The *Vita nuova* had been punctuated by visions, and by that marvelous nexus of terms that denote the life-renewing capacity of the contemplative eye: "mirare," "miracolo," "ammirazione"; a gazing at the unexpected, a filling of the mind with light. I am not forgetting that the narrative of the *Commedia* represents a journey back to Beatrice. Nor am I ignoring the passage in the *Convivio* where Dante speaks in unambiguously epiphanic *and* sacramental terms of his own use of vernacular Italian as a radiant "new sun," offered, as in the miracle of loaves and fishes, to a hungry multitude.[3] Yet the shift in genre to epic narrative remains profoundly significant in assessing his understanding of language and indeed of thought itself. Epic poems take time—and are often about our use of time in destroying or founding cities. And poetry takes time especially when seen under another aspect that Dante constantly emphasizes—which is to say, his interest in the painstaking and time-consuming processes of the poetic craft. The emphasis in the *Convivio* and *De vulgari eloquentia* falls less upon poetic vision than upon poetic workmanship—as it does also throughout the *Commedia* itself. The poet, for Dante, is one who labors in the "workshop of rhetoric," who files and polishes or else who weaves subtle textures out of words that, in Dante's own analogy, are as shaggy or silken as the fabrics of the Florentine clothing industry.[4] The *Paradiso* is his final labor—his "ultimo lavoro"—requiring the poet often to "put his back into it," as in *Paradiso* 23:

> Se mo sonasser tutte quelle lingue
> che Polimnía con le suore fero
> del latte lor dolcissimo piu pingue,
>   per aiutarmi, al millesmo del vero
> non si verria, cantando il santo riso
> e quanto il santo aspetto facea mero;
>   e così, figurando il paradiso,
> convien saltar lo sacrato poema,
> come chi trova suo cammin riciso.
>   Ma chi pensasse il ponderoso tema
> e l'omero mortal che se ne carca,
> nol biasmerebbe se sott' esso trema.
>
>   (55–66)

[Even if all those voices were to sound / that Polyhymnia and her sister muses / fed on their sweetest milk so richly once, / and aid me, singing of that holy smile / and how her holy look grew purer still, / I'd still not reach one thousandth of the truth. / And so, imagining this Paradise, / the sacred epic has to make a leap, / as when we find the road ahead cut off. / Yet no one if they've gauged that weighty theme— / and seen what mortal shoulders bear the load— / would criticize such trembling backing-out.]

When Dante does speak of vision and prophetic *furor*—alluding in *De vulgari eloquentia* 2.4 to the journey of Aeneas to the underworld in *Aeneid* book 6—his attention falls less upon the eagle-flight of prophetic rapture than upon the sheer difficulty of getting back into the temporal world: that is the "opus" that is the "labor," the strenuousness that poetry demands. To use Hopkins's phrase, "shéer plód makes plough down sillion / Shine" ("The Windhover"). The ploughshare glitters through the friction of the furrow. Grace shines, however unexpectedly and unconstrainedly, on our pedestrian works. Not perhaps on works that are "good" by any human standard, but on the working evidence of human potentiality, on those textured manifestations of being which demonstrate that we are alive. It greatly complicates the issue that Hopkins was a priest. Dante was not. But Dante did know how to render up the work of human hand for whatever benediction may then fall upon it. Few passages in the *Commedia* are more moving than the opening of *Paradiso* 25, in which Dante imagines the remote contingency, scarcely calculable within the parameters of temporal cause and effect, that his poem might win for him not a heavenly crown but a return to Florence, and that in returning he will receive the laurel crown in the very place where, at baptism, his name was first given him. The analogy is plain: in terms of theological hope, Dante submits to the sacraments, but in terms of poetry, he depends for his temporal identity on the responses of those who read him in his work.

There is, however, another way in which the poetry of Hopkins as well as Dante demands that we be cautious in our employment of the epiphany trope. For in Hopkins, poetic epiphanies are almost invariably—and literally—manifestations of the person of Christ. The whole birth-narrative of "The Wreck of the Deutschland" illustrates this, as do these lines from "As kingfishers catch fire . . .":

> for Christ plays in ten thousand places,
> Lovely in limbs and lovely in eyes not his
> To the Father through the features of men's faces.

This is a rather different epiphany from those that, say, T. S. Eliot might encourage. Eliot, influentially, was concerned with seeing the transfiguration of *things*, whereby the dry pools of the wasteland bloom with light and roses and fire intertwine. Notoriously, however, he is hopeless (in every sense of the word) with people. But Dante is not. From the

encounter with Francesca in *Inferno* 5, Dante is often disappointedly—
but hopefully—seeking that shining-forth of personhood that he first
experienced in his meeting with Beatrice and which, finally, he represents in the faces that are described in *Paradiso* 31 immediately before he
arrives at the vision of God's human features ("Vedea visi a carità suadi, /
d'altrui lume fregiati e di suo riso, / e atti ornati di tutte onestadi" [49–51]
[I saw there faces swayed to *caritas*, / arrayed in their own smiles and
light not theirs / and all they did adorned with dignity]).

The epiphany of persons must surely be a very different matter, theologically, from the epiphany of things. If Hopkins's Harry Ploughman
can be an epiphany, if the banker's wife Bice Portinari can also be Beatrice, who is Dante's God-bearing image, then anybody—poet, prophet,
or even the odd academic—may likewise be enlisted, wholly out of the
blue, to corruscate as such an image.

Propositions and Persons

Such possibilities—and responsibilities—point directly to the second
and third of my introductory *P*s, namely, persons and propositions, and
certainly deny us any such thing as might be described as "intellectual
property." But to see how these *P*s are enacted, let me focus on these lines
from *Paradiso* 14.

> Qui vince la memoria mia lo 'ngegno;
> ché quella croce lampeggiava Cristo,
> sì ch'io non so trovare essempro degno;
>   ma chi prende sua croce e segue Cristo,
> ancor mi scuserà di quel ch'io lasso,
> vedendo in quell' albor balenar Cristo.
>   Di corno in corno e tra la cima e' l basso
> si movien lumi, scintillando forte
> nel congiugnersi insieme e nel trapasso:
>   così si veggion qui diritte e torte,
> veloci e tarde, rinovando vista,
> le minuzie d'i corpi, lunghe e corte,
>   moversi per lo raggio onde si lista
> talvolta l'ombra che, per sua difesa,
> la gente con ingegno e arte acquista.
>   (103–17)

[And here remembering surpasses skill: / that cross, in sudden flaring, blazed out Christ / so I can find no fit comparison. / But those who take their cross and follow Christ / will let me off where, wearily, I fail, / seeing in that white dawn, as lightning, Christ. / From horn to horn, from summit down to base, / there moved here scintillating points of light, / bright as their paths met, bright in passing on. / So minute specks of matter can be seen— / renewing how they look at every glance, / straight in their track, oblique, long, short, swift, slow— / moving through sunbeams that will sometimes streak / the shade that people, to protect themselves, / have won through their intelligence and art.]

The epiphanic characteristics of this passage are immediately apparent, in its flashes of lightning, its sudden brilliancies and scintillations. Yet there is also a precise theological point at issue here, which is enforced not by the rhapsodic lyricism of the passage alone but also by its place in the continuing narrative and logical efflorescence of the *Paradiso*. These lines mark the point of transition from the episode in which Aquinas and Solomon have appeared to that in which Dante describes an encounter with his own forebear, Cacciaguida. And the crucial point is that this moment both interrupts a sequence and reintegrates it in a deeper understanding of persons and of their place in the temporal world. This, as in Hopkins's epiphanies, is a vision of the person of Christ. But it is not an invitation to contemplation of the Passion, either intellectual or affective. Dante at no point in his poem produces any such invitation. Rather, its call is to Christian practice. The Cross here becomes the underlying pattern in which the souls of the courageous display themselves to Dante. And, by analogy, even the motes of dust dancing in a beam of light—the tiny fragments of body, of skin loss—are enlisted to clarify that understanding. Dante here seems to echo Lucretius and yet to propose a wholly un-Lucretian approach to the knowable universe.[5] For Dante's world is posited on the mystery of the Cross. And the splendor of any created being in time is likewise posited on that. The dust may be a reality. Not, however, because in itself it reveals the design of divine creation—or any argument from design—but rather because it can march, in the columns of Dante's human text, as a similitude illuminating the human persons of the Heaven of Mars. So, more knowingly, must Dante's readers march, who are counseled here at line 106 to form a cross-bearing relationship with their author. Neither vision nor science releases us from time-bound sequences. They drive us back into the very passion that animates our otherwise dusty deaths.

A further word on persons and propositions. If, for Dante, reality is actually constituted by the Trinity, by the Cross, and by the Resurrection, then all that we are and all that we say must be held forward in a spirit of dispossession and deference towards those three creative principles. And theologians, too, knowing this for two millennia, have a great deal to teach literary critics who have worried over the fragmentation of the self, or the construction and deconstruction of the subject. There may be a need for humility or penitence. Indeed, humility and penitence are exact expressions of our existential condition. But there is no need for *worry* or for the naughty intellectual terrorism that delights in shaking the foundations of our comfortable selfhood. That selfhood never was comfortable. It is just what theologians and theorists alike maintain it is: a cultural accretion. And if we *are* words, then we are not "mere" words or prisoners of language, but sentences in the discourse of the Logos. The trick—the "comedy"—is to want to say that we *are* part of the discourse of the Logos and thus convert our solemn self-importance into an agreement to play the creational language game.

These obvious points have a very particular relevance to our reading of Dante's work. It is as common now as it was in the nineteenth century to see in the *Commedia* evidence of poetic titanism, megalomania, or at least an ambition to encompass systematically the whole universe of knowledge and experience. Or else, in some highly sophisticated versions of this interpretation, Dante is seen as a wonderfully adroit trickster, who mentions God only to assert a covert authority born of his own creative talent over the unsuspecting reader. I am not going to deny that Dante was perhaps the first poet in modern cultural history to envisage such Promethean gestures as the raised eyebrow of Farinata (*Inf.* 10.35) or the heroic obscenity of a Vanni Fucci, flicking his Italian V-signs at God (*Inf.* 25.1–3). I would, however, want to say that, properly read, in the very moment of cultivating such an imagination, Dante in the *Commedia* submits his own imaginings to equally powerful criticism. Thus the *Paradiso*, above all, offers not only a more Christian but actually a more realistic account of what human beings are than anything the *Inferno* has to offer. Dante's Hell is a place of mere identity, a realm of self-definition where the apparently heroic voices of Francesca, Farinata, and even Ulysses are shown asserting their own (undoubtedly real) virtues.

In Paradise, however, human *beings* are *being* human—displayed, that is, through their activities rather than in pseudo-monumental attitudes of self-aggrandizement. We do not know anything about Beatrice's height—or girth—or whether her hair was really a Pre-Raphaelite ginger. We *do* know that, in Dante's imagination, she is a source of motion and that she talks in the *Paradiso* about topics that engage at least Dante's attention, all the time smiling—intelligently, one likes to think. The underlying mode of the *Paradiso* is praise, directed to the Trinity as the paradigm of personhood, in songs such as that in *Paradiso* 14.28–33, which annihilates and consummates numerical identity into pure melody: the one and two and three; the three and two and one.[6]

But, finally, are propositions, proofs, or even precepts likely to sustain any such understanding? Are there professional arguments to persuade us to be better at being persons? I doubt it, and again I take some strength in my doubts from the calming deliverances of theologians. Rowan Williams, drawing on Hans Urs von Balthasar, speaks of at least one of the functions of theology as being "celebration."[7] In saying so, Williams does not disallow the interest that theologians might take in analysis and intellectual history. His words do, however, suggest that academic discourse need not always and forever be second-order comment, devoted to the assessment or production of plausible opinion. It may be just as valid for us, in our academic lives no less than in our domestic and interior existences, to be preparing for *performance*, in rehearsing words that will subsequently be used in the first-order discourses of creeds, prayers, hymns, and liturgies. And that, I take it, is consistent with an acceptance, running through Williams's writings, of language as the element in which human beings live, move, and have their being, as it is also with his recognition of play as the subtlest expression of human freedom. All of this is music to the ears of the literary critic. For decades now we have been in thrall to historical and philosophical models of discourse. Yet, without some such understanding as Williams offers, the fundamentally first-order character of literary criticism—by which I emphatically do *not* mean the cultivation of private sensibility—is likely to be lost. In their own sphere, literary critics, too, are preparing for performance, even for celebration. The brightest products of any literary course are likely to be those who have learned through their reading to *write* or at least learned the celebration of continuing exemplars.

Would Dante agree with this? One might be forgiven for thinking he would not, to judge from the centuries of scholarly comment on the nuances and positionings of the poet's intellectual affiliations. Dante himself does not make it any easier by offering in the *Monarchia* a work written in Latin for a professional audience. Yet I would strongly resist any suggestion that the *Monarchia* can be used to provide an explanation of—or alternative to—the *Commedia*. Once again, if Dante is a theologian, then his contribution lies less in any definition of doctrinal nicety than in the *form* of what he says—in his ability to make us reflect upon and appreciate the linguistic and narrative action of a Christian performance. After all, judged from our own professional point of view, the *Monarchia* appears to be not only very bad history—in its deeply distorted view of the Roman Empire—but also pretty feeble theology, paling beside Augustine and even beside recent writings that stress that there can be no talk of politics without talk of the Body of the Church and the community of Resurrection. There are, indeed, references in book 3 of the *Monarchia* to the Church as the true Body of Christian Truth.[8] Yet these suggestions come to fruition only when Dante turns to the sequences of metrical narrative. Such themes as these are not always explicitly addressed, even in the *Commedia*. But they are brought into play sometimes by imagery, sometimes by verbal suggestion, and always by an interrogative and *self*-interrogative narrative that forms itself in a confessional spirit and offers itself not as a last word in anything but as part of a narrative that its readers respond to and continue to expand. When, for instance, Dante is examined in Faith, Hope, and Charity in *Paradiso* 24–26, nothing is at stake. Dante is never going to botch his answers and so return in dudgeon to the dark wood of *Inferno* 1. The whole thing is a performance. This is to say that, just as the Creed is performative, as a promise of a way of life made in a communal context, Dante here likewise speaks to be heard by others, including the Otherness of God, and to be at one with the response that Otherness alone—whether divine or human—can offer.

A more extended anticipation of this theological disposition is offered at an earlier stage in the intellectual narrative of the *Paradiso*, in Dante's depiction of those Christian philosophers, including Aquinas, who might—one supposes—be most profoundly wedded to the validity of propositional statement. Yet Dante's Aquinas is concerned above all to identify, as the exemplar of utmost wisdom, King Solomon, who is indeed a lover of Wisdom but is here emphatically portrayed as a ruler devoted to the well-being of his subjects in time. The whole thrust of Aquinas's speech is thus to displace any speculative appetite for intellectual system and to concentrate attention on the *ways* in which we think and conduct ourselves within a world of "brevi contingenze" (13.63) [brief contingencies], of time and decay, of growth and change. In such a world, says Aquinas, we are bound to proceed with leaden feet, with a cautious attention to the limits of our own nature. Solomon is displayed, not "in all his glory," but as a "voce modesta" (14.35) [modest voice], like the angel's voice in announcing God's will to Mary ("forse qual fu da l'angelo a Maria" [14.36]). The height of Wisdom lies in such an understanding. Solomon in his own speech delivers not a prudent review of fiscal possibilities but an ecstatic hymn to the Resurrected Body (*Paradiso* 14.43–66). Our ultimate point of arrival is to return to our limits, yet to know, in the community of resurrection, that they were never limits at all.

Until that time, there is the plod that Aquinas promised and the secular vision of witness and martyrdom as modes of performance, which Dante then proceeds to explore in the Cacciaguida episode (*Paradiso* 14–18). These cantos at the central point of the *Paradiso*—which at first demonstrate a surprising emphasis upon temporal rather than eternal existence—directly translate the implications of Solomon's wisdom into a consideration of the forms of activity—ethical, civic, linguistic, and poetic—that for Dante seem to stand as the truest expression of Christian theology. Here, as one began to see in *Paradiso* 14.88–124, Dante shifts from the consideration of Christian wisdom to that of Christian courage and imagines an encounter with Cacciaguida, his own grandfather thrice-removed, his *trisavolo*. Cacciaguida had died as a crusader on the Second Crusade. But there is no bellicose triumphalism here or tales of derring-do in foreign fields. On the contrary, the first canto of the sequence is concerned with the peace that once prevailed in Florence—and which now has been lost forever under the impact of rapid economic expansion. In Cacciaguida's day, Florence had something of the character of a tribal homeland. It lived within the tiny circuit of its ancient walls, designated, significantly, in a sort of acoustic geometry, by the limits of the echoes resonating from the Church of the Badia ("Fiorenza dentro da la cerchia antica, / ond' ella toglie ancora e terza e nona, / si stava in pace, sobria e pudica" [*Par.* 15.97–99] [Florence, within the ancient ring, from which / she takes the bell-sound still of terce and nones, / lived on in modesty, chasteness and peace]). Within such a circuit all Florentines could be sure of their place within the sanctified rectilinearities of cradle and table, bed and grave.[9] But this primal organization of our brief contingencies has been shattered by the influx of economic migrants and by the restless centrifuge of mercantile activity, as bankers and merchants pursue their busy lives, not on crusades but in commercial traveling to their deaths in foreign fields. In canto 17, Dante proceeds to place his own misfortunes as an exile and his own mission as a poet at the center of these agitations. Here, as elsewhere, he represents himself as the victim of the political strife that arose in these changing times, and begins to envisage his own text as the only true homeland for those who seek a return to what Florence once was.

In all of this, Cacciaguida, as the ideal father, represents the courage as much to sustain the ethic of former civility as to fight and die for his cause. And this is a courage needed for facing life as well as death, for living in that austere attachment to age-old limits that was characteristic of the Florentine citizenry—says Dante—in Cacciaguida's day. Now that such virtue has been desecrated, the poet will require a similar courage, first of all to face the day-to-day martyrdom of exile; he must live bitterly dependent on patrons and every night climbing another man's stair.[10] But the poet is also called upon to engage directly and dangerously with these contingencies. For his witnessing to the truth will involve no secluded reading of comforting phrases in some universal book but rather a word-by-word descent into the temporal world. In *Paradiso* 17, Dante calls upon himself to speak out boldly against the destroyers of peace, to name names and risk the consequences of offence to those very families to which he may need to resort for his earthly crust. And his words will be as earthy as the extremely earthy phrase in which he purposes to "lascia pur grattar dov' è la rogna" (129) [let them all scratch wherever they itch].

In terms of poetics, the naming of names and the scratching of itches may well prove central in the Cacciaguida episode. But one is also bound to recall—for its theological resonance—that all such ordinary virtue is set against and supported by the image of the Cross. Although the whole of this episode is located in the planetary orbit of Mars, the configuration that here replaces the circular dances of the Heaven of Christian philosophy is neither the sword nor the scimitar but the many-edged outline of the cruciform. I need not belabor the point. Our truth, with the Cross, lies in our response to the limits that define our nature. Our city is our exile. Our characteristic existence, from this Dantean perspective, lies in time and in language, themselves both modes of exile. So much to say, so little time to say it, and so much, anyway, that is unsay-able. The Cross confirms all that and gives it, quite undeservedly, some meaning.

Polemics of Praise

All this leads us to reflection on the first part of my essay's title, which as yet remains unexplained. A full appreciation of Dante's understanding of propositions and persons will require reflection on the notion that praise—as the foundational relationship in liturgy and thought between creature and Creator—lies at the very heart of Dantean poetics. Dante himself suggests as much in *De vulgari eloquentia*, where he argues that the first word, rationally speaking, that Adam ever uttered was the word "God"—"*El*"—thereby recognizing his maker in the mode either of question or response (*Dve* 1.4). More importantly, the *stilo della loda*—the praise style—is the very style that Dante identifies as characteristically his own when, at a crucial moment in the *Vita nuova*, he realizes that his role as poet is not to flatter Beatrice or seek any benefit from knowing her, but rather to speak in praise of the fact that she exists at all. This is not to say that Beatrice ever becomes for Dante an idolatrous alternative to God. On the contrary, the praise of Beatrice, as a creature of God, is seen as an exercise, within the sphere of language, of that very virtue that Beatrice throughout the *Vita nuova* most clearly exemplifies—the virtue of humility. Thus, in pursuing his specific activity, the poet will not suppose that his words can ever encompass or possess the reality of a divinely created person, still less the person of God. Indeed, as the opening lines of "Donne ch'avete intelletto d'amore" suggest, any attempt to write as if that were possible would render the poetry "vile"—ignoble—destroying that very delicately poised manifestation of nobility that Beatrice herself displays, paradoxically, in grounding her being in humility:

Donne ch'avete intelletto d'amore,
I' vo' con voi de la mia donna dire,
non perch'io creda sua laude finire
ma ragionar per isfogar la mente.
             (*Vn* 19.4, vv. 1–4)

[You ladies who have intelligence of love / I wish to speak of my lady with you / not so that I should ever conclude her praises / but speaking to give my mind an outlet.]

This position has implications that many Dantists are likely to resist. After all, to speak of humility in Dante runs against a view that, with some reason, celebrates the encyclopedic ambition of the poet to offer a total—and to some, a totalizing—view of the knowable universe. Yet I persist in this, particularly when the text under consideration is the *Paradiso*. This *cantica* is punctuated at every turn by passages insisting that the poet's words cannot exhaust the reality of his own vision, let alone the reality of God. (The opening of *Paradiso* 23, discussed above, emphasizes this: "Ma chi pensasse il ponderoso tema / e l'omero mortal che se ne carca, / nol biasmerebbe se sott' esso trema" [64–66] [Yet no one if they've gauged that weighty theme— / and seen what mortal shoulders bear the load— / would criticize such trembling backing-out].

I propose, simply enough, that instead of regarding Dante's words as a rhetorical topos, we should accept that Dante means what he says. It is an aspect of both praise and of humility that he should. And theologians can supply any number of examples from the apophatic tradition where the religious seriousness of such protestations simply cannot be questioned.

Yet to acknowledge this is not to embrace mere silence but rather to recognize the field in which we as language-animals most effectively graze and frolic. So, at the crystalline boundaries of linguistic possibility, Dante turns back and enters—to use his own phrase—the workshop of rhetoric and finds there a whole range of instruments, lenses and scalpels, mirrors, and even skewers, to employ in his dealings with other human beings in a range of semiotic functions. The *Commedia* shows the virtuoso at work, the craftsman at his forge; and the credit of course is his. It would be poor praise, however, that obscured with fantastic claims to cosmic domination the conditions of humility under which, realistically, craftsman-like work is always done, or the lessons in ethical and linguistic craft that our observation of Dante may teach us.

The perception of the authorial act implied in the poetics of praise is, I hope, consistent with that conception of the human person as essentially relational that I offered in the earlier part of this essay. But the question remains as to what there is in all this for the reader, now deprived of visionary information or of simplistic assumptions regarding the nature of doctrinal propositions. And here again theology has much to offer. As Rowan Williams writes:

> Language about God is kept honest in the degree to which it turns on itself in the name of God and so surrenders itself to God . . . [And] it is speaking *of* those who have spoken to God and who have thus begun to form the human community . . . that is the only kind of universal meaning possible without the tyranny of a "total perspective".[11]

Among the many implications of this argument is the suggestion that religious practice requires a willing acceptance that religious language is metaphorical and traditionary in its character and that, as such, it requires and contributes to a communal understanding carried within the ecclesial body. Liturgy—in which performative and even phatic utterance prevails—is the primary expression of this understanding. Or else, once more, we can take Dante seriously. Dante is prepared to regard his words as an "olocausto"—a burnt offering (*Par.* 14.89). We may also recall that from canto 4 of the *Paradiso* onwards, Dante and his reader are required to recognize that what they see in Dante's Heaven is emphatically *not* what they will get.[12] It is as much a metaphor to speak of souls neatly disposed in the planetary spheres as it is to speak of the hands and feet of God.

But this is why only certain people are advised to read the *Paradiso*. Thus in *Paradiso* 2:1–18 we are invited to choose whether or not we read the *cantica*. These lines have sometimes been read as an appeal to a spirit of intellectual élitism, to a certain relish for abstraction and difficulty. But nothing, in my view, could be more mistaken. For, taking Dante seriously, this address to the readers, portrayed as following Dante's ship in their little boat, emphasizes a peculiarly human freedom. It is notable, for instance, that Dante's lines here run parallel to those of *Inferno* 26, in which Ulysses, seeking a total view of the wisdom of the world, spurs his crew on to a voyage that ends in disaster, a mad flight where all are "smarriti," as Dante was in the dark wood—"the right way blurred and lost" (*Inf.* 1.3). But Ulysses' rhetoric allows his crewmen no choice in the matter; they utter no word in response to his "orazione picciola" (122) [little speech]. Dante now speaks in terms of affection rather than disparagement to those in the little boat. There is no shame in *not* reading the *Paradiso*. But there *is* a decision involved. Can we bear the cross of a work where much will *not* be told us, where not knowing and shared dispossession themselves prove to be the condition of freedom? Can we accept what is given as a gift? That is what the *Paradiso*—and the cosmos itself—both are, in their way: pure gifts; not some maddening mechanical toy that we are constantly trying to get to function, but a field of human action in which intelligence and imagination are always at play in total freedom from the pressure to make things work.

It is perhaps the function of any work of art to restore our freedom and refresh our capacity for play. But notably, Dante in the *Convivio* (1.8) speaks of language, or more specifically the *vernacular* language, as a gift—wholly unexpected (though useful when received) and above all able to establish a bond of good will between person and person. In the *Paradiso* the poet speaks, through Beatrice, of freedom of will as the greatest gift that God, in creating, gave to us—and God throughout the *Paradiso* is constantly seen in terms of his "larghezza," his generosity in the creation of space and time. Correspondingly, the theological gift of Dante's poem is that he offers—in the spirit of the praise-style—the opportunity for the renewal of such "large" or generous action in the confines of space and time. And here perhaps Dante has something to teach the theologian. For while the notions of "gift" and "praise" are central and entirely comprehensible within the act of worship, they take on a certain strangled embarrassment in secular contexts, often denoted by epiphanic italics—"what a wonderful word"—as if the point were to pluck some metaphor to illuminate our theological understanding. I cannot see that theological argument is going to solve this rhetorical problem. For what we need is a wholly secular effort to evacuate the word of its secular application and offer it up as an "olocausto" for those meanings that it might acquire in the language-game of liturgy. And here the lay-poet, battling against the grain of presumptuous usage, may be of service in preparing words for such sacramental uses. Thus in *Paradiso* 24, when St. Peter asks whether Dante possesses the virtue of faith "ne la tua borsa" (85) [in your purse], Dante immediately resorts with flamboyant irony to the language of the department store: "Sì ho, sì lucida e sì tonda, / che nel suo conio nulla mi s'inforsa" (86–87) [Yes! Round and bright. Nothing in how it's minted p'rhapses me]. Satire and scandal are enlisted in the service of praise. Credit and fiduciary coinage are here seen for what they are—perverse analogies for our true relationship in faith to the ground of our being. The world at its worst—seen with the eye of scandalous comedy—can lose its grip and provide at least the "altri pochi" (*Par.* 2.10) [other few] with a cup to carry hopefully into the unknown.

Praise and polemic are not unrelated after all. But turning now to polemics, perhaps I can say something about an issue in Dante studies, which, if left unanswered, would threaten to undermine the whole basis on which a volume such as this rests. This issue is developed in Teodolinda Barolini's *The Undivine Comedy*, where Barolini offers to "detheologise" Dante's poem, by emphasizing the play of pure fiction and narratorial virtuosity in what she calls Dante's "hall of mirrors." A soft answer to such a project is called for. Indeed, in dealing with a passage such as the Cacciaguida episode, where Dante obviously invents his own ideal father-figure, there can be no ignoring the striking—and possibly ethical—illusionism that Dante displays.

Nonetheless, the very title of Barolini's work cries out for theological examination and conveniently brings me to the final phase of my argument. For Dante's *Commedia* never was "Divine." That is a sixteenth-century soubriquet, probably reflecting an egotist appetite for stupendous imagery and a desire to enter into Faustian shadow-fights with the merely human projections of what divinity might look like. As theologians are well aware, better be "undivine" than idolatrous. Christianity, moreover, is not so much a "mystery" religion as a "history" religion; and the *Commedia* might be seen as a direct reflection of this fact. As Nicholas Boyle puts it: "*The Divine Comedy* is not just *a* Christian poem; it is the paradigm of what Christian poetry is . . . [not] the representation of a timeless ideal nor a self-contained fiction, but part of the process of history, which it (partially) depicts."[13]

Considerations such as this are as new for me as they are striking—and also very necessary. There is what we may call second-order history, where as rulers or popes—or even scholars—we attempt to possess time and make it authoritatively ours. But there is also the history of those first-person performances that look to the past only to ensure a sustaining interest in the future. Another name for such history is tradition, another still is liturgy. And increasingly, it seems to me that the essential factor in Dante's mind and work is an unremitting attempt to release tradition—and even liturgy—from the dead hand of historical power. The words of Osip Mandelstam help towards a conclusion. During the 1920s, Mandelstam saw in Dante's poetry a model of civilization and a supreme example of what poetic language should be. For him, the very universe in which Dante moves and writes is a universe of value, not of fact. It is not a "mechanical clock" but a mode of relationship, even of love: "Dante's planetarium is far removed from the conception of the mechanical clock, for the prime mover of this great crystal set works not on transmissions or cog-wheels, but is indefatigably concerned with the translation of power into quality."[14] Dante's poem, devoted to the "love that moves the sun and other stars," is also concerned polemically to reveal the many obstacles that impede our participation in such a universe. This is the dark wood in which the *Commedia* begins. It is also the world to which, in the Cacciaguida episode, Dante contemplates his return. The year is 1300. This may not be a date that particularly interests historians. But for Dante it was the year when, with his politician's eye, he could reasonably see the beginning of history in the direst sense of that word, the beginning of that translation of quality into power that still afflicts us and complicates our freedoms whenever, as politicians, popes, or even scholars we attempt to possess time and make it authoritatively dance to our tune. The year 1300 was a Jubilee year, with freedom from sin as its fundamental theme. It was also, however, the year in which Pope Boniface VIII was stirring the Machiavellian mix of Italian and European politics in a way that would lead directly to Dante's exile. The remedy proposed by Dante in the *Commedia* is to call us, in the Cacciaguida episode and throughout, to attend to the words and names that may illuminate our futures and wrench them back from the possession of history in its direst sense. We are thus invited to read anew, with all that attention to detail, voice, rhythm and tone, image and suggestion, and irony and ambiguity that literary critics used to practise and Dante still demands we should.

Notes

Translations from the *Commedia* are from Dante, *Divine Comedy*, tr. Kirkpatrick.

1. Hopkins, "God's Grandeur."
2. Heaney, *Seeing Things*.
3. "Questo sarà quello pane orzato del quale si satolleranno migliaia, e a me ne soverchieranno le sporte piene. Questo sarà luce nuova, sole nuovo [...]" (*Conv.* 1.13.12) [This ... will be that fine barley bread on which thousands will amply satisfy their hunger, whilst for me there will be basketsful left over to enjoy. This will be a new light, a new sun. ...].
4. *Dve* 2.7.
5. See Lucretius, *De rerum natura* 2.14–19, a text which Dante probably knew through Lactantius, *De ira Dei* 10.3. The image of the motes of dust is also found in Aristotle, *De anima* 1.2, 404a, where it is attributed to Democritus. See Chiavacci Leonardi, *Commedia*, 3:406–7.
6. "Quell' uno e due e tre che sempre vive / e regna sempre in tre e 'n due e 'n uno, / non circunscritto, e tutto circunscrive, / tre volte era cantato da ciascuno / di quelli spirti con tal melodia, / ch'ad ogne merto saria giusto muno" [that one and two and three who always lives / and always reign in three and two and one, / uncircumscribed and circumscribing all, / had, three times now, been lauded in the songs / of every spirit there, the melody / a condign prize, however great the worth.]
7. R. Williams, *On Christian Theology*, xii–xvi.
8. *Mon.* 3.15.3.
9. "Oh fortunate! ciascuna era certa / de la sua sepultura, e ancor nulla / era per Francia nel letto diserta. / L'una vegghiava a studio de la culla, / e, consolando, usava l'idïoma / che prima i padri e le madri trastulla; / l'altra, traendo a la rocca la chioma, / favoleggiava con sua famiglia / d'i Troiani, di Fiesole e di Roma" (*Par.* 15.118–26) [How fortunate these were, each being sure / of where her grave would be! None yet was left / alone in bed by men who'd gone to France. / One, still awake, would watch around the crib / and soothe the baby, babbling in the tongue / that parents thrill to in the early days. / Another, drawing tresses from the spool, / sat with her family and told them tales / of Trojans, of Fiesole and Rome].
10. "La colpa seguirà la parte offensa / in grido, come suol; ma la vendetta / fia testimonio al ver che la dispensa. / Tu lascerai ogne cosa diletta / più caramente; e questo è quello strale / che l'arco de lo essilio pria saetta. / Tu proverai sì come sa di sale / lo pane altrui, e come è duro calle / lo scendere e 'l salir per l'altrui scale. / E quel che più ti graverà le spalle, / sarà la compagnia malvagia e scempia / con la qual tu cadrai in questa valle; / che tutta ingrata, tutta matta ed empia / si farà contr' a te; ma, poco appresso, / ella, non tu, n'avrà rossa la tem-

pia." (*Par.* 17.52–66) [Shrill cries of blame will chase the ones who lose—/ they always do. But vengeance, when it falls, / will speak of that same Truth that deals it out. / You'll leave behind you all you hold most dear. / And this will be the grievous arrow barb / that exile, first of all, will shoot your way. / And you will taste the saltiness of bread / when offered by another's hand—as, too, / how hard it is to climb a stranger's stair. Yet what will weigh upon your shoulders worst / is all the foul, ill-minded company / that you, in that dark vale, will fall to keep. / For that ungrateful, crazy, vicious crew / will turn as one against you. Yet it's them / whose brows before too long will blush with shame.]

    11. R. Williams, "Theological Integrity," in *On Christian Theology*, 8.

    12. "Qui si mostraro, non perché sortita / sia questa spera lor, ma per far segno / de la celestïal c'ha men salita. / Così parlar conviensi al vostro ingegno, / però che solo da sensato apprende / ciò che fa poscia d'intelletto degno. / Per questo la Scrittura condescende / a vostra facultate, e piedi e mano / attribuisce a Dio e altro intende." (*Par.* 4.37–45) [They did, here, show themselves, but not because / this sphere has been allotted them as theirs. / They signify celestial power least raised. / To speak in this way fits the human mind. / For you can only grasp through things you've sensed / what mind will then present as fit for thought. / For this same reason, Scripture condescends / to your capacities, and says that God / has hands and feet—though meaning otherwise.]

    13. Boyle, "The Idea of Christian Poetry," 290, 293.

    14. Mandelstam, "Conversation about Dante," 450.

2

All Smiles
Poetry and Theology in Dante's *Commedia*

PETER S. HAWKINS

Milton dubbed Edmund Spenser "our sage and serious poet," praising him as a better teacher about virtue and vice than "Scotus or Aquinas."[1] Literary history subsequently transferred this laurel crown to Dante, who continues to be read, translated, and reimagined by modern writers to a degree that has eluded the author of *The Faerie Queene*.[2] "Sage and serious," however, is not a tag to be accepted lightly. It comes with baggage—the earnest expectation of instruction and the prospect of tedium. No one, of course, could bring this charge against *Inferno*. Horace Walpole might despise Dante as "extravagant, absurd, disgusting, in short a Methodist parson in Bedlam"; Nietzsche might disdain him as a "hyena that writes poetry in tombs"; but has anyone ever found his Hell a bore?[3] There is too much passion, too much demonic mischief to enjoy: mud wrestling among the wrathful (*Inf.* 8.52–60), a demon's fart as call to arms (*Inf.* 21.139), and a malicious put-down of Virgil by an ironic hypocrite with attitude (*Inf.* 23.142–44).

Once one is past the excitement of *Inferno*, however, two-thirds of the poem remains, and in that stretch of sixty-six cantos is a slew of philosophical and theological longueurs—a surplus of virtue—that in sheer accumulation can be dauntingly "sage and serious." *Paradiso* in particular seems to defy pleasure with dense passages of *non-poesia*, famously despaired over by Benedetto Croce. There is Beatrice delivering herself on moon spots (*Par.* 2), for instance, or, in her magisterial role as theologian, giving the rationale for the Incarnation (*Par.* 7). Too much information—

and all of it, despite the *Commedia*'s title, apparently at the farthest remove from a laugh or a smile.

Yet such *non-poesia* passages contain flashes of humor, which often yield remarkable insights into what Dante is centrally up to in his poem. An example is the apparent throwaway line in *Purgatorio* 29, "Giovanni è meco," in which Dante adjudicates between two biblical visionaries. Exactly how many wings have the creatures that accompany the griffin-drawn chariot in the pageant of revelation? The poet tells us that what he saw on the other side of Lethe was what Ezekiel describes at the opening of his prophecy, except that when it comes to the number of their wings—a total of six, not four—"Giovanni è meco e da lui si diparte" (105) [John's with me / as to their wings; with him, John disagrees]. In other words, John the Divine gets it right not because a New Testament seer takes in more of the truth than an Old Testament prophet but because his Apocalypse accords with the *Commedia*. John is *with* the poet, and Dante's vision has the last word. What can the observant reader do in the face of such chutzpah but smile?

Another such moment of truth occurs in the Primum Mobile, in *Paradiso* 28.[4] First, the larger setting: twice in the heaven of the fixed stars, as Dante and Beatrice rotate in the constellation of Gemini, the pilgrim looks down from his lofty vantage in the material universe to behold the seven concentric planetary spheres just traversed. From the Stellatum in the eighth heaven, therefore, he peers down at Saturn, Jupiter, Mars, the sun, Venus, Mercury, the moon—only to see at the center of this cosmos "l'aiuola" [the little threshing floor] of our world. Noting how small and insignificant it seems from the perspective of the heavens, "io sorrisi del suo vil sembiante" (22.135) [I smiled at its scrawny image].

When Dante next ascends to the Primum Mobile, he looks into Beatrice's eyes—as he has done throughout his paradisiacal ascent—and beholds a dazzling version of this planetary Chinese box. He sees, however, the addition of a ninth, outermost circle. Presumably, this represents the ninth sphere, the Primum Mobile, in which he now rotates. Again, the center he beholds, reflected first in Beatrice's eyes and then in the sphere all around him, is immobile; but whereas before, the nine circles revolved faster and faster as they moved outward toward the tenth sphere, that of the Empyrean, now the circle closest to the center moves with the greatest speed. The revolutions of the others slow as distance from the still point increases.

Dante is dumbfounded when he views this light show, because it is the inverse of what he found in the *mondo sensibile*. Instead of being the tenth heaven, lying beyond the boundaries of the universe, the Empyrean is signified by the still *center* of the turning world; instead of moving with increasing speed in their centrifugal spin, the outer spheres slow, and the circle closest to the center moves fastest and burns brightest with love. The cosmos is turned not upside down but inside out: center and circumference switch places.

Beatrice explains to the bewildered Dante that he must shift gears from flesh to spirit, and move from a notion of God's transcendence to one of his immanence. What Dante now beholds is the spiritual universe that ultimately governs the material according to a "mirabil consequenza" (28.76) [wonderful accord] between less and more. The angelic intelligences closest to God govern the sphere farthest away from the earth, and so on. Beatrice then goes on to name the celestial hierarchies in a sweeping survey. Starting with the three orders closest to the divine center, she names Seraphim, Cherubim, and Thrones. In doing so, she spends six tercets largely to establish—in a move that shows her in a Dominican rather than a Franciscan light—that the *vision* of God gives rise to love (and then successively ardor, brightness, and motion), not that the love of God inspires vision and the rest.[5] That theological debate expeditiously resolved, Beatrice continues her survey of the *angelico templo* with the next descending triad—Dominions, Virtues, Powers—to which she accords only three tercets. The final grouping—Principalities, Archangels, Angels—is dispatched in a bare three lines.

These nine angelic denominations are all to be found in scripture, but helter-skelter. Although angels fly throughout both testaments, the rest of the heavenly host are named only in scattered texts—seraphim and cherubim in the Old Testament, archangels in 1 Thessalonians (4:16) and Jude (1:9), and the rest of the choir in two listings given by Paul in his epistles to the Ephesians (1:21) and the Colossians (1:16). Yet if these various angelic beings are all to be found in the Bible, they are never once named together or assembled in any particular order. Thus, when Beatrice straightforwardly lists them in a hierarchal succession, she offers what she *sees*, not what she reads in scripture.

Throughout Beatrice's discourse in *Paradiso* 28, there is no sense of the tentative "forse" [perhaps] that elsewhere in the *Commedia* indicates we are in the realm of surmise. Dante's personal angelic doctor tells us what is. Yet in the Middle Ages the ordering of the angels was the subject of various accounts and therefore a matter of dispute.[6] For a long time, Gregory the Great was the main authority on the subject; even so, angelologists eager for his word on the hierarchy had to choose between the ordering given in a sermon on Luke 15 and another found in his *Moralia in Job*.[7] After Dionysius the Areopagite was translated into Latin by John Scotus Eriugena and John of Salisbury and subsequently taken up by both Victorines and Scholastics, his *Celestial Hierarchy* provided another authoritative account, one that was bolstered by the universal assumption that Dionysius (known to us with historical hindsight as "Pseudo") was a more ancient authority than Gregory—that he was, indeed, the very Dionysius mentioned in Acts 17 as being among Paul's initial converts in Athens.[8]

Both Thomas Aquinas and Bonaventure note the disparity between the angelic orders in Gregory and Dionysius.[9] Thomas treats it as nothing of importance; Bonaventure, although acknowledging the genuine authority of Gregory, throws his lot in with Dionysius because of the latter's relationship with Paul, who, according to medieval readings of *The Celestial Hierarchy*, confided in Dionysius his knowledge of the "third heaven," about which the apostle otherwise refused to speak in 2 Corinthians 12.[10]

Whereas Thomas and Bonaventure (along with Peter Lombard and Bernard of Clairvaux)[11] made up their minds about the order of the angels on the basis of this or that human authority, Dante stakes his claims on his own firsthand vision. Nothing is left to surmise or debate in *Paradiso* 28, which from start to finish is preoccupied with assertions of truth. *Vero* and its derivatives appear six times in the canto, clustered at its opening and at its close. Moreover, when Beatrice dispels the pilgrim's confusions about the relation between model and copy, we are told that "come stella in cielo il ver si vide" (87) [like a star in heaven—truth was seen].

But how does Dante handle the question of truth so crisply in these matters, when the best theological minds of the Middle Ages disagreed? For the reader of *Paradiso* 28 who is adept in angelology, it is evident that the poet's spokeswoman, Beatrice, is following Dionysius to the letter. But instead of acknowledging a debt to an authoritative theologian, the poet makes it appear that Dionysius is in accord with Dante/Beatrice and not the other way around. *Dïonisio è meco*. Dante sets the theological record straight when he concludes *Paradiso* 28 with an elaborate marshaling of authority, in which personal experience, face-to-face vision, trumps everything else:

> E Dïonisio con tanto disio
> a contemplar questi ordini si mise,
> che li nomò e distinse com' io.
>   Ma Gregorio da lui poi si divise;
> onde, sì tosto come li occhi aperse
> in questo ciel, di sé medesmo rise.
>   E se tanto secreto ver proferse
> mortale in terra, non voglio ch'ammiri:
> che chi 'l vide qua su gliel discoperse
>   con altro assai del ver di questi giri.
>   (130–39)

[And Dionysius, with much longing, set / himself to contemplate these orders: he / named and distinguished them just as I do. / Though, later, Gregory disputed him, / when Gregory came here—when he could see / with opened eyes—he smiled at his mistake. / You need not wonder if a mortal told / such secret truth on earth: it was disclosed / to him by one who saw it here above—/ both that and other truths about these circles.]

Dionysius first made an entrance in the *Commedia* in *Paradiso* 10, in the heaven of the sun and among the *sapienti* of the church. Thomas Aquinas celebrated him there as the one who, while still "in carne," in the flesh, "più a dentro vide / l'angelica natura e 'l ministero" (116–17) [beheld most deeply the angels' nature and their ministry]. In *Paradiso* 28, we get another perspective on that encomium. In the first place, Dionysius is to be judged correct because he named and distinguished the angels "com'io"—as I do, says Beatrice, who of course speaks for the poet in her capacity as his celestial "front." Second, it was not Dionysius "in carne" who saw most deeply into the secrets of the angels and their ordering. It was not he who was enraptured to the third heaven "sive in corpore sive extra corpus nescio Deus scit" (2 Cor 12:3) [whether in the body, or out of the body, I know not: God knoweth], nor did Dionysius himself hear the *arcana verba* that are unlawful for a man to utter. Rather, Paul had the direct experience of heaven's "secret truth," the "truths about these circles" and much more. Dionysius recorded what Paul confided to him when both men were "in carne"; thus, what Dionysius spoke he spoke on the authority of another. Dante, however, is like Paul in that he claims to have seen reality for himself—the secret truth, the truths about these circles, the truth of the *Commedia*'s revelation to us.

In *Paradiso* 28, the foil for Dionysius is Gregory the Great—the one who miscalculated the angelic orders, and not only once but twice. We are told that after dying and arriving where Dante and Beatrice now stand—where Paul stood before them all—Gregory saw the truth and immediately acknowledged his error. Whereas Dionysius had been working on the basis of experience (albeit someone else's), Gregory resorted to that holy guesswork which theologians offer when scripture and tradition offer no definitive word, when they must take an imaginative leap. Gregory was looking through a glass darkly, not seeing face-to-face as Dante can do in the Primum Mobile when, after staring at the spinning spheres reflected in Beatrice's eyes, he turns to see, "come stella in cielo," the truth of the heavenly spheres *as they are*.

It was not always thus: at the time when he wrote the *Convivio*, Dante, like Gregory, miscalculated—and did so by following Gregory's "authoritative" ranking of the celestial order given in *Moralia in Job*. In book 2 of the *Convivio*, Dante moves the reader through a discussion of the material heavens (in which he notes, in 3.4, that in an early work, *On the Heavens and the Earth*, Aristotle made a mistake in numbering the heavens that he later corrected in his *Metaphysics*). He then addresses the question of the spiritual creatures that govern the material spheres. In this sequence, we anticipate the move from matter to spirit, from copy to model, that we later find in *Paradiso*'s transition into the Primum Mobile. In contrast to Aristotle and Ptolemy, Dante says, Christians have insight into the truth of the heavens because they have been "amaestrati da colui che venne da quello, da colui che [le] fece, da colui che le conserva, cioè dallo Imperadore dell'universo, che è Cristo" (2.5.2) [instructed on the realm of the spiritual creatures by him who came from there, by him who made these creatures, by him who conserves them in being, that is, by the Emperor of the Universe, Christ Himself].

Since Christ is never recorded as having said much about angels, Dante must be ingenious in his examples of this instruction. Christ's first "revelation" (which took place, oddly, before his birth) is the archangel Gabriel, who comes to Mary at the Annunciation; his second is the reference by Satan in the wilderness of temptation to the legions of angels that the Father would surely have put at the Son's disposal. Perhaps realizing that neither of these examples even remotely provides instruction on the angelic hierarchy, Dante turns next to Christ's "sposa e secretaria" [spouse and confidant], the church, which "dice, crede e predica ... tiene e afferma" [states, believes, and preaches ... holds and affirms] that there are nine orders of spiritual creatures (2.5.5). Where did the church put forth this teaching? In the breviary, perhaps, or in various prefaces to the Mass, but most probably for Dante in *Moralia in Job*, where Gregory begins at the bottom of the ladder with the angels and ascends to the seraphim at the top and where he specifies the lineup exactly as the *Convivio* later gives it: Angels, Archangels, Thrones, Dominions, Virtues, Principalities, Powers, Cherubim, and Seraphim.

Wrong! Following those who have been to the Primum Mobile and seen for themselves, one should begin at the top and work one's way down or move from center to circumference, just as the divine light makes its heavenly *exitus* to stimulate the creaturely *redditus*. And as for the relative position of the ranks: Thrones and Principalities, now as evident as a radiant star shining in a flawless heaven, occupy positions quite different from the ones Gregory surmised. By following Gregory, the Dante of the *Convivio* missed the truth.

Paradiso 28 entails an implicit auto-correction by Dante—a looking backward at an earlier work, at a previous appeal to authority, and at a mistaken assumption about truth.[12] The *Convivio* was well-intentioned guesswork, based on the venerable but erroneous authority of tradition; by contrast, the *Commedia* sees the truth for itself. Seeing, therefore, is the ultimate validation of believing—and *Paradiso*, in James Merrill's words, is "pure Show and Tell."[13]

Given the *Commedia*'s penchant for an unannounced looking back to the *Convivio*—most famously, the Casella episode in *Purgatorio* 2 and the moon spots of *Paradiso* 2—we have every reason to expect a palinodic chastening at this precise moment. There should be a frown by Dante as by Gregory, as the shadow of the *Convivio* or *Moralia in Job* falls on the crystalline clarity of *Paradiso*'s Primum Mobile. Instead of frowning, however, Gregory—and presumably Dante with him—breaks forth in a smile that Rachel Jacoff has aptly characterized as "post-palinodic."[14] Among the blessed in *Paradiso*, as Jacoff demonstrates, the backward glance toward a sinful life once lived (or an intellectual error once committed) carries with it no sense of recrimination. In the Heaven of Venus, the notorious Cunizza confides that the erotic self-indulgence that characterized her in the world has long ago been happily "indulged," or pardoned—"e non mi noia" (9.35) [and I do not grieve]. Similarly, Folco of Marseilles, in the same canto and star, confesses the imprint of Venus on his former life. He adds, "Non però qui si pente, ma si ride, / non de la colpa, ch'a mente non torna, / ma del valor ch'ordinò e provide" (103–5) [Yet one does not repent here; here one smiles— / not for the fault, which we do not recall, / but for the Power that fashioned and foresaw]. An occasion that might understandably summon regret over what had been done or thought once in the world instead summons a smile. "Non si pente, ma si ride," says Folco, just as Gregory, realizing that when he "divided himself" from Dionysius he unwittingly left the truth behind, laughs at his own error: "si divise ... di sé medesmo rise."

What are we to make of this smiling? On the one hand, Dante as *theologus* is providing fellow practitioners of the queen of sciences with some role models. Dionysius/Paul is meant to remind us that only when we see face-to-face rather than through a glass darkly can we behold the truth as clearly as we behold a star in the heavens. Seeing trumps believing, and there is much about the faith that cannot be seen: one must wait in all humility for revelation. And then there is Gregory, who in all good faith believed but did not see. When the time for vision comes, he realizes his error but does so with joy: he smiles when experience corrects him. Viewed in this light, the recognition scene that closes *Paradiso* 28 recalls the happy spirit of the theological academy set forth in the heaven of the sun, in *Paradiso* 10–14. There, former rivals and opponents on Earth (Thomas Aquinas and Siger of Brabant, Bonaventure and Joachim, Dominicans and Franciscans) dance together in a round of mutual regard, a concord of *l'uno e l'altro*, of the one and the other. No one cares who once got it wrong now that all behold the truth held in common.

Having said this, we need also to be aware that Dante is contrasting his certain vision of truth with the theologians' mere speculation about it. Like him, they have scripture and tradition as their authorities; but Dante—like Paul—sees for himself. Theologians do their best with their summas, with their careful winnowing of tradition, but the poet beholds the "secret truth" of the angels and in the vernacular lines of his *Commedia* discloses "that and other truths about these circles." He goes on to do exactly this in the following canto, through Beatrice, who tells us, for instance, that Jerome was very wrong to think that the angels were created a long stretch of ages before the universe was made. Why would they be deprived of their God-given task as movers of the celestial wheels; what would they do with eternity on their hands (29.37–68)? Beatrice claims she has scriptural authority on her side, "li scrittor de lo Spirito Santo" (29.41) [scribes of the Holy Ghost]; she also has reason itself (43). But, here as elsewhere, the poet's authority counts most. Either you are with the *Commedia* or you are not: if you are not, you are wrong.

And, perhaps, you smile. Smiling is, in fact, the hallmark gesture of the "sage and serious" Dante, and a sign of his distinctive originality as a Christian poet.[15] If one were to judge solely by the dominant iconography in the Middle Ages, there was nothing much to smile about before the mid-thirteenth century, at least not in the sacred sphere that dominated public art and imagination.[16] There was no place there for anything like those serenely radiant representations of the Buddha or the occasionally raucous bodhisattvas that come to us from Southeast Asia; instead, people in ecclesiastical circles from the time of early Christianity to the late medieval period debated (as at the thirteenth-century University of Paris) whether Christ had ever once laughed during his lifetime. The pious could make a decision on how to conduct themselves properly. On the advice of both Franciscans and Dominicans, Saint Louis vowed to refrain from any show of mirth on Fridays, in honor of the day of the Crucifixion.[17]

The text of choice on the subject might well have been scripture's shortest verse, John 11:35: "et lacrimatus est Iesus," Jesus wept. In this spirit, the Rule of Saint Benedict takes a dim view of humor, denouncing it as the companion of mockery and lewdness, the enemy of the cloister's silence, the antithesis of humility. The Rule speaks about the need for vigilance against humor, about "the bolt of the mouth" and "the barrier of the teeth."[18] Thomas Aquinas, although making place for playfulness as a tonic for the soul, puts the jocose under wraps.[19]

"Jesus wept." Yet, with the rise of the laity and the development of vernacular literatures, laughter and smiling began to work their way into legitimacy. Philippe Ménard's monumental study *Le rire et le sourire dans le roman courtois en France au moyen âge* shows an explosion of both expressions between 1150 and 1250. Ménard also offers something of an anatomy, moving from the full-bellied feudal roar of the macho *gab* (the poetry of male banter) to the refinement of the courtly lady's nuanced *sourire;* to the prophetic laugh of the young woman that foretells the glorious future of Perceval in the poem of that name by Chrétien de Troyes.[20]

It is no doubt significant that this vernacular literature is all secular. But in the same period that Ménard studies, 1150–1250, we also find some extraordinary developments in the sacred sphere. Not surprisingly, Saint Francis celebrates *hilaritas* and tells his brothers, the *ioculatores Domini*, that the outward and visible sign of joy should be a characteristic of their Christian calling. In fact, "in tribulations, in the presence of those who torment you, always remain *hilari vultu*"—of a joyful countenance—which is another way of saying, Don't forget to smile.[21] There was also the ritual of laughter at Easter, the *risus paschalis*, which established that under certain circumstances, and in the light of Christ's triumph over death and the grave, an outburst of laughter was meet, right, and the Christian's bounden duty.[22]

Most important of all, for our purposes, is the appearance in the ecclesiastical art of the mid-thirteenth century—though largely in the north—of what has come to be called "the Gothic smile."[23] An angel in the northwest porch of Reims Cathedral—now known as *Le sourire de Reims*—is taken to be the vanguard of this new movement toward heightened subtlety, expressivity, and (if one can speak thus of an angel) joie de vivre. Also at Reims is an angel of the Annunciation, dated c. 1255, who, in the Gospels' spirit of good news, greets a very serious Virgin Mary portrayed in the old style.

The smiles of Reims Cathedral turned out to be contagious, as we can see in the cathedral at Bamberg, and not only in its famous *Lachengel*. There is Saint Stephen, a radiant proto-martyr happily bearing the stones that killed him, and a cohort of jovial souls who appear in the Last Judgment scene at Christ's right hand. In Magdeburg the wise virgins of the Gospel parable in Matthew 25:1–13 show the joy they feel at being admitted to the marriage feast; in Naumburg the statue of Reglindis, one of the founders of the cathedral there, smiles benignly from her niche; and in Regensburg a serenely happy Gabriel beams at a very blessed Virgin Mary, mutually joyful partners in the Annunciation. In England there is the Angel choir at Lincoln (begun around 1256) and in Toledo, dating from the last quarter of the thirteenth century, the *Virgen Blanca*.

Scholars debate whether this sudden outbreak of smiling grew out of a new sense of psychological nuance that was essentially secular in spirit or, given the sacred context of so many of these images, whether such work shows the spirit through the flesh: the smile "registers an important shift in the discourse of medieval art towards the recognition of the expressive face and body as a coherent locus of ideas: the body becomes the unambiguous sign of the inner moral resources of the protagonist."[24] In the mid-thirteenth century, beatitude became something to smile about.[25]

The greatest master of the Gothic smile, however, was not one of the anonymous visual artists who made these remarkable images, but rather a poet whose birth in 1265 is roughly coincident with the new appeal of the "upturning of the mouth and . . . brightening of the face and eyes."[26] Dante's interest is evident from his first work, the *Vita nuova*, when Beatrice's giving or withholding her *salute*, which I take to mean her smile, means the world: "Quel ch'ella par quando un poco sorride, / non si pò dicer né tenere a mente, / sì è novo miracolo e gentile" (21) [When she a little smiles, her aspect then / no tongue can tell, no memory can hold, / so rare and strange a miracle is she]. Here we see the poet take some liberty with scripture as he invokes Paul's disclaimer in 1 Corinthians 2:9 (itself a citation of Isaiah 64:6) that "eye hath not seen, nor ear heard, neither hath it entered into the heart of man, what things God hath prepared for them that love him." For the apostle, what escapes the comprehension of eye, ear, and heart is the inscrutable divine plan; for the poet of the *Vita nuova*, it is Beatrice's smile.

In the third book of the *Convivio*, the poet presents us with a canzone, "Amor che ne la mente mi ragiona" [Love, which discourses to me in my mind], that also makes much of the beloved's smile. Only now it falls on him not from Beatrice, a flesh-and-blood woman, but rather from Philosophy's allegorical countenance. The canzone speaks of the lady's "dolce riso" as the way Love drew him into its domain (57–58). The ensuing commentary then argues that whenever a "sweet smile" appears on the human face, the soul manifests itself most clearly and indeed uniquely: no two smiles are exactly alike. Taken together, mouth and eyes constitute the "balconi" [balconies] of the soul; they are the means by which a lady steps out of her body and displays her inner self—the way she opens up. "Dimostrasi ne la bocca quasi come colore dopo vetro. E che è ridere se non una corruscazione de la dilettazione de l'anima, cioè uno lume apparente di fuori secondo sta dentro?" (3.8) [The soul reveals itself in the mouth rather like colour behind glass. And what is laughter if not a coruscation of the soul's delight, that is, a light appearing externally which corresponds to the state of being within?]. Nor is this all that a smile can do. The lady's radiant face may even give her lover a foretaste of beatitude: "Cose appariscon nello suo aspetto / che mostran de' piacer di Paradiso" (lines 55–56), says the canzone; things appear in her countenance that show some of the pleasures of Paradise.[27]

By the time of the *Commedia*, the *dolce stil nuovo* hyperbole of the *Vita nuova* and the *Convivio* becomes sheer narrative fact: Beatrice's smile *is* the way that Dante journeys toward the beatific vision of God. *Sorriso/sorridere* and *riso/ridere*—as noun or verb, and apparently interchangeable in meaning—appear over seventy times in the poem, in a wide variety of contexts. The first instance is toward the beginning of *Inferno*, as Virgil smiles upon Dante in Limbo when the great poets of antiquity turn to the pilgrim with a sign of greeting, welcoming him as one of their own ("volsersi a me con salutevol cenno, / e 'l mio maestro sorrise di tanto" [4.98–99] [they turned to me, saluting cordially; / and having witnessed this, my master smiled]). In the following canto, Francesca recalls that single moment in the Lancelot romance when the longed-for smile of Guinevere—her "disïato riso" (5.133)—draws the knight into her embrace (and Paolo and Francesca to their doom). Thereafter, *sorriso* and *riso* are reserved for the province of redemption: over twenty instances in *Purgatorio* and more than double that number in *Paradiso*.

Occasionally, the smile appears on a cosmic scale, as we see in the cases of the planets Venus (*Purg.* 1.20), Mercury (*Par.* 5.97), Mars (*Par.* 14.86), and Jupiter (*Par.* 20.13). The ante is upped in *Paradiso* 27 when Dante's successful completion of his three-part theological examination at the outset of the canto provokes something even more extensive—"un riso / de l'universo" (4–5) [a smile / the universe had smiled]. The poet likens this panorama of joy to the sudden clearing of a misty sky: "sì che 'l ciel ne ride / con le bellezze d'ogne sua paroffia" (28.83–84) [so that the heavens smile with loveliness / in all their regions].

Often, however, smiling emphasizes a distinctly human connection between the dead and the living, a bond of easy affection that works against the tragic failed embrace that Dante found in Virgil's epic tradition. In the antepurgatorial "waiting room" of the second kingdom, for instance, Casella (*Purg.* 2.83) and Manfred (3.112) both smile on seeing Dante suddenly appear in their temporary niche of the afterlife. In canto 4, the pilgrim in turn can barely repress a grin when he discovers that Belacqua, in word and deed, is among the heaven-bound but still his lazy old self (122). Samuel Beckett, in *The Lost Ones*, says of this meeting that it "wrung from Dante one of his rare wan smiles."[28] In fact, the Beckett Collection, in Reading, includes a notecard keeping score of Dante's smiles in the poem.[29] But there is no reason to assume anything wan about the encounter with Belacqua—or about any of the others that follow in *Purgatorio*.

Indeed, the smiles exchanged in the second canticle contribute as much as the presence of the sun to its new atmosphere of light, color, and emotional warmth. For instance, after Dante's sojourn on the terrace of pride, he discovers by touch that there are now only six remaining *P*'s on his forehead. Virgil delights to watch him: "a che guardando, il mio duca sorrise" (12.136) [and as he watched me do this, my guide smiled]. He does so yet again when Dante passes through the refining fire of lust on the final terrace, lured through the flames by one Virgilian blandishment after another: "indi sorrise / come al fanciul si fa ch'è vinto al pome" (27.44–45) [then smiled / as one smiles at a child fruit has beguiled].

The encounter with Statius in *Purgatorio* 21, moreover, is a veritable profusion of heartfelt smiles. Hearing Statius praise Virgil to the skies but enjoined to keep the master's identity concealed, Dante struggles against a flash of a smile—"un lampeggiar di riso" (114)—which he cannot quite conceal and must in the end explain. "Forse che tu ti maravigli, / antico spirto, del rider ch'io fei; / ma più d'ammirazion vo' che ti pigli" (121–23) [Ancient spirit, you / perhaps are wondering at the smile I smiled: / but I would have you feel still more / surprise]. The Statius episode is not only a scene of smiles first suppressed and then expressed; it is also a stimulus for our own smiling. It is difficult to imagine a reader of *Purgatorio* 21's recognition scene failing to mimic the textual "lampeggiar di riso."

Higher up on the purgatorial mountain, in the Garden of Eden, Matelda is repeatedly all smiles (28.67, 76, 96). When she suggests that the ancient poets who sang of the golden age might have dreamed of this very place, Virgil and Statius take her words as a compliment to their kind. They then acknowledge her gracious "corollary" to them by breaking into their own smiles: says Dante, "Io mi rivolsi 'n dietro allora tutto / a' miei poeti, e vidi che con riso / udito avëan l'ultimo costrutto" (28.145–47)

[Then I turned around completely, and I faced / my poets, and saw that with a smile they had heard these last words].

At the climactic moment of the pilgrim's Edenic reunion with Beatrice, it can only be a smile that breaks forth with the grace of "viva luce etterna," as the lady unveils not only her "holy eyes" but also the "seconda bellezza" of her mouth (31.133–45). As she does so, the "balcony" of her smiling face displays not only her soul but also God's light:

> O isplendor di viva luce etterna,
> chi palido si fece sotto l'ombra
> sì di Parnaso, o bevve in sua cisterna,
>   che non paresse aver la mente ingombra,
> tentando a render te qual tu paresti
> là dove armonizzando il ciel t'adombra,
>   quando ne l'aere aperto ti solvesti?
> (31.139–45)

[O splendor of eternal living light, / who's ever grown so pale beneath Parnassus' shade / or has drunk so deeply from its fountain, / that he'd not seem to have his mind confounded, / trying to render you as you appeared / where heaven's harmony was your pale likeness— / your face, seen through the air, unveiled completely?]

The lady's smile is ineffable: it confounds the mind, evades the poet's powers of representation.

Finally, when Dante protests after his immersion in Lethe that he does not recall ever having made himself a stranger to Beatrice (33.91–92), the lady responds to him not with a barbed reproach but with a smile ("sorridendo rispuose" [95]). It is none other than a holy version of the one she used to flash on Earth: "così lo santo riso / a sé traéli con l'antica rete!" (32.5–6) [with its old net, / the holy smile so drew [my eyes] to itself]. Like the machinery of courtly love—the repertoire of eyes and mouth, the "old net" of physical beauty—Beatrice's smile continues to work conventionally, albeit in the new context of the afterlife.

Beatrice goes on to smile throughout *Paradiso*. Sometimes she does so out of impatience or in amusement over Dante's incomprehension of beatitude (e.g., 1.95; 2.52; 3.24; 3.25). So too does Piccarda in the heaven of the moon, who, her eyes smiling ("con occhi ridenti" [3.42]), goes on to "smile a little" ("sorrise un poco" [3.67]) when Dante wonders if she might not be happier in some more exalted place. More often the blessed, otherwise invisible in their beatitude, are experienced by the pilgrim (and signified by the poet) as coruscations of light, or even as smiles *tout court:* Justinian (5.126), Gratian (10.103), Orosius (10.118), Thomas Aquinas (11.17), and Cacciaguida, who is said to be "chiuso e parvente del suo proprio riso" (17.36) [at once hidden and revealed by his smile]. Only the fully visible "dolce riso" of Beatrice appears again and again, however, as an expression of joy over Dante's spiritual progress: 7.17; 10.61; 10.62; 15.34; 18.19; 23.59; 27.104; 29.17; 30.26; 31.92. Because the light that flashes forth from her eyes and mouth is a reflection of God's splendor, a quintessence of Paradise, her smile can easily *dazzle* and overwhelm ("vincendo me col lume d'un sorriso" [18.19] [conquering my will with her smile's splendour]).

There is even one occasion when she withholds the expression that customarily lifts Dante to a higher celestial sphere. In the heaven of Saturn, not wanting him to become like Semele, incinerated on beholding Jove in his divinity, she refuses to smile (21.4–12). Yet two cantos later, in the heaven of the fixed stars, Dante is able not only to withstand Beatrice's "santo riso" (23.59) but also, at her express invitation, to take it all in: "Apri li occhi e riguarda qual son io; / tu hai vedute cose, che possente / se' fatto a sostener lo riso mio" (46–48) [Open your eyes and look on what I now am; / the things you witnessed will have made you strong / enough to bear the power of my smile].

The pilgrim's struggle to express the power of that smile carries over into the Empyrean. Indeed, there Dante reprises his entire relationship to his lady as a move from *riso* to *riso*. In *Paradiso* 30, he recalls what her "dolce riso" meant to him in the *Vita nuova*, when everything depended on a smile's being granted or withheld. As it was in the beginning of his career, so it is now at its end: the poet is overcome by the lady's power: "così lo rimembrar del dolce riso / la mente mia da me medesmo scema" (26–27) [so does the memory of her sweet smile / deprive me of the use of my own mind]. In the next canto, after Beatrice has resumed her allotted place in the heavenly rose, Dante thanks her for her willingness to leave her footprints in Hell in order to liberate him for Heaven. She listens as Dante speaks, "e quella, sì lontana / come parea, sorrise e riguardommi; / poi si tornò a l'etterna fontana" (31.91–93) [and she, however / far away she seemed, smiled, and she looked at me. / Then she turned back to the eternal fountain].

Nor is Beatrice the only one to smile in the Empyrean: indeed, smiling, we are told, is the signifier of the beatific vision. Dante realizes this when he takes in the whole of the heavenly rose with a glance and sees that the blessed have faces "a carità süadi, / d'altrui lume fregiati e di suo riso" (31.49–50) [given up to love— / graced with Another's light and their own smile]. The phrase "di suo riso," each one adorned with his or her own smile, suggests that the joyful expression of eyes and mouth is, like a fingerprint, unique to each of the blessed—as person-specific as the individualized seating in the hierarchy of the heavenly rose. The *Convivio* made it clear that no two faces are alike because each reveals a unique soul. Here we realize the beatific truth of this statement: by their smiles ye shall know them in eternity.

At the apex of the *candida rosa* (*Par.* 31.1), the Blessed Virgin Mary brightens at the sight of more than a thousand "angeli festanti," each distinct in splendor and skill: "Vidi a lor giochi quivi e a lor canti / ridere una bellezza, che letizia / era ne li occhi a tutti li altri santi" (31.133–35) [And there I saw a loveliness that when / it smiled at the angelic songs and games / made glad the smiles of all the other saints]. Mary's smile inspires a flash of recognition in the blessed: the "bellezza" of her mouth rejoices in the angels' sublime play and in turn calls forth "letizia" in all their eyes. When Bernard offers his prayer to her at the outset of the poem's final canto, and before she too, like Beatrice, looks upward to the eternal fountain of divine light, the Virgin's face expresses her joy at his words on behalf of the pilgrim: "Li occhi da Dio diletti e venerati, / fissi ne l'orator, ne dimostraro / quanta i devoti prieghi le son grati" (33.40–42) [The eyes that are revered and loved by God, / now fixed upon the suppliant, showed us / how welcome such devotions are to her]. Once again her smile has a ripple effect, this time on Bernard, who in turn "m'accennava, e sorridea, / perch' io guardassi suso" (49–50) [was signaling—he smiled—to me to look upward]. Yet upward is a spiritual direction in which Dante is already moving on his own, drawn as he is from the smiling faces of Mary and Bernard to the ultimate face-to-face vision of God.

In the final moment of illumination, when the pilgrim beholds the incarnate Christ at the heart of the Trinity, we are not told if any expression falls across the face of "la nostra effige," our image and likeness (131). The Byzantine aesthetic of *Paradiso*, not to mention the sublimity of the moment, argues against this possibility: an iconic Pantocrator's bold, impassive stare comes most readily to mind. And yet the poet had hinted that the inner life of the Trinity, of God's own self, is nothing less than the sharing of a smile. The First Person begets the Second, we are told at the opening of *Paradiso* 10, by "[g]uardando nel suo Figlio con l'Amore / che l'uno e l'altro etternalmente spira" (1–2) [gazing upon His Son with that love / which One and the Other breathe eternally].

Does this mean that the divine gaze is breathing forth a smile and, therefore, that the Holy Spirit "is" the smile of the Father mirrored in the face of the only begotten Son? One thinks in this regard of Meister Eckhart (d. 1327), a contemporary to the north, who also understood that "[w]hen the Father laughs at the Son and the Son laughs back at the Father, that laughter gives pleasure, that pleasure gives joy, that joy gives love, and that love is the Holy Spirit."[30]

This sense of God's own joy is Dante's elaboration on the theological notion of perichoresis, the internal "dance" of the three persons of the Trinity.[31] Indeed, in the closing canto of the poem the poet praises God as one who smiles upon himself: "O luce etterna che sola in te sidi, / sola t'intendi, e da te intelletta / e intendente te ami e arridi!" (33.124–26) [Eternal Light, You only dwell within / Yourself, and only You know You; Self-knowing, / Self-known, You love and smile upon Yourself!]. It is a Trinitarian commonplace to speak of the divine persons as knowing and loving one another. The distinctive Dantean touch is found in the notion of a self-reflecting divine smile—"te . . . arridi"—and with it the idea of God as a community of eternal, spontaneous delight. With this shared joy, this triune smiling, it would not be out of keeping if the divine face that Dante beholds at the end of his vision smiled. After all, even if Jesus of Nazareth wept during his earthly life, might not the Second Person of the Trinity by contrast be all about joy? Many medieval commentators identified that person as the true speaker of Wisdom's words in Proverbs 8:30–31: "cum eo eram cuncta conponens et delectabar per singulos dies ludens coram eo omni tempore; ludens in orbe terrarum et deliciae meae esse cum filiis hominum" [I was with him forming all things: and was delighted every day, playing before him at all times; Playing in the world: and my delights were to be with the children of men].

Given this identification with play and delight, might not Christ, when finally seen face-to-face in the Empyrean, appear under the aspect of joy? Since we know that the blessed in the heavenly rose become most uniquely themselves when they smile, when soul configures face, might not every one of them be following the example of the Word made flesh? Might not the *imago Dei* consist in the uniquely human ability to laugh, for, as Aristotle said, humankind "is the only one of the animals that laughs"?[32] Might not *sorriso* and *riso* constitute the *imago Dei* as much as reason and will do; might not the great gift of the beatific vision, the end for which humankind was made, be the infinite mirroring of God's smile?

Note my persistent resort to rhetorical questions and to the hypothetical "might not?" as I move across the (s)miles of Dante's universe from assertions of seeing to the realm of surmise, from the *Commedia*'s relentless truth claims to its sheer playfulness. Every smile given, received, or exchanged signifies that someone was there to notice—Dante the character in the poem, who first saw for himself and then told us about his vision. But every smile also asserts the imaginative activity of Dante the poet, draws attention to his sustained act of invention, his bringing into this drama of salvation an expression that over the course of the poem he made into his hallmark. The massive structure of the text, its ponderous claim to authority, is constantly alleviated by a gesture that flashes with the imagination's quicksilver—yet another sign that despite the graven aspect of the poem, by the end of *Paradiso* Dante is writing on bright air.[33]

The *Commedia* combines scripture's assurance about historicity with fiction's freedom to raise an eyebrow, conceal a guffaw, and introduce a spirit of sublime play (angelic and otherwise) into an ultimately serious journey of redemption. The smiles that accumulate faster and faster as the poem moves toward its conclusion may even be a sign that the poet is emulating the *lieto fattore*, the happy divine creator.[34] As God brought existence into being with joy, he provided in the cosmos a divine model for the fictive copy, for the poem whose name, after all, is "commedia."

As this review of *riso* and *sorriso* should suggest, the smile is not only Dante's signature gesture but perhaps his most original and indeed useful contribution to medieval theology—and indeed to the Christian tradition itself, which has long found it easier to recall that "Jesus wept" than to imagine that he might have laughed as well. Despite the degree to which Dante is associated with the infernal, it is his creation of a "smile of the universe," radiant throughout Purgatory and Paradise, that shows his spin on the ancient religion he inherited. To be told that God the Trinity smiles upon himself; to see Gregory smiling at his former error; to catch the delight in Mary's eye, which spreads like lightning throughout the heavenly rose; to consider that the resurrection of the body might mean the raising up of one's own distinctive smile; or to imagine seeing God face-to-face as an encounter with holiness that does not require eyes averted and lips closed tight but rather entails the spontaneity of a smile returning a smile—to entertain any of these possibilities requires a "new life" for the Christian imagination, one that did not take place in Dante's fourteenth century and is now (sadly) long overdue.

Paul Binski notes that in the medieval world of images, even in what he calls "'the humane' post-1300 era," Italian faces "for the most part resolutely refuse to smile"; by contrast, "the smiling image, especially that of the Virgin Mary, had become ingrained in the visual culture of northern Europe."[35] One wonders in the end if the smile was the best gift Dante received from the north—that is, from the territory of a Holy Roman Empire that otherwise failed him so miserably. In any event, rather than the imperial eagle, the smile in effect became the *Commedia*'s "sacrosanto segno," its "sacred sign" (*Par.* 6.32). It is the gesture that moves us from *Inferno* to *Paradiso*, from the human to the divine, and from time to eternity.

Notes

An earlier version of this essay was delivered as a lecture at the University of Cambridge conference from which this volume originated. It was first published as "All Smiles: Poetry and Theology in Dante," *PMLA* 121, no. 2 (2006): 371–87. Translations of the *Commedia* are from Dante, *Divine Comedy*, tr. Mandelbaum.

1. Milton, *Areopagitica*, 311.
2. See the essays gathered in Hawkins and Jacoff, *The Poets' Dante*; McDougal, *Dante among the Moderns*; Havely, *Dante's Modern Afterlife*.
3. Walpole, letter to William Mason, 25 June 1782 (cited in Toynbee, *Dante in English Literature*, 1:340); Nietzsche, "Skirmishes," 60.
4. For readings of *Paradiso* 28, see Chiavacci Leonardi's commentary; Contini, "*Paradiso* XXVIII"; Cosmo, "I ministri"; Frattini, "Il canto XXVII del *Paradiso*"; Padoan, "Il canto XXVIII del *Paradiso*"; Psaki, "*Paradiso* XXVIII"; Scrivano, "Intelligenza del cosmo"; Spera, "La poesia degli angeli"; Taddeo, "Il canto

XXVIII del *Paradiso*"; and Vandelli, "Il canto XXVIII del *Paradiso*." Contini (who emphasizes the reiterated truth claim of the canto) and Psaki are especially insightful.

5. In *Paradiso* 28.106–14, Beatrice establishes that the acuity of the angels' intellectual vision of God determines their capacity to love, to shine, and to move. Bosco and Reggio in their notes to *Paradiso* 28.109–11 (469) point to *ST* IaIIae.3.1–8; *Supplement* 92, ad1–3. See also Dante, *Mon.* 3.16.7.

6. A sense of the extent of subsequent theological discussion can be found in the "Index of Angels" in *Patrologia Latina* 39–40, which moves from the second to the twelfth centuries. For Dante on the angels, especially in the context of dispute about their hierarchy, see especially Mellone, "Gerarchia angelica"; also Mellone, "Gli angeli in Dante," as well as Fallani, "Le gerarchie angeliche"; Boyde, *Dante Philomythes and Philosopher*, 172–201; and the superb discussion by David Keck, who investigates (and does much to elucidate) the thicket of diverse angelic rankings (*Angels and Angelology*, 53–58).

7. In his sermon on Luke 15:8–10, the thirty-fourth of his *Homiliae in evangelia*, Gregory the Great lists the nine orders of angels as follows: Seraphim, Cherubim, Thrones, Dominions, Principalities, Powers, Virtues, Archangels, and Angels (305). In *Moralia in Job*, bk. 32, ch. 48, however, they are given as Angels, Archangels, Thrones, Dominions, Virtues, Principalities, Powers, Cherubim, and Seraphim (1666).

8. See Rorem, *Pseudo-Dionysius*; also Keck, *Angels and Angelology*, 53–58. The *Celestial Hierarchy* actually gives two rankings. In one passage, we find Thrones, Cherubim, Seraphim, Powers, Virtues, Dominions, Angels, Archangels, and Principalities (bk. 6, ch. 2). In just a few chapters, however, Dionysius gives what becomes his "standard" list: Seraphim, Cherubim, Thrones, Dominions, Virtues, Powers, Principalities, Archangels, Angels (bk. 6, chs. 7–9).

9. Thomas writes, "gradus angelicorum ordinum assignant et Gregorius et Dionysius, quantum ad alia quidem convenienter, sed quantum ad principatus et virtutes differenter. Nam Dionysius collocat virtutes sub dominationibus et supra potestates, principatus autem sub potestatibus et supra Archangelos, Gregorius autem ponit principatus in medio dominationum et potestatum, virtutes vero in medio potestatum et Archangelorum. Et utraque assignatio fulcimentum habere potest ex auctoritate apostoli" (*ST* Ia.108.6.ad) [Gregory and Dionysius are in agreement in arraying the angelic orders, except for Principalities and Powers. For Dionysius ranks Virtues below Dominions and above Powers; Principalities, below Powers and above Archangels. But Gregory puts Principalities between Dominions and Powers; Virtues, between Powers and Archangels. Both arrangements can draw on the authority of St. Paul for support]. Likewise, "virtutes, secundum Gregorium, videntur esse idem quod principatus secundum Dionysium. Nam hoc est primum in divinis ministeriis, miracula facere, per hoc enim paratur via Annuntiationi Archangelorum et Angelorum" (Ia.108.6.resp.4) [Virtues in Gregory's sense seem to be the same as Principalities

in Dionysius's sense, for the first among divine ministries is the working of miracles that prepares the way for the messages of Archangels and Angels]. Bonaventure sees more at stake here than Thomas and opts for Dionysius's reckoning because of his connection to Paul's firsthand account: "Quia enim diversimode distinctionem *hierarchiarum* consideraverunt, ideo et divisiones *ordinum* in ipsis diversimode assignaverunt ... Sed cum utrumque horum simul non possit esse verum ... Et dicendum ad hoc, quod magis innitendum est dicto Dionysii, tum quia ipse didicit, sicut dicitur, a Paulo, et ita tradidit, sicut audivit ... Dionysius distinctionem hierarchiarum sumsit penes ea quae sunt ipsis angelicis spiritibus *intrinseca* et *essentialia;* et ideo sic ordines distinxit, sicut habent collocari in caelis. Gregorius vero plus pensavit *opera* et *officia;* et ideo sic distinxit, secundum quod plus potest valere ad eruditionem nostram." In translation, "[Gregory and Dionysius] think differently about the characteristics of the angels in the celestial hierarchy, and for that reason they ascribed the divisions of the order differently.... But since both of these divisions cannot simultaneously be true ... there must be an examination of which belief is true and which belief should be relied on more, so that the hierarchies and orders are not confused. The answer to this question must be that Dionysius's beliefs ought to be relied on more ... because he learned his knowledge, as it must be reported, from Paul and handed down this knowledge just as he heard it.... Also, Dionysius understood the division of the hierarchies to rest on those qualities that are interior and that determine the essence of the angelic spirits themselves. Gregory, to be sure, considered the works and duties of the angels to be of greater importance, and therefore he divided the hierarchies so as to give more weight to our own earthly concerns [i.e., works and duties]" (*Sententiarum* bk. 2, dist. 9, art. 1, question 1; trans. mine). Keck contrasts the theological methodologies of Thomas and Bonaventure "to show the extent to which theologians disagreed about the approach to the angelic hierarchies" (*Angels and Angelology,* 56).

10. *The Golden Legend* of Jacobus de Voragine, completed in 1260, puts the relationship between Dionysius and his "source" this way: "It is said that Paul revealed to Dionysius what he, in ecstasy, had seen in the third heaven, as Dionysius himself seems to insinuate in more than one place. Hence he discoursed upon the hierarchies of the angels, their orders, ranks, and functions, so brilliantly and clearly that you would not think that he had learned all this from someone else, but that he himself had been rapt to the third heaven and there had looked upon all he described" (2:239).

11. Peter Lombard gives two hierarchies: in *Sententiae,* bk. 2, dist. 9, ch. 1, he follows Dionysius's standard listing in *The Celestial Hierarchy,* bk. 6, chs. 7–9, whereas in *Sententiae,* bk. 2, dist. 9, ch. 2, he follows Gregory's sermon, falsely attributing the ranking to Dionysius. Bernard of Clairvaux in the fifth book of his *Five Books on Consideration* follows Gregory's sermon in one passage (ch. 10) and in another comes up with yet a different sequence (ch. 7): Angels, Archangels, Virtues, Powers, Principalities, Dominions, Thrones, Cherubim, and Seraphim.

12. Zygmunt Barański warns against making too much of the reader's alleged knowledge of the *Convivio*, which Pertile has argued Dante not only left unfinished but wanted actively to suppress. Nonetheless, as Barański also says, this does not mean that the *Convivio* has no role to play in our understanding of the poem: "Even if Dante had wanted to keep the treatise quite a private affair, the very fact that he authored both books means that—at least as far as one privileged reader was concerned—the earlier text could not but be significant for the later one. And thanks to the art of allusion, this is indeed the case" ("The 'New Life' of 'Comedy,'" 20; see also Pertile, "Dante's *Comedy*").

13. From "M" in "The Book of Ephraim," the first part of *The Changing Light at Sandover*.

> The resulting masterpiece takes years to write;
> More, since the dogma of its day
> Calls for a Purgatory, for a Hell,
> Both of which Dante thereupon, from footage
> Too dim or private to expose, invents.
> His Heaven, though, as one cannot but sense,
> Tercet by tercet, is pure Show and Tell.
>
> (45)

For more on these two poets, see Merrill's essay on Dante, "Divine Poem," in Hawkins and Jacoff, *The Poets' Dante*, 227–35, and Jacoff, "Merrill and Dante."

14. Jacoff, "Post-Palinodic Smile." For Dante's characteristic use of the palinode, see also Freccero, "Casella's Song"; Ascoli, "Palinode and History."

15. A place to begin any inquiry of the smile in Dante is with the word studies in the *ED* for *ridere* (4:920–21), *riso* (4:977–78), *sorridere* (5:336–37), and *sorriso* (5:337). For the most extensive treatment of the smile in Dante heretofore, see Burrows, *Gestures and Looks*, 156–79.

16. Paul Binski writes: "Christianity is not the most jocular of iconic religions, and offers us nothing at its heart to compare with the serene smile of the Buddha, or the fecund cheer of the Hindu pantheon. The phenomenon of smiling seems at odds with the expressive character of the Christian religion as chartered in the Gospels, apocryphal and hagiographic literature, and indeed much in Christian art: Jesus wept, but no one in the canon of 'authentic' early Christian literature smiles, though smiling does occur in later hagiography" ("The Angel Choir," 354). See Braet, "What about Medieval Humour?"; Trumble, *A Brief History of the Smile*; and, especially interesting, LeGoff, "Laughter in the Middle Ages."

17. LeGoff, "Laughter in the Middle Ages," 44. LeGoff's interest in the study of medieval laughter began with Curtius's excursus on "jest and earnest in medieval literature" (*European Literature*, 417–35) and "the church and laughter" (420–22), especially the latter's discussion of whether Jesus ever laughed during his earthly life.

18. LeGoff writes, on the Rule of Saint Benedict and its conception of the human body in relation to good and evil: "Eyes, ears, and mouth are the filters of good and evil and must be used in order to let the good enter or express itself and to block the road for evil. The *Regula magistri* speaks of the 'bolt of the mouth,' the 'barrier of the teeth,' etc. When laughing is starting, it must at all costs be prevented from expressing itself. So we see how, of all the forms of expression which come from the outside, laughter is the worst, the pollution of the mouth" ("Laughter in the Middle Ages," 46). The *risus monasticus* was denounced as an occasion of sin, yet the existence of *joca monacorum* collections from the eighth century on suggests that the brothers often succumbed to the temptation. So too, of course, did preachers in the pulpit, eager to keep their congregations engaged.

19. To combat the notion of a grim Middle Ages, Luiz Jean Lauand intends to show that "*ludus* pervaded medieval culture" and to argue that Thomas had great respect for *eutrapalia*, or "good play." Yet when one looks at the 356 instances of *ludus* in Thomas's writings that Lauand amassed, it is clear that most of them refer to the dangers of bad play. See Lauand, "*Ludus*." For a twentieth-century exploration of this issue, see the objections of the rigorist monk Jorge de Burgos in Umberto Eco's novel *The Name of the Rose*.

20. See Ménard's chapter "L'expression du rire et du sourire," in *Le rire*, 420–64, esp. 426–47. See also his essay "Rires et sourires."

21. LeGoff speaks of laughter as a form of Franciscan spirituality and comportment ("Laughter in the Middle Ages," 51).

22. On the *risus paschalis*, see Jacobelli, *Il risus paschalis*; and Wendland, *Ostermärchen*. The documentation we have comes from the north (Bavaria) and from the seventeenth century. A Google search on the Web reveals that the practice is currently being revived, though largely (and surprisingly) by Presbyterians.

23. On the Gothic smile, see Binski, "The Angel Choir"; Svanberg, "The Gothic Smile"; Sauerländer, *Cathedrals and Sculpture*, vol. 2; and Trumble, *A Brief History of the Smile*, 103–32. Ménard (*Le rire*) connects the advent of the smiling saints and angels to the new frequency of the word *sourire* over *rire*. Binski contrasts laughter and smiling: "Because true expressivity requires control, the nuanced smile lies essentially within the sphere of muscular control, and hence of acculturated bodily dispositions. Laughter, though also culturally variable, tends in contrast toward the sphere of nature; to the loss of, or denial of, control" (354).

24. Binski, "The Angel Choir," 355–56.

25. "What is light in the heavens?" asks the Neoplatonist Marsilio Ficino in the fifteenth century: "Abundance of life from the angels, unfolding of power from the heavens, and laughter in the sky?" (cited in Gage, *Colour and Culture*, 78).

26. According to *Webster's New World Dictionary of the American Language*, a smile is "a facial expression indicating usually pleasure, favor, or amusement ... characterized by an upturning of the mouth and usually accompanied, especially in indicating pleasure, by a brightening of the face and eyes."

27. The *Convivio* continues its discussion of the smile in bk. 3, ch. 15, where Dante glosses the notion of the lady's smile as an adumbration of the joys of Paradise. In this passage, it becomes fully clear that the lady in question is Wisdom, or Philosophy.

28. Beckett, *The Lost Ones*, 14.

29. Knowlson, *Damned to Fame*, 279, n. 31. My thanks to Christopher Ricks for making this connection for me.

30. *Meister Eckhart*, 245.

31. *Perichoresis* (from a Greek word for "dancing around"), or *circumincession*, denotes the mutual interpenetration of the three persons of the Trinity, the common ground of God. *Perichoresis* is related to the term *co-inherence*, used extensively by Charles Williams in his Dante criticism.

32. "For those who are tickled laugh quickly because of the motion that quickly reaches this location [i.e., the midriff]. And though they heat up gently, nevertheless they manifestly act and move though independent of choice. And mankind alone is ticklish both because of the thinness of his skin and because he is the only one of the animals that laughs." *On the Parts* 3.10, 672b.

33. Follow the sequence of *Paradiso* 33.58–66, an extended simile in which the poet describes the difficulty of saying anything about an increasingly ineffable experience: a solid becomes liquid before evaporating, unsealing or "unsigning" itself ("si disigilla") into the wind ("al vento").

34. "Letizia" [joy] and the adjective "lieto" occur over fifty times in the *Commedia* (only seven of which are in *Inferno*). Joy is usually registered in the face, in the eyes particularly, or through an expression or a gesture; it is closely related, therefore, to the smile. When God is described as "lieto" [joyful], it is often in his capacity as the "lieto fattore" (*Purg.* 16.89) [happy maker].

35. Binski, "The Angel Choir," 352.

3

In Unknowability as Love
The Theology of Dante's *Commedia*

VITTORIO MONTEMAGGI

"Nulla vedere e amor mi costrinse"

The debate over the question of the relationship between theology and narrative poetry in the *Commedia* is one of the oldest and most controversial surrounding Dante's text. And while it would be possible to trace a broad seven-hundred-year-old critical consensus as to the importance of this relationship, it would be impossible to trace any consensus as to its nature. In relation to current scholarship, moreover, it could even seem contentious to propose that the *Commedia* may, in its entirety as a narrative poem, be read as theology. There seems to be wide scholarly agreement that theology and narrative poetry are intimately related in the *Commedia* and that this relationship is one of the most important structuring principles of Dante's poetics, but there has been relatively little exploration of the idea that this principle underlies every aspect of Dante's poem. It is for this idea that I argue in the present essay.

The reason is that underlying Dante's work is not only a theological understanding of the value of narrative and poetry, but also a theological understanding of language itself: of language intended as that aspect of human nature through which human beings relate to each other, to the world, and to God. For Dante, as we shall see, to be human, to speak, to love, and to be related to God are, if properly conceived, one and the same thing. As I will propose, this recognition requires a threefold perspective on attempts to think about the relationship between theology and poetry in the *Commedia*. It goes without saying that any reading of the *Commedia*, and therefore even of the *Commedia* as theology, ought to respond, as should be the case with all poetry and all narrative, to the work's form as well as to its content. This is an important idea in itself, and one that chimes well with much contemporary theology and with many recent revaluations of medieval thought. But with Dante we can go further than this. In the *Commedia* it is not just the case that form mirrors and enhances content. It is also the case that reflection on the relationship between form and content is brought deliberately to the fore by Dante, and given explicit theological grounding in his understanding of language. Given the theology of language underlying the *Commedia*, any attempt to read the work as a theological poem, I propose, must take three things into account: first, the dynamics which, as Dante's narrative suggests, define properly oriented relationships between human beings and between human beings and God; second, the idea of language which, for Dante, is at one with these dynamics; and, third, the way in which Dante consciously presents the *Commedia* as an example or model of such a kind of language.

This threefold perspective has important implications for the way we read the *Commedia* as theology. More generally, it also has significant implications for how we might think about theology finding fruitful and illuminating expression as poetry. For this perspective provides a compelling invitation to engage with the idea that if it is true that there is more to theology than propositional objectivity, factual description, or mimetic representation; and if it is true that in theology, form matters as much as content; then this is because God, as the unfathomable ground of all existence, is intimately related not only to how one might understand or represent divine being but to the acts of intellection and representation themselves; and because, as love, God is intimately related not only to what one might say about divine being but also to the ethical nature and value of one's utterances.

Specifically, I contend that the theological dynamics of the *Commedia* are governed by a twofold recognition. Dante insists that God is beyond the constrictions and power of human reason and language; and, equally, that God *is* the love which sets the universe in motion and sustains it in its being. I propose that by exploring the inextricable relationship between these two ideas, we will better understand the theological nature of the *Commedia*. On a most basic level, these two recognitions point to a fusion in the *Commedia* of cataphatic and apophatic impulses. On the one hand, the *Commedia* appears to be a monument to Dante's belief that the human mind can—and, indeed, as far as possible should—attempt to construct a comprehensive picture of the universe and its relationship to its Creator; on the other hand, Dante seems to want to point to the inadequacy of the human being fully to comprehend or speak about God. Although commentators have tended to emphasize the cataphatic aspect of the *Commedia*, the apophatic dimension has attracted appreciation in recent years.[1] Yet such appraisals are often limited in their application to the text of the poem (concentrating, for the most part, on the *Paradiso*) and often do not address in any great detail the relationship in the *Commedia* between apophatic and cataphatic impulses. I suggest that a theological hermeneutics for the *Commedia* as a whole may find its foundations in the way in which apophatic and cataphatic intersect in the text's particular poetic and narrative form.

The point is that for Dante, negative and affirmative theological discourses are not mutually exclusive. Neither discourse is properly meaningful if understood in isolation from the other. In this, Dante is at one with the medieval theological tradition as a whole, in which the polarization of apophatic and cataphatic would have made little sense at all.[2] In particular, however, I suggest that in the *Commedia*, apophatic and cataphatic meet in the ethical dimension of the poem. It is probably no coincidence that Dante's and Beatrice's entrance into the light and love constituting the Empyrean is inaugurated by a line—"nulla vedere e amor mi costrinse" (*Par.* 30.15)—which, in describing how Dante is constrained to turn his eyes towards Beatrice "from seeing nothing—and in love—," seems narratively and poetically to be paraphrasing 1 John 4:12: "Deum nemo vidit umquam si diligamus invicem Deus in nobis manet et caritas eius in nobis perfecta est" [No man hath seen God at any time. If we love one another, God abideth in us: and his charity is perfected in us]. *Paradiso* 30.15 thus seems to make explicit a basic theological principle underlying the writing of the *Commedia*: man ultimately cannot and will not, even in Heaven, fully come to know God; what man can and ought to do, and most perfectly will do in Heaven, is to participate in the love which God is. And, for Dante, human beings may participate, may *be*, the love which God is through their relationships with one another, relationships which ought to be modeled on and partake in the life of Christ.

The other side of the coin of the (brilliant) darkness in which God dwells in relation to the human intellect is that of sin and suffering, which led Christ to cry, "My God, my God, why have you forsaken me?"

The reflections that follow consist of two main sections. In the first, I outline—primarily through reference to passages from the *Paradiso* and the *Purgatorio*—what I take to be the dynamics of Dante's theology of language, and of the way in which language, for Dante, is at one with love. In the second, I suggest how such an understanding of Dante's theology can both enhance and be enriched by reflection on Dante's encounters with Ulysses and Ugolino in the *Inferno*, and on some of their echoes across the rest of the poem.

THE THEOLOGICAL LANGUAGE OF THE *COMMEDIA*

There can be no doubt that Dante's idea of love plays a role of fundamental importance in the theology of the *Commedia*. One need only think of Dante's famous reference to God, in telling us of his union with God at the very end of the *Commedia*, as "l'amor che move il sole e l'altre stelle" [the love that moves the sun and other stars]. The account of creation in *Paradiso* 29 provides a valuable starting point for considering the importance of Dante's idea of God as love:

> Non per aver a sé di bene acquisto,
> ch'esser non può, ma perché suo splendore
> potesse, risplendendo, dir "*Subsisto*",
>   in sua etternità di tempo fore,
> fuor d'ogne altro comprender, come i piacque,
> s'aperse in nuovi amor l'etterno amore.
> (13–18)

[Not seeking any good that He had not— / there can be none— but so his shining-out / could in return shine back and say: "I am", / in His eternity beyond all time, / beyond our understanding, as He pleased, / to new loves Love Eternal opened out.]

Strictly speaking, this passage is about the creation of the angels—"nuovi amor." Yet it tells us much about Dante's understanding of God and of how, as love, God relates to creation. For Dante, the love which God is, and through which everything that is has its being, reflects itself into creation, finding new and particular expression in creatures capable of loving. This is very significant for our purposes. For while no explicit mention is made here of human beings, and while there is no doubt that for Dante human beings are quite different from angels, human beings for Dante are the only other creatures endowed with intellect and will and therefore capable of loving. This is a valuable passage to keep in mind, for the theological dynamics it beautifully embodies can help illuminate our understanding of the relationship that exists, as love, between human beings and God. In this respect, it is extremely interesting to note that even though, for Dante, angels are in essence without the need for language, the idea of language plays an important role in the passage: it is as language—"*Subsisto*"—that Dante chooses metaphorically to represent the re-reflection, in and as the angels, of the love which God is.[3]

Before turning to the question of human beings and language, however, it is worth giving Dante's angels some further consideration. A different point, made through reference to angels, has important implications for Dante's idea of the relationship between human beings and God. In meeting Peter Damian in *Paradiso* 21, Dante the character asks him to explain the workings of divine will. Peter Damian replies that he is not in a position to do so because not even the angel closest to God has full comprehension of the will and being of God, as this is something that cannot pertain to any created being (83–102). It would be difficult to overestimate the importance of this idea in Dante's theology. It is often assumed that for Dante, the inability fully to comprehend God applies only to corruptible or fallen human beings and disappears when redeemed human beings reach Heaven. For Dante, however, this inability does not disappear in Heaven, since it pertains to created beings not as fallen or even as corruptible but simply as created. All being, for Dante, originates in God and is constantly sustained in existence by God, who is existence itself. As such, full comprehension of God ultimately eludes the grasp of all created intellectual beings—angelic or human—since that which is the ground of all existence cannot itself ultimately be reduced to an object of intellectual comprehension. As the ground of all existence, God is as intimately related to the *act* of intellection as to any *object* of intellection. Or, to phrase this in terms of the metaphor of light dear to medieval theologians, and which Dante employs in *Para-*

diso 29, the light through which one sees cannot fully become an object of sight.[4]

This does not, of course, imply that for Dante, human beings cannot meaningfully speak about God. Dante would not have written the *Commedia* if he thought this was the case. It does imply, however, that the meaning of theological utterances always lies in more than their objective accuracy. To speak meaningfully about God, for Dante, is also always to convey an invitation to others to consider what it might mean to think of one's being as intimately related to the unfathomable and ultimately non-objectifiable love that sets the universe in motion and sustains it in existence. Significantly, while for Dante the life of the blessed is not characterized by full comprehension of God, it is characterized by full union with God and by perfect participation in the love which God is. When in *Paradiso* 3 the pilgrim meets Piccarda Donati—sister of one of his dearest friends—he is baffled to hear from her that she is perfectly happy even if she is in the lowest of the degrees of blessedness that Dante will witness on his way to God. Piccarda responds to Dante's bafflement by reassuring him that while she might be in the lowest group of souls, she is nonetheless perfectly at one with divine being and love.

> "Frate, la nostra volontà quïeta
> virtù di carità, che fa volerne
> sol quel ch'avemo, e d'altro non ci asseta.
>   Se disïassimo esser più superne,
> foran discordi li nostri disiri
> dal voler di colui che qui ne cerne;
>   che vedrai non capere in questi giri,
> s'essere in carità è qui *necesse*,
> e se la sua natura ben rimiri.
>   Anzi è formale ad esto beato *esse*
> tenersi dentro a la divina voglia,
> per ch'una fansi nostre voglie stesse;
>   sì che, come noi sem di soglia in soglia
> per questo regno, a tutto il regno piace
> com' a lo re che 'n suo voler ne 'nvoglia.
>   E 'n la sua volontade è nostra pace:
> ell' è quel mare al qual tutto si move
> ciò ch'ella crïa o che natura face."
>   (70–87)

[Dear brother, we in will are brought to rest / by power of *caritas* that makes us will / no more than what we have, nor thirst for more. / Were our desire to be more highly placed, / all our desires would then be out of tune / with His, who knows and wills where we should be. / Yet discord in these spheres cannot occur— / as you, if you reflect on this, will see— / since charity is *a priori* here. / In formal terms, our being in beatitude / entails in-holding to the will of God, / our own wills thus made one with the divine. / In us, therefore, there is, throughout this realm, / a placing, rung to rung, delighting all / —our king as well in-willing us in will. / In His volition is the peace we have. / That is the sea to which all being moves, / be it what that creates or Nature blends.]

We learn here that for Dante, the blessed cannot but be in a state of perfect charity; and that this means that the very form and essence of heavenly being is defined by the coming together of the individual will of the blessed and the will of God, as one will.

For Dante, then, it is in the nature of the truth that God is, that such a truth cannot be fully comprehended *and* that it can fully be participated in. As the "alta carità" which brings all there is into existence, God necessarily lies beyond the full grasp of created intellects; but intellectual beings can fully come to partake in the very essence of that same love. All this gains greater theological depth if we turn to the *Purgatorio*. And the most convenient place to start, in this respect, is Dante's encounter with Forese—Piccarda's brother—on the terrace of gluttony.[5] Most significant for our purposes are the words with which Forese describes the driving force behind the actions of the souls in Purgatory. About the pain suffered by the gluttons—who are constantly kept in a state of thirst and hunger by mysterious odors coming from two inverted trees—Forese says:

["]E non pur una volta, questo spazzo
girando, si rinfresca nostra pena:
io dico pena, e dovria dir sollazzo,
    ché quella voglia a li alberi ci mena
che menò Cristo lieto a dire '*Elì*',
quando ne liberò con la sua vena."
                  (*Purg.* 23.70–75)

[Nor once alone, in circling round this space, / is agony and pain refreshed in us. / I call it pain. Rightly, I should say solace. / For that same yearning leads us to the tree, / that led Christ, in his joy, to say '*Elì*', / when through his open veins he made us free.]

The souls of Purgatory—who are learning in the afterlife what, ideally, they should have learned during their earthly life—prepare themselves for heavenly being by conforming their will to that of Christ, who on the cross, in conforming to the will of God, cried out—as Dante puts it—"*Elì*":[6] "Heli Heli lema sabacthani" (Mt 27:46).[7] If human beings are to partake in the perfect charity which is the life of Heaven, they must learn to conform their will to that of Christ. The union of divine and human willing, spoken of by Piccarda as the essence of Heaven, has its theological grounding in the Christology of *Purgatorio* 23. It is significant, moreover, that Dante should choose in *Purgatorio* 23 to foreground Christ's cry from the cross, and with it the idea that, in the very process of embodying the love which is to redeem mankind, Christ too feels unable fully to comprehend God. We thus find another powerful expression of the interconnection in Dante's thought between love and the unknowability of God. And we do so in conjunction with finding a powerful expression of Dante's idea that when it comes to thinking about the relationship between human beings and God, the interconnection between love and the unknowability of God ought to be configured in a Christological key.

We thus begin to see in more specific terms how, according to Dante, it might be possible for human beings, too, to think of their own being as a reflection of the splendor of the love which God is. The references to the cross and to physical suffering, however, also point to the fact that the way in which human beings may partake in divine love and may be expressions of that love cannot be the same as the manner in which angels do so. For human beings are embodied beings.[8] They are the only beings to partake at once of the immaterial and the material aspects of creation and the only beings to be at once temporal and eternal.[9] In Dante's understanding of the hylomorphic relationship of body and soul, it is simply not possible, when it comes to human beings, to think of the soul not in conjunction with the body, and vice versa. For Dante, the human soul is the form of the body. This is why, in the *Commedia*, Dante—who emphasizes the importance of this question more than most of his medieval contemporaries—presents us with the view that even between death and resurrection, human souls exist in embodied fashion: upon reaching the afterlife, they generate a body from the air around them.[10] Whether or not this view was meant by Dante to be taken literally, it nonetheless compellingly makes the point that a soul which does not inform an individual human body is not, for Dante, a properly *human* soul.

The significance of all this for our purposes lies in the fact that for Dante, to be human is not only to be an embodied being endowed with intellect and capable of loving, but also to be a linguistic being: humans are one because of the other. As made clear in *De vulgari eloquentia* 2.3, language, for Dante, is a direct counterpart of human hylomorphism and is inseparable from the particularities and limitations of individual embodied existence. Words are both physical and rational signs, and in this they are emblematic of the way in which, given their embodiedness, human beings communicate. To be human is to be an embodied, rational, linguistic, and social being. It is impossible, on Dantean terms, to think of any one of these aspects of human existence in any other way than in conjunction with the others.

It is thus extremely interesting to note that Dante's encounter with Forese leads, in the narrative, to the *Commedia*'s most extended reflection on how human beings come to be human in the first place. Having witnessed Forese's suffering, Dante asks his guides Virgil and Statius how it is that souls in the afterlife can be affected in material terms. Statius provides the most complete answer to Dante's question and explains how the souls produce an aerial body upon reaching the afterlife. But in answering Dante's question, Statius also provides a full lesson on the generation of the body and on the creation of the soul. He first explains how in the womb the embryo develops into a vegetative and then into a sensitive soul. He then says:

> Ma come d'animal divegna fante,
> non vedi tu ancor: quest' è tal punto,
> che più savio di te fé già errante,
> sì che per sua dottrina fé disgiunto
> da l'anima il possibile intelletto,
> perché da lui non vide organo assunto.
> Apri a la verità che viene il petto;
> e sappi che, sì tosto come al feto
> l'articular del cerebro è perfetto,

> lo motor primo a lui si volge lieto
> sovra tant' arte di natura, e spira
> spirito novo, di vertù repleto,
>   che ciò che trova attivo quivi, tira
> in sua sustanzia, e fassi un'alma sola,
> che vive e sente e sé in sé rigira.
>   (*Purg.* 25.61–75)

[This creature will become a speaking child. / Yet *how*, you don't yet see. And this same point / led someone far more wise than you astray, / who in his teachings set the soul apart / from *intellectus* as *possibilis*, / finding no organ taken up by that. / Open your heart. Receive the coming truth. / Know this: when once the foetal brain is brought / to full articulation in the womb, / the Primal Cause of Motion turns in joy / to see so much of nature's art, and breathes / new breath of spirit filled with power within, / which draws all active elements it finds / into its being and thus forms one soul / which lives and feels and turns as conscious self.]

The first thing to note about this passage is the word "fante"—"child" or "infant" but, without the prefix "-in," etymologically "a speaking being," a being capable of speech. Thus Dante chooses to speak of the moment in which the embryo becomes human through reference to language. We also find that the moment the embryo becomes human is the moment in which the individual soul is created directly by God ("motor primo") and breathed by God into the womb. To be human, for Dante, is to enjoy a direct relationship with God, a relationship defined by the creation of the individual soul by God and by the fact that, in being so created, the human being is capable of speech. This truth is, moreover, tied to the image of an open or pierced chest (67). And this could suggest that it might fruitfully be thought of in terms of the physical suffering of the crucifixion. The significance of this suggestion is enhanced by the fact that in line 70 the joy with which God wonders at the generation of every individual human body is referred to with the same term ("lieto") that Dante uses in *Purgatorio* 23.74 to refer to Christ's joy on the cross. The gladness of the love that brings each human being into existence as a linguistic being is the same as the gladness of the love embodied in Christ, the same love which Forese's words highlight as that to which human beings can and ought to conform so as to be worthy of Heaven. As we shall see, this may be related to Dante's understanding of the Trinity. But before we turn to this idea, let us consider the relevance of what has been said so far for understanding the poetics of the *Commedia*.

Poetry, for Dante, is one of the highest expressions of language. And, given his understanding of language as both a physical and a rational phenomenon, one can see why Dante might have regarded poetry, with its conscious foregrounding of the physical as much as the rational features of language, as among the noblest forms of human communication. Given the importance ascribed by Dante to the embodied nature of human beings, moreover, one can see why he might have been profoundly attracted not simply by poetry but specifically by *narrative* poetry, with the possibility this entails for the representation of the ways in which language not only speaks, but also generates community; and of the ways in which language not only expresses understanding but embodies understanding as individual human beings move and interact in space and time (and, in the Empyrean, even beyond space and time); and finally, of the ways in which language might be related not only to saying and knowing but also to loving.[11]

That said, we can turn to what is often regarded as the most important statement of poetics in the *Commedia*. It occurs between Dante's encounter with Forese and Statius's lesson in embryology, and it takes the narrative form of an exchange between Dante and Bonagiunta da Lucca. Dante is praised by Bonagiunta for giving birth to a new kind of poetry, identified with reference to "Donne ch'avete intelletto d'amore," a poem of central importance in the *Vita nuova*. Bonagiunta speaks:

> ["]Ma dì s'i' veggio qui colui che fore
> trasse le nove rime, cominciando
> '*Donne ch'avete intelletto d'amore*'".

to which Dante replies:

> "I' mi son un che, quando
> Amor mi spira, noto, e a quel modo
> ch'e' ditta dentro vo significando".
> (*Purg.* 24.49–54)

[(")But tell me: do I see the man who drew / those new rhymes forth, whose opening line ran so: / 'Ladies, who have intelligence of love . . .?" / And I to him: "I am just one who, when / Love breathes in me, takes note and then goes on / showing the meaning that's ordained within."]

Let us recall that for Dante the creation of the human person is defined as the creation of a "fante," or "speaking being." To become human is to be made, through the divine breath that is the source of all existence, a being capable of speech. One cannot but note the parallel with the passage from *Purgatorio* 24: proper poetic language—poetic language of the kind crafted by Dante—issues from the breath of love: "quando / Amor mi spira." What one makes of the parallel clearly depends on how one understands "Amor." On the one hand, this is undoubtedly the courtly and earthly love analyzed and idealized in the Italian poetic tradition inherited by Dante and transformed by him in the *Vita nuova*. On the other hand, lines 52–54 recall traditional imagery used to refer to the inspiration of scripture, and commentators have shown that they are remarkably similar to how a twelfth-century treatise talks about the possibility of speaking accurately about charity.[12] No contradiction need be seen between these readings. One of the defining characteristics of the *Vita nuova*, in relation to which Dante is identified by Bonagiunta, is its fusion of reflection on earthly and divine love. Thus "Amor" is accurately read here as referring not only to the love of love poetry but also to God, the prime mover of *Purgatorio* 25.70. Indeed, as we saw earlier, "amore" is one of the ways in which Dante refers to God in the *Paradiso*.

From this perspective, the parallel between the passages from *Purgatorio* 24 and 25 is of high theological significance: just as human—that is, linguistic—existence is breathed into being by the source of all that is, similarly, proper poetry—that is, one of the highest expressions of human language—issues forth from the love which the source of all being is. As we have seen, moreover, the love which is ontologically one with the source of all being may be defined in terms of the dynamics of the cross—in terms, that is, of the love that is a self-giving response to the will of God and that finds a heavenly counterpart in the *caritas* in which Piccarda says human beings may be perfectly at one with each other and with divine being itself.[13] On the one hand, therefore, poetic language is presented by Dante as truthful to the extent that it is an expression of the love for existence and for others that is at one with the source of all being. On the other hand, it is precisely insofar as human beings are directly related, as embodied beings, to the love that is the source of all being that they can enter into language, and therefore into properly human existence, in the first place. While clearly marking a theological development with respect to the *Vita nuova*, this view is consistent with the "poetics of praise" introduced by Dante in his earlier work in connection with "Donne ch'avete intelletto d'amore." In commenting on this poem in the *Vita nuova*, Dante tells us that poetic language ought to be shaped by one's praise of the God-given goodness and beauty of that which one loves, not—as was more customary in the poetry of his day and in his own earlier work—by reflection on the extent of one's being able to possess or achieve the object of one's desire (*Vn* 18–19). In the *Vita nuova* it is of course the figure of Beatrice who inspires this reflection; a figure which, as commentators invariably point out but rarely attempt to explain in theological detail, must be interpreted both in the *Vita nuova* and the *Commedia* in Christological terms. And if the figure of Beatrice is Christical in both works, this is because she is related to and inspires an understanding of language and of human relationships according to which one's words, one's actions, and one's whole being are defined by a self-giving love for God and others that is at one with the ground of human—indeed of all—existence.

Lines 49–54 of *Purgatorio* 24 thus present Dante's poetry as issuing from, and as an embodiment of, the love in which God and human existence are perfectly at one. In the light of what has been said so far, the three cantos from the *Purgatorio* which we have taken into consideration provide a narrative sequence that inextricably links reflection on the crucifixion, on love and love poetry, and on the relationship between human and divine existence.[14] Although unable fully to comprehend the source of their existence, human beings may, by acting in self-giving love, partake in the divine will which gives them being; human beings speak most truthfully when speaking in self-giving love and praise for God and others; insofar as they are linguistic beings, human beings are at one with God.

All this allows for a fuller articulation of an answer to the question with which we began—that of the terms according to which the *Commedia* may be read, in its entirety, as theology. If, for Dante, to be human is to be a linguistic being, which is to be an embodied being enjoying a direct relationship with her Creator; if enjoying a direct relationship with God is being able to partake in the love which God is, while at the same time not being able fully to comprehend God; and if, finally, the language of the *Commedia* both issues from and as an action partakes in the love which is God; then it would seem to follow that Dante would have regarded the narrative poetry of the *Commedia* as not only one of the highest forms of human poetry and language but also, therefore, in itself a legitimate mode of theological expression, of expression revealing, in form and content, the nature of the relationship between divine and human existence. Dante, then, would have regarded the *Commedia* as possessing theological value not merely because of what it says about God and about the relationship between human beings and God. Its theological value would also derive from its invitation to the reader to engage with a certain understanding of language, whereby the latter expresses the love in which God and human beings may be at one; and from its presentation of itself to the reader as an instance of such a language. Dante, in other words, would have identified the theological value of his poem as its invitation to the reader to establish a relationship with the text defined by an understanding of how—as with Forese and Piccarda—one's actions and utterances may, in failing to allow for full comprehension of truth, allow one fully to partake in nothing other than the love which truth itself is.

In another passage from the *Paradiso* that expresses Dante's idea of creation as love, we find:

> Guardando nel suo Figlio con l'Amore
> che l'uno e l'altro etternalmente spira,
> lo primo e ineffabile Valore
>   quanto per mente e per loco si gira
> con tant' ordine fé, ch'esser non puote
> sanza gustar di lui chi ciò rimira.
>   (*Par.* 10.1–6)

[Looking within his Son through that same Love / that Each breathes out eternally with Each, / the first and three-fold Worth, beyond all words, / formed all that spins through intellect or space / in such clear order it can never be, / that we, in wonder, fail to taste Him there.]

God creates all there is through the Son, with the love that Father and Son eternally breathe forth.[15] "Spira" (2) is the same as the expression used in *Purgatorio* 25.71 for the creation of the human soul and in *Purgatorio* 24.53 for the inspiration of Dante's poetry. The word "amore," however, is now a specific reference to the Holy Spirit. It could be argued, therefore, that for Dante, *this* is the love which, lying at the origin of all existence, is also the ground of human existence and language and with which human beings may, in Christlike self-giving, be perfectly at one. This line of reasoning seems to come extremely close to the idea that Dante thought that his poetry, like scripture, was directly inspired by the Holy Spirit. And indeed Dante comes remarkably close to saying this in the *Commedia*.[16] In suggesting that his poetry might be at one with the Holy Spirit, however, Dante is not trying to set up the *Commedia* as a rival or even an equal to scripture. His claim should rather be interpreted as a humble expression of belief that good theology is language which, informed by the truth embodied by scripture and therefore by the work of the Holy Spirit, does not claim full comprehension of truth; language which, conscious of its particularity and provisionality, presents as theologically valuable its attempt to be, as an ethical gesture, at one with the Trinitarian love that moves the sun and other stars.

Ulysses, Ugolino, and the Theology of the *Commedia*

The theological dynamics outlined above regarding the relationship in the *Commedia* between language, love, and the unknowability of God are brought to the fore at the beginning of the *Purgatorio*. On the shores of Purgatory, Dante the character does not see Virgil's shadow on the ground next to his; he is taken aback and thinks he has been abandoned by his guide. His discomfort, however, prompts Virgil to explain that there is only one shadow because he, Virgil, is no longer embodied in flesh that may act as a barrier to the sun's rays (*Purg.* 3.16–27). He then says:

> Ora, se innanzi a me nulla s'aombra,
> non ti maravigliar più che d'i cieli
> che l'uno a l'altro raggio non ingombra.
>   A sofferir tormenti, caldi e geli
> simili corpi la Virtù dispone
> che, come fa, non vuol ch'a noi si sveli.
>   Matto è chi spera che nostra ragione
> possa trascorrer la infinita via
> che tiene una sustanza in tre persone.

State contenti, umana gente, al *quia;*
ché, se potuto aveste veder tutto,
mestier non era parturir Maria . . .
                              (28–39)

[If nothing now is shadowed at my feet, / don't wonder any more than when the rays / the heavens project don't block each other out. / To suffer torments both of heat and chill, / the Utmost Power gives bodies, fit for that, / not wishing *how* it does to be revealed. / It's madness if we hope that rational minds / should ever follow to its end the road / that one true being in three persons takes. / Content yourselves with *quia,* human kind. / Had you been able to see everything, / Mary need not have laboured to give birth.]

These lines are characterized by a somewhat ambiguous logic.[17] For the Incarnation both is, and is not, presented as satisfyingly counterbalancing the pronounced deficiency of human reason to grasp ultimate truth. On the one hand, these lines may be read as stating that, even given the Incarnation, human beings still cannot "veder tutto." On the other hand, however, the Incarnation is presented as that which offers human reason a way out of this impasse. What this passage represents, I think, is not only an attempt to define the relationship between human reason and truth with reference to the Incarnation, but also the beginning of an attempt to question and define, with reference to the Incarnation, the very idea of truth. The Incarnation, in the *Commedia,* is presented as counterbalancing reason's inadequacy not so much because it offers reason answers that reason may otherwise not be able to reach, as because it reveals that it is constitutive of reason that certain answers should not be available and that one's understanding of truth will always be put into question and redefined by one's encounter with other people. It does so by revealing an understanding of human personhood in which the recognition that certain answers are not available may go hand in hand with an understanding of the way in which one's actions may partake in the very truth that reason may not be allowed fully to fathom.

As we saw above, for Dante, human actions may partake in that truth by sharing in the dynamics of the cross—at one and the same time a statement of human inability fully to comprehend God and the world, and a statement of the fact that readiness to take suffering upon oneself for others' sake is the basis for coming to terms with human personhood and for understanding how persons should act towards each other. The cross, in other words, defines human nature as having less to do with being able fully to understand God and the world than with how one may have one's actions defined by the will of God, thereby becoming—as Piccarda says—able fully to conform to the will and needs of others. As such, Dante's understanding of the crucifixion unfolds the ambiguous logic of *Purgatorio* 3.28–39.

It comes as no surprise, therefore, that in the *Paradiso* Dante should link the dynamics of the cross to his poetic voice, to the latter's deficiency in describing heavenly truth, and to the relationship the reader may establish with the *Commedia*:

> Qui vince la memoria mio lo 'ngegno;
> ché quella croce lampeggiava Cristo,
> sì ch'io non so trovare essempro degno;
>   ma chi prende sua croce e segue Cristo,
> ancor mi scuserà di quel ch'io lasso,
> vedendo in quell' albor balenar Cristo.
>   (*Par.* 14.103–8)

[And here remembering surpasses skill: / that cross, in sudden flaring, blazed out Christ / so I can find no fit comparison. / But those who take their cross and follow Christ / will let me off where, wearily, I fail, / seeing in that white dawn, as lightning, Christ.]

On the basis of this and earlier observations, I propose that for Dante, an important part of the theological value of the poem is its narrative creation of communities that Christically participate (in *Purgatorio* and *Paradiso*) or fail to participate (in *Inferno*) in the love which God is. Related to this, moreover, is the way the reader is invited to establish with the *Commedia*, and its presentation of itself as language, a relationship at one with the love through which, as the text itself shows, one should relate to God and to other human beings. In the remaining part of this essay, I support this twofold suggestion by looking at how, through his presentation of his encounters with Ulysses and Ugolino, and through some of their echoes across the *Commedia*, Dante seems to negotiate the possibility of doing theology.

The first of the two aspects of my suggestion—that the poem creates communities that participate or fail to participate Christically in God's truth—finds articulation in Dante's encounter with Ulysses in *Inferno* 26. Dante raises a challenge for himself in this canto, since he puts in Hell a figure who is said to have died in pursuit of exactly that which Dante pursues in writing his poem: the ultimate truths of virtue and knowledge. It was in order to pursue these truths, Ulysses tells Dante, that he proposed to sail in exploration around the world and to embark on a journey beyond the Pillars of Hercules and the known, inhabited world. During this journey, Ulysses further tells Dante, he and his companions, on seeing Purgatory, were shipwrecked by a divinely ordained storm (90–142). Dante's Ulysses thus calls into question the theological coherence of the *Commedia*. He forces us to ask in what way, if any, the poem's project may be defended: after all, while Dante's search for virtue and knowledge leads him to talk about the ultimate truths about God, the cosmos, and human beings, Ulysses meets with death.

Ultimately, Dante appears to meet the challenge by inviting readers to interpret his journey in the *Commedia* and that of Ulysses beyond the Pillars of Hercules as quite different kinds of journey. Common to both journeys, however, is a strong affirmation that the pursuit of knowledge and the pursuit of virtue are interwoven. As Ulysses puts it to his companions when he tries to convince them to trespass the geographical limits of the known world, human beings were made "per seguir virtute e canoscenza" (120) [(to) go in search of virtue and true knowledge]. Accordingly, he says, his burning desire was to "divenir del mondo esperto / e delli vizi umani e del valore" (98–99) [understand how this world works, / and know of human vices, worth and valour]. And yet, to quench this desire, he leaves behind some of the most important relationships of love a man may find in his life—abandoning son, father, and wife (94–96)—and proposes to gain experience, as he puts it, of the "mondo sanza gente" (117) [worlds where no man dwells]. Ulysses' pursuit of virtue and of knowledge, therefore, is both born out of and leads into a world without people, a world that does not give due importance to the unfolding of communal relationships. And a world without people, without community, a priori undermines the flourishing and understanding of virtue.[18] From a Dantean perspective, Ulysses may be right to state that knowledge and virtue are interwoven. But he is mistaken in thinking that an understanding of virtue may be abstracted from its flourishing within a communal context, or that it may be arrived at following the apprehension of those ultimate truths regarding the world and human beings which Ulysses believes are there for him to grasp beyond the Pillars of Hercules.

The Pillars of Hercules for Dante's Ulysses are a boundary designed to keep human beings from a comprehension of the world and human existence that would elevate them to a divine status. Or, to put it differently, from a Ulyssean perspective, knowledge of ultimate truth is in principle available to human beings but is jealously kept by God away from them. My suggestion, however, is that from Dante's perspective, the Pillars of Hercules are a reminder that ultimate comprehension of the world is not *even in principle* available to human beings. To think otherwise would be to misunderstand what it means to say "God," or the fact that God is love. The Pillars of Hercules are a reminder that in one's pursuit of knowledge, one should never lose sight of the proper dynamics of community. The latter emerge from the recognition that, because ultimate truth is inscrutable, one must abandon the presumption of explaining the world or of asserting one's will over and against that which grounds it and which, ultimately, gives it its proper sense of direction.

Significantly, Ulysses refers to the cause of the shipwreck in which he died simply by saying that it occurred "com' altrui piacque" (141) [as pleased Another's will]. This is almost invariably interpreted as a reference to God. The expression, however, is ambiguous. While it is certainly a reference to God, it also (and perhaps primarily) presents us with the fact that Ulysses can only think of his death as having been caused by a will other than his own. As such, moreover, it implies an equation between the pursuit of truth and the assertion of the individual will over and against that which is perceived as opposing it.

The significance of this is enhanced by the recurrence of the same expression, "com' altrui piacque," in *Purgatorio* 1. On arriving in Purgatory, Dante and Virgil meet Cato, who instructs Virgil to cleanse Dante's face from the marks of the journey through Hell and to gird him with one of the reeds growing on Purgatory's shore (*Purg.* 1.28–108). After a description of Virgil washing Dante's face with dew (121–29), we find:

> Venimmo poi in sul lito diserto,
> che mai non vide navicar sue acque
> omo, che di tornar sia poscia esperto.

>   Quivi mi cinse sì com' altrui piacque:
> oh maraviglia! ché qual elli scelse
> l'umile pianta, cotal si rinaque
>   subitamente là onde l'avelse.
> (*Purg.* 1.130–36)

[We then came out across an empty shore / that never saw its waters sailed upon / by any man who knew how to return. / There, at another's will, he girded me. / And this was marvellous: that, as he chose / that simple plant, another like it rose, / reborn the instant that he plucked it out.]

As spoken by Dante the poet in *Purgatorio* 1.133, "com' altrui piacque" presents us with a radically different perspective from that offered us by Ulysses. In both *Purgatorio* 1 and *Inferno* 26, "com' altrui piacque" is a reference to the will of God. But in *Purgatorio* 1, it is also a reference to the will of another human being. In fact, it is impossible distinctly to ascribe "altrui" in *Purgatorio* 1.133 either to God or Cato. The will to which Dante conforms in starting his journey through Purgatory is at once that of God and that of another human being, one through the other. In Purgatory, pursuit of virtue and knowledge is bound not to the assertion of individual will over and against that which is perceived as opposing it, be it the will of God or the needs of others; it is bound, rather, to one's willingness to conform one's will to that which may, in love and humility, redefine it. *Purgatorio* 1.130–36 thus begins to prepare us for *Purgatorio* 23.70–75, discussed above, and for the idea that the will of the individual might conform to Christ's own conforming his will, for the sake of others, to that of God. This idea is what Dante's Ulysses does not appreciate. For Ulysses, that which limits the assertion of one's will cannot but be a cause of death, and of joy turning into tears (*Inf.* 26.136). From the perspective of the *Purgatorio*, however, that which, in love and humility, may limit the assertion of one's will cannot but be the cause of new life, and of the possibility for tears to qualify, but not ultimately to undermine, joy and laughter (as Forese's words make clear in *Purgatorio* 23.70–75).[19]

Such a perspective is more fully articulated in the narrative following *Purgatorio* 1. Using another term crucial in Ulysses' story ("esperto"),[20] Virgil explains to the first group of souls whom he and Dante the character meet in Purgatory:

> Voi credete
> forse che siamo esperti d'esto luoco:
> ma noi siamo peregrin come voi siete.
>   Dianzi venimmo, innanzi a voi un poco,
> per altra via, che fu sì aspra e forte,
> che lo salire omai ne parrà gioco.
>   (*Purg.* 2.61–66)

[You may think that we / possess experience of where we are. / But we, like you, are pilgrim foreigners. / We came a little while before yourselves, / taking a different, hard and bitter road. / So now the climb will seem to us a game.]

Lines 62 and 63 imply that the abandonment of claims to full knowledge of otherworldly truths is the precondition for being able to compare one's condition to that of a soul traveling on a journey that will inevitably lead to God. As the narrative of this and the following canto makes clear, moreover, this recognition is inseparable for Dante from the recognition that a condition of uncertainty may also be the basis for the readiness to help and be helped by others on one's way.[21] As with Ulysses, then, so also from the perspective of the *Purgatorio*, pursuit of virtue and pursuit of knowledge are intertwined. But the relationship between the two is now inverted. An understanding of virtue is no longer dependent on a pursuit of knowledge that leads one to neglect one's communal existence. Rather, the flourishing of virtue, of the dynamics of community beautifully rendered by "gioco" (66), is dependent on one's ability to abandon the presumption to comprehensive knowledge. Significantly, the same word, "gioco," will be used again in the *Commedia* to refer both to the life of Eden and to that of Heaven itself (*Purg.* 28.96; *Par.* 20.117).

Significantly, moreover, immediately following the word "gioco" we find:

> L'anime, che si fuor di me accorte,
> per lo spirare, ch'i' era ancor vivo,
> maravigliando diventaro smorte.
>   E come a messaggier che porta ulivo
> tragge la gente per udir novelle,
> e di calcar nessun si mostra schivo,

così al viso mio s'affisar quelle
anime fortunate tutte quante,
quasi obliando d'ire a farsi belle.
　Io vidi una di lor trarresi avante
per abbracciarmi, con sì grande affetto,
che mosse me a far lo somigliante.
　Ohi ombre vane, fuor che ne l'aspetto!
tre volte dietro a lei le mani avvinsi,
e tante mi tornai con esse al petto.
　Di maraviglia, credo, mi dipinsi;
per che l'ombra sorrise e si ritrasse,
e io, seguendo lei, oltre mi pinsi.
　Soavemente disse ch'io posasse;
allor conobbi chi era, e pregai
che, per parlarmi, un poco s'arrestasse.
(*Purg.* 2.67–87)

[The souls who were aware (because I breathed) / that I was still alive, now blenched in awe, / and, wondering at the sight, grew very pale. / And, as around some messenger who bears / an olive branch in hand, crowds form to hear / the news—none shy to trample to the fore— / so these souls, too, stare fixed upon my face, / forgetting almost (all so fortunate!) / to go ahead and make themselves more fine. / And one drew forward now, I saw, to me / to take me in his arms with such great warmth / it moved me, so I did the same to him. / Ah shadows, empty save in how they look! / Three times I locked my hands behind his back. / As many times I came back to my breast. / Wonder, I think, was painted over me. / At which the shadow smiled, and so drew back, / while I, pursuing him, pressed further on. / Gently, he told me I had better stop. / And then I knew who this was, so I prayed / that he should speak and pause there for a while.]

In the light of all that has been said so far, it is important to note that the encounter between Dante and his friend Casella seems to qualify the inversion of a Ulyssean perspective on the pursuit of virtue and knowledge. It does so by bringing to the fore the sense of wonder that may follow one's encounter with others, and the way this sense of wonder may be at one with the attention paid to language and to bodily appearance and expressions; the way bodily expressions such as the smile may bring persons into relation with one another. Dante's arms returning to beat his chest (80–81) might also be connected with the recognition scenes at the crucifixion described in Luke 23:47–48 and Matthew 27:54, thus relating the encounter with Casella to the recognition that God made himself man.[22] Moreover, Dante's encounter with Casella is, of course, the narrative prelude to the explicit questioning in the next canto regarding the nature of the corporeality of the shades of Purgatory, which, as we have seen, in *Purgatorio* 3.28–39 explicitly brings together reflection on human embodiedness, on the inability fully to grasp ultimate truth, and on the Incarnation.

Inferno 26 and some of its later echoes in the poem thus remind us of the idea expressed by Dante in the *Convivio* that human beings cannot even desire to have full knowledge of ultimate truth, and if they think they do so, they are in fact misunderstanding what it is that they desire (3.15.6–10). We are pointed, in other words, to the idea that precisely insofar as one is confident that in principle it is possible fully to understand God, one undermines the possibility of being able meaningfully to talk about God. At the same time, we are pointed towards the idea that for Dante, this recognition enables one to see that virtue and knowledge are most appropriately pursued within a particular understanding and unfolding of community. From this perspective, understanding of truth is determined by the extent to which one is willing to have one's actions defined, and one's understanding of truth constantly refined, by the presence and needs of others; by the "gioco" that characterizes human community at its best.

To complement the above readings by returning to an explicit consideration of Dante's understanding of language, consider Dante's invitation to the reader to reflect on the relationship between infant speech and the theological value of the *Commedia*.[23] We saw above that Dante refers to the creation of the human soul as the moment of the creation of a "fante," a being capable of speech. We also saw that this idea can be related to Dante's understanding of love, of the unknowability of God, and of the relationship between the two. All this is integrally related in the *Commedia* to an understanding of language, in which each utterance is viewed as an ethical gesture, requiring, in receiving and speaking every word, the apophatic and infant-like ability to learn how to speak anew. It may also be seen, in turn, as integrally related to Dante's presentation of his poem as such a gesture.

Consider, for example, the opening of *Inferno* 32:

> S'ïo avessi le rime aspre e chiocce,
> come si converebbe al tristo buco
> sovra 'l qual pontan tutte l'altre rocce,
>   io premerei del mio concetto il suco
> più pienamente; ma perch' io non l'abbo,
> non sanza tema a dicer mi conduco;
>   ché non è impresa da pigliare a gabbo
> discriver fondo a tutto l'universo,
> né da lingua che chiami mamma o babbo.
>   Ma quelle donne aiutino il mio verso
> ch'aiutaro Anfïone a chiuder Tebe,
> sì che dal fatto il dir non sia diverso.
> (1–12)

[If I had rhymes that rawly rasped and cackled / (and chimed in keeping with the cacky hole / at which, point down, all other rock rings peak), / I might then squeeze the juices of my thought / more fully out of me. But since I don't, / not without dread, I bring myself to speak. / It's not (no kidding) any sort of joke / to form in words the universal bum, / no task for tongues still whimpering 'Mum!' and 'Dad!' / The Muses, though, may raise my verse— women / who once helped Amphion lock Thebes in walls— / so fact and word may not too far diverge.]

In describing the last circle of Hell, Dante laments his lack of adequate language for the task. Such a language, he tells us, would not be one "che chiami mamma o babbo," but one in which there would be a perfect coincidence between facts and the words used to describe them. This is usually interpreted simply as an expression of Dante's awareness of his language's limitations, of the kind of language he does not possess. Dante, however, might also be telling us something quite specific about the language he feels he does possess, and about its theological value.

What Dante might mean by a "lingua che chiami mamma o babbo," and by a language in which words perfectly coincide with the facts they describe, is suggested by the narrative of Dante's encounter with Ugolino, soon after the above passage. In telling Dante about his and his children's imprisonment and starvation, Ugolino famously says:

Quando fui desto innanzi la dimane,
pianger senti' fra 'l sonno i miei figliuoli
ch'eran con meco, e dimandar del pane.
   Ben se' crudel, se tu già non ti duoli
pensando ciò che 'l mio cor s'annunziava;
e se non piangi, di che pianger suoli?
   Già eran desti, e l'ora s'appressava
che 'l cibo ne solëa essere addotto,
e per suo sogno ciascun dubitava;
   e io senti' chiavar l'uscio di sotto
a l'orribile torre; ond' io guardai
nel viso a' mie' figlioui sanza far motto.
   Io non piangëa, sì dentro impetrai:
piangevan elli; e Anselmuccio mio
disse: "Tu guardi sì, padre! che hai?".
   Perciò non lagrimai né rispuos' io
tutto quel giorno né la notte appresso,
infin che l'altro sol nel mondo uscìo.
   Come un poco di raggio si fu messo
nel doloroso carcere, e io scorsi
per quattro visi il mio aspetto stesso,
   ambo le man per lo dolor mi morsi;
ed ei, pensando ch'io 'l fessi per voglia
di manicar, di sùbito levorsi
   e disser: "Padre, assai ci fia men doglia
se tu mangi di noi: tu ne vestisti
queste misere carni, e tu le spoglia".
   Queta'mi allor per non farli più tristi;
lo dì e l'altro stemmo tutti muti;
ahi dura terra, perché non t'apristi?
   Poscia che fummo al quarto dì venuti,
Gaddo mi si gittò disteso a' piedi,
dicendo: "Padre mio, ché non m'aiuti?".
   Quivi morì; e come tu mi vedi,
vid' io cascar li tre ad uno ad uno
tra 'l quinto dì e 'l sesto; ond' io mi diedi,
   già cieco, a brancolar sovra ciascuno,
e due dì li chiamai, poi che fur morti.
Poscia, più che 'l dolor, poté 'l digiuno.
                     (*Inf.* 33.37–75)

[I woke before the day ahead had come, / and heard my sons (my little ones were there) / cry in their sleep and call out for some food. / How hard you are if, thinking what my heart / foretold, you do not feel the pain of it. / Whatever will you weep for, if not that? / By now they all had woken up. The time / was due when, as routine, our food was brought. / Yet each was doubtful, thinking of their dream. / Listening, I heard the door below locked shut, / then nailed in place against the dreadful tower. / I looked in their dear faces, spoke no word. / I did not weep. Inward, I turned to stone. / They wept. And then my boy Anselmo spoke: / "What are you staring at? Father, what's wrong?" / And so I held my tears in check and gave / no answer all that day, nor all the night / that followed on, until another sun came up. / A little light had forced a ray into / our prison, so full of pain. I now could see / on all four faces my own expression. / Out of sheer grief, I gnawed on both my hands. / And they—who thought I did so from an urge / to eat—all, on the instant, rose and said: / "Father, for us the pain would be far less / if you would choose to eat us. You, having dressed us / in this wretched flesh, ought now to strip it off." / So I kept still, to not increase their miseries. / And that day and the day beyond, we all were mute. / Hard, cruel earth, why did you not gape wide? / As then we reached the fourth of all those days, / Gaddo pitched forward, stretching at my feet. / "Help me," he said. "Why don't you help me, Dad!" / And there he died. You see me here. So I saw them, / the three remaining, falling one by one / between the next days—five and six—then let / myself, now blind, feel over them, calling / on each, now all were dead, for two days more. / Then hunger proved a greater power than grief.]

These lines arguably present us with instances of both the kinds of language referred to in *Inferno* 32.1–12. Faced by his sons' suffering and by the inevitability of their and his own death, Ugolino falls silent. Nothing he could say, his decision seems to imply, can change their situation or be more than a further expression of the reality of their impending death. Faced with the inevitability of death, language is paralyzed, since ultimately it may do nothing more than point to a reality—death—that collapses all meaning onto itself. This could be seen as a way of defining language, characterized by the idea of a perfect coincidence between facts and the words used to describe them. For one way to read the phrase "sì che dal fatto il dir non sia diverso" [so fact and word may not too far diverge] (*Inf.* 32.12) is to regard it as referring to language's loss of any notion of ultimate meaning: language can do nothing more than coincide with the facts it describes, since anything language could describe is a mere fact with no meaning if not that defined, ultimately, by death. On such a view, language is merely useful or instrumental—so much so that when faced with certain death, Ugolino can only feel that human communication and interaction are best dispensed with.

An alternative to Ugolino's silence is the cries of his sons, who in calling to their father qualify the idea of a "lingua che chiami mamma o babbo" (*Inf.* 32.9). They cry for help that will not be delivered, and they respond to the reality of death by offering to die for Ugolino. As far as being able to counter impending death, these actions are as effective as Ugolino's silence. Yet they call into question that which Ugolino's silence seems to imply—namely, that death ultimately empties language of all meaning except that of death itself. They do so by asserting that the certainty of death does *not* make human interaction dispensable, and that this is so because one human being may offer to die for another.

Inferno 32.1–12 can thus be read, on the one hand, as stating that a language adequate for describing Hell would be in line with the idea of meaning embodied in Ugolino's silence; and on the other hand, as implying that the language in which the *Commedia* is written is closer to the actions of Ugolino's sons. That the actions of Ugolino's sons may be related to Dante's understanding of truth is strongly suggested by the fact that they might be interpreted in a Christological key.[24] Particularly significant, especially in the light of the passage from *Purgatorio* 23 considered above, is the fact that Gaddo's "Padre mio, ché non m'aiuti?" (*Inf.* 33.69) parallels Jesus' cry on the cross. If Gaddo's cry qualifies *Inferno* 32.9, then *Inferno* 32.9 may also be related to the fact that in the Ugolino episode, Dante wishes to foreground the crucifixion; and to the fact that, through the crucifixion, Dante foregrounds the ideas embodied in Christ's cry from the cross: namely, that death disqualifies human attempts fully to comprehend God or grasp ultimate meaning, and that, nonetheless, all notions of God and ultimate meaning are not meaningless, because one human being may offer to die for another. In Trinitarian terms, *Inferno* 32 and 33 foreground the idea that God, and therefore truth, are equally the silence faced by Jesus crying on the cross, the person crying, and the love for which he dies.

On this reading, *Inferno* 32.1–12 does not so much express the wish for an accurate description of Hell as suggest what kind of language would qualify for such a description and why the *Commedia* should not be seen as an instance of it. Two things in particular follow. First, when talking about the theology of the *Commedia*, one should not speak of an individual's attempt to conceive of and present as objectively accurate a picture of God, or of the experience of God, or of the relationship between human beings and God, as humanly possible. For Dante, a theology so conceived a priori fails to grasp the basic distinction between creature and Creator, between that which can be spoken *of* and that which is the ground of human speech and existence.[25] Rather, one should speak about a text embodying an understanding of theology in which the aim is to invite others to realize that appreciation of truth rests on one's ability to recognize that one's understanding of truth is defined and constantly redefined by one's readiness to respond in love to the will and needs of another. For, as we have seen, from a Dantean perspective, human beings may partake in truth itself by shaping their words and deeds according to the dynamics of the Incarnation and Crucifixion of the Word.

Second, it follows that when, in *Inferno* 32 as well as the passage from *Paradiso* 14 examined above, Dante declares the inadequacy of his language to speak about the subject at hand, he is saying something specific not only about the nature of truth and its relationship to the human mind, but also about the relationship the reader is invited to have with the *Commedia*.[26] By apophatically foregrounding the *Commedia*'s particularity, provisionality, and frailty, among other things through reference to infant speech, Dante invites the reader to read his poem not (as it is often read) simply as a mimetic masterpiece but as a narrative and poetic exploration of the ultimately unrepresentable mystery of man's relationship with God; an exploration which, as voice, aims to display those same ethical dynamics which, as narrative, it suggests may allow human beings to partake in the life of God.[27]

As suggested by the opening lines of *Inferno* 32, then, a language that may claim to have theological value is for Dante comparable to that of a child crying out for its parents, as Christ on the cross cried out for his own father. In this light, it is no doubt significant that, in the strongly autobiographical narrative context of *Purgatorio* 11, Dante is asked by Oderisi:

> Che voce avrai tu più, se vecchia scindi
> da te la carne, che se fossi morto
> anzi che tu lasciassi il "pappo" e 'l "dindi",
>   pria che passi mill' anni? . . .
>   (103–7)

[What more renown will you have if you strip / your flesh in age away than if you died / before you'd left off lisping "Din-dins!", "Penth!" / when once a thousand years have passed . . .]

Oderisi's question could be read—at least in one of its meanings—as an invitation to view Dante's poetic voice as that of a child barely beginning to speak; as wanting to be a language caught, in its attempt to come to terms with the eternal truths it attempts to depict, in a constant state of redefinition determined by its existence alongside other individual voices;[28] and as wanting to be of the same kind as that which the narrative of the *Commedia* suggests should characterize all human relationships partaking in the "gioco" of truth itself.[29]

Also significant is the way Dante introduces us to his final vision of God:

> Omai sarà più corta mia favella,
> pur a quel ch'io ricordo, che d'un fante
> che bagni ancor la ligua a la mammella.
>   Non perché più ch'un semplice sembiante
> fosse nel vivo lume ch'io mirava,
> che tal è sempre qual s'era davante;
>   ma per la vista che s'avvalorava
> in me guardando, una sola parvenza,
> mutandom'io, a me si travagliava.
>   (*Par.* 33.106–14)

[And now my spark of words will come more short— / even of what I still can call to mind— / than baby tongues still bathing in mum's milk. / But not because that living light on which, / in wonder, I now fixed my eyes showed more / than always as before and one sole sight. / Rather, as sight in me, yet looking on, / grew finer still, one single showing-forth / (me, changing mutely) laboured me more near.]

Dante thus gives voice to the idea that full interaction with God is necessarily a constant source of transformation for the human person, and requires a conception of language in which the latter is in a constant state of redefinition and for this reason comparable to infant speech (note again the use of the word "fante"). The significance of this idea is enhanced by the fact that the vision to which these words usher us is that of truth as constituted by the human person—Christ, Dante, all individual persons (*Par.* 33.115 ff.): by the human person as seen in the light of the love which God is, and in which, as Piccarda had said, individual human beings come to recognize how their acting towards each other can be at one with divine being.

It is important, in this respect, that Dante's name is registered for the first and only time in the *Commedia* when he is reduced to child-like sobbing and stuttering by Beatrice in the Earthly Paradise (*Purg.* 30.22–31.90; for "Dante," 30.55).[30] This episode opens with Dante turning to Virgil as a "fantolin" would turn to his "mamma" and being reprimanded by Beatrice for doing so (30.40–57). Beatrice's reproach should be seen not as a reproach directed at child-like behavior as such, but rather as an invitation to reflect on what it truly means to compare one's adult voice to that of a child—reflection which, as the final cantos of the *Purgatorio* suggest, must begin in confession, with recognizing one's shortcomings before others. As Beatrice puts it, what Dante has to do is not so much stop crying as learn how to cry properly (30.55–57). The moment in which Dante moves from Virgil to Beatrice, often dubbed as the movement from reason to faith, could therefore more accurately be seen as the moment in which one fully begins to learn that to speak properly is to be ready constantly to learn how to speak anew, and that this is so because human nature may be perfected and made worthy of Heaven only when the individual is ready to have his or her will shaped by the will of another—"Come anima gentil, che non fa scusa, / ma fa sua voglia della voglia altrui" (*Purg.* 33.130–31) [As noble souls incline to do—they make / another's will, without excuse, *their* will].

This brings us back to the Ugolino episode. Although they recall Christ's words and actions, Ugolino's sons do not directly address God. They address another human being. This suggests two things. First, and most obviously, for Dante the love of one human being for another is properly defined from a theological perspective. Second, and conversely, one's sense of what it means to talk about God ought to be grounded in an understanding of how human beings can relate to one another. It is often said that, at least in one of its aspects, the *Inferno* may be read as an account of human wrongdoing that could stand, to borrow Kenelm Foster's phrase, "in any world that is human at all."[31] Although Dante is clearly not trying to construct this account without reference to scripture or the Christian tradition, in episodes such as his encounter with Ugolino he seems to negotiate the possibility of talking about God in terms that could stand without the aid of revelation. I am suggesting that, for Dante, the actions of Ugolino's sons allow one to accept the proposition that, because one can offer to die for another, human personhood has in essence more to do with love than it has with death; and that this would be for Dante *quod omnes dicunt deum*, or rational proof that it is meaningful to talk about God. I am also suggesting that this reveals Dante's understanding of theological language. One gets one's theology wrong, according to Dante, unless one's sense of what it means to talk about God is grounded in the recognition of what it would mean for human communication and interaction to be seen merely as useful or instrumental. Talk about God is meaningful not because one can be sure of the meaning of anything one says about God; it is meaningful because it is not meaningless to suggest that, ontologically, human personhood is closer to love than to death.

Having thus presented at the end of the *Inferno* the possibility of meaningful talk about God, in the *Purgatorio* and the *Paradiso* Dante moves, as we have observed, to negotiate the terms according to which it may be possible to shape one's language in full theological fashion. We now find confirmed the extent to which, in presenting his language as theological in the *Commedia*, Dante presents it, by highlighting the link between ethical and theological reflection, at the intersection between what can and what cannot meaningfully be grasped and between what is made and what grounds the existence of all that is made. This idea finds its most beautifully succinct expression in Dante's statement at the beginning of *Paradiso* 33 that in Mary the human being was so perfected "che 'l suo fattore / non disdegnò di farsi sua fattura" (5–6) [Its maker, then, / did not disdain to make himself his making]. This is the theological perspective that lies behind passages such as *Purgatorio* 3.28–39 and *Paradiso* 14.103–8; that ultimately reveals the tragic incoherence between the words and deeds of Dante's Ulysses; and that ultimately grounds, in allowing apophatic and cataphatic to meet, the possibility for the *Commedia* to be read, in its entirety as a narrative poem, as theology.

It is no coincidence that, shortly before the lines from *Paradiso* 14 examined above, Dante the poet should use the notion of infant language—indicated by the word "mamme"[32]—to refer to hope in the Resurrection; to hope in that perfect union of body and soul for which all human beings are made, and in which the blessed will be perfectly at one with each other and with God:

> Tanto mi parver sùbiti e accorti
> e l'uno e l'altro coro a dicer "Amme!",
> che ben mostrar disio d'i corpi morti:
>   forse non pur per lor, ma per le mamme,
> per li padri e per li altri che fuor cari
> anzi che fosser sempiterne fiamme.
> (61–66)

[So ready and alert they seemed to me—/ those double choirs— to add their plain "Amen" / they showed their keen desire for long dead bones, / not only for themselves but for their mums, / their fathers, too, and others dear to them, / before they were these sempiternal flames.]

To be at one with divine being, for Dante, is to give full expression to one's existence as defined by one's love for God and others, and therefore also to an understanding of communication grounded in one's sense that language and love might, if properly conceived, be one and the same thing. The hope presented by Dante is that the *Commedia* might be read as an instance of such communication.

Notes

I am extremely grateful to Zygmunt Barański, John Barnes, Piero Boitani, David Burrell, Florencia Cano, Sarah Coakley, Oliver Davies, David Ford, Ben Fulford, Kristen Pinto Gfroerer, Marco Giani, Manuele Gragnolati, the late Dan Hardy, Douglas Hedley, Rachel Hill, Thirza Hope, Robin Kirkpatrick, Christian Moevs, George Pattison, Tamara Pollack, Russell Re Manning, Gregory Seach, Janet Martin Soskice, Matthew Treherne, and Denys Turner for their comments on earlier versions of this essay. It follows and expands on the paper delivered at the conference. Some of the material, however, is new and follows from papers more recently delivered at the Systematic Theology Seminar of the University of Cambridge and at the University of Notre Dame. In its present form, moreover, some of the material follows closely from work completed since the conference, which deals in more detail and with broader bibliographical reference with some of the questions raised here: "'La rosa,'" "'Padre mio,'" and "'Nulla vedere.'" Translations of the *Commedia* are taken from Dante, *Divine Comedy*, tr. Kirkpatrick.

1. See Botterill, *Dante and the Mystical Tradition* and "Mysticism and Meaning in Dante's *Paradiso*"; Carugati, *Dalla menzogna al silenzio* and "Dante 'mistico'?"; Colombo, *Dai mistici a Dante*; F. Ducros, "L'esigenza poetica"; Franke, *Dante's Interpretive Journey*; Jacomuzzi, "Il *topos* dell'ineffabile"; Meekins, "The Study of Dante, Bonaventure and Mysticism"; Pertile, "A Desire of Paradise"; Tambling, *Dante and Difference*.

2. See Burrell, *Knowing the Unknowable God*; Lash, "Creation, Courtesy and Contemplation"; Sells, *Mystical Languages of Unsaying*; Turner, *The Darkness of God* and *Faith, Reason and the Existence of God*.

3. See Moevs, *Metaphysics of Dante's "Comedy,"* 148–51.

4. See Bonaventure, *Itinerarium mentis in Deum* 5.4; also Aquinas, *ST* Ia.12.2. See also *Par.* 21.83–90.

5. See Boitani, *Dante's Poetry of the Donati*. Note also the structural parallel between *Purg.* 23.74 and *Par.* 29.15.

6. This is the only instance in the *Commedia* in which Christ's words are quoted in what would have been his mother tongue. See the comments on infant speech later in this essay and *Par.* 26.124–38.

7. See also Mk 15:34 and Ps 21:2.

8. For a more detailed discussion, especially as relating to the significance in the *Commedia* of the figure of Ulysses, see my "'La rosa.'"

9. See *Mon.* 3.16.

10. See Gragnolati, *Experiencing the Afterlife*.

11. For language and love, see also Lombardi, *Syntax of Desire*, and Soskice, *The Kindness of God*.

12. Barolini, *Undivine Comedy*, 52–54; Carugati, *Dalla menzogna al silenzio*, 4–56; Chiavacci Leonardi, *Commedia*, 2:710–11, 725–26; Moevs, *Metaphysics of Dante's "Comedy,"* 88–89; Scott, *Understanding Dante*, 10–13.

13. See also *Par.* 20.94–99.

14. A broader study of the questions at hand would clearly have to take into consideration how this narrative sequence finds further articulation in Dante's reflection on poetry in *Purgatorio* 26 and, in turn, how this all prepares for Dante's ascent into the Earthly Paradise.

15. Compare *ST* Ia.45.7.

16. See Hawkins, *Dante's Testaments*.

17. A full analysis of this passage, as of *Purgatorio* 2.61–66, needs to take into consideration the significance of the fact that the character speaking is Virgil. This raises the question of the extent to which such passages may be seen as accurate expressions of Dantean theology. In line with *Purgatorio* 22.64–73, I suggest that Virgil's words may be taken as accurate representations of Dantean theology but not without qualification. For example, one could suggest that in the narrative dynamics of both *Purgatorio* 2.61–66 and 3.28–39, Virgil's words, while of great theological significance, are spoken without full awareness of their theological implications.

18. See also Honess, "Communication and Participation."

19. All of this in turn also prepares, of course, for the "come i piacque" in the passage from *Paradiso* 29 from which we began.

20. See also *Purg.* 1.132.

21. See *Purg.* 2.52–133 and 3.1–105. See also Lash, "Anselm Seeking," 161–63.

22. "Videns autem centurio quod factum fuerat / glorificavit Deum dicens / vere hic homo iustus erat / Et omnis turba eorum qui simul aderant ad spectaculum istud et videbant quae fiebant / percutientes pectora sua revertebantur" (Lk 23:47–48) [Now the centurion, seeing what was done, glorified God, saying: Indeed this was a just man. And all the multitude of them that were come together to that sight, and saw the things that were done, returned striking their breasts]; "Centurio autem et qui cum eo erant custodientes Iesum / viso terraemotu et his quae fiebant timuerunt valde dicentes / vere Dei Filius erat iste" (Mt 27:54) [Now the centurion and they that were with him watching Jesus, having seen the earthquake and the things that were done, were sore afraid, saying: Indeed this was the Son of God]. The moment in which in Matthew Jesus is recognized as the Son of God coincides in Luke's narrative with the moment marked by the crowd's striking their breasts. See also Mk 15:39.

23. See also Cestaro, *Dante and the Grammar of the Nursing Body*; Hollander, "Babytalk in Dante's *Commedia*"; and Honess, "Expressing the Inexpressible."

24. For more detailed discussion of this, and of the related question of Dante's understanding of the Eucharist, see my "'Padre mio.'"

25. My interpretation of the theological implications of the Ugolino episode is indebted to the theological studies referred to above, as well as to Beyer, "The Love of God"; Davies, "The Sign Redeemed"; Eagleton, "'Decentring' God"; Foster, "Dante as a Christian Poet"; F. Kerr, "Derrida's Wake" and "Charity as Friendship"; Lash, "When Did the Theologians Lose Interest in Theology?"; McCabe, "Sacramental Language"; Milbank, "The Name of Jesus"; Pattison, *The End of Theology*; Soskice, "Monica's Tears"; R. Williams, "Poetic and Religious Imagination."

26. See also Pertile, "La *Commedia* tra il dire e il fare."

27. See also Barański, "Dante's Biblical Linguistics."
28. Consider, in this respect, the significance of *Purgatorio* 11.94–99. These lines are generally read simply as an expression of the idea that later artists supplant the fame of earlier ones. The syntax, however, also allows for the opposite reading. "Colui" (96) could, grammatically, refer to either Cimabue or Giotto; "l'uno a l'altro Guido" (97) does not specify which Guido supplants the other; and the subject of "caccerà" (99) could be either Dante (if indeed it is Dante to which "chi" [99] refers) or "l'uno e l'altro" (compare *Purg.* 11.37; *Par.* 10.9; *Par.* 29.5–6).
29. See also chapter 3 of my "'Nulla vedere.'"
30. See Kirkpatrick, *Dante's "Inferno,"* 31–32. See also 363–67, 391–413.
31. Foster, "The Theology of the *Inferno*," 54.
32. See *Dve* 2.7.3–4.

4

The Poetry and Poetics of the Creation

PIERO BOITANI

Dante's first mention of the Creation in the *Commedia* is at the beginning of the *Inferno*, when the protagonist has put the dark wood behind him and finds himself at the foot of the hill of virtue, where he is stopped by the leopard of lust. We are immediately given the hour of the day and season of the events about to unfold: a spring morning with the sun in the constellation of Aries, namely, the spring equinox, precisely the time of year when, according to medieval tradition, God had created the universe; a morning when the sun "montava 'n sù con quelle stelle / ch'eran con lui quando l'amor divino / mosse di prima quelle cose belle" (1.38–40) [was mounting with those stars which were with it when Divine Love first set in motion those fair things].

For one moment, as the sun of this first spring lightens the landscape, external and internal, the terror that had seized Dante in the dark wood seems to give way to hope. Light and hope are shot through with longing, made explicit in the two past tenses of the verbs, enacting the distance between the world's Beginning and its present. Dante clearly feels this nostalgia for the Beginning as some essential aspect of his own self, a feeling which is both sensual and intellectual. The idea of the beginning of all things allows him, imaginatively, to see and enjoy the sun and stars as "cose *belle*," *fair* things, and not simply "good," as Genesis has it. This first firmament possesses a *pulchritudo* of intimate and pristine aesthetics, like the dawn and the aura that the "things" shed on everything surrounding them.

What this introductory canto of the *Inferno* is also doing is attributing the Creation to divine "love," in an operation both poetic and evangelical. Dante is possibly thinking of Thomas Aquinas's commentary on Aristotle's *Metaphysics*, where he states that the poet Hesiod, "before the time of the philosophers," had placed love as "principium rerum."[1] The act of Creation is then envisaged by Dante, following Aristotle, as a first, primordial ("di prima") impulse to the movement imparted by the Prime Mover to the celestial bodies, setting time and space in motion. The verb "mosse" in line 40 is a precise philosophical term, which, followed by "cose belle," is also perceived as an effortless gesture, as if God had given a gentle flick at some slender circle of light that nevertheless supported the entire weight of gravity of the universe. Genesis's "Fiat lux" (1:3) [Let there be light], "fiat firmamentum" (1:6) [Let there be a firmament], and "fiant luminaria" (1:14) [Let there be lights] are thus translated from words into one silent, luminous touch, reflected by the light of the sun and the stars.

It is difficult, then, to maintain that Dante has no specific poetics of Creation when these verses begin the wonderful rainbow which is completed in the very last line of *Paradiso*: "l'amor che move il sole e l'altre stelle" [the Love that moves the sun and the other stars]. Here, the "desire and will" that Dante speaks of three lines before the end are finally fulfilled by the vision of God, and are directed by that same "love which moves the sun and the other stars"; here, Dante himself becomes, with the "cose belle" of *Inferno* 1, an object of the Creation—of a Creation in whose end is its new and present Beginning.

The rapt poetry of the Creation will return, as we shall see, in the *Paradiso*, but Dante is too subtle and complex a thinker to remain infatuated by "fair things." Immediately after their creation, God turned His Hand to something else: to the gates of Hell and the reign of eternal pain, which the lost souls "abandon all hope" on entering (*Inf.* 3.1–9). The modern world tends to take a dim view of this duality in a God of love; for Dante, however, there is no ambiguity: it is indeed the "divina podestate" (5) [divine power], the Father, the "somma sapïenza" (6) [supreme wisdom], the Son, and the Holy Ghost, defined "primo amore" (6) [primal love],[2] which have produced these gates, in a display of both immense power and infinite wisdom and love. Wisdom, because the moral economy of the universe needs a place or state to contain the evil of the primordial past and all the evil to come, and love, because this confinement of evil is a supreme good. It was "justice," we are informed, that moved (the same verb, "mosse") the "alto fattore" (4) [the most high maker] to create the gruesome abyss, the same justice that punishes evil and rewards good. Imperfect on earth, without Hell justice would remain forever unfulfilled, and God's work incomplete. To paraphrase Dostoevsky: if Hell did not exist we would have to invent it. So essential is it in the global economy, as it were, that Dante pronounces its creation and eternal duration immediately after the creation of the first things, the angels, the heavens, and the first matter. The poetics of Creation as awed admiration of "fair things" is complemented, then, by Creation as an expression of unfathomable Justice producing terrifying things, fair only in the sense of "justified." In other words, the theology and poetics of Creation justify the poetry of the *Inferno* and *Paradiso*.

Dante is fascinated by the creation of all things eternal. In the *Purgatorio*, the reign of the human and the "beautiful," between the horror of the *Inferno* and the sublimity of *Paradiso*, he twice speaks of the creation of the immortal soul. The two passages are strictly interlinked, but their underlying poetics are fundamentally different. In the first, *Purgatorio* 16.85–93, the deftness and delicacy of God's movements are transmitted to the soul, here conceived as a young girl, crying and laughing in turn, "l'anima semplicetta," which turns in delight to whatever catches its eye:

> Esce di mano a lui che la vagheggia
> prima che sia, a guisa di fanciulla
> che piangendo e ridendo pargoleggia,
>   l'anima semplicetta che sa nulla,
> salvo che, mossa da lieto fattore,
> volontier torna a ciò che la trastulla.
>   Di picciol bene in pria sente sapore;
> quivi s'inganna, e dietro ad esso corre,
> se guida o fren non torce suo amore.

[From his His hand who regards it fondly / before it is, comes forth, like a child / that sports, tearful and smiling, / the little simple soul that knows nothing, / but, moved by a joyful Maker, / turns eagerly to what delights it. At first it tastes the savour of a trifling good; / it is beguiled there and runs after it, / if guide or curb do not divert its love.]

The soul issues "from [God's] hand" effortlessly, a bubble materializing on the divine palm, or a spark released for some dance or game. But the Creator's loving glance was fixed on "her" even before her creation, "prima che sia: con piacere e diletto la considera e mira, quasi in essa, la quale è immagine sua, specchiandosi" [before it is: with pleasure and delight he considers her and gazes at her, as if mirroring himself in her, who is his image].[3] This divine "fondness," as Sinclair translates Dante's verb "vagheggiare," is a response to the soul's ineffable beauty, its "vaghezza," and its simplicity: simple, innocent, and pure to the point of knowing nothing; the *tabula rasa* evoked by Aristotle and Aquinas.[4]

Having caught a glimpse of God's hand and his delighted and loving glance, we now learn that he is a joyous ("lieto") maker, moving the soul of each individual as, in *Inferno* 1 and *Paradiso* 33, he moves the sun and the other stars. The delight God feels in creating the human soul is clearly an essential aspect for Dante, who returns to it (as we shall see below) in *Purgatorio* 25, and again in Bernard's words, almost at the end of the poem:

> Lo rege per cui questo regno pausa
> in tanto amore e in tanto diletto,
> che nulla volontà è di più ausa,
>   le menti tutte nel suo *lieto* aspetto
> creando, a suo piacer di grazia dota
> diversamente ...
>   (*Par.* 32.61–66; my emphasis)

[The King through whom this kingdom rests / in such love and delight / that desire can dare no farther, / creating all minds in his *glad* sight, / bestows his grace variously at his pleasure ...]

Nothing so stirs divine joy as the creation of a human soul, which then reverberates with the same joy, unconsciously recognizing a spontaneous desire to turn back to the father-figure who in *Purgatorio* 16 "dandles" or "cuddles" it ("trastulla"). The soul naturally desires happiness, Aristotle would say, and if it fails to turn to its Maker for this happiness, it tries the taste "di picciol bene" [of a trifling good] and rushes to the pleasures of the flesh.[5] In other words, the principle of *eudaimonia* governing Aristotelian ethics is replaced by the pleasure principle which Freud perceives as governing the mechanisms of the psyche.

What interests me, however, is more the poetry of the passage. The central image, of the soul as a young child, may be remotely inspired by Proverbs (8:30), where Wisdom describes how it was conceived by God before the Beginning and amused itself by playing in His presence. At the end of his life, the Emperor Hadrian wrote a childlike lyric which is quoted in the *Historia Augusta*: "Animula vagula, blandula, / hospes comesque corporis, / quae nunc abibis in loca / pallidula, rigida, nudula? / nec, ut soles, dabis iocos!" [Little wandering soul, body's guest and companion, to what place are you going now? Cold, dark and gloomy, never again to joke or play].[6] Hadrian's soul is like a playful small girl, wandering about and charming, the body's guest and companion, but ready to leave off all play and fly, naked, stiff, and pale, towards bare, bleak spaces. If Dante had been aware of the emperor's melancholy lines, he might have conceived this passage in *Purgatorio* 16 as Wisdom speaking out in joyous counterpoint to it, or written a medieval version of the *Animula* that is one of T. S. Eliot's *Ariel Poems*.[7] He probably was not, however. Perhaps we should read his passage, then, as sudden empathy with the concrete, referential actions of a child—possibly his own daughter—who cries and laughs as she plays. The memory of this simple spontaneity then fused with his perennial aspiration towards primordial innocence: the soul before original sin, or Eve in her childhood.

The process of Dante's inspiration is actually much more complex. In the *Convivio* (4.12), to describe the soul following first the lesser, then the greater good, he had used the image of the *parvuli*, the small boys, reaching first for an apple, then some small bird, then, when they grow up, a woman and a horse—an image deriving from Brunetto Latini's *Trésor* and, ultimately, Horace's *Ars poetica*.[8] At this point, association would have led him to his soul-child image. The idea was not unknown in the Middle Ages, however; in the *Passio Petri et Marcellini*, for example, the souls are elegantly dressed young women, and in two cases at least, the *Dormition of the Virgin* in the Byzantine mosaics (of the Norman period) in the church of Santa Maria dell'Ammiraglio in Palermo, and the mosaics by Pietro Cavallini in Santa Maria in Trastevere, Rome, the soul is represented as a child.[9]

The theological tradition goes back to Origen and his *Commentary* and *Homilies* on the Song of Songs, and thence to Guillaume de Saint Thierry's *Commentary* and Bernard's *Sermones in Cantica*: the perfect soul is a Bride, ardently desiring her Bridegroom, the Word, and being desired by him in return. For Origen, the "young girls" accompanying the Bride represent the souls of believers who, although faithful, have still to reach perfection.[10] Even more interestingly, when Origen speaks of God "creat[ing] man to his own image . . . male and female he created them" (Gn 1:27), he maintains that the verse can be interpreted allegorically, as the creation of the "inner man" uniting the "spirit" (male) and the "soul" (female). Wherever they find "concord" and "consent" (St. Paul's *symphonia* between husband and wife [1 Cor 7:5]), they increase and multiply, generating "good motions," thoughts and reflections with which to "replenish the earth." The soul, however, "is conjoined and, as it were, coupled with the spirit, and can occasionally sink to the level of bodily pleasures ("di picciol bene in pria sente sapore; / quivi s'inganna, e dietro ad esso corre" [At first it tastes the savour of a trifling good; / it is beguiled there and runs after it]), tainting itself with "bodily adultery," in which case it can neither increase nor multiply.[11] The "double Creation" which Origen reads in Genesis 1:26–27 and 2:7 posits a "primordial existence" for man, namely, "the being according to the creator's image," and an existence "deriving from sin, moulded out of the mud of the earth."[12] This element created "according to the creator's image" Origen reads as the soul.

The soul, then, occupies center stage in Origen's theology, so often revisited in the Middle Ages.[13] Created by God in his own image, with the spirit it forms part of Paul's "inner man." Though it can be diverted towards earthly matters, it is also the Bride seeking the Bridegroom, and "turns eagerly" back ("volontier torna") to him who "regards it fondly" ("la vagheggia"). Every created soul is naturally small, and can only grow with experience and the gradual knowledge of God. The image of the children thus emerges quite naturally, reinforced and directed by the echo of the Gospel in which Jesus invites the disciples to "suffer the little children, and forbid them not to come unto me, for such is the kingdom of heaven" (Mt 19:14) ("Sinite parvulos ["parvuli" is the word used by Dante in the above passage from the *Convivio*] et nolite eos prohibere ad me venire; talium est enim regnum caelorum").

Origen, for example, in his *Commentary on Matthew*, compares these "little children" to Christ himself, who became a "child," and we are instructed to "become as little children" if we are to be saved.[14] He then combines Luke's synoptic account with the First Epistle of St. Paul to the Corinthians, to exhort the wise "not to put themselves above those that are small in the church and not to despise those who are children and infants in Christ: *Verily I say unto you, Whosoever shall not receive the kingdom of heaven as a little child* [Lk 18:17]: although an adult, and no longer a child, who has *put away childish things* [1 Cor 13:11], he *becomes as a child* among children, and tells them that: *I, brethren, could not speak unto you as unto spiritual, but as unto carnal, even as unto babes in Christ. I have fed you with milk, and not with meat* [1 Cor 3:1–2]." The "babes in Christ" are thus the ideal for humanity in its ascent and spiritual progress, because, as Origen later explains, quoting Matthew (18:5), Jesus states: "Whoso shall receive one such little child in my name receiveth me." And Matthew also writes that, when asked by the disciples who was the "greatest" in the kingdom of Heaven, "Jesus called a little child unto him, and set him in the midst of them. And said, Verily I say unto you, Except ye be converted, and become as little children, ye shall not enter into the kingdom of heaven. Whosoever therefore shall humble himself as this little child, the same is greatest in the kingdom of heaven" (18:1–4). Origen, followed by Jerome, glosses that this child is the Holy Ghost, "become small for the salvation of men" and sent with the Saviour by the Father.[15] The Trinity evoked by Dante for the creation of Hell is now reflected in the spiritual child described by Origen and Jerome. Indeed, the Christian's very goal is identified with the state of childhood. Quoting Luke 18:17 again, Origen maintains that the text has a dual meaning: "either he who receives the kingdom of God becomes as a child, or he receives the kingdom of God, which for him has become as a child. And perhaps those here on earth who receive the kingdom of heaven receive it as if it were a child, while in the next world they will no longer accept it as such, but according to the greatness of perfection which in spiritual maturity (so to speak) reveals itself to all those who in the present time have received the kingdom of God, which was like a child."[16]

Origen is tracing a great circle, departing from God's creation of the human soul, in his own image, in the form of a woman, and returning to the Logos as the desired Bridegroom of the Child-Bride. Within this circular rhythm there is both the moment in which the soul can turn aside from its divine *telos*, and, equally, the possibility to become as a child and enter the kingdom of God, which is also a child. It is this sort of theological conception that forms the backdrop to Dante's lines in *Purgatorio* 16, where we find exactly this same circle, going from Creation to its return towards the Maker, and from the Creator's love for his creature to the return of that love: a strictly human trajectory against the cosmic backdrop of the Beginning and the End. If we then ask ourselves what the poet adds to the theologian, the answer will certainly center around the weeping, smiling, playing child ("fanciulla / che piangendo e ridendo pargoleggia" [child / that sports, tearful and smiling]), the simple soul ("l'anima semplicetta" [the little simple soul]), and the "trastulla" that, as it were, entertains the soul, but that is also connected to the power of speaking, singing, and poetry:[17] all expressions with connotations of the nature, activities, and language of or about children. From the *Convivio* on, this is then the poetry of the "parvuli," the poetics of a writer who becomes an evangelical child.

At the same time, at the center of such a poetics lies, *a parte subiecti*, the "vagheggiare" Dante attributes to the creating God—a loving contemplation, an enraptured love of the first things. It is significant that this "vagheggiare" will, in the *Paradiso*, be ascribed to the soul of Adam, the first man God ever created, and again, by virtue of syntactical ambiguity, to God himself:

> . . . Dentro da quei rai
> vagheggia il suo fattor l'anima prima
> che la prima virtù creasse mai.
> (26.82–84)

> [Within these rays / looks with love on his Maker the first soul / the First Power ever created]

"Vagheggiare" (the verb courtly poetry employs for human eros) is also the very aim of what I would call the "theological aesthetics" of Dante. When he ascends to the fourth Heaven, the Heaven of the Sun and the *Sapientes*, he invites his readers to lift up their eyes with him "to the lofty wheels [of the celestial equator and of the ecliptic] and direct them where the motion of the one strikes the other: there they should begin to 'vagheggiar' the art of that Master who so loves it in his heart that his eye never leaves it":

> Leva dunque, lettore, a l'alte rote
> meco la vista, dritto a quella parte
> dove l'un moto e l'altro si percuote;

>   e lì comincia a vagheggiar ne l'arte
>   di quel maestro che dentro a sé l'ama,
>   tanto che mai da lei l'occhio non parte.
>   (*Par.* 10.7–12)[18]

The object of such a "vagheggiar" is the *art* of God, in other words the created universe, the cosmos in which we live and which Dante portrays in his poem: lifting his eyes, the reader will encounter not only God's art but also the poet's. While man's loving contemplation of the work of the divine Maker corresponds to the love which He bears to it within Himself, Dante immediately afterwards returns to the *reader*'s pleasure in following him: "Or ti riman, lettor, sovra 'l tuo banco, / dietro pensando a ciò che *si preliba*, / *s'esser vuoi lieto* assai prima che stanco" (10.22–24; my emphases) [Stay now, reader, on your bench, / thinking over this of which *you have a foretaste*, / and you shall have much *delight* before you are tired]. And he finally points to himself, the scribe who writes down God's art: "Messo t'ho innanzi: omai per te ti ciba; / ché a sé torce tutta la mia cura / quella materia ond' io son fatto scriba" (25–27) [I have set the food before you, now feed yourselves, for the theme of which I am made the scribe bends to itself all my care]. "[Q]uella materia ond' io son fatto scriba": this, finally, is the object of the readers' "vagheggiare," to lift your eyes *with me*. Dante places his poetry as the intermediary between God and human kind.

Of quite a different nature is the language Dante uses to describe the creation of the intellectual soul in *Purgatorio* 25.61–78:

>   Ma come d'animal divegna fante,
>   non vedi tu ancor: quest' è tal punto,
>   che più savio di te fé già errante,
>   sì che per sua dottrina fé disgiunto
>   da l'anima il possibile intelletto,
>   perché da lui non vide organo assunto.
>   Apri a la verità che viene il petto;
>   e sappi che, sì tosto come al feto
>   l'articular del cerebro è perfetto,
>   lo motor primo a lui si volge lieto
>   sovra tant' arte di natura, e spira
>   spirito novo, di vertù repleto,

> che ciò che trova attivo quivi, tira
> in sua sustanzia, e fassi un'alma sola,
> che vive e sente e sé in sé rigira.
>
> E perché meno ammiri la parola,
> guarda il calor del sol che si fa vino,
> giunto a l'omor che de la vite cola.

[But how from animal it becomes a child / you do not yet see; this is the point / which once made one wiser than you to err, / so that in his teaching he separated / the possible intellect from the soul, / because he did not see an organ appropriated by it. / Open your breast to the truth that follows / and know that as soon as in the embryo / the articulation of the brain is perfected / the First Mover turns to it, rejoicing / over such handiwork of nature, and breathes / into it a new spirit full of virtue, / which draws that which it finds active there / into its own substance and becomes one single soul / which lives and feels and turns itself within itself. / And, so that you may wonder less at my words, / consider the sun's heat which becomes wine / when it is joined to the juice that pours from the vine.]

Here Dante is keen to distinguish between the generation of the vegetative and sensitive souls, on the one hand, and the creation of the rational soul, on the other: to demonstrate how the human foetus "d'animal divegna fante." He is also keen to confute Averroes, who "fé disgiunto / da l'anima il possibile intelletto." The whole passage, like the parallel one in *Convivio* 4.21, attests that Dante's source on this subject is not only Aristotle's *De generatione animalium* but also Albert the Great's *De natura et origine animae*.[19] In other words, here he is speaking not "as a child" but as a scholar and philosopher; and the register is sustained until the point when Statius, now his Christian mouthpiece, turns to the question of the creation of the intellectual soul. At the very moment where the Aristotelian influence shows how "al feto / l'articular del cerebro è perfetto," a subtle but swift change occurs in Dante's imagination. The Aristotelian "motor primo" turns to the human embryo in a way that is equally Aristotelian,[20] but simultaneously Christian, on account of both its turning (for Aristotle it would be immobile) and, above all, its joyousness: "lieto" once again, and now "sovra tant' arte di natura" [over such handiwork of nature], almost as if it were now contemplating with love ("vagheggiando," so to speak) the work of art that nature has generated in the foetus.

From this Aristotelian-Christian sequence the directly biblical inspiration of the "second" Creation follows,[21] "e spira / spirito novo": as the climax to the entire process, the divine breath breathes an immortal soul into the embryo. But Dante stays with Genesis for only a second. This new spirit, "di vertù repleto" [full of virtue], attracts into its substance what is already "active" in the vegetative-sensitive soul, fusing with it, according to Albert, to become "un'alma sola." It is living, like the being in Genesis, and sentient, but it also possesses the supreme capacity for contemplation: "che vive e sente e sé in sé rigira" [which lives and feels and turns itself within itself]. It "turns" as God turned towards the foetus, but now on itself, revolving like a wheel, not only contemplating the truth but also, as Dante states in the *Convivio*, following Aristotle's *Metaphysics* Book Lambda,[22] contemplating its own contemplation "and the beauty of it, turning about itself and with itself falling in love, for the beauty of its first view." Here the soul falls in love not only with God, the main object of its "trastullar" in *Purgatorio* 16, but above all with itself, the subject and object of philosophy, within the contemplation of which Aristotle placed God in the same book of the *Metaphysics*.

The passage ends with another leap; stupefying and difficult as it is by Statius's own admission, it requires careful glossing. Dante uses the famous analogy of the "calor del sol che si fa vino, / giunto a l'omor che de la vite cola" [the sun's heat which becomes wine / when it is joined to the juice that pours from the vine]. Nardi was the first to link this image "materially" with Cicero's *De senectute* (15.53), but inserting it "ideally" into the vast context of the comparable metaphor of the union of the light of the sun and that of fire in the air, employed by Alexander of Hales, Jean de la Rochelle, and a number of others.[23] Cicero's description of the old man's joy in the flourishing vine and grape,[24] "et suco terrae et calore solis augescens"—the pleasure of the senses and of life—is almost transformed into the delight of the primordial elements of light and fire, the two together then helping to fulfill the pleasure in contemplating contemplation, which belongs to the now complete soul. Dante's sureness of poetic foot—in all senses—has no problem in dealing with exactly how the spiritual is embedded in the corporeal, however. He foregrounds the dizzying distance between the celestial, immaterial heat of the sun and the earthly, filtering humours of the vine, at the same time indicating the inevitable and perfect encounter between the two (corporeal) elements, which infallibly produces a new substance, wine. This marvelous and most natural metamorphosis needs no Cicero or medieval philosopher to explain it: the nous of a farmer will do just as well—or, equally, the biblical knowledge of the average Christian, who will immediately think of the marriage of Cana, where the earthly element of water is transformed into wine, the "sign" of the Eucharist (Jn 2:1–12), and remember Christ's statement that "I am the true vine, and my Father is the husbandman" (Jn 15:1) [ego sum vitis vera et Pater meus agricola est]. And so, after a most learned kind of poetry, honed by the technicalities of Aristotle and Albert, the confutation of Averroes, and the inspiration of the Bible, Ciceronian satisfaction, cosmic exultation, and contemplative pleasure all reach their perfect *kairós* in wine: not the refined toast of poets, but the liquid drunk in Tuscany, the Veneto, and Romagna. The complete soul of man is no longer a child caught between laughter and tears, but a simple, thick, aromatic and inebriating wine. Philosophy and theology create their own poetics: that of the winemaker after that of the child.

The leap in register from *Purgatorio* to *Paradiso* is nearly paralyzing for the reader. It is no simple return to the cosmic nostalgia of *Inferno* 1, or to the philosophical discourse on the creation of the human soul in *Purgatorio*. *Paradiso* is not for the philosophically fainthearted: it gives a Neoplatonic reading of the scriptures which makes no concessions to the uninformed. This is poetry for the "few" who "reached out early for the angels' bread" (*Par.* 2.10–11) [Voialtri pochi che drizzaste il collo / per tempo al pan de li angeli], and who can "put forth [their] vessel on the salt depths, holding [Dante's] furrow before the water returns smooth again" (13–15) [metter potete ben per l'alto sale / vostro navigio, servando mio solco / dinanzi a l'acqua che ritorna equale]—for the few who have fed on divine wisdom and the Word, which is Christ. This type of poetry had never been heard before.[25] It is the result of an *agon*, a struggle with the philosophical, theological, and not least verbal raw materials,[26] creating an unprecedented effect on his readers.[27] In a word, as I have maintained elsewhere,[28] this is a new, unique, and sublime form of poetry.

It is beyond my present scope to give a detailed analysis of the poetics of Creation in the *Paradiso*. I intend to concentrate on two seminal passages, in cantos 19 and 29, and call other lines to witness where relevant. Canto 19 is part of the long, extraordinary sequence of the Eagle, which extends from canto 18 to canto 20. Now in the sixth Heaven, the Sphere of Jupiter, the pilgrim watches, amazed, as the head and neck of an eagle are picked out in fiery sparks, and begin to illustrate the mysteries of divine justice. Throughout the episode comprising *Paradiso* 18–20, Dante returns continuously to the theme of poetry ("canto") and art that was announced in *Paradiso* 18 by the last motion of Cacciaguida, "tra i cantor del cielo artista" (51) [singer among the singers of that heaven]. He creates a scale of *poietai*, from the supreme Painter and Architect of the universe down to David, "cantor de lo Spirito Santo" (20.38) [singer of the Holy Ghost], and then to the "buon cantor" [good singer] who closes canto 20, afterwards reascending to the unique and extraordinary voice of Dante Alighieri, *poietes* of Paradise and the *Paradiso*.

The first position is occupied, in *Paradiso* 18.109–11, by "He that designs the heavens":

> Quei che dipinge lì, non ha chi 'l guidi;
> ma esso guida, e da lui si rammenta
> quella virtù ch'è forma per li nidi.

> [He that designs there has none to guide Him. / He Himself guides, even as we recognize to be from Him / that power which is form for the nests.]

With "none to guide him" according to any predesigned model, "He Himself guides," and from him, recognizably, derives the "virtù" that shapes all creatures in embryo—"that power which is form for the nests." Dante the Platonist now, as in *Paradiso* 13, sees within the divine mind the archetypes of all existing forms, but in reminding us of the "virtù ch'è forma," the informing principle by which God creates all beings, he will not forget the *tode ti*, Aristotle's particular-universal: "per li nidi" has both a general value, as the place where the living being is formed and grows from seed, and a singular, applying to *this* particular celestial eagle, painted in Heaven by God and the model of all the eagles on earth. What is presented to us is, in sum, the Idea of an Eagle in tangible form; and it must inevitably strike us that, if God was drawing without a model, it is the poet Dante who is now inventing and drawing this celestial eagle, and who is thus implicitly arrogating for himself divine painterly powers.

The image of the Divine Architect in canto 19, on the other hand, is absolute: the geometer "turning His compass about the bounds of the world," filling it with any number of things, manifest and hidden, but without infusing them with his own "valore"—his power as the creating Father—to avoid making his idea and word (the Son) appear "in infinito eccesso," infinitely exceeding, with respect to the created world. In just two *terzine*, the Creation is evoked in all its theological and philosophical complexity (with the whole structure of the universe, in which all things visible and invisible are contained, in discrete order), and with the great biblical image of the compass as a beguilingly visual introduction that "encompasses" the reader and stuns him into acceptance of the difficult cosmic ride ahead.[29] This is Dante's rewriting of the beginning of Genesis and John's Gospel:

> Poi cominciò: "Colui che volse il sesto
> a lo stremo del mondo, e dentro ad esso
> distinse tanto occulto e manifesto,
>   non poté suo valor sì fare impresso
> in tutto l'universo, che 'l suo verbo
> non rimanesse in infinito eccesso.
> (*Par.* 19.40–45)

[Then it began: "He that turned His compass / about the bounds of the world, and within it / devised so variously things hidden and manifest, / could not make His power to be so impressed / on the whole universe that His Word / should not remain in infinite excess.]

At the human level of *poiein* there is, in *Paradiso* 18–25, no higher "maker" than David, traditionally considered the author of the Psalms; here he is actually the "cantor de lo Spirito Santo" (20.38), and "sommo cantor del sommo duce" (25.72) [the sovereign singer of the sovereign Lord]. Dante acknowledges David's inspiration as coming directly from God ("cantor de lo Spirito Santo," meaning, of course, both that David sings of the Holy Ghost and that his song is dictated by it); he also recognises that this "tëodia" (25.73) was a fundamental human experience for himself, in that it was the first means by which hope was "first distilled in [his] heart"—"quei la distillò nel mio cor pria / che fu sommo cantor del sommo duce" (25.71–72) [he first distilled it in my heart / who was the sovereign singer of the sovereign Lord]. *Theody* is a hymn to God, a song in his honor, the monotheist's equivalent of the Greek ode to winning athletes and to the gods; it is the highest lyrical model that the *Paradiso* enacts as narration.[30]

The challenge is met head-on in the Eagle sequence, as evinced in two passages from *Paradiso* 18 and 19, in which Dante as poet demonstrates full self-awareness of both his attempt and his success. The first comes just before the *terzina* dedicated to the celestial Painter, and invokes the Muse to illumine the human painter and enable him to represent the letters and words formed by the spirits of the just *as he conceived them*. The author is certainly God: but the writer is equally certainly Dante, and the Muse confers glory and long life on *human* genius, which in its turn, jointly, confers fame on the cities and kingdoms of the world:

> O diva Pegasëa che li 'ngegni
> fai glorïosi e rendili longevi,
> ed essi teco le cittadi e ' regni,
>   illustrami di te, sì ch'io rilevi
> le lor figure com' io l'ho concette:
> paia tua possa in questi versi brevi!
>   (*Par.* 18.82–87)

[O Pegasean goddess, you who to genius / give victory and long life / as it does through you to cities and kingdoms, / illumine me with yourself that I may set forth / their shapes as I deciphered them. / Let your power appear in these brief lines!]

Dante, of course, is perfectly aware to what extent the Muse's power is displayed in the present cantos: at the beginning of canto 19 he states proudly that what he is about to relate of the Eagle was never sung by any voice, written by any pen, or conceived by any imagination:

> E quel che mi convien ritrar testeso,
> non portò voce mai, né scrisse incostro,
> né fu per fantasia già mai compreso . . .
>   (7–9)

[And that of which I have now to tell / never tongue conveyed, nor ink wrote, / nor ever was conceived by fancy.]

Here is a totally new element, then, in Dante's poetry: no models can exist for an imagination which, to celebrate divine justice and attack the knotty problem of pagan salvation, reinvents the eagle of Ezekiel and John, fleshing it out into a unity and, simultaneously, plurality of movements and arabesques, in a flash of gold on silver: fire, water, sun, birds. This is the poetry and poetics of Creation *as justice*, as in *Inferno* 3: but how different! Dante's poetry here is the delicate, purified, blissful murmur of contemplation.

Let me now skip to *Paradiso* 29, my other major text on the Creation — a canto which is absolute, which speaks with one voice alone, that of Beatrice, sweeping down from before the beginning to the earthly world of the fourteenth century and back again to the fullness of the heavens. Canto 29 predicates being in its primeval forms, and moves through time and space to hover over out-of-time and outside-space; it moves constantly from the instant to eternity, from the "point" to the celestial waters and on to the final "eccelso" [height] and "larghezza" [breadth]. It also boldly re-scripts Scripture, rewriting the Hebrew-Christian Genesis and the prologue of John's Gospel in the Greek-Latin-Scholastic language of the Platonists and the Aristotelians, and roundly dismissing any anthropomorphism from the Beginning in favor of metaphysics and the categories of thought. The canto is divided into three clear parts (lines 1–81; 82–126; 127–45), proceeding like an inverted parabola, the third part returning to the subject and heights of the first.

Paradiso 29 is linked by situation to the previous canto (Beatrice and Dante are in the ninth, the last of the physical heavens, the crystalline or "aqueous" *caelum angelorum*, or Primum Mobile) and continues both its themes and its means. After describing the angelic orders, Beatrice now continues with their creation, her tone briskly changing from irony to anger as she anathematizes the foolishness of the theologians. Canto 28 had ended with Pope Gregory, who, on meeting the angels face to face, "di sé medesmo rise" (135) [smiled at himself] and at his erroneous theories on the angelic orders (Dante in fact follows Dionysius the Areopagite). Here, all those daring to hold other opinions as to angels get very short shrift indeed.

The canto opens with one of the instants that underscore it: a long, suspended moment as Beatrice pauses in her description; an almost imperceptible threshold as we climb the invisible step marking off the Beginning. This limen is evoked through a perfect scientific image and names from myth: the children of Latona, Apollo (sun) and Diana (moon). When the sun is in Aries and the moon in Libra, they "make a belt of the horizon," as Dante puts it, the sun rising and the moon setting. The celestial zenith then holds them in balance ("'inlibra," in Dante's specially coined term) for a split second, each one in the next moment changing hemispheres as the sun rises above and the moon dips below the horizon, "liberating" itself from (but also "unbalancing," "dilibra," in Dante's punning coinage) the "girdle." From a scientific viewpoint, this instant is seen as a mathematical point, while the images used to describe it evoke huge cosmic scales, as if the two parts of Beatrice's disquisition on angels were connected with the rising of the sun (*Paradiso* 29) and the setting of the moon (*Paradiso* 28), here meeting on the horizon in one moment's smiling silence. In this silence is contained all the joy of contemplation, and of the meditation on the essence of things:

> Quando ambedue li figli di Latona,
> coperti del Montone e de la Libra,
> fanno de l'orizzonte insieme zona,
>   quant' è dal punto che 'l cenìt inlibra
> infin che l'uno e l'altro da quel cinto,
> cambiando l'emisperio, si dilibra,
>   tanto, col volto di riso dipinto,
> si tacque Bëatrice, riguardando
> fiso nel punto che m'avëa vinto.
>   (29.1–9)

[When the two children of Latona, / covered by the Ram and by the Scales, / both at once make a belt of the horizon / as long as from the moment when the zenith holds them balanced / till the one and the other, / changing hemispheres, are unbalanced from that girdle, / for so long, her face illumined with a smile, / Beatrice kept silent, looking / fixedly at a point that had overcome me.]

The image of the point immediately returns.[31] In the previous canto, Dante had glimpsed God as "un punto . . . che raggiava lume" (16) [a point which radiated light], and heard the angels singing hosannas to the "punto fisso che li tiene a li *ubi*, / e terrà sempre, ne' quai sempre fuoro" (95–96) [the fixed point, which holds and shall ever hold them in the place where they have ever been]. Beatrice had immediately defined it as the point from which "depende il cielo e tutta la natura" (42) [from that point hang the heavens and all nature]. Now, in canto 29, it is Beatrice who looks fixedly at the point ("that had conquered me," Dante admits, "che m'avëa vinto") and begins to speak, "telling, not asking" him what he desires to hear, knowing it perfectly well already because she had "seen it there where every *ubi* and every *quando* is centred" (10–12) [Io dico, e non dimando, / quel che tu vuoli udir, perch' io l'ho visto / là 've s'appunta ogne *ubi* e ogne *quando*], namely, in the Point, which is God Himself. *Ubi* (already used in canto 28) and *quando* are adverbs used as nouns,[32] but they are relative, the first standing for "the place where," and the second for "the time/moment in which." Human space and time are *relations*, not absolutes. But relations of place and time are "centred," that is, they converge in the Point of God, the Absolute. Dante thus immediately delineates the different horizons—human and divine—on which he will articulate his account of the Creation, and gives some explanation for the inconceivable similarity between Beatrice's silence (of the duration of a mathematical point) and the concentration of space and time in God (a "point" where they are "centred"). Silence, it appears, is God's: only in silence can an adequate account of Him begin, albeit in the human verbs and rational words which are all we have. And indeed it is here, in *Paradiso* 29, that Dante's long consideration of the divine Creation finally ends, in a meditation that is not without reason, since creation by God of all that exists represents the central foundation, the intellectual pivot, of a religious understanding of the cosmos. This canto contains all his impassioned analysis of the theme, in passages that encompass a number of philosophical traditions and hover at the threshold of the ontologically unutterable.

From the relatives of where and when, *ubi* and *quando*, Beatrice now moves beyond the "point" to the absolutes of beyond-time, beyond-space—"di tempo fore, / fuor d'ogne altro comprender" (16–17) [beyond time, beyond every other bound]. She moves towards the eternity which is God's, which is beyond any need and any desire to increase: "[n]on per aver a sé di bene acquisto" (13) [not to gain any good for Himself]; but which is also beyond any other bound of human comprehension ("fuor d'ogne altro *comprender*"). For the pure pleasure of it and according to His desire ("come i piacque," 17), "s'aperse in nuovi amor l'etterno amore" (18) [the Eternal Love unfolded Himself in new loves]. His only aim is to multiply existence into new, self-conscious lives, "perché suo splendore / potesse, risplendendo, dir '*Subsisto*'" (14–15) [that His splendour, shining back, might say *Subsisto*]. This Latin verb, which Beatrice uses, includes not mere existence, of course, but the whole and complete state of Being, a Scholastic echo of the *Ego sum qui sum* [I am who am] through which God reveals His being to Moses, concealing it in absolute mystery (Ex 3:14).

The creation of the angels is a reflection of light, an opening out of Love into new loves, a blossoming and "breaking," as the last lines of the canto will have it, of the "Eternal Goodness" into "so many mirrors," "remaining in itself one as before" ("Vedi l'eccelso omai e la larghezza / de l'etterno valor, poscia che tanti / speculi fatti s'ha in che si spezza, / uno manendo in sé come davanti" [142–45] [See now the height and the breadth / of the Eternal Goodness, since so many / mirrors it has made for itself in which it is broken, / remaining in itself one as before]). This is the Neoplatonism of Dionysius the Areopagite, but with an "aesthetic" consistency lacking in its models; it is a powerful affirmation of being requiring no divine hand (unlike, for example, *Purgatorio* 16 or Michelangelo's God in the Sistine Chapel), nor, surprisingly, John's Logos or Word.[33]

The scriptures, Dante states in *Paradiso* 4 (37–48), "condescend" to human capacity and lend God "hands and feet," but they have a very different significance. Dante's re-scripting of Scripture has no intention of "condescending" and no longer needs any "sign" to communicate to our "sense perception," since it speaks directly to the "intellect"—to humans as potential angels.[34] It now signifies something "other." When Goethe's wretched Faust attempts to translate the *incipit* of the fourth Gospel, he tries out four different expressions to render into modern thought-systems the *Verbum* that was already an adaptation, via *Logos*, of the Hebrew *dabhar*: *Wort, Sinn, Kraft*, and *Tat*.[35] Dante, for his part, is having nothing of semantic speculations: he goes confidently to tradition, and in the place of Word, Sense, Might, and Action, he consecrates Love, the love that unites all things, the "etterno amore," which in *Purgatorio* 3 (134) saves Manfredi and in *Paradiso* 7 (33) designates the Incarnation of the Word—supreme Eros and Charity. That Love was never inactive ("né ... quasi torpente si giacque" [*Par.* 29.19] [nor ...

did he lie as it were inert]), but had always ("né prima né poscia" [20] [there was no 'before' or 'after']—since time only came into existence after the Creation) proceeded as a "discorrer di Dio sovra quest' acque" (21), as God's moving over the face of "these" waters.

I intend to stop here for the moment and examine Dante's moves more closely. The only phrase of Genesis he "misquotes" is the idea of God's moving over the waters. As the Vulgate puts it, "In principio creavit Deus caelum et terram. Terra autem erat inanis et vacua, et tenebrae super faciem abyssi, et spiritus Dei ferebatur super aquas. Dixitque Deus: fiat lux. Et facta est lux" (Gen 1:1–3) [In the beginning God created heaven and earth. And the earth was void and empty, and darkness was upon the face of the deep; and the spirit of God moved over the waters. And God said: Let there be light. And there was light]. God then divides light from dark, which He calls day and night: "and there was evening and morning one day" (4–5) [factumque est vespere et mane dies unus]. On the second day He creates the firmament in the middle of the waters, to divide "the waters that were under the firmament from those that were above the firmament" (6–7) [aquas quae erant sub firmamento ab his quae erant super firmamentum].

Dante has virtually eliminated all this: in particular, he has no "earth without form and void," no "darkness upon the face of the deep," and no Word to pronounce "Let there be light." Even the movement of the Spirit over the waters takes on a different significance, since the whole sequence has been changed.

In the Bible, God's moving over the waters *precedes* creation proper, which begins when God states "Let there be light." At most, this hovering over the waters is symbolic of incubation, the interpretation given by part of the exegetical tradition. When Milton, for example, evokes the Spirit at the beginning of *Paradise Lost*, he writes: "thou from the first / Wast present, and with mighty wings outspread / Dove-like sat'st *brooding* on the vast abyss / And *madest it pregnant*" (1.19–22). Again, later, in the magnificent account of Creation in Book 7, when the Son in His chariot rides out into the ocean of Chaos, he calms it, takes a compass to circumscribe the universe, and rolls it around the vast deeps, creating heaven and earth: "Matter unformed and void: darkness profound / Covered the abyss"; "but"—and here he gets to our point—"on the watery calm / His *brooding* wings the spirit of God outspread, / And vital virtue *infused*, and vital warmth / Throughout the fluid mass," pushing back into the depths "the black tartareous cold infernal dregs / adverse to life: then founded, then conglobed / Like things to like, the rest to several place / Disparted" (218–42).[36]

Dante, then, considerably alters the single biblical phrase he quotes, "et spiritus Dei ferebatur super aquas" [and the spirit of God moved over the waters]. In the first place, the waters become "these waters," "*quest'*acque." Following a tradition that gained considerable currency in the thirteenth century, he takes them as the waters above the firmament, those of the ninth heaven above the stars, in the Crystalline or Primum Mobile.[37] Beatrice and Dante are now above the same primeval waters over which the *ruah elohim* of the Beginning moved: *these* waters; and from this giddy height, Beatrice (i.e., Dante) dares to re-script Holy Scripture.

In the second place, Dante boldly cuts across centuries of controversy over the expression "spiritus Dei" (which in the original could mean terrible storm or gust of wind, or the breath or spirit of God) and simply attributes the action to God Himself. Third, he eliminates the neutral form of the verb "ferebatur" of the Vulgate, ignores the "incubabat" and "fovebat" (i.e., the incubating and brooding, which are the origins of Milton's version), and opts for a verb that is simultaneously powerful and delicate, "discorrer," the movement implied in the English noun and verb "course," and suggested by the "irruebat" of other traditional interpretations. Although he may have Ovid in mind ("ipse deus velox discurrere gaudet in altis / montibus" [The god himself loves to scamper, fleet of foot, about the high mountains]),[38] I believe the meaning here is closer to the "perlabitur" Virgil uses to describe Neptune's calming of the seas by skimming the surface of the waves with the light wheels of his chariot: "rotis summas levibus perlabitur undas."[39] Furthermore, in classical and medieval Latin, "discurrere" also stands for the orator's exploration of the ramifications of an argument (as in "discourse"). The first would agree with the opening of Eternal Love into new loves; the second would refer indirectly to the action of God's word, which is fundamental to Genesis and John but notably absent from *Paradiso* 29. Note, too, that in the *Convivio* (3.7.3), when Dante cites the *Liber de causis* to state that "la prima bontade manda le sue bontadi sopra le cose con uno discorrimento" [the Primal Goodness sends its bounties upon all things with a single diffusion], the word "discorrimento" replaces the original "influxio." Once again, God descends among His creatures by means of the movement of "discorrer." In his commentary on *Paradiso* 29, Cristoforo Landino makes an explicit parallel between God's "course," his "trascorrere," and the "discourse of creation."[40]

In the Vulgate the spirit of God is carried or proceeds ("ferebatur") above the waters. A tradition running from Augustine to Thomas Aquinas, aptly summarized by Peter Lombard, interprets this as the "voluntas artificis quae superfertur materiae quam vult formare," the will of the creator which "passes above" the matter it wishes to shape.[41] Dante, who was certainly at home within this tradition, is thus describing the action whereby the supreme Agent-Artisan-Artist is preparing to give shape to shapeless matter, to the *res fabricandae*, the things to be created.

Dante's is a complete rewriting of Genesis, then, as we adduce from the echo here. It continues as the six days wear on, or fail to, since Dante subverts the divine "discourse," replacing these days yet again by the single moment—the Divine Being "raggiò insieme tutto / sanza distinzïone in essordire" and without "intervallo" (*Par.* 29.29–30 and 27) [creation flashed into being from its Lord all at once without distinction in its beginning; without interval]. That is, the creation of the universe was both simultaneous and instantaneous. The point is that Dante rejects the anthropomorphic imagery that dominates the account in Genesis and so many other myths of creation to start a philosophical *mythos* of his own. He is interested not in the single creatures, species, or types (trees, fish, reptiles, etc.) but in the prime essences, created directly and immediately ("sanza mezzo," as stated in *Paradiso* 7.70) by God, which Dante then collects under philosophy's capital letters of Form and Matter, and analyzes within the context of the equally uppercase categories of Act and Potency.

To grasp the fascination (and indeed value) of these capitals, it will perhaps be sufficient to review, briefly, their meanings within the philosophical tradition. "Form" indicates the basic, necessary essence or substance of the things that possess matter; the cause or *raison d'être* whereby a thing is what it is; and the act or actuality of the thing itself, the beginning and end of its becoming. "Matter" can be taken as both the "subject" (i.e., that which "lies below") and the potency. For Plato, matter, the "mother" of all natural things,[42] is the raw, amorphous, passive, receptive material of which all natural things are composed. For Aristotle, matter is subject: formless, indeterminate, unknowable—such is prime matter, the raw material not in the sense of bronze, wood, and so forth of which an object is made, but the subject common to all materials. As to potency, for Plato, matter "never loses its potency."[43] Aristotle, on the other hand, identifies matter with potency: "all things produced by both nature and art possess matter since the possibility each has of being or not being in itself, for each, constitutes its matter."[44]

Thus when Dante orders the creation of the universe into these categories (starting at *Par.* 29.22), he is moving to the heart of the matter, the substance of things. He refers to form and matter, each in absolute, singular purity or united ("congiunte e purette"); that is to say, pure form (or pure act), namely, angelic intelligence; pure matter (or pure potency), namely, prime matter; and form-and-matter together, a compound of both, namely, the heavens. The three things together take the place of the biblical heaven and earth, constituting the object of the Big Bang and the foundations of the universe. The instant had been announced in *Paradiso* 7, when the long and fascinating argument of Plato's *Timaeus* had been filtered through metrum 9, book 3 of Boethius's *Consolation*. To the Bible's *bonum* ("et vidit Deus quod esset bonum") is added the Greek *kalon* (*pulchrum*) to achieve the perfect *kalokagathon*:

> La divina *bontà*, che da sé sperne
> ogne livore, ardendo in sé, sfavilla
> sì che dispiega le *bellezze* etterne.
>   (*Par.* 7.64–66; my emphases)

[The divine *Goodness*, which spurns / all envy from itself, burning within itself so sparkles / that it displays its eternal *beauties*.]

At Dante's objection that the elements—air, fire, water, and earth—and their compounds are corruptible, although created by God, Beatrice in *Paradiso* 7 had answered that the angels and heavens were created "in loro essere intero" (132), as whole beings, while the elements and compounds "da creata virtù sono informati" (135) [are informed by created virtue] and thus receive their form from a created force between God and themselves—the influence of the heavens. The same idea, imagery (luminous rays, mirrors, and splendor), and vocabulary (love, goodness, one-and-many, substance, potencies, act, and contingencies) are all used by Thomas Aquinas in *Paradiso* 13, in the magnificent lines in which he distinguishes between direct and indirect divine Creation, before describing generation:

> Ciò che non more e ciò che può morire
> non è se non splendor di quella idea
> che parturisce, amando, il nostro Sire;
>   ché quella viva luce che sì mea
> dal suo lucente, che non si disuna
> da lui né da l'amor ch'a lor s'intrea,
>   per sua bontate il suo raggiare aduna,
> quasi specchiato, in nove sussistenze,
> etternalmente rimanendosi una.
>   Quindi discende a l'ultime potenze
> giù d'atto in atto, tanto divenendo,
> che più non fa che brevi contingenze;
>   e queste contingenze essere intendo
> le cose generate, che produce
> con seme e sanza seme il ciel movendo.
>   (52–66)

[That which dies not and that which can die / are nothing but the splendour of that Idea / which our Sire, in Loving, begets; / for that living Light which so streams / from its shining source that it is not parted / from it nor from the Love which with them makes the Three, / of its own goodness gathers its beams, / as it were mirrored, in nine subsistences, / remaining forever one. / Thence it descends to the last potencies, / passing down from act to act and becoming such / that it makes nothing more than brief contingencies; / and by these contingencies I mean / things generated, produced with or without seed, / by the motions of the heavens.]

At the same time, there is a significant difference between *Paradiso* 7 and 13 on the one hand, and *Paradiso* 29 on the other: the former are in present time, the latter in the past. The first two describe and explain the creative act as it *always* is in the universe, from substances, "subsistences," to generated things; the third, the creative act *in principio*, that out-of-time instant from which time began: constant and continuous creation, as it were, and primitive creation and order.

This is why the beginning was simultaneous and instantaneous creation, "come d'arco tricordo tre saette" (*Par.* 29.24) [like three arrows from a three-stringed bow], or a radiant bursting out of all things, like a ray of light shining in transparent glass, amber, or crystal (25–30—for our medieval ancestors, light propagated instantly). The double image is one and three, like the Creator and the three original substances (angels, matter, heavens); three-string bow and three arrows; the ray in glass, amber, and crystal. In both cases, it takes place at an astounding speed, echoing the moving ("discorrer") over the waters, while the effulgence of the second mirrors the splendor and primordial brightness of the angels. This is a Beginning of absolute Light, which only in this aspect recalls the biblical "Fiat lux." Note, too, that Dante uses "usciro ad esser" (23) [came into being] for the first, and "dal venire / a l'esser tutto" (26–27) [from its coming to its completeness] for the second. The argument and the poetry are radically ontological, as the third *terzina* confirms, using "sustanze" (32); form is substance, too, for Aristotle.

Being was created with structure: the "ordine" (31) [order]. which arranges it according to hierarchical degree, and the "costrutto" (31) [construct], the construction in which the degrees are interrelated. At the top, then, are the substances in which the pure act was produced, created as pure forms, namely, the angelic intelligences; at the base, pure potency, formless prime matter; in between, potency and act, tied in the heavens by an indissoluble knot.

We would be wrong to imagine any gap in time between the creation of the angels and that of the heavens and prime matter, which was the mistake made by Jerome, the prince of the Latin Fathers. The Bible itself—"li scritter de lo Spirito Santo" (29.41) [the scribes of the Holy Ghost]—states the opposite,[45] and reason also proves it: it is implausible for the angels, the heavenly "movers," to have passed a considerable period in a state of imperfection, that is, without lending movement to all the rest as their function and hence their perfection requires. Beatrice is here lightly rapping the knuckles of Jerome and a number of others, as she had with Gregory at the end of *Paradiso* 28 (and as she is soon to do rather virulently). But while noting that for Beatrice, too, as for Dante, human logic and the scriptures are considered not at variance, we also have to note that "questo vero" (*Par.* 29.40) [this truth], declared here obliquely, places Dante the poet on the same level as the "scritter de lo Spirito Santo." Scripture and its rewriting have a similar status and inspiration: indeed, the rewritten Word knows better than the original (no canonical book gives us a blow-by-blow account of the creation of the angels!) "dove e quando questi amori / furon creati e come" (46–47) [where and when these loving spirits were created].

This, then, is the instant beginning of the cosmos and the angels' place in it; and perhaps those of us who live in the third millennium need to remember what Massimo Cacciari, following Wallace Stevens, calls the "necessity" of angels,[46] not only within a classical and medieval context—which requires more than mere bodies and compounds of body and spirit (i.e., humans) for the plenitude of the universe—but on our own modern horizon. In the second of the *Duineser Elegien*, Rilke maps, with a near-Dantesque enchantment, Creation's first peaks ("Höhenzüge") and first dawn-like mirrors ("Spiegel") of creation—blossoming, being, and beauty:

> Frühe Geglückte, ihr Verwöhnten der Schöpfung,
> Höhenzüge, morgenrötliche Grate
> aller Erschaffung,—Pollen der blühenden Gottheit,
> Gelenke des Lichtes, Gänge, Treppen, Throne,
> Räume aus Wesen, Schilde aus Wonne, Tumulte
> stürmisch entzückten Gefühls und plötzlich, einzeln,
> *Spiegel*: die entströmte eigene Schönheit
> Wiederschöpfen zurück in das eigene Antlitz.

[Fortunate first ones, creation's pampered darlings, / ranges, mountain tops, morning-red ridges / of all Beginning—seed of a blossoming god, / hinges of light, hallways, stairways, thrones, / spaces of being, force fields of ecstasy, storms / of unchecked rapture, and suddenly, separate, / *mirrors:* each drawing its own widespread / streaming beauty back into its face].[47]

The rest, after the beginning of time, is history, albeit in the most rapid of sequences. Before we can count to twenty—not even twenty seconds after Creation—a part of the angels fall, devastating earth, through the pride of Lucifer, whom Dante has seen at the bottom of the cosmos, crushed by the weight of the universe. Dante's time-scale is as dizzyingly rapid (in Milton, the fall alone lasts for nine days, and for nine more, "nine times the space that measures night and day," the rebel angels lie stunned and defeated) as his spatial scale is immense: Lucifer falls from the peak to the "suggetto d'i vostri alimenti" (*Par.* 29.51—i.e., the earth beneath all the other elements or even all elemental matter) to the most profound of the abysses. The angelic colleagues of the fallen band, recognizing that their being and supreme intellect come from His goodness, were content to remain on the opposite peaks of the Empyrean, circling in blessed and constant contemplation around God. Their reward was to undergo the opposite motion and be elevated. Their visual and intellectual faculties are illuminated by grace, and their ability to receive it, their perfect, now stable will, is unable to look towards evil. In a word, the faithful angels are granted the beatific vision; they receive that "velle," that achieved sight and understanding for which humanity, and in a few moments Dante as *dramatis persona*, is also destined (*Par.* 33.142–45). This seems to be precisely what Beatrice is announcing when she emphasizes (in *Par.* 29.64–66) that while grace is necessary for the vision of God *in sua essentia*, it is given to the creature, human or angel, "secondo che l'affetto l'è aperto" [in the measure that the heart is open to it], so that, she assures, "ricever la grazia è meritorio" [there is merit in receiving grace].

Dante is now able to contemplate the angelic "consistorio" (*Par.* 29.67) [consistory] directly and unaided. But Beatrice is a very fundamental—some might say fundamentalist—*lector*. She reviews the world's Schools ("le vostre scole," 70), in which "si legge" (71) [it is taught] that the angels possess intellect, will, and memory. All such teaching is confusion, misunderstanding, and error, she glosses. In their blessed contemplation of God's countenance, the angelic substances see everything, since nothing is hidden from them, and their understanding is "sine interpolatione":[48] "però non hanno vedere interciso / da novo obietto, e però non bisogna / rememorar per concetto diviso" (79–81) [their sight is never intercepted / by a new object and they have no need / to recall the past by an abstract concept]. If this sentence robs the angels of memory, it impresses itself on ours, reminding us to what extent our existence is, at best, a wild goose chase for slippery scraps of concepts fragmented in time. It contains, it seems to me, all the tension of the end of the *Commedia* as an act of poetry. The *Paradiso*, especially in its last cantos, from canto 28 to 33, is—inevitably, given human capacity and human narration—one long "rememorar per concetto diviso," while the vision is "never intercepted" from the moment Dante receives the *lumen gloriae* in canto 30.

Beatrice, our fundamentalist *lector*, is now "là giù" (*Par.* 29.74) [down there] and making short work of the world and its human content. Her polemic moves through its various stages, first intellectual, then prophetic, with the inexorable drive of a sermon. "Là giù," our strict teacher raps out, "non dormendo, si sogna" (82) [men dream while awake], and on the subject of the memory of the angels they speak falsehoods either in complete sincerity or, worse—"ne l'uno è più colpa e più vergogna" (84) [but in the one case is the greater blame and shame]—in total bad faith.

The second part of canto 29 begins here. Beatrice's descent proceeds, with some doubling back and internal repetition, in a rhythm of increasing invective, from the creation of the angels all the way down to the swine of St. Anthony. I have traced this descent and its motivations elsewhere,[49] and I will therefore not retrace it here. Two reasons for Beatrice's invective, however, are worth noting in the present context. The first is to fight the battle of intellectual honesty and responsibility.[50] Beatrice's speech on the creation of the angels constitutes supreme evidence of Dante's passional and rational engagement with being, and her attack is directed against all those who believe—or, worse, do not believe—that they are "speaking the truth" (83)—those who teach in the "schools" and "philosophize" (85), and those who love and preach appearances. These are clerics, above all, but also secular intellectuals, whose task it should be to follow one only path to truth, an authentic wisdom founded on the Gospel. If sowing it in the world costs blood (91), "chi *umilmente* con essa s'accosta" (93; my emphasis) [he who approaches it with *humbleness*] truly pleases (God and man). Those for whom "thinking" is a professional occupation (and these include, as we shall see shortly, illustrious names) have before them the way of humility vis-à-vis Scripture, which should be interpreted without "invenzioni" (95) [inventions] (Platonic and Aristotelian doctrines are not such, but rather the fruit of the meditation of the greatest "lovers of wisdom"). Theirs, like that of the first disciples', is the intellectual responsibility of the "verace fondamento" (111) [true foundation], which they have inherited. Beatrice's "scandal" is in this sense holy, for it concerns the human being's faithfulness to human intellect, to his or her behavior towards Being, towards a text, towards the word.

The second reason for Beatrice's invective is to authenticate and endorse, to make absolute and irrefutable Dante's negative opinion on the memory of the angels and above all his account of the Creation. In other words, Dante uses the beginning of Beatrice's tirade to announce his version of the Beginning as the one true version. Translated into the vernacular, what he is saying is "I'll set you straight: this is what really happened." This is why Beatrice's account refutes all the big names, directly or indirectly: Thomas Aquinas, on the number of substances first created;[51] Jerome and Aquinas, on the time elapsing between the creation of the angels and the creation of the "other world," the rest of the universe;[52] Augustine and Aquinas again on the memory of the angels, as we have just seen; and Aquinas again, among others, on the presumed eclipse during Christ's Passion.[53]

Dante is telling us that he can now do without his *maestri*. At the same time as he runs to the scriptures for support, he is freely dipping into Plato and Aristotle, not with hybris but out of a desire for complete clarity, for full honesty. In fact, the whole passage on the Creation in *Paradiso* 29, with the exception of the memory of the angels, is faithfully following *distinctio* 2, book 2 of Peter Lombard's *Sententiae*: the sequence, allusions, problem of time, and reference to Jerome are almost identical.[54] But Dante is far more daring: Peter quotes Genesis, Ecclesiasticus, the Book of Wisdom, the Psalms, Job, and Isaiah; Dante injects the Hebrew prophets and Hebrew wisdom with Greek wisdom in the shape of Platonic images and Aristotelian concepts. In doing this he is, of course, following a time-honored Christian technique, but in a much more advanced form than his predecessors, be they Church Fathers, twelfth-century Platonists, or Scholastics. Hence Beatrice's dictum, "Voi non andate giù per *un* sentiero / filosofando" (85–86; my emphasis) [You below do not follow a *single* path in your philosophizing]: because he thinks, in total intellectual responsibility, that the one true path is *his*, his new philosophico-biblical syncretism.

Once we have touched bottom, the upward trajectory in the third part of the canto is equally steep. Here the *plenitude* of the angels is finally stated, namely, their number is such that the human mind and tongue are unable to reach it. *Milia milium*, Daniel proclaims (Dan 7:10), concealing a finite number beneath infinity: thousands of thousands, a genitive which seems to bespeak exponential multiplication and the result of which is not even a plurality, but a "natura" [nature], a species initially seen as one (*Par.* 29.130–35) but then, immediately afterwards, as discrete individuals according to their ability to understand and, therefore, to love. The primal light, Beatrice continues, which "raia" [irradiates] all the species of angels, "per tanti modi in essa si recepe, / quanti son li splendori a chi s'appaia" (136–38) [is received by them in as many ways as are the splendours with which it is joined], since the ability to conceive the divine light differs for each. The affections, then, are also different, she explains, "d'amar la dolcezza / diversamente in essa ferve e tepe" (140–41) [love's sweetness glowing variously in them, more or less].

We return, then, to the Beginning, to the resplendent splendor. However, this is not the beginning of Creation, which, for the sake of convenience, I shall call "before-time." All this radiating and responding, looming and loving, is *now and always*, in that outside-time which Dante as *dramatis persona* has finally reached and with which Dante the poet increasingly struggles. Here all the height and extension, as well as the excellence and generosity, of the "etterno valor"—its pure sublimity—can be comprehended, precisely because it became the many mirrors into which it broke, multiplying itself and yet "uno manendo in sé come davanti" (145) [remaining in itself one as before].

In conclusion, there is one question that cannot be avoided: what sort of poetry is it, which uses imagery and concepts of this kind? One very reasonable definition, well beyond Croce's distinction between "poetry" and "non-poetry," is "philomythic."[55] But this immediately requires another question: why does poetry such as this still exert such a singular attraction on the averagely cultivated reader who is no philosophy specialist? Because, Patrick Boyde maintains,[56] "difficult concepts are conveyed through metaphor in such a way that they capture the imagination even when they are imperfectly understood." I would absolutely agree, but would also add a comment inspired by the passage in which Aquinas glosses Aristotle's *Metaphysics* regarding the philosopher and the "philomythes." Taking wonder as the start of all philosophy, Aristotle maintained that the mythically inclined (the poet, the *philomythes*) is in a sense also a philosopher, since myths deal with wonderful things. Aquinas reverses the terms, stating that the philosopher is in a sense *philomythes*, the quality proper to the poet. "Unde primi, qui per modum quemdam fabularem de principiis rerum tractaverunt, dicti sunt poetae theologizantes, sicut fuit Perseus, et quidam alii, qui fuerunt septem sapientes."[57] Dante thus emerges as a *poeta theologizans*, who treats *de principiis rerum poetice et fabulariter*: a "metaphysical" poet in the original, Aristotelian sense.

Seven hundred years on, however, the expressions take on a rather different significance. The whole *Commedia* reads as *fabula*, and not only in the sense of a fiction containing innumerable other fictions, but because it is now a myth of Western consciousness and the modern imagination. It is not simply the journey through the three realms, or Virgil, Beatrice, and the various characters encountered that comprise the *fabulae* and *mythoi*, but also, for us, Dante's system of logic and philosophical lexis, underpinning both the individual passages and the whole structure of the poem.

It is not a question of the extraordinary imagery—Boyde's "metaphor"—that Dante employs to illustrate his concepts: Love unfolding like a flower, the triple-strung bow, the three arrows, or the ray shining inside glass, amber, or crystal. While totally necessary, they would not explain the work's aesthetic reception *today*. What conquers the modern reader is the dissonant echo of the scriptures, on the one hand, and the philosophical register, on the other. The echo is "dissonant" in that it restores a significantly rewritten Word, Dante having no scruples about placing himself on the level of the "scrittor de lo Spirito Santo" and making free with Genesis, the Book of Wisdom, and the fourth Gospel to produce a new text, his own (re)Scripture. It is this echo and simultaneous transformation, text speaking to and through text, that captivates the modern reader. When Dante is examined in *Paradiso* 26 by St. John about charity, he answers that what prompted his love to God was both "filosofici argomenti" and "autorità" (25–26), philosophical reasoning and Scripture. And by these he means first Aristotle ("colui che mi dimostra il primo amore / di tutte le sustanze sempiterne" [38–39] [he ... who established for me the primal love of all the eternal beings]); then the voice of the "verace autore" (40) [true Author], God, who tells Moses in Exodus, "Io ti farò vedere ogne valore" (42) [I will make you see all goodness];[58] and finally John himself, "l'aguglia di Cristo" (53) [the eagle of Christ], "incominciando / l'alto preconio che grida l'arcano / di qui là giù sovra ogne altro bando" (43–45) [in the beginning / of the sublime announcement (contained in his Gospel) which proclaims the mystery / of God on earth, more than any other heralding]. This, precisely, is the poetry that the *poeta theologizans* creates, and his poetics of the "poema sacro / al quale ha posto mano e cielo e terra" (*Par.* 25.1–2) [sacred poem / to which both heaven and earth have set their hand], now therefore going beyond David's *tëodia*: Aristotle's philosophy,[59] the Old and the New Testament. It is significant that, among the texts of the latter, Dante should choose the beginning of John's Gospel, "In principio erat Verbum" [In the beginning was the Word], for those lines not only rewrite the Creation but have a sublime aura acknowledged by all commentators and speak the language of Hellenic philosophy as much as that of Judaic theology.

The philosophic register on which the Creation is re-created, on the other hand, is beguiling in its use of canonical categories, which effortlessly "universalize" the immense variety of individual creatures. Furthermore, it seems to me that words such as "form" and "matter," "potency" and "act," "being" and "substance," have a significance that in part differs from the present one, and differs again from the very precise meaning they had for a thirteenth-century Aristotelian. They lie, so to speak, halfway between "alterity" and "modernity." They are alien yet comprehensible, surprising yet expected—an ideal situation for the reception of a work of poetry. Classical statements, almost archetypes of the Western (and not only Western)[60] mind and culture, they possess a philosophical aura which is part of our conceptual framework, in representing ideas with which our reason and our language have lived for twenty-five centuries. At the pre-philosophical, pre-specialist level, they work for us in the same manner as Homer's epithets for the sea or dawn, "wine dark" and "rosy fingered"; they work at the pre-philological level, as myths embedded in our cultural DNA or in the *logos* of our subconscious.[61]

A similarly "metaphysical" modern poet has no similarly evocative models; modern culture has replaced being with scientific becoming and a discourse of quantity. The Big Bang hardly lends itself to poetry; it has to be quantified and mathematically analyzed for the first three seconds, minutes, or million years. Democritus has won, and the barion, quark, and photon are not forms but elementary particles of matter: "brevi contingenze," Dante would say. As far as we know, only Lucretius was able to make poetry of them, more than two thousand years ago. When a modern poet—Rilke or Eliot, for example—writes poems of being, he has to enlist the angels, or situate himself at "the point of intersection of the timeless with time,"[62] the point of the Incarnation and the rose.

Notes

An earlier, much shorter version of this essay has been published as "The Poetry and Poetics of the Creation," in Jacoff, *The Cambridge Companion to Dante* (2nd ed.). Translations of the *Commedia* are taken—and slightly modified—from Dante, *Divine Comedy*, tr. Sinclair.

1. 1 Jn 4:8: "Deus caritas est"; Aquinas, *In Duodecim Libros Metaphysicorum Aristotelis* 1.4, 984b29, lect. 5, 102 (p. 29). On love, see also Dronke, "'L'amor che move il sole e l'altre stelle.'" For the general theme of Creation, particularly in Dante, I refer readers to Steiner, *Grammars of Creation*, in particular, 77–106.

2. Compare *ST* Ia.39.8.

3. Bernardino Daniello, quoted by Natalino Sapegno, ad loc., in Dante, *Divina Commedia*, ed. Sapegno, 2:183.

4. Aristotle, *De anima* 3.14; *ST* Ia.79.2.

5. Compare *Purgatorio* 18.19–21. On *Purgatorio* 16, see Malato, "'Sì come cieco,'" and the references therein.

6. *Hadrian*, in *Scriptores Historiae Augustae*, 25, 5–9; and see Yourcenar, *Mémoires d'Hadrien*, ch. 1.

7. In this poem, T. S. Eliot wrote in perfect modern counterpoint to Hadrian's and Dante's lines: "Issues from the hands of God, the simple soul."

8. Brunetto Latini, *Trésor* II, 74, 6 (p. 251); Horace, *Ars poetica* 156–78.

9. See "anima" in *Enciclopedia dell'Arte Medievale*, 1:810.

10. Origen, *Commentarius in Canticum* I, 1, 2, XXXIII; *Omelie sul Cantico dei Cantici* I, i, 50–53; I, 3, 25–35; I, 6, 14–19. In his commentary on the Song of Songs, Gregory the Great, for instance, follows Origen faithfully (*Commentaire sur le Cantique des Cantique* 10 and 15 (pp. 86–97).

11. Origen, *Homelies sur la Genèse* 1.15 (p. 67).

12. Origen, *Commentarius in Iohannis* 20.182.

13. de Lubac, *Exégèse médiévale*, 1:207–38, and in particular p. 234 and n. 12.

14. Origen, *Commentarius in Matthaei* 15.7–8.

15. Origen, *Commentarius in Matthaei* 13.18; Jerome, *In Matthaei* 3.137.

16. Origen, *Commentarius in Matthaei* 13.19.

17. "Trastulla" will be used in *Paradiso* 9.76 of the voice of Folchetto da Marsiglia, which, together with the song of the Seraphim, gives joy to Heaven; but Folchetto was also one of the most famous troubadours. The same "trastulla" is employed by Cacciaguida in *Paradiso* 15.121–23, when he describes the Florentine women of his age, when mothers kept watch tending their children's cradles, using "the tongue that first delights [trastulla] fathers and mothers." Note that for Dante this childish "idioma" [tongue] gives delight in the first place to parents, not to children. The "trastulla" of *Purgatorio* 16.90 is anticipated by Guido del Duca in his "del ben richesto al vero e al trastullo" in *Purgatorio* 14.93. An ethics and poetics of "trastullare" are therefore present as well, the latter coming close to that of "vagheggiare."

18. Compare *Paradiso* 9.106–7; see also Took, *L'Etterno Piacer*.

19. See Nardi, "L'origine dell'anima umana secondo Dante," in *Studi di filosofia medievale*, 9–68.

20. See Aristotle, *De generatione animalium* 2.3, 736b, according to whom the intellect does not come from nature by generation, but "from outside," "et divinum esse solum."

21. Gen 2:7: formavit igitur Dominus Deus hominem de limo terrae et inspiravit in faciem eius spiraculum vitae et factus est homo in animam viventem [And the Lord God formed man out of the slime of the earth: and breathed into his face the breath of life, and man became a living soul].

22. *Conv.* 4.2.18; *Metaphysics* 1072b. In his edition of the *Convivio*, Cesare Vasoli recalls *De anima* 430a and Thomas Aquinas, *Exp. Eth.* 10, lect. 10, 2092, besides the *Liber de causis*, Prop. 15, 124–27, and Albert the Great, *De causis* 2, tr. 2, 43. But surely a treatise that begins by quoting Aristotle's *Metaphysics* would not, at such a crucial moment, forget one of the climaxes of that work.

23. Nardi, *Studi di filosofia medievale*, 56, n. 3, and 156–59.

24. Cicero asks himself, "qua quid potest esse cum fructu *laetius*, tum aspectu *pulchrius*?"—what can be more delicious to the taste, or more alluring to the eye?

25. "L'acqua ch'io prendo già mai non si corse" (*Par.* 2.7) [The waters I take were never sailed before].

26. On this *agon*, see Kenelm Foster, "The Mind in Love," 52. In *Paradiso* 2 its icon is the allusion to "Iasón . . . fatto bifolco" (18) [Jason turned ploughman] and its comparison with Dante's work: the effort of taming the oxen and plowing corresponds to Dante's, in writing of such difficult matters. See Curtius, *European Literature*, 313–15.

27. "Que' glorïosi che passaro al Colco / non s'ammiraron come voi farete" (*Par.* 2.16–17) [Those glorious ones who crossed the sea to Colchis / were not amazed as you shall be].

28. See Boitani, *The Tragic and Sublime*, 223–78, and "Dante's Sublime."

29. From Prov 8:27–29, already employed by Dante in *Conv.* 3.15.16.

30. See Hawkins, *Dante's Testaments*, 81–87, and the references in the notes therein.

31. On this, and on the whole of *Paradiso* 28, see Contini's memorable pages now in his *Un'idea di Dante*, 191–213, in particular 205–6.

32. This is the reading of virtually all modern commentators, including, among the most recent, Anna Maria Chiavacci Leonardi in Dante, *Commedia*, ed. Chiavacci Leonardi, 3:798.

33. It is indirectly present, on the other hand, in *Paradiso* 13, where the same splendor attaches to the Idea "che partorisce, amando, il nostro Sire" (54) [which our Sire, in loving, begets]: the Son, the Word.

34. See Chiavacci Leonardi's penetrating reading, in her important introduction to the canto, in Dante, *Commedia*, ed. Chiavacci Leonardi, 3:792.

35. See Frye, *The Great Code*, 17–19. On the many versions of Creation in different cultures, see Van Wolde, *Stories of the Beginning*.

36. Milton, who uses both Plato and Neoplatonism, closely follows the account of Genesis, beginning with light and then following the six days. See Alastair Fowler's commentary in *Paradise Lost*, ad loc.

37. See Nardi, "Lo discorrer di Dio sovra quest'acque," in his *Nel mondo di Dante*, 307–13; Pépin, *Théologie*, 390–422.

38. In Ovid, *Fasti* 2.285–86, where the subject is Pan.

39. *Aeneid* 1.147.

40. Landino, *Comento*, 4:1966.

41. Augustine, *De Genesi contra Manichaeos* 1.7.12; Peter Lombard, *Sententiae* l. II, d. 12, c. 3; *ST* Ia.66.1.ad2.

42. *Timaeus* 50b–d.

43. *Timaeus* 50b.

44. *Metaphysics* 7.7, 1032a20.

45. Gen 1:1; Sir 18:1.

46. Stevens, "Angel Surrounded by Paysans," in *Collected Poems*, 496–97, and *The Necessary Angel*; Cacciari, *L'angelo necessario*.

47. Rilke, *Duino Elegies*, 12–13. See Calvo, "Le api dell'invisibile," 177–216.

48. *Mon.* 1.3.7.

49. See my "Creazione e cadute di *Paradiso* XXIX." I use here the part of that essay which deals with the Creation of *Paradiso* 29.

50. I owe this consideration to Giuseppe Bonfrate.

51. "*Quatuor* enim ponuntur simul creata, scilicet caelum empyreum, materia corporalis (quae nomine *terrae* intelligitur), tempus, et natura angelica" (*ST* Ia.46.3.resp) [The four following are commonly supposed to have been created at once and together, namely the empyrean heavens, bodily matter (in other words, the earth), time, and angelic natures]. The whole of *quaestio* 46 is of relevance to Dante's account.

52. Jerome, on Titus 1:2, *In ad Titum*, 691; *ST* Ia.61.3 and resp.

53. *ST* IIIa.44.2.

54. The sequence of the *distinctio* is as follows: "quando [angelica natura] creata fuerit, et ubi, et qualis facta dum primo conderetur; deinde qualis effecta aversione quorundam et conversione quorundam" [when angels were created, and where, and what kind of nature was made, when the first was founded, then what kind of effects came from the aversion of certain ones and the conversion of certain others]. Chapter 2 in particular states: "quod nihil factum est ante caelum et terram, nec etiam tempus: cum tempore enim creata sunt, sed non ex tempore" [That nothing was made before heaven and earth, not even time: they were created with time, and not out of time]; chapter 3.1 states: "quod simul cum tempore et cum mundo coepit corporalis et spiritualis creatura" [That together with time and with the world the spiritual and corporal creature began]; chapter 3.2 then takes issue with Jerome on the question of the time that elapsed between the creation of the angels and the rest of the universe; chapter 4 explains "ubi angeli mox creati fuerint: in empyreo scilicet, quod statim factum, angelis fuerit repletum" [Where were the Angels then created? In the splendid Heaven which is said to be the "empyrean," which as soon as it was made was filled with Angels];

chapter 5, "quod simul creata est visibilium rerum materia et invisibilium natura, et utraque informis secundum aliquid, et formata secundum aliquid" [That the matter of things visible and the nature of invisibles was created together, and each was formless according to something, and formed according to something]; chapter 6 deals with Lucifer and his pride. In *distinctiones* 3–6, Peter specifically examines the creation and fall of the angels. In *distinctio* 3, chapter 1, Peter attributes to the angels, from the beginning of creation ("in initio *subsistentiae* suae" [at the start of the their subsistence]; Dante's "subsisto" has a model, then), "essentia simplex, id est indivisibilis et immaterialis; et discretio personalis; et per rationem naturaliter insitam intelligentia, *memoria* et voluntas sive dilectio; liberum quoque arbitrium" [simple essence, that is an indivisible and immaterial essence; and a discretion of persons; and through a reason naturally engrafted in to each an intelligence, memory and will or choice; also free will]. Translations given are based on the English text available on http://www.franciscan-archive.org/lombardus/opera/.

55. Boyde, *Dante Philomythes and Philosopher*; see also, on the anti-Croce polemics, Kirkpatrick, *Dante's "Paradiso."*

56. Boyde, *Dante Philomythes and Philosopher*, 266.

57. *In Duodecim Libros Metaphysicorum Aristotelis* 1.3, 55.

58. Ex 33:19: "Ego ostendam omne bonum tibi" [I will shew thee all good]. Dante's translation of Exodus is Cavalcantian, from the sonnet "Vedeste, al mio parere, onne valore," which is Cavalcanti's answer to the first sonnet in Dante's *Vita nuova*.

59. Some commentators identify the subject of *Paradiso* 26.37–39 as Dionysius, referred to in *ST* Ia.6.1. Dionysius's attribution of "bonum" to God "sicut ex quo omnia subsistent" (*De divinis nominibus* IV) would not contrast with Aristotle's statement, in *Metaphysics* bk. 12 (Lambda), 7, 1072b, that the Prime Mover moves the heavens through love, "quasi desideratum." In *Conv.* 3.2.4–7, Dante quotes in this regard the *Liber de causis*, which was then attributed to Aristotle, the "maestro di color che sanno" (*Inf.* 4.131) [master of them that know].

60. Suffice it to remember Arabic thinkers such as Avicenna and Averroes, who figure prominently in Dante's Limbo, *Inf.* 4, next to the greatest Greek and Roman philosophers, and who were essential mediators between Aristotelian and medieval Christian philosophy.

61. One would of course need to qualify this statement with regard to our reception of Homer, specifying that in this instance what is involved is the *mythos* in our subconscious.

62. T. S. Eliot, *Four Quartets*, "The Dry Salvages," V. I wonder if Eliot's "point" might not be an echo of Dante's "punto" in *Paradiso* 29.

5

Liturgical Personhood
Creation, Penitence, and Praise in the *Commedia*

MATTHEW TREHERNE

To speak of "liturgical personhood" is to draw a link between liturgical practice and subjectivity that requires careful formulation. The notion that liturgy might in some sense shape personhood, while not new, has been sharpened over the last fifteen years or so in theological studies. Scholars have addressed—often in highly sophisticated ways—the manner in which liturgical performance can be seen, not as empty formula or inert ritual, but rather as a rich mode of religious language, which establishes complex relationships between the subject engaged in liturgical performance, the God to whom liturgy is offered, and the words of the liturgy itself. Catherine Pickstock, for instance, offers a rich analysis of the late medieval mass, which emphasizes the ways in which it leads the participant to experience the contrast of time and eternity, and shifts between different types of utterances—constative, performative, self-referential, and doxological—none of which predominates.[1] As a result of this modulation, a particular type of human agency emerges which is neither wholly active nor fully passive.[2] In a Heideggerian vein, Jean-Yves Lacoste argues that liturgy is best understood as a field of action and a site of distinctive experience. Liturgy is, he argues, "tout ce qui incarne la relation de l'homme à Dieu. . . . La liturgie est en effet ce concept qui nous interdit la dissociation ruineuse de l'intérieur et de l'extérieur, du 'corps' et de l'"âme'" [all that embodies the relationship of man to God. . . . Liturgy is indeed the concept which forbids us from making a ruinous dissociation of interior and exterior, of "body" and "soul"].[3]

Such strongly stated accounts warn us against any temptation to write off liturgy as a merely decorative, exterior practice.[4]

At the same time that the implications of liturgy for religious practice are being reexamined in theological studies, Dante scholarship is increasingly acknowledging the importance of liturgy to the *Commedia*,[5] although the focus has been primarily on the penitential aspects of the liturgical performances of *Purgatorio*, and the relevance of certain aspects of religious practice—in particular, the sacraments—to Dante's poem remains contested.[6] If we are willing to engage with the claims of theologians such as Pickstock and Lacoste, we must entertain the possibility that the liturgical performances Dante describes in the *Commedia* are not merely an add-on, nor simply part of the "coloring" of the poem; rather, they might be theologically significant in their own right. Indeed, there are very good textual reasons to take Dante's presentation of the liturgy seriously. In his account of Purgatory, the very presence of liturgy marks an innovation with regard to the view of Purgatory that had emerged in late medieval culture. (According to Aquinas, for instance, the souls of Purgatory had no need to pray at all.)[7] This innovation stands alongside a number of other strikingly original aspects of Dante's Purgatory. These include the physical structure of Purgatory, which figures the movement of the souls as a movement towards the Earthly Paradise and thus towards the condition of prelapsarian humanity in Eden; and— through the principle of vice, which informs the division of Purgatory proper into seven terraces and underlies the processes of purgation that Dante describes—the importance of psychological change. It is my contention that these innovations are closely tied with Dante's presentation of liturgy in the *Commedia*. In particular, I wish to show that the restoration of the proper relationship between creature and creator is central to this presentation, and that the movement of souls to God is suggested through a consistent set of references to the sacramental and through a shift in liturgical performance towards praise, a shift that takes place throughout Purgatory and is fulfilled in Paradise.

LITURGY, PERSONHOOD, AND CREATEDNESS IN *PURGATORIO*

A subtle but important distinction must be drawn between the liturgical performances witnessed by the pilgrim in Ante-Purgatory and those of Purgatory proper, a distinction which helps alert us to Dante's concerns in presenting liturgy in *Purgatorio*. In Ante-Purgatory—a place where "tempo per tempo si ristora" (*Purg.* 23.84) [restitution comes to time through time], with its emphases on waiting rather than on moral change—liturgical performances are closely related to the liturgical cycles on earth, especially the daily office. Thus, in the Valley of the Negligent Princes, hymns associated with the Compline service are performed in the evening: *Te lucis ante* (8.13), alongside *Salve Regina* (7.82).[8] In this sense, the use of liturgy in Ante-Purgatory is similar to the earthly liturgy, although the order of the Compline service performed here is slightly different from that on earth.[9]

In Purgatory proper, the emphasis changes considerably: the souls appear to be engaged in the ongoing repetition of fragments of liturgy. The first sign that the pilgrim and Virgil encounter of the souls of the wrathful is the sound of the singing of *Agnus Dei*: "Pur '*Agnus Dei*' eran le loro essordia" (16.19) [The words they uttered first were "*Agnus Dei*"]; the plural exordia imply ongoing repetition. The souls of the lustful, in the purifying fire of the seventh terrace, sing *Summae Deus clementiae*, call out an example of chastity, then begin the hymn again; Dante-poet says that "questo modo credo che lor basti / per tutto il tempo che 'l foco li abbruscia" (25.136–37) [This form of song will serve for them, I think, / throughout the time the fire is scorching them]. (In the earthly liturgy, the hymn was sung once, on Saturday at Matins.)[10] Moreover, on no occasion is there any particular indication that hymns associated with a specific time of day are being sung. Unlike Ante-Purgatory, this is a realm of moral change (and scholars continue to explore in fruitful ways the rich dynamics of this change). Liturgy is closely tied to this change.[11]

As even a superficial reading of the *Purgatorio* shows, on all but one of the terraces of Purgatory the souls utter prayers that relate to the vice of which they are being purged. On the first terrace, in the opening lines of canto 11, Dante's additions to the biblical version of the *Pater Noster* set out in Matthew 6:9–13 emphasize the souls' dependence on God and diminish any sense of their own strength and ability. Thus, in their prayer the penitent souls say that they cannot reach the kingdom of God alone, even using all their own wit ("Vegna ver' noi la pace del tuo regno, / ché noi ad essa non potem da noi, / s'ella non vien, con tutto nostro ingegno" [7–9] [May peace, as in Your realm, come down to us. / For we ourselves cannot attain to that]); they ask to be forgiven without their merit being considered ("non guardar lo nostro merto" [18] [do not look upon what we deserve]); their strength, they say, is easily subdued ("Nostra virtù che di legger s'adona" [19] [The powers we have (so easily subdued)]). On the second terrace, the envious cry out a litany of the saints (13.50–51), as though to emphasize the value of generosity of spirit on the part of the saints. The wrathful pray for peace (16.17–19). Not only does the content of the prayer relate to the moral change undergone by the souls, but the manner of the liturgical performances also suggests a model of behavior which can be viewed as a corrective to the souls' particular vice. As the wrathful pray for peace, they do so collectively, each in harmony with the others: "Pur '*Agnus Dei*' eran le loro essordia; / una parola in tutte era e un modo, / sì che parea tra esse ogne concordia" (16.19–21) [The words they uttered first were "*Agnus Dei*"— / the self-same text and tune from all of them, so that, it seemed, at heart they sang as one]. The version of the *Pater Noster* of the penitent proud is not sung by any particular individual; the communal performance of the prayer undermines any residual egotism on their part.

Having passed through the terrace of the slothful, where no liturgy is performed (I shall suggest a reason for this shortly), the pilgrim and Virgil reach the last three terraces of Purgatory. Here, a different type of vice is being purged, and accordingly, the liturgy that is being performed has different emphases. The three liturgical songs refer strongly to the rejection of attachment to material goods. In the case of the avaricious, Psalm 118 is sung (19.73). Augustine interpreted this psalm as a prayer against attachment to earthly things: "Si tamquam unam quamdam domum magnam universum mundum velimus accipere, videmus velut ejus cameram coelum: terra erit igitur pavimentum" (*Enarrationes in Psalmos* 118.25) [If we look upon the whole world as one great house, we see that the heavens represent its vaulting, the earth therefore will be its pavement].[12] In the case of *labïa mëa, Domine*, lines from Psalm 50 performed on the terrace of gluttony (23.11), the souls are reminded of the use of the mouth in gluttony. Finally, the words of the *Summae Deus clementïae*, performed by the lustful (25.121), emphasize the transient nature of the earthly body—"lumbos iecurque morbidum / adure igne congruo, / accincti ut sint perpeti, / luxu remoto pessimo" [Our loins and liver, diseased, / burn out with suited fire, / so may they ever be girt up, / all sinful lust put away]—and remind the souls of the dependence of the body upon the creator ("Summae Deus clementiae, mundi factor machinae" [God of highest clemency, maker of the fabric of the world]).[13]

The "relevance" of the prayers of Purgatory to the vices being purged is dependent upon Dante's conception of Purgatory as a place of moral change. The liturgy of Purgatory forms part of the broader process of purgation, which is conceived as a transformation of the will through the physical (or virtually physical) suffering undergone by the souls, as well as through the use of exempla. This is a basic but important principle: in linking moral change with prayer, Dante ensures that the prayers either remind the penitent souls of the vice being purged—and thereby introduce a confessional element—or inculcate an opposing virtue. When the souls pray, not only do they ask for help, but the prayers themselves and the manner of praying offer models of behavior. The fact that the liturgy of Purgatory proper is repeated over and over thus ties in with the notion of vice underlying Purgatory: a vice for Dante, following Aristotle and Scholastic thinkers, is a *habit* that can be corrected by new habits.[14]

This moral change, as the *Commedia* makes clear, is linked with a recovery of the proper relationship between creature and creator. This is evident in canto 17, when Virgil presents an overview of the structure and rationale of Purgatory (85–139). He begins by explaining that natural love—defined by Aquinas as love for God[15]—cannot err, whereas elective love can err, either in pursuing objects with the wrong degree of love, or in loving evil done against others. Although there are clear distinctions between the vices, what they all have in common is that they distort the relationship between creator and creature, whether in directing love towards secondary goods, or in directing love towards the ill-being of others, or—in the case of the slothful—in displaying a lack of love for any goods at all. As Virgil puts it, through such love "contra 'l fattore adovra sua fattura" (102) [what's made then works against its maker's plans]. It is the excessive love of secondary goods that is purged in the upper three terraces of Purgatory:

> Altro ben è che non fa l'uom felice;
> non è felicità, non è la buona
> essenza, d'ogne ben frutto e radice.
> L'amor ch'ad esso troppo s'abbandona,
> di sovr' a noi si piange per tre cerchi . . .
> (17.133–37)

[And other goods will not bring happiness, / not happy in themselves, nor that good source / of being, seed and flower of all that's good. / The love that gives itself too much to these / is wept for in the circles still above.]

This love is an excessive attachment to that which will be described by Aquinas in *Paradiso* 13 as "brevi contingenze" (63) [brief contingencies], as passing, ephemeral things (a notion which informs the pilgrim's own confession in *Purgatorio* 31 of his distraction by "[l]e presenti cose / col falso lor piacer" [34–35] [Mere things of here and now / and their false pleasures]). Within Virgil's scheme outlined in *Purgatorio* 17, the love of "[a]ltro ben" (133), purged in the upper terraces of Purgatory, can be seen as the love of such "brevi contingenze" for their own sake. Reading back from Aquinas's discussion of creation in the final *cantica*, the love that gives itself excessively to those things, this attachment to "contingenze," ignores the fact that all depends upon its creator for its very existence, as Dante's Aquinas will put it in a Neoplatonic, Trinitarian formulation (which in turn adds nuance to the opening of *Paradiso* 10):[16] "Ciò che non more e ciò che può morire / non è se non splendor di quella idea / che partorisce, amando, il nostro Sire" (*Par.* 13.52–54) [Those things that cannot die and those that can / are nothing save the splendours of that One / Idea that, loving, brought our Lord to birth].

The vices purged in the first three terraces, by contrast, can be viewed as the failure of the human being to recognize *its own* source as God. The pilgrim learns from Beatrice in *Paradiso* 29 that Lucifer turned away from God in an act of pride (55–57), a pride that is contrasted in Beatrice's explanation with the attitude of those angels who remained modest and recognized God as the source of their being (58–59). Failure to recognize God as the source of being explains the emphasis on the self in the first three vices purged in Purgatory proper. As Virgil puts it, "chi, per esser suo vicin soppresso, / spera eccellenza" (*Purg.* 17.115–16) [Some hope, by keeping all their neighbours down, / that they'll excel]; "chi podere, grazia, onore e fama / teme di perder perch' altri sormonti" (118–19) [some will fear that, if another mounts, / they'll lose all honour, fame and grace and power]; "chi per ingiuria par ch'aonti, / sì che si fa de la vendetta ghiotto" (121–22) [some ... when hurt, bear such a grudge / that they crave only to exact revenge].

The performance of liturgy in Purgatory proper, then, alongside the other aspects of penance, is directed towards putting right that relationship between creator and creature—specifically, by redirecting souls away from attachment to secondary goods for their own sake, and away from attachment to the notion of the self as independent from its source.[17]

PURGATORIO AND THE ANTICIPATION OF DOXOLOGY

So far, I have emphasized the "corrective" aspect of liturgical performance in Purgatory proper: the liturgy tends to have a penitential tone and forms part of the souls' rejection of vice. Doxology—the direction of prayer towards the praise of God—is instead largely reserved for *Paradiso*. But it would be wrong to suggest that the praise of God—or, better, the notion of praising God—is entirely absent from *Purgatorio*. In particular, four instances are highly suggestive of doxology, either by referring to others' praise of God or by seeming to offer praise to God, in ways that require us to reflect on the nature of praise. These are the singing of "*Te Deum laudamus*" in canto 9 (140); sections of the vernacular rewriting of the *Pater Noster* in canto 11 (1–24, especially lines 10–12); the *Gloria in excelsis Deo* of canto 20 (133–41); and the "*Labïa mëa, Domine*" of canto 23 (10–12), which asks for the souls' lips to be opened in order for praise to occur. The presence of such suggestions of doxology does not mean that Dante is confused about the respective roles of praise and penitence in liturgical prayer in Purgatory. In fact, their presence has much to tell us about Dante's understanding of the conditions in which praise might occur.

The first and second examples are relatively clear. *Te Deum laudamus* is sung, not by the penitent souls of Purgatory, but by an unspecified, possibly angelic, choir. The second example, the version of the *Pater Noster*, refers specifically to the wish that God's name be praised, and is not itself an act of praise. There is a wish that human beings might sing Hosanna, but this is in a subjunctive mood; the only beings described as engaged in doxology are the angels. There is a wish that praise might happen, but the only place it can be sure to happen is in Paradise.

The other two examples are more richly suggestive of the conditions under which humans can engage in doxology. First, the *Gloria in excelsis Deo* of canto 20 requires careful analysis. It stands out as an example, for it is a doxological hymn in its own right (rather than the expression of a wish that doxology might take place), and it is enunciated by the penitent souls, who otherwise seem unable to engage in doxology.

To understand what is actually happening in the shouting of "*Gloria in excelsis Deo*" here in Purgatory, where doxology is only anticipated, we must first ask what might appear to be an obvious question (a question that Catherine Pickstock asked searchingly of the Greater Doxology in the earthly liturgy).[18] What does it mean to say, sing, or shout "*Gloria in excelsis Deo*"? Is it a constative utterance? In other words, is it a statement of the fact of God's glory? The latter part of the hymn suggests so: "Gratias agimus tibi propter magnam gloriam tuam" [thanks we give to You because of Your great glory], referring to God's preexisting glory. Or is it an optative wish, the expression of a desire that God should be glorious? It is clearly this—at least in some sense. Or is it an offering of glory? It is this, too—as the hymn says, "glorificamus te"; we make You glorious.

There is a further, crucial aspect to the *Gloria in excelsis Deo*: it is a citation of angelic song, recalling the song of the angels who announced Christ's birth to the shepherds (Lk 2:8–14), and is explicitly acknowledged as such by the poet (20.140). It aspires to a mimetic participation in angelic song. But in its liturgical use in the mass, it also refers back to the status of sinful mankind. There is a shift in the hymn from the doxological to the appeal to mercy: the hymn ends with the words "Domine Deus, Agnus Dei, Filius Patris, Qui tollis peccata mundi, miserere nobis" [Lord God, Lamb of God, Son of the Father, who take away the sins of the world, have mercy on us]. Although the enunciation of the *Gloria* is an imitation of the angelic choirs, it ends with a reminder of the condition in which the words are spoken: that of humanity not yet freed from vice and in need of Christ's mercy. Its status as imitation is thus highlighted; its enunciators do not become angels but only take on, temporarily, the angelic voice.

Within the earthly liturgy, the Greater Doxology is not only an act of praise but an act of acknowledging the sinful nature of the enunciator. It is an offering of glory to God, but it also depends upon God's mercy and on the acknowledgement of the inadequacy of the speaker. In *Purgatorio* 20, Dante suggests this. The words "*Gloria in excelsis Deo*" are cried out by the penitent souls at the moment when the earthquake shakes Mount Purgatory; the souls know (although the pilgrim and Virgil only learn this in 21.58–60) that the earthquake signifies the release of a soul from Purgatory.

> "*Gloria in excelsis*" tutti "*Deo*"
> dicean, per quel ch'io da' vicin compresi,
> onde intender lo grido si poteo.
>   No' istavamo immobili e sospesi
> come i pastor che prima udir quel canto,
> fin che 'l tremar cessò ed el compiési.
> (20.136–41)

["*Gloria in excelsis Deo!*" and all / were speaking out these words, so I could tell / the meaning of the cry from those close to. / We stood unmoving, caught there in suspense— / as were the shepherds who first heard this song— / until the tremor ceased and all was done].

Dante emphasizes here the gap between the angelic choir and the penitent souls. The words are *shouted* by the souls, in contrast with the "canto" of the angels. Moreover, the pilgrim can only just make out the cry, emphasizing the chaotic nature of its enunciation.

But what is it about the souls' condition in Purgatory that makes doxology so difficult? And what are the conditions under which praise of God can occur? The fourth example of an allusion to doxology in the liturgy of *Purgatorio*—the singing of Psalm 50 in canto 23—offers the beginnings of an answer to these questions. Before we turn to the psalm, it is important to note that the canto as a whole, while specifically concerned with the purgation of gluttony, is marked by sustained allusion to a general movement away from attachment to the contingent secondary goods in favor of the source of being itself. This is evident from the opening of canto 23, which describes the pilgrim glancing about him, like someone chasing after birds: "li occhi per la fronda verde / ficcava ïo sì come far suole / chi dietro a li uccellin sua vita perde" (1–3) [I, through these green boughs, fixed searching sight / (as might some hunter tracking little birds, / who spends his life in vain on that pursuit)]. Significantly, in the moral context of the terrace of gluttony, this image is the first in a series of images that are shared between this passage of the *Commedia* and a commentary on the foolishness of desiring material goods in book 4 of the *Convivio*.[19] The human soul, Dante says, desires to return to its maker, just as all things desire to return to their origins (*Conv.* 4.12.14). Setting out on life's path, the human soul seeks that ultimate good; however, on seeing the first thing which seems to be good, she believes she has found it: "dirizza li occhi al termine del suo sommo bene, e però, qualunque cosa vede che paia in sé avere alcuno bene, crede che sia esso" (4.12.15) [the soul is always on the look-out for its ultimate goal, the highest good; and so whenever it sees anything in which some good appears, it thinks that it is that highest good]. (The same principle is elucidated in Marco Lombardo's discussion of free will in *Purgatorio* 16.64–105, which describes how the newborn "anima semplicetta" "di picciol bene in pria sente sapore" [88, 91] [little simple soul] [tastes the flavour, first, of some small good].) Dante then goes on to give examples of that which the human finds:

> Onde vedemo li parvuli desiderare massimamente *un pomo*; e poi, più procedendo, desiderare *uno augellino*; e poi, più oltre, desiderare bel vestimento; e poi lo cavallo; e poi *una donna*; e poi ricchezza non grande, e poi grande, e poi più. E questo incontra perché in nulla di queste cose truova quella che va cercando, e credela trovare più oltre. (*Conv.* 4.12.16, my emphases)

> [So we see small children desiring above all else an apple; then, when they are somewhat older, desiring a little bird; then, still later, desiring fine clothes; then a horse; then a woman; then riches in small measure; then riches in large measure; then even more riches. This happens because people find in none of these things what they are actually seeking, and think they will find it a little way on.]

Thus people move from desiring small things to desiring ever greater material things; but because none of those things is God, their desire is not fulfilled. The examples given in the *Convivio* of these lesser goods— an apple, a bird, a woman—are echoed strongly in *Purgatorio* 23. The canto opens, as noted above, with the pilgrim glancing about as if chasing after birds (1–3), a distraction he must overcome on his own journey through Purgatory (which is also, of course, his own journey to God). And later in the canto Forese Donati refers to the dangers of sexual desire, describing the female body in crude terms, condemning "le sfacciate donne fiorentine" [bare-faced Florence girls] who go about "mostrando con le poppe il petto" (101–2) [with blatant breasts and both their boobs on show]. (He blames the Florentine women rather than the men who desire their bodies.) But most significant of all, here, is the apple, the first thing the child desires, according to the *Convivio*. For this is the terrace on which gluttony is purged; and of course purgation—as Forese Donati explains in lines 61–75—takes place through the desire for the sweet-smelling fruit. It is "in fame e 'n sete" [thirsting, hungering] that each soul "qui si rifà santa" (66) [(is) here remade as holy]; in circling the tree, "si rinfresca nostra pena" (71) [agony and pain are refreshed in us].

Thus, according to the logic of the *Convivio* passage cited above, people seek out "contingenze"—things far from the source of being—thinking they have found what will provide satisfaction, but being ultimately frustrated. But the fruit that smells sweet on the inverted tree of *Purgatorio* 23 is actually directly inspired by divine power. It rains down into the tree—as Forese Donati puts it, "De l'etterno consiglio / cade vertù ne l'acqua e ne la pianta" (61–62) [There falls . . . from the Eternal Mind / a virtue in that water and that tree]. In purging themselves of the excessive desire for food, people are also moving towards something that is directly caused by divine power. The rejection of "contingenze" is directly associated with the desire to move closer to the source of being itself.

Psalm 50 is sung in this context. As mentioned already, the words of the psalm Dante chooses to cite—"Labia mea, Domine"—are particularly apposite for the souls of the gluttons, and suggest a reflection on the vice of which the souls are being purged. There is more at stake, however, since the phrase "Labia mea, Domine" involves a desire to praise: "Domine labia mea aperies; *et os meum adnuntiabit laudem tuam*" (Ps 50:17, my emphases) [O Lord, thou wilt open my lips: and my mouth shall declare thy praise]. This is not, in itself, an act of praise; but it is an *anticipation* of praise—a request that praise might be made possible—at the same time that it is a reflection on the attachment to the contingent of which the souls are being purged. The move towards freedom from vice is thus also presented as a move towards praise.

There is another anticipation of praise in canto 23, however, and this enriches further our understanding of the conditions under which doxology can occur. When Forese Donati describes the souls' movement around the tree, he explains that the smell on the tree arises directly from "l'etterno consiglio," and then says:

> E non pur una volta, questo spazzo
> girando, si rinfresca nostra pena:
> io dico pena, e dovria dir sollazzo,

> ché quella voglia a li alberi ci mena
> che menò Cristo lieto a dire "*Elì*",
> quando ne liberò con la sua vena.
>
> (70–75)

[Nor once alone, in circling round this space, / is agony and pain refreshed in us. / I call it pain. Rightly, I should say solace. / For that same yearning leads us to the tree / that led Christ, in his joy, to say "*Elì*", / when through his open veins he made us free.]

As we have seen, this episode of purgation involved a rejection of attachment to the contingent for its own sake; and linked with this, through the performance of the psalm, was the notion of *praise*. In that rejection, the individual not only is purged of the desire for the contingent, but is also disposed to praise. Moral change is not only a removal of a negative disposition; it is also a preparation for that praise. In the same move that the lips are turned from gluttony, they are turned towards praise. And here, the moment when such liberation from attachment to the contingent became possible, namely, Christ's sacrifice on the Cross, is radically rewritten by Dante as a joyful calling of God's name rather than, as in the "Heli, Heli, lema sabacthani" of Matthew 27:46, an anguished lament.

This joyful calling of God's name, understood in light of the freedom from attachment to the contingencies of the material world (which is also a return to that first condition of union between creature and creator), is a close echo of the first word of human language by prelapsarian man, the naming of God by Adam, described in the *De vulgari eloquentia*. In that work, Dante had argued—contradicting the account of the *primiloquium* in Genesis—that the first word spoken by Adam must have been the name of God, "*El*" (1.4.4).[20] This is in contrast with the first sound made by humans following the Fall, which is "heu." The first word was joyful, and Dante says that such a word must have named God, since outside of God is no joy:

> Nam, sicut post prevaricationem humani generis quilibet exordium sue locutionis incipit ab 'heu', rationabile est quod ante qui fuit inciperet a gaudio; et cum nullum gaudium sit extra Deum, sed totum in Deo, et ipse Deus totus sit gaudium, consequens est quod primus loquens primo et ante omnia dixisset 'Deus'. (1.4.4)

[For if, since the disaster that befell the human race, the speech of every one of us has begun with 'woe!' it is reasonable that he who existed before should have begun with a cry of joy; and, since there is no joy outside God, but all joy is in God, and since God himself is joy itself, it follows that the first man to speak should first and before all have said 'God'.]

This links to Christ's word described in *Purgatorio* 23. (Although Dante corrects aspects of the *De vulgari eloquentia* in the *Commedia*, for instance, in the idea that language change occurred in the garden of Eden and is therefore a natural phenomenon rather than a punishment for an act of transgression (*Par.* 26.124–38), he does not distance himself from the idea that the first word spoken by Adam was the name of God. The first name of God is different, however: in Adam's account in *Paradiso* it is described as "*I*," rather than "*El*" (134–36).) The strength of the link between Adam's condition in the Garden of Eden and Christ's utterance of God's name is strengthened still further by the fact that the tree on the terrace of gluttony is described as deriving from the tree of knowledge in the Earthly Paradise (24.115–17). The reference to Christ's word on the cross, which marks the transition from pain to joy, from "pena" to "sollazzo," is a return from the "heu" of post-lapsarian humanity, tempted by contingent apples, to the "*El*" of Adam in "gaudium," in relation with his maker, in the form of the "lieto" cry of "*Elì*." That Dante saw Adam's utterance in Eden as a form of praise is clear from his explanation of why Adam should speak: "voluit tamen et ipsum loqui, ut in explicatione tante dotis gloriaretur ipse qui gratis dotaverat" (*Dve* 1.5.2) [He still wished that Adam should speak, so that He who had freely given so great a gift should be glorified in its employment].

One of the possible models for Adam's *primiloquium* is Augustine's *De Genesi ad litteram*, in particular, its analysis of the first day, in which the angels are created:[21]

Si lux illa, quae primitus creata est, non corporalis sed spiritalis est, sicut post tenebras facta est, ubi intelligitur a sua quadam informitate ad Creatorem conversa atque formata, ita et post vesperam fiat mane, cum post cognitionem suae propriae naturae, qua non est quod Deus, refert se ad laudandam lucem, quod ipse Deus est, cuius contemplatione formatur; . . . ut vespera primi diei sit etiam sui cognitio non se esse, quod Deus est, mane autem post hanc vesperam, quo concluditur dies unus et inchoatur secundus, conversio sit eius, qua id, quod creata est, ad laudem referat Creatoris et percipiat de Verbo Dei cognitionem creaturae. (4.22.39)

[... if the light originally created is not material but spiritual, then this light [namely, the company of the angels] was made after the darkness in the sense that it turned from its unformed state to its Creator and was thus formed. Consequently, after evening, morning is made, when after its knowledge of its own nature as something distinct from God, this light directs itself to praise the Light that is God, in the contemplation of which it is formed ... Evening of the first day, therefore, is the knowledge spiritual beings have of themselves, inasmuch as they know they are not God. The morning following the evening that concludes the first day, the morning, that is, which begins the second day, is the conversion of spiritual beings, by which they direct to the praise of their Creator the gift of their creation, and receive from the Word of God a knowledge of the creature next made, namely, the firmament.]

Just as, in Augustine's account, the angels immediately turn to God in an act of praise, so too, in Dante's discussion, Adam's first word is a joyful naming of God. And in *Purgatorio* 23, there is a return to the condition in which Adam found himself in union with his creator. This is associated now with the figure of Christ, whom the souls imitate in their suffering. In canto 23 we are learning that doxology takes place in the union with God, which is to say, in the union between creature and creator that is restored when distorted forms of elective love are redirected towards God.

Such a doxology, Dante suggests, is Christological: at this stage of the *Commedia*, it is clear that restoration of the relationship between creature and creator within which praise of God can occur is possible through Christ's sacrifice and through assimilation to that sacrifice. These ideas are all suggested in the Bible. The second person of the Trinity was associated biblically with creation, being described as the means by which creation occurs.[22] And the notion that praise is offered through Christ was present in the Bible; as Hebrews 13:15 puts it, in terms that are particularly loaded in relation to *Purgatorio* 23, with its ideas of praise, lips, fruit, and Christ: "Per ipsum [Christ] ergo offeramus hostiam laudis semper Deo, id est fructum labiorum confitentium nomini eius" [By him therefore let us offer the sacrifice of praise always to God, that is to say, the fruit of lips confessing to his name]. All that Dante does in *Purgatorio* 23 in linking creation, Christ, and praise, therefore, draws on ideas present in Christianity. But Dante's text links the ideas particularly closely, through imagery and allusion rather than through theological argument.

The theme of praise recurs in the next canto, where the pilgrim presents one of the clearest statements of Dante's poetic practice in the *Commedia* (clear, that is, only in the sense that it obviously *is* a statement of poetic practice: its implications have proved controversial).[23] It relates directly to the notion of praise. Bonagiunta asks whether the pilgrim is the person who wrote the poem "Donne ch'avete intelletto d'amore" (*Purg.* 24.51) [Ladies, who have intelligence of love]—the first poem, according to the prose of *Vita nuova*, to be written according to the principles of praise. The pilgrim responds that "I' mi son un che, quando / Amor mi spira, noto, e a quel modo / ch'e' ditta dentro vo significando" (52–54) [I am just one who, when / Love breathes in me, takes note and then goes on / showing the meaning that's ordained within]. Bonagiunta replies that he has now seen the difference between his work and Dante's: whereas Dante's pen followed the dictations of love, his and that of his associates did not (58–60). Bonagiunta says that now he can see "il nodo / che 'l Notaro e Guittone e me ritenne" (55–56) [the knot / that kept the Brief, Guittone and me]; that which held them back was a "nodo"— the same word that has been used twice by Virgil in *Purgatorio* to describe vices (16.24; 23.15), and which was used by the angel at the gate in describing a key that frees one from vice by allowing entry into Purgatory (the key "'l nodo digroppa" (9.126) [gets the knot undone]). It will also be used by Beatrice to describe the pilgrim's doubts, which prevent him from understanding her explanation of creation (*Par.* 7.53).[24] Just as a "nodo" can impede doxology, because it distorts the relationship between creature and creator, so too, Bonagiunta acknowledges that his and his associates' inability to respond to the dictates of love in a praise style is a "nodo" that has held them back.

Creation, Generation, and the Eucharist: *Purgatorio* 23

The Christological dimension of praise that emerges in canto 23 is evident in a further aspect of this section of the poem. The movement towards a rejection of excessive attachment to secondary, contingent goods is linked with a particularly dense set of allusions to the Eucharist. I have argued elsewhere that at key moments in the pilgrim's journey, an awareness of God's creative power is linked—allusively but with striking consistency—to the sacrament of the Eucharist.[25] This process begins as early as *Inferno* 3, where the pilgrim is faced with the declaration inscribed on the gate to Hell that

> fecemi la divina podestate,
> la somma sapïenza e 'l primo amore.
>   Dinanzi a me non fuor cose create
> se non etterne, e io etterno duro.
>   (5–8)

> [I am a creature of the Holiest Power, / of Wisdom in the Highest and of Primal Love. / Nothing till I was made was made, only / eternal beings. And I endure eternally]

The pilgrim's response—"Maestro, il senso lor m'è duro" (12) [Their meaning, sir, for me is hard]—echoes the disciples' response to Christ's description of himself as the bread of Heaven, and his injunction to them to eat of his flesh: "durus est hic sermo" (Jn 6:61) [this saying is hard]. In *Purgatorio* 10, faced with the carvings on the terrace of pride, which are realistic beyond anything produced by human beings and are made by "Colui che mai non vide cosa nova" (94) [The One who sees no thing that's new to Him], the pilgrim finds himself bewildered, his senses divided. The description strongly echoes medieval accounts of the Eucharist and is charged with references to the Incarnation, thus drawing a link between the sacrament, Christology, and the question of creation.

On the terrace of gluttony (*Purg.* 22–24), as we saw in the previous section, a rejection of attachment to contingent goods for their own sake in favor of the source of being is a central dynamic, which I linked with the movement towards praise figured in these canti. The Eucharist is a key presence in this dynamic. Although it is not named directly, the allusions to the Eucharist are strikingly consistent in linking the sacrament to the condition of createdness. The first suggestion of the Eucharist in canto 23 is in the performance of Psalm 50, which Dante describes the souls as both singing and weeping at the same time.[26]

> Domine, labïa mea aperies et os meum adnuntiabit laudem tuam. Non enim sacrificio delectaris, holocaustum, si offeram, non placebit. Sacrificium Deo spiritus contribulatus, cor contritum et humili-

atum, Deus, non spernit. Benigne fac Domine in bona voluntate tua Sion et aedificentur muri Hierusalem. Tunc acceptabis sacrificium iustitiae oblationes et holocausta tunc inponent super altare tuum vitulos. (Ps 50:17–21)

[O Lord, thou wilt open my lips: and my mouth shall declare thy praise. For if thou hadst desired sacrifice, I would indeed have given it: with burnt offerings thou wilt not be delighted. A sacrifice to God is an afflicted spirit: a contrite and humbled heart, O God, thou wilt not despise. Deal favourably, O Lord, in thy good will with Sion; that the walls of Jerusalem may be built up. Then shalt thou accept the sacrifice of justice, oblations and whole burnt offerings: then shall they lay calves upon thy altar.]

Two types of sacrifice are evoked here: first, a form of self-sacrifice, found in the "contrite and humiliated heart"; second, the sacrifice of cattle, which will only be acceptable to God in his grace. These two sacrifices were reconciled by the Christian Psalm commentators, who understood them typologically. As Augustine put it, "In illo tempore erat David, quando sacrificia uictimarum animalium offerebantur Deo, et uidebat haec futura tempora. Nonne in his uocibus nos agnoscimus? Erant illa sacrificia figurate, praenuntiantia unum salutare sacrificium" (*Enarrationes in Psalmos* 50.21) [David was living at that time when sacrifices of victim animals were offered to God, and he saw these times that were to be. Do we not perceive ourselves in these words? Those sacrifices were figurative, foretelling the one saving sacrifice]. The sacrifice mentioned in the psalm prefigures the crucifixion.

Augustine's commentary reminded his medieval readers that the notion of sacrifice of Psalm 50 had to be linked to the Eucharist. Dante's description of hearing the psalm in canto 23 is also suggestive of this link. The pilgrim hears the singing "per modo / tal, che diletto e doglia parturìe" (11–12) [so tuned / it brought both happiness and pain to birth], thus associating the psalm with a paradoxical experience of birth, suffering, and joy—an experience with obvious affinities to the place of the Incarnation and the Eucharist in medieval Christian life. According to Augustine's commentary on the psalm, the crucifixion of Christ did not remove the need for the sacrifices David had mentioned; it recasts the sacrifice as one involving the will of the subject: "Nihil ergo offeremus? . . . Noli extrinsecus pecus quod mactes inquirere, habes in te quod occidas"

(50.21) [shall we therefore offer nothing? ... Do not seek from without cattle to slay; you have in yourself what you may kill]. Part of what is happening in the singing of the psalm, then, is that the souls are purging themselves in a form of self-sacrifice. There is a confessional element in the reflection on the vice of gluttony inherent in the reference to lips in the words of the psalm that Dante cites; and this confessional element is also suggested by the contrition that the psalm proposes as the condition acceptable to God. This contrition is linked by the Psalm commentators to the Eucharist. But in the context of canto 23, there is a still stronger link made between the Eucharist and the self-sacrifice involved in the purgation of the souls; that link has to do with the rejection of attachment to the contingent in favor of an approach to the source of being itself. For as the souls are weeping and singing this psalm, they are passing around the tree, which is informed directly by the divine mind, which is pouring down onto it; and the suffering that this involves is linked directly by Forese Donati to Christ's sacrifice on the Cross. It is the same desire that leads the souls around the tree "che menò Cristo lieto a dire 'Elì', / quando ne liberò con la sua vena."

The ephemeral contingencies produced by nature—the desirable apples, birds, and objectified bodies of *mediate* creation—are rejected in favor of moving closer to the source of being, *immediate* divine creation. The rejection of gluttony, says Donati, is the same self-sacrifice that Christ made on the cross; and the liberation this gives to mankind he describes by reference to Christ's blood. This self-sacrifice was the same as that which led Mary to notice the lack of wine at the wedding of Cana, as a voice from the tree reminds the souls—"Più pensava Maria onde / fosser le nozze orrevoli e intere, / ch'a la sua bocca, ch'or per voi risponde" (22.142–44) [Maria thought far more / of how the wedding might be full and fine / than of that mouth by which she prays for you]—which led to Christ's first miracle, turning water into wine, itself a prefigurement of the Eucharist. These Eucharistic allusions are also suggested negatively, by the figure of another Mary, a woman who in the siege of Jerusalem in 70 AD ate her son through hunger: "Ecco / la gente che perdé Ierusalemme, / quando Maria nel figlio diè di becco!" (23.28–30) [Just look! The folk who lost Jerusalem / when starving Mary pecked her son to death]. We have been reminded of the Virgin Mary's contrasting selflessness at Cana in the previous canto. And Dante makes a significant alteration to the primary source for this story, book 6 of Flavius

Josephus's *De bello judaico*, using the trope "diè di becco" [pecked] for eating. In so doing, he hints at and reverses a further Eucharistic image, that of the pelican, which was believed to feed its own flesh to its young, an image Dante will recall in *Paradiso* (25.113).

The allusions to the Eucharist in Dante's description of the terrace of the gluttons thus display continuity in relation to the question of creation. In each case they involve a rejection of selfish desire for "contingenze"; this rejection then leads to the sacramental. To restate the examples: Mary does not think of her own thirst (22.142–44); the miracle at Cana, prefiguring the Eucharist, occurs. The penitent souls sing the words of Psalm 50, which most strongly reinforce their purgation of gluttony (23.11); the psalm goes on to refer to a sacrifice, and a self-sacrifice which (in Augustine's view) is a figure for Christ's sacrifice on the cross. The pilgrim is reminded of Mary of Jerusalem, who, in an inversion of the Eucharist, ate her own son (23.28–30). The souls on the terrace of the gluttonous process around a tree, which worsens their hunger; but the tree is directly dependent on God's power, and the desire that leads them to do so is the same desire Christ felt when he liberated humankind with his blood, his blood being the sign of that liberation, its manifestation in the world, the Eucharist (23.61–75).

CREATION AND DOXOLOGICAL SUBJECTIVITY IN *PARADISO*

The liturgical performances in *Purgatorio* are closely tied to the models of personhood enacted there. First, as we have seen, the use of liturgy is in keeping with the broader processes of penance in Purgatory; a key aspect is the restoration of the proper relationship between creature and creator. Second, in canto 23 this redirection of love towards the creator was marked by allusions to the Eucharist, which occurred in the context of the rejection of attachment to the contingent. Finally, the liturgy of *Purgatorio* anticipates—but does not yet fully take part in—doxology. My analysis of canto 23 suggests that, through that redirection of love and through an assimilation to Christ, doxology becomes possible.

Understood in this light, the penitential liturgy of *Purgatorio* clearly anticipates the doxology of *Paradiso*. How does that doxology develop the themes suggested by the second *cantica*? In the most thorough published survey of the liturgical "vestiges" in the *Commedia*, John Barnes finds little to indicate a substantive connection between the action of *Paradiso* and the doxology performed there, but rather sees the heavenly liturgy as conferring a certain mood on the poem. Thus, for instance, in the case of canto 26.69, where a version of the Sanctus is performed, "there seems to be no obvious connection between this and Dante's declaration on charity"; perhaps "its function is to confer solemnity on the gratitude of the blessed at this point."[27] Similarly, the Greater Doxology of 27.1–2 "seems to be used here ... as a magnificent punctuation mark between episodes."[28] Such descriptions attribute a largely decorative function to the liturgical praise of God in Paradise. However, as I have suggested in my discussion of the anticipations of doxology in *Purgatorio*, the poem has built carefully towards this praise, which—far from being mere mood music—has been bound up Christologically with the notion of the restoration of the relationship between creator and creature.

There are many doxological formulations in *Paradiso*: *Hosanna* (7.1; 28.94; 28.118; 32.135); *Sanctus* (7.1; 26.69); "Dio Laudamo" (24.113); and a version of the Greater Doxology, *Gloria in excelsis* (27.1–2; Dante's version emphasizes the praise of the Trinity). In addition, there are other, less well-defined acts of praise: the song to Christ of 14.118–26 is "d'alte lode" (124) [(of) high praise]; the souls forming the Eagle of canto 19 sing songs of praise (34–39); souls are described as "laudando il cibo che là sù li prande" (25.24) [praising ... the feast at which they sat]. What does it mean for a soul in Paradise to engage in an act of praise?

"Glory" is a key notion for the doxology represented in *Paradiso*,[29] for it opens up several problems associated with the offering of praise to God. By working through these problems we will be in a position to establish the dynamics governing heavenly doxology as a whole. Although in *Paradiso* there is only one occasion where a version of the Greater Doxology is performed in praise of God, the notion of offering glory to God is in many ways typical of doxological prayer in *Paradiso*. The idea of glory is present in the liturgical Sanctus (a version of this is performed in *Par.* 26.69; and an element of it is present in 7.1): "pleni sunt caeli et terra gloria tua"; Durand describes the Sanctus as a celebration of God's glory (*Rationale divinorum officiorum* 4.34.1). When the souls sing "Dio laudamo" (14.113), the reader might recall the *Te Deum laudamus*, which had been sung in *Purgatorio* 9, though probably not by penitent souls: "Pleni sunt celi et terra maiestatis gloriae tuae; Te gloriosus apostolorum chorus."

Beyond the weight of allusions to glory in the liturgy described in *Paradiso*, however, there are two important conceptual reasons why glory raises questions important to my argument here. First, as Dante makes very clear in *Purgatorio* 11, glory is a notion that can be misused, especially by the prideful. Second, glory is fundamentally related to the question of creation, which I have been arguing is central to the question of praise. All of creation, as we shall see, is for Dante and for medieval theologians a manifestation of the glory of God. If we are to understand the dynamic of doxological subjectivity in *Paradiso*—the ways in which human personhood is constituted in the utterance of praise to God—then we need to understand the way in which the offering of glory to God occurs in relation to these two notions.

Purgatorio 11 raised the problem of praise in Purgatory, in that the penitent souls do not offer praise in their prayer, but rather express a wish that others might praise God (10–12). There is a hint as to why this might be so in the use of the word "Gloria" later on in this canto. The term or a derivative of it is used three times by Oderisi, each time as a negative term. Oderisi talks of the "vana gloria de l'umane posse" (91) [vainglorying in human powers], manifested in pride as the desire to possess glory. Thus, any desire on the part of Guido Cavalcanti or Guido Guinizelli to take possession of the "gloria del la lingua" (98) [glory of language] is inevitably thwarted, as that glory passes inevitably from one person to another. Provenzano Salvani left the condition in which "vivea più glorïoso" (133) [he lived in glorious fame] to commit the act of humility that enabled him to progress so far in Purgatory, as Oderisi explains in response to a question from the pilgrim. Glorious living—understood as the grandeur of earthly power—is a condition that Salvani had to leave for the sake of his salvation. This is an understanding of glory as self-aggrandizement—a glory humans can only seem to possess, even though the human soul—as Dante had put it in the *Convivio*—"sempre desideri gloria d'acquistare" (4.4.3) [always desires to acquire glory]. Aquinas explains in more detail the circumstances in which glory is vain and therefore sinful. In each case, these circumstances are inimical to the relation between creator and creature that Dante's Purgatory seeks to restore. Glory is vain, first, when a person seeks it for frail and perishable reasons; second, when the judgment of an inadequate person is sought; and, finally, when it is desired egotistically rather than for God's honor or for the spiritual welfare of one's neighbor (*ST* IIaIIae.132.1).

What is the difference between that kind of glory and the glory of God? First of all, there must be a qualitative difference between it and the glory of a God who is "colui che tutto move" [who moves all things that are]. The glory of God cannot be possessed by any human but rather is God's reflection, apparent to a greater or lesser degree in creation. This is linked, in *Paradiso* as in medieval Christianity generally, to the image of light.[30] That much is clear even from the opening lines of canto 1, where glory is a quality that is resplendent: "La gloria di colui che tutto move / per l'universo penetra, e *risplende*" (1.1–2, my emphasis) [Glory, from Him who moves all things that are, / penetrates the universe and then *shines back*].[31]

By virtue of being a reflection of God's light, creation is, in itself, a manifestation of the glory of God. But if so, we are left with the problem of what it means to *sing* glory to God, to offer him glory in an act of praise. A useful distinction can be found in Aquinas between the glory in which all created beings participate by virtue of being created, and a more participative glory that is available only to intelligent creatures. The glory of unintelligent creatures, Aquinas argues, is a reflection of God's goodness simply because they are created ("in hoc ipso quod creatura aliqua habet esse, repraesentat divinum esse et bonitatem eius" [*ST* Ia.65.2.ad1] [In the very fact of any creature possessing being, it represents the Divine being and Its goodness]). In this sense all of creation is a reflection and manifestation of God's glory, as the opening words of *Paradiso* state. Intelligent creatures, however, because of their reason, are capable of recognizing the goodness of the Creator. This type of glory, or beatitude, consists in the recognition by an intelligent being of its source in and as God. As Aquinas explains, "sed bonum hominis dependet, sicut ex causa, ex cognitione Dei. Et ideo ex gloria quae est apud Deum dependet beatitudo hominis sicut ex causa sua" (*ST* IaIIae.2.3) [On the other hand, man's good depends on God's knowledge as its cause. And therefore man's beatitude depends, as on its cause, on the glory which man has with God]. Aquinas contrasts this glory with earthly fame, explaining that "fama nullo modo potest facere hominem beatum" (*ST* IaIIae.2.3.ad2) [fame can in no way make man happy].

Angelic praise, as we saw earlier, is a key example of this glory in Augustine's commentary on Genesis: in turning to God as their source, the angels utter praise. In Dante, angelic bliss is clearly linked to this recognition of God as the cause of creation. The angels who did not fall, Beatrice explains, "furon modesti / a riconoscer sé da la bontate" (*Par.* 29.58–59) [restrainedly / acknowledged of themselves the utmost good]. God created the angels, Beatrice also explains, not to acquire any good for himself ("Non per aver a sé di bene acquisto" [13] [Not seeking any good that He had not]), but as an act of *subsistence*, as light reflecting back to light ("perché suo splendore / potesse, risplendendo, dir '*Subsisto*'" [14–15] [but so his shining-out / could in return shine back and say: "I am"]; see also the description of God's light by Dante's Aquinas, "quasi specchiato" (*Par.* 13.59) [as mirrored]). In discussing the anticipation of praise in *Purgatorio* 23, I argued that this canto suggested the need to renounce an attachment to "contingenze" for their own sake, as a necessary prerequisite to doxology. The full reflection of God's glory and splendor back to him, as Beatrice's discussion of the angels shows, is a participation in the opposite of contingency: subsistence.

The human being, too, is capable of reflecting the light of divine being back to God. However, sin makes humanity unlike God and blocks that light, as Beatrice explains in *Paradiso* 7 (73–81). Similarly, she explains in canto 29, those angels who remain in Heaven and who acknowledge their maker as they had been created to do (58–60) are lit by grace and enter into the beatific vision (61–62); whereas those who grew proud, fell (55–57). Pride is thus specifically associated with the refusal of the fallen angels to recognize their status as created.

A link between these principles and doxology is suggested in the Heaven of the Sun. Canto 10 ends with a sound similar to the Matins bell, and with the souls moving in a "glorïosa rota" (145) [wheel in glory], singing and dancing. Canto 11 then opens with an invective against the "insensata cura de' mortali" (1) [idiotic strivings of the human mind], which includes a catalogue of the principles of sin and attachment to the flesh. The pilgrim, in contrast, "da tutte queste cose sciolto, / con Bëatrice m'era suso in cielo / cotanto glorïosamente accolto" (10–12) [released from all that sort of thing, / was gathered up on high with Beatrice / in glorious triumph to the heavenly spheres]. The opening lines recall Lucifer's action but also, once again, the terrace of pride, where the poet had lambasted human pride as an inability to put wings to proper use ("non v'accorgete voi che noi siam vermi / nati a formar l'angelica farfalla, / che vola a la giustizia sanza schermi?" [*Purg.* 10.124–26] [do you not recognize that you are worms / born to become angelic butterflies / that fly up to justice with no veil between?]). The acceptance into Paradise, "glorïosamente," where a "glorïosa rota" sings praise to God, is possible because of Dante's distance from that sin.

We have seen that for Dante in the *Commedia*, God's glory cannot be possessed by humans, and therefore in offering glory to God, humans are not offering something that is fully theirs, as in an exchange between two discrete entities, but are rather reflecting glory back as they receive it from God. God's glory, moreover, is reflected in creation, and most fully in those beings most similar to him; Beatrice at different points explains that the angels and human beings offer an example of the ways in which that glory either can be blocked through pride or sin, or can be fully reflected. And the full reflection of God's glory, as evident in the relationship between the angels and God, demonstrates a relationship with God in which God's eternal existence is enunciated as "subsistence" in the divine "subsisto."

These principles shape the dynamic of doxology in *Paradiso* as a whole. In my discussion of *Purgatorio*, I suggested that what appears to be a clear instance of doxology in the second *cantica*, the *Gloria in excelsis Deo* of canto 20, is in fact a flawed doxology, an imperfect impersonation of the angelic praise, which, in its imperfection, points back to the condition of the souls in Purgatory. Taken together with the anticipations of doxology found in *Purgatorio*, it is clear that the excessive attachment to self and to secondary goods is the barrier to a full participation in God's glory. Such a participation is, however, completed in Paradise, where the souls of the blessed do not block that light but rather reflect it back fully to God.

If we compare the *Gloria in excelsis* of *Purgatorio* 20 with the climactic singing of praise to God at the opening of *Paradiso* 27, the contrast between the flawed doxology of Purgatory and the heavenly doxology is clear. The words are sung just before the "entry" of the souls into the Empyrean:

> "Al Padre, al Figlio, a lo Spirito Santo"
> cominciò, "gloria!" tutto 'l paradiso,
> sì che m'inebrïava il dolce canto.
>   Ciò ch'io vedeva, mi sembiava un riso
> de l'universo; per che mia ebbrezza
> entrava per l'udire e per lo viso.

> Oh gioia! oh ineffabile allegrezza!
> oh vita intègra d'amore e di pace!
> oh sanza brama sicura ricchezza!
> (27.1–9)

["To Father and Son and the Holy Ghost, / glory on high!" all Heaven here began, / till I, at that sweet song, reeled drunkenly. / And what I saw, it seemed, was now the laughter / of the universe. So drunkenness, for me, / came in through hearing and, no less, through sight. / The joy of that! The happiness beyond all words! / A life of peace and love, entire and whole! / Riches all free of craving, troubleless!]

The song's intoxicating beauty and the immediate clarity of the words mark a clear contrast with the chaotic, barely comprehensible shout of "*Gloria in excelsis*" of *Purgatorio* 20. We might also note that these words come at the end of an episode of *Paradiso*—that of the Heaven of the Fixed Stars—which contains very strong echoes of the terrace of gluttony in *Purgatorio*. *Purgatorio* 23 had reflected upon the dangers of attachment to the contingent for its own sake, opening with the pilgrim glancing through "fronde"; and here the pilgrim offers an account of charity that draws on such language, presenting the created world as worthy of love not for its own sake but precisely because it is dignified: "Le fronde onde s'infronda tutto l'orto / de l'ortolano etterno, am' io cotanto / quanto da lui a lor di bene è porto" (*Par.* 26.64–66) [every leaf, en-leafing all the grove / of our eternal orchardist, I love / as far as love is borne to them from Him]. And, just as Christ's naming of God on the cross recalls Dante's description of the *primiloquium* in the *De vulgari eloquentia*, so too, the episode draws to a close—just before this climactic singing of praise—with Adam's discussion of the nature of language in the garden of Eden.

It is, moreover, important to note that the pilgrim sees the performance of the song as a smile of the universe, "un riso / de l'universo." This smile of the universe represents a bringing together of the notions of formal glory—the glory manifested by all of creation simply by virtue of being—and participative glory—the glory in which the intelligent soul recognizes God as its source. The utterance of glory is a full, active participation in God's glory. And that participation is described by the poet as complete, without need, "sanza brama."

The smile of the universe can be related to this union with God in two ways. First, the smile is frequently associated in *Paradiso* with an outpouring of light. Aquinas speaks of "[q]uell' altro fiammeggiare," which "esce del riso / di Grazïan" (*Par.* 10.103–4) [The next flame blazes out from Gratian's smile]; the red light of the planet Mars is an "affocato riso" (14.86) [flares of a smile]; in Beatrice's eyes "ardeva un riso" (15.34) [a smile was burning]. To smile, in *Paradiso*, is to reflect light. The smile of the universe is therefore a vision of the universe reflecting God's light/glory back to him in that act of praise. This act of praise is also, however, presented as similar to God's own act of smiling. God is described by the poet in *Paradiso* 33, in an image that links light and the smile, as smiling on himself ("O luce etterna che sola in te sidi, / sola t'intendi, e da te intelletta / e intendente te ami e arridi!" [124–26] [Eternal light, you sojourn in yourself alone. / Alone, you know yourself. Known to yourself, / you, knowing, love and smile on your own being]). When the pilgrim witnesses the universe smile in an act of praise, he is witnessing the universe returning itself to God, returning light to light. He is experiencing all of creation in its condition of createdness — a condition in which creation happily returns praise to God.

The pilgrim's own response is also indicative of this involvement of the created world in the life of the Trinity. At the utterance of the "gloria," he describes an experience of inebriation (*Par.* 27.3, 5). This echoes closely mystical language on the union with God, described, for instance by Bernard, as a drunkenness that occurs as human desire enters into the divine will.[32] On the brink of entering the Empyrean — presented in the *Commedia* as the mind of God — the souls themselves are about to enter that union; and the pilgrim too is in this state, as he is to find. The utterance of "gloria" is thus bound up with that union. We might note, too, that the reaction of the pilgrim is climactic: he has experienced profound responses to liturgical singing previously in the *Commedia*, but this case is slightly different. In *Purgatorio* 8, the *Te lucis ante* was sung "con sì dolci note, / che fece me a me uscir di mente" (14–15) [each note so sweet / it made me wonder out of conscious thought], reflecting a moment of abandonment of self; in *Purgatorio* 23, the sound of singing mixed with weeping was such "che diletto e doglia parturìe" (12), which is akin to the paradoxical experience of pain and joy of Purgatory, as described later in the canto by Forese Donati ("io dico pena, / e dovria dir sollazzo") (72). In other words, these are merely stages on the way to ecstatic union, whereas in hearing the "gloria" at this moment of *Paradiso*, the pilgrim experiences something close to an understanding of that union itself.

The climactic doxological performance of canto 27 can be understood, I suggest, as a paradigm for all of the heavenly praise of God described in *Paradiso*. Because the souls of Paradise are in that condition of blessedness in which they are in no way separated from God's will, and in which they recognize God as the source of their being, they are not offering anything to God that is not already God's. They are, instead, willingly reflecting God's glory back to him, in a smiling relationship; they are bound up in that same relationship God has with himself, as a light which reflects and smiles on itself. The reason why this is climactic, and why only this act of praise seems to be a "riso de l'universo," has to do with the progress of the pilgrim, who is now himself almost prepared to experience the beatific vision and union with God. He is almost prepared to be united with the point where all the universe, in its spatial and temporal dimensions, comes together at the source of creation—as Beatrice describes it, "là 've s'appunta ogne *ubi* e ogne *quando*" (29.12) [where every "when" and "where" attains its point]. That the universe *seems* to him ("mi sembiava") to be smiling in that act of praise is a late stage on the path to that union.

The act of praise of *Paradiso* 27 comes after the link between personhood and liturgy has been carefully signalled and elaborated by Dante throughout the *Purgatorio*. In particular, the shift from the penitential mode of liturgy performed in Purgatory to the doxological mode described in *Paradiso* is grounded in the way in which the relationship between creature and creator is understood. This relationship is a key theme of the *Commedia* as a whole. But there is a close link between that relationship and the dynamics of penitence and praise, which is perhaps most clearly evident in *Purgatorio* 23. Here, the penitent souls purge themselves of the love of secondary goods, which distract them from love of the supreme good; they do so in a move presented, precisely, as a move towards praise. This is evident both in the words of the psalm they sing and in the self-sacrifice of Christ, which is a restoration of the condition of humankind in the garden of Eden. In *Paradiso*, that relationship between creator and creature is restored, in particular in the idea of glory.

In offering praise to God, the souls of Paradise are reflecting God's glory back to God. This reflection is a manifestation of their awareness of their condition of createdness. In this condition, doxology occurs as naturally as the blessed souls reflect their creator's light.

NOTES

I extend warm thanks to Zygmunt Barański, Simon Gilson, Claire Honess, Ben King, Robin Kirkpatrick, Vittorio Montemaggi, and Victoria Treherne, who commented on earlier versions of this essay. Except where otherwise noted, translations from the *Commedia* are taken from Dante, *Divine Comedy*, tr. Kirkpatrick.

1. Pickstock, *After Writing*.
2. In the Roman rite, Pickstock argues, a "constant play of differences modulates through narrative, dialogue, antiphon, monologue, apostrophe, doxology, oration, invocation, citation, supplementation and entreaty. This manifold genre disarms in advance any assumption of an authoritarian or strategic voice of command" (ibid., 213).
3. Lacoste, *Expérience et Absolu*, 26–27.
4. Useful accounts of medieval liturgical practice include Harper, *Forms and Orders*; Jungmann, *Mass of the Roman Rite*; Klauser, *A Short History of the Western Liturgy*; Righetti, *Manuale di storia liturgica*.
5. Among studies of liturgy in Dante, Barnes, "Vestiges of the Liturgy" is notable for the breadth of its coverage and its appendix, which contains a useful list of liturgical references from the *Commedia* and suggestions as to their sources; Martinez, "Poetics of Advent Liturgies" breaks new ground in demonstrating the depth and richness of Dante's use of liturgical references. Robert Durling and Ronald Martinez's commentary and notes to the *Purgatorio* are particularly sensitive to the liturgical connotations of the poem. Other useful works include La Favia, "'Ché quivi per canti'"; Ardissino, "I canti liturgici"; McCracken, "*In Omnibus Viis Tuis*." See also Treherne, "Liturgical Imaginations." The liturgical texts performed in Dante's Purgatory have been recently collected by Paul Walker. See his "Texts and Translations for Chants Mentioned by Dante."
6. A strong body of opinion is that the sacraments should not be regarded as present in any important sense in the *Commedia*. The fact that there are no explicit discussions of the sacraments in the poem has led some critics to suggest that Dante had little interest in them. See, for instance, Truijen, "Sacramento," and Took, "Dante's Incarnationalism" (16)—although Took argues that Dante presents every significant human encounter as "sacramental." Peter Armour makes perhaps the most cogent argument against seeking sacramental

meaning in the *Commedia*. He maintains that the sacraments "pertain solely to man's life on earth" and therefore have no place in Dante's afterlife (*Door of Purgatory*, 4). However, see also Treherne, "Ekphrasis and Eucharist" and "Art and Nature."

7. *ST* IIaIIae.83.11.ad3.

8. See McCracken, "*In Omnibus Viis Tuis*," and Robert Durling's essay "The Canonical Hours: Compline" in his edition and translation of the *Purgatorio*, 600–602, for a summary and discussion of the service.

9. Barnes, "Vestiges of the Liturgy," 231.

10. *Analecta hymnica*, 51:30–32.

11. For recent discussions of the psychological changes undergone by the souls of Purgatory proper, see, for instance, Teodolinda Barolini's account of the redirection of desire towards God (*Undivine Comedy*, 99–121); Marc Cogan's discussion of vice (*Design in the Wax*, 77–147); and Manuele Gragnolati's examination of physical suffering in Purgatory, in particular what he describes as "productive pain," and the assimilation to Christ which occurs in Purgatory (*Experiencing the Afterlife*, 109–37).

12. Cited from the edition by Eligius Dekkers and Johannes Fraipont.

13. *Analecta hymnica*, 51:32. Translations from Durling, *Purgatorio*.

14. Cogan, *Design in the Wax*, 77–147.

15. *ST* Ia.60.5.ad4; Ia.60.1.ad3.

16. "Guardando nel suo Figlio con l'Amore / che l'uno e l'altro etternalmente spira, / lo primo e ineffabile Valore / quanto per mente e per loco si gira / con tant' ordine fé" (1–5) [Looking within his Son through that same Love / that Each breathes out eternally with Each, / the first and three-fold Worth, beyond all words, / formed all that spins through intellect or space].

17. Liturgy's role in these terraces as a corrective to wrong uses of elective love may help explain the lack of liturgy on the terrace of sloth (*Purg.* 17–18). Liturgy in Purgatory serves to redirect elective love towards the creator; in the case of the vice purged on the fourth terrace, however, the problem is a lack of elective love, not its misdirection.

18. Pickstock, *After Writing*, 203.

19. It is unlikely that Dante would have expected most of his readers to know the *Convivio*; and the extent to which in the *Commedia* Dante wishes to distance himself from the *Convivio* remains a controversial topic (on this debate, see Scott, "Unfinished *Convivio*"; Pertile, "Lettera aperta"; and, for a discussion of the ways in which the early commentators were aware of the *Convivio*, Azzetta, "La tradizione"). Basile ("Il viaggio") and Barolini (*Undivine Comedy*) see this passage as paradigmatic for the *Commedia* as a whole, establishing the model for the pilgrim's journey to God.

20. On the daring nature of Dante's rewriting of Genesis, see Barański, "*Sole nuovo, luce nuova*," 93–106. As Barański puts it, the name of God "era il mezzo con cui Adamo riconosceva il suo Creatore e ne celebrava l'onnipotenza" (103).

21. Cited in Raffi, *La gloria del volgare*, 147–49.

22. See Jn 1:3 ("omnia per ipsum [Christ] facta sunt: et sine ipso factum est nihil" [All things were made by him: and without him was made nothing that was made]); 1 Cor 8:6 ("unus Dominus Iesu Christus, per quem omnia et nos per ipsum" [one Lord Jesus Christ, by whom are all things, and we by him]); Heb 1:2 ("quem [Christ] constituit heredem universorum, per quem fecit et saecula" [whom he hath appointed heir of all things, by whom also he made the world]).

23. For a summary of some of the issues, see Martinez, "Pilgrim's Answer."

24. The term "nodo" is also used differently, indeed positively, in the *Commedia*, in particular to describe the binding together of the universe in the vision of and union with God of *Paradiso* 33 ("La forma universal di questo nodo" [91] [the knotting-up of universal form]); in Purgatory proper, however, its meaning is only associated with vice. For a discussion of the "nodo" and the term's relation to medieval falconry, see Pertile, "Il nodo."

25. See Treherne, "Ekphrasis and Eucharist" and "Art and Nature."

26. The lines were frequently used elsewhere in the liturgy—in particular as a versicle and response.

27. Barnes, "Vestiges of the Liturgy," 252.

28. Ibid., 253.

29. On the idea of glory throughout Dante's works, see Agliano, "Gloria."

30. Perhaps the most obvious example of the linking of glory and light in medieval theology is the notion of "lumen gloriae," a concept invented by Albert the Great of a light that enters the intellect and gives it power to see God. Aquinas retains the concept, and Dante's Peter Damian describes a similar idea, although without calling it the "light of glory" (*Par.* 21.83–87). See Gilson, *Medieval Optics*, 252–56.

31. The link between light and glory has already been raised by Dante in describing Beatrice as "O luce, o gloria de la gente umana" (*Purg.* 33.115) [You light and glory of the human race].

32. *De diligendo Deo* (10.27). On Bernard's imagery of divine union, see Moevs, *Metaphysics of Dante's "Comedy,"* 64; on Bernard more generally, see Botterill, *Dante and the Mystical Tradition*.

6

Dante's *Commedia* and the Body of Christ

OLIVER DAVIES

The systematic theologian inevitably approaches a theological poet such as Dante with a certain amount of trepidation and, hopefully, with some caution. After all, to read a literary text as theology (as though it were theology?) is to cross a boundary that resonates at many different levels. There is, first, the question of genre, and second, that of intent. Do we read literary texts with the same kinds of expectations with which we read theological ones? What kind of reading does the literary or theological text itself promote? (We are speaking here of traditions of reading which any tutored reader will already inhabit, but there is a sense nevertheless in which we can say that a text "calls out" to be read in a certain way, on account of subtle signs and forms of organization on and below the surface of the text.)

On the face of it, theological and literary texts need to be read in different ways: the former communicate ideas, clarify, and instruct—although some theology will also develop the expressivity of certain thematic and doctrinal topoi; the latter may also communicate ideas, clarify, and instruct, but will tend to do so in the light of the autonomy of the text itself. Crudely stated, we may legitimately request of the theologian some account of what they mean at any particular point in their text—there is immediate responsibility here for what is communicated—while the poet will or may turn the request back to the text itself. No theologian worth their salt would set out to complicate their thought in such a way and to such an extent that the reader interpretively struggles, as with a literary text, to determine exactly what are the ideas being communicated by the author. The literary text, on the other hand, stands as an end in itself; however rich its readings and resonances, there has to be a sense in which the form of the literary work of art cannot be dissolved into conceptual systems of communication without at that point stepping out of what we ordinarily understand to be the act of reading literature—whereby we give ourselves over to the text, and allow it, for the duration of the reading and sometimes long afterwards, to be our world. That said, these initial, cautious thoughts are complicated by the far-reaching crossover between theology and literature in the modern period, which suggests that theology must in fact learn the indirectness of the literary text if it is properly going to be able to communicate what must be communicated—something so elemental and primary that it simply cannot be communicated in any other way but indirectly. (Such a view of the theological text is outrightly modern, belonging to early Romanticism in general and to one of the greatest figures of that period, Søren Kierkegaard, in particular.)[1]

So how should a systematic theologian read Dante's *Commedia*? The initial answer to this must of course be "as literature." And if we did not read it in that way, then perhaps we would not be reading it at all. Surely, if we want to come to grips with Scholastic theology, then we would best look at Thomas Aquinas and his *Summa Theologiae* and not at Dante, for whom, in this respect at least, Thomas is a "source." But while it may be fascinating to discern where the influence of Thomas in Dante may lie, such an interpretive exercise is not in itself theology: it is the business of tracking Dante's theological sources for sensible historical purposes. There is clearly more than that to reading Dante's *Commedia* "as theology." The approach characterized in this essay is thus entirely other than the tracking of sources (though perhaps we will do a little of that); but nor does it simply aim to offer a literary understanding of Dante's text *qua* literature (although I hope it will not be too unsubtle in this regard). It is, rather, an approach that presupposes the centrality of both theology and literariness in the reading of Dante's text.

The approach to Dante's *Commedia* presented here takes the act of reading—the act of reading this text—to be already caught up in the nature of the text itself, in such a way that to read it from a perspective which is not intensely theological and literary at the same time would be to read it wrongly. This does not mean that readings of a kind other than the one gathering pace here might not be infinitely more interesting or rewarding. But it does mean that the failure to grasp the extent to which, for Dante, the act of reading the *Commedia* must itself be as theologically determined as anything in the text, calls into question the extent to which we, as readers, are properly reading *this* text. From this perspective, it is a condition of readership that we should conform ourselves as far as possible to the expectations of the reader as implied in the authorial act itself. Books are written for an audience, and Dante's great book was written for an audience who understood that the world was more or less as Dante depicted it, at least from the point of view of ultimacy. Thus we, too, should seek to inhabit that place as best we may, in order to see this text from new and possibly hitherto unacknowledged angles.

So where are we to begin? Let us start with language. In the early chapters of book 1 of the *De vulgari eloquentia*, Dante gives us an intriguing account of the nature of language. Several points of principle emerge. In the first place, language in its most primary form is not that which is akin to "gramatica" (*Dve* 1.1.3), by which Dante means a language, such as Latin, which is acquired through learning, a process which Dante holds to be an artificial form of language acquisition. Language in its most primary form is, rather, the common or vernacular language which we learn as young infants by imitating those closest to us, in immediate physical proximity or community. This is a material and social conception of language, based upon interaction with and care for very young children, and involving the distinguishing of words, or "voces," which is to say, words as perceptible or sensible *sounds* that are uttered directly to us (*Dve* 1.1).

Further, language in this sense is part of our humanity. As Dante puts it:

> Cum igitur homo non nature instinctu, sed ratione moveatur, et ipsa ratio vel circa discretionem vel circa iudicium vel circa electionem diversificetur in singulis, adeo ut fere quilibet sua propria specie videatur gaudere, per proprios actus vel passiones, ut brutum animal, neminem alium intelligere opinamur. Nec per spiritualem speculationem, ut angelum, alterum alterum introire contingit, cum grossitie atque opacitate mortalis corporis humanus spiritus sit obtectus.

Oportuit ergo genus humanum ad comunicandas inter se conceptiones suas aliquod rationale signum et sensuale habere: quia, cum de ratione accipere habeat et in rationem portare, rationale esse oportuit; cumque de una ratione in aliam nichil deferri possit nisi per medium sensuale, sensuale esse oportuit. Quare, si tantum rationale esset, pertransire non posset; si tantum sensuale, nec a ratione accipere nec in rationem deponere potuisset.

Hoc equidem signum est ipsum subiectum nobile de quo loquimur: nam sensuale quid est in quantum sonus est; rationale vero in quantum aliquid significare videtur ad placitum. (*Dve* 1.3)

[Since, therefore, human beings are moved not by their natural instinct but by reason, and since that reason takes diverse forms in individuals, according to their capacity for discrimination, judgment, or choice—to the point where it appears that almost everyone enjoys the existence of a unique species—I hold that we can never understand the actions or feelings of others by reference to our own, as the baser animals can. Nor is it given to us to enter into each other's minds by means of spiritual reflection, as the angels do, because the human spirit is so weighed down by the heaviness and density of the mortal body.

So it was necessary that the human race, in order for its members to communicate their conceptions among themselves, should have some signal based on reason and perception. Since this signal needed to receive its content from reason and convey it back there, it had to be rational; but, since nothing can be conveyed from one reasoning mind to another except by means perceptible to the senses, it had also to be based on perception. For, if it were purely rational, it could not make its journey; if purely perceptible, it could neither derive anything from reason nor deliver anything to it.

This signal, then, is the noble foundation that I am discussing; for it is perceptible, in that it is a sound, and yet also rational, in that this sound, according to convention, is taken to mean something.]

Only human beings have speech. Baser animals do not have need of communication, and the angels already communicate without speech. Angels have an immediate, spiritual or reflective form of communication (they know each other's minds). This is a nondiscursive form of communication that will be very important for Dante in the *Commedia*. It is the materiality of our bodies, by which we are "weighed down," which makes the use of words necessary for human beings. (At this point, Dante seems to be in line with Thomas Aquinas's outline of the distinction between human and angelic knowledge and communication in *Summa Theologiae* I, questions 57 and 107.) In a further exegesis of language, Dante describes speech as exhibiting both material and conceptual or rational dimensions: it therefore reflects back to us the character of our own humanity. The first element that constitutes the word is reason, or meaning, by which we too are governed as human beings; and the second is materiality, which Dante describes as the sensible or perceptible element ("sensuale"). Without materiality, rational communication could not take place between one human being and another, and without rationality, the passage of material sounds ("sonus") would be meaningless.[2]

Finally, we must note one further aspect of Dante's theory of language. He declares in *De vulgari eloquentia* 1.5.1 that "homine sentiri humanius credimus quam sentire" [it is more truly human for a human being to be perceived than to perceive]. This appears to sum up what he wishes to say about language in its relation to the human. While recognizing the indispensable role of reason in human life and communication, Dante wants to remove language from the hegemony of reason, by arguing for the primacy of language as received, rather than acquired by our own efforts (as in learning a language later on in life). He also wants to stress the extent to which language is part of human society: it not only communicates the social but constitutes it. And finally, Dante wants to show us that language is always material, and thus *always part of the external world*.

In this—his unequivocal identification of the material nature of the sign—Dante is most radical and innovative.[3] The materiality of signs is what we see last, since the whole point of using signs is to communicate meanings. The communication of meaning through signs inevitably has as one of its effects the veiling of the materiality of the signs. We tend to be aware of the material properties of signs only when they prove inadequate for the purposes of communication.[4] The moment that we identify and acknowledge the materiality of the signs by which we construct and communicate meanings, however, a new possibility is given for understanding the nature of language. Language now belongs to the world by virtue of its materiality, and thus becomes part of the externality, or reality, of the world. Its locus cannot therefore be confined purely to human internality. By virtue of its materiality, language can now be thought and indeed applied in ways that are outrightly concerned with the material world order, which is to say that language can now become *cosmological*.

Dante's insight regarding the material nature of the sign and thus the materiality, or externality, of language opens up a new cluster of interrelated themes. Language, body, and world are thematically unified in Dante's thought. Language and body are related in that in both, the expressivity of signs comes to the fore in their material form. Word *means;* body *lives.* A dead body no longer lives but is still material; an unheard or uncomprehended word sounds but does not mean. Language, further, is utterance from within the body, which, according to Merleau-Ponty, makes us "like crystal."[5] Words are formed in breath. And both the living body and the meaningful word are situated at the border between the subjective and objective orders of experience. Our words and our bodies exist for us but also for others. The hand that touches is itself touched, as Merleau-Ponty has it, and the word uttered expresses my own mental states, which are communicated to the mind of another. This borderland between subjectivity and objectivity is another way of speaking about "world," as the place where I exist as a self-aware, sentient being in a shared space and time, which is the ground of community with others.

None of this will be surprising to phenomenologists concerned with perception, but nevertheless the link between language and body through the material nature of the sign is a deeply unmodern way of conceiving of things. It frankly contradicts, for instance, the immensely influential account of signs by another phenomenologist, Edmund Husserl, as set out in his *Logical Investigations,* which (paralleling the work of Gottlob Frege) disassociates language from the material world. It does, however, begin to resonate with the "turn to the letter" which we have seen recently in the work of Geoffrey H. Hartman and Jacques Derrida.[6]

The first place in the *Commedia* at which language as human communication comes strikingly into view in all its materiality is in canto 3 of the *Inferno* (where the uncommitted and pusillanimous are). The sounds of Hell that meet the pilgrim's ears include "sospiri, pianti e alti guai" (22) [sighings and complaints and howlings]. Later in canto 3 we have a classic description of the language of the damned:

> Diverse lingue, orribili favelle,
> parole di dolore, accenti d'ira,
> voci alte e fioche, e suon di man con elle

> facevano un tumulto, il qual s'aggira
> sempre in quell' aura sanza tempo tinta,
> come la rena quando turbo spira.
>
> (25–30)

[A jumble of languages, deformities of speech, / Words which were pain, with intonations of anger, / Voices which were deep and hoarse, hands clapped together, / Made altogether a tumult, round and round, / Unceasingly in that air in which all was colourless, / Just as it might be in a perpetual sandstorm.]

Let us note: this description in fact places the material properties of the communicating signs over the meaning of the signs. In other words, matter destroys communication and, with it, the sociality of language. Language has become like "sand," deadening, homogeneous in the sense of admitting no distinctions, and dry. The "language" is expressive, indeed deeply so, of human conditions of lament and pain, though generally it is a debased humanity made present to us in this way. In canto 6, for instance, where Cerberus is, there is a reference to spirits who "[u]rlar ... come cani" (19) [howl like dogs]. The angry and sullen of canto 7 "[q]uest'inno si gorgoglian ne la strozza" (125) [gurgle this hymn in their throats]. In Hell, even Virgil, Dante's enlightened guide (and shining example of natural reason), stumbles in his speech at the confrontation with evil when they come to the gates of the City of Dis, so that the pilgrim surmises that he may have misread his guide's "parola tronca" (9.14) [broken phrase]. And in canto 24, as they proceed into deeper Hell, the pilgrim hears "una voce ... / a parole formar disconvenevole" (65–66) [a voice / which did not seem designed for forming words]. This is the same episode in which sinners exchange their bodies for that of serpents and burn up.

What the *Inferno* teaches us, therefore, is that human language cannot survive the distortions, fragmentations, and inversions of the human body which the pilgrim witnesses there, and which reflect different degrees and kinds of sin. Human language in Hell seems vulnerable to the same merciless, unconstrained natural forces that beat upon the bodies of the damned. The breakdown of language thus signals the collapse of community, leaving only isolated and fractured instances of individual subjectivity (still communicated in the bare expressivity of the sounds); and this breakdown is itself intrinsically part of the failed human interaction that characterizes Hell as a whole and that we witness as the pilgrim struggles to understand and communicate with those he meets on this part of his journey through the medieval cosmos.

Purgatorio, on the other hand, begins to show sound and language in a quite different light. The earlier cantos include references to the singing of penitential psalms as the souls labor up the side of the mountain of Purgatory. Here, language returns to its sociality and becomes the shared resource of the "work song" and of psalms which express penance and thanksgiving for divine mercy. Later cantos include many more songs of praise and thanksgiving. In canto 12, Dante the pilgrim offers a commentary on the distinction between the language of Purgatory and Hell when he says:

> Noi volgendo ivi le nostre persone,
> '*Beati pauperes spiritu!*' voci
> cantaron sì, che nol diria sermone.
>   Ahi quanto son diverse quelle foci
> da l'infernali! ché quivi per canti
> s'entra, e là giù per lamenti feroci.
> (109–14)

[While we were turning our bodies there / Voices were singing: '*Beati pauperes spiritu*,' / And no words can tell how sweetly they sang. / Ah, how different these approaches are / From those of hell! For here we have songs / As we go in, and there ferocious laments.]

In *Paradiso* the singing becomes multipart and aetherial, the musical quality of the human voice is enhanced, and dance becomes a central motif which integrates the voice and the body in a total act of rejoicing, praise, and celebration. *Paradiso* 12, with its description of the dancing theologians, is a fine example:

> Sì tosto come l'ultima parola
> la benedetta fiamma per dir tolse,
> a rotar cominciò la santa mola;
>   e nel suo giro tutta non si volse
> prima ch'un'altra di cerchio la chiuse,
> e moto a moto e canto a canto colse;
>   . . . .

> Poi che 'l tripudio e l'altra festa grande,
> sì del cantare e sì del fiammeggiarsi
> luce con luce gaudïose e blande,
>   insieme a punto e a voler quetarsi,
> pur come li occhi ch'al piacer che i move
> conviene insieme chiudere e levarsi . . .
> (1–6, 22–27)

[As soon as the blessed flame had taken / The last word up, to speak it, there began / A revolution of the sacred millstone; / And it had not turned once completely / Before another circle closed around it, / So joining movement with movement, song with song . . . / When the dance and the great festival / Alike of singing and of glowing lights, / One with another, in joy and gentleness, / Had reached, in a single will and moment, its end, / Like eyes which, in the pleasure that directs them, / Cannot help being raised and closed in unison . . .]

A significant new, though related, point of departure appears at this point: we encounter, in the reference to "eyes," a motif arising from the field of nonverbal communication.

As we recall from Dante's comments in *De vulgari eloquentia*, angels do not need language to communicate; they do so immediately. Here, Dante is in line with medieval angelology, specifically that of Thomas Aquinas, who says of angels that they do not need to speak at all but choose to speak when either praising God or teaching.[7] Angels, like baser animals, stand as a definitional limit with respect to what constitutes the human. The *Commedia* shows us that human nature shades towards animality at the lower pole and towards the angelical at the higher. The new communicative thematic I am suggesting here, to complement that of ordinary speech, is not the angelic, however, although it is intimately bound up with angelic communication, specifically in respect to its ability to function directly or nondiscursively, from mind to mind, without looping through the body, as it were. But angels, who are still substances, have no need of bodies. Theirs is an intelligence that is powerful enough to know and to communicate without dependence upon the knowledge that comes to us through the senses. This is one of the critical differences between ourselves and angels, again for both Thomas Aquinas and Dante. Thomas speaks of angels as creatures who retained the full power of the original goodness of creation—they are unfallen as it were, with some celebrated exceptions—and thus signify to us, who *are* undoubtedly fallen and compromised in all manner of ways, what it is that we can one day become. This is an important point, for in *Summa Theologiae* I, question 57, Thomas draws an analogy between the communicative luminosity of the angelic mind and our own resurrected bodies of the future. He says of the latter: "the brightness of the risen body will correspond to the grace and glory in the mind; and so will serve as a medium for one mind to know another." In other words, in our ultimate corporeal state, we will communicate as the angels do, but of course we will do so through the transparency of the now glorified human body (glorified through the glorification of Christ's own body).

This angelogical background gives us a way of understanding something that seems to play a fundamental role in Dante's embodied semiotics: the smile and light from the eyes (or "flashing eyes"). This theme is introduced very early on, with the first appearance of Beatrice, who is ultimately to teach and to lead the pilgrim on his journey. As Virgil tells him, in explaining how Beatrice came to ask Virgil to rescue Dante,

> Lucevan li occhi suoi più che la stella;
> e cominciommi a dir soave e piana,
> con angelica voce, in sua favella . . .
> (*Inf.* 2.55–57)

[The shining of her eyes was more than starlight; / And she began to speak, gently and quietly, / With the voice of an angel, but in her own language . . .]

Beatrice's eyes, or more precisely, the light or brightness in her eyes, will play a critical role at several points in the pilgrim's ascent towards God. He seems to see *through* her eyes at *Paradiso* 1.64–69, where we read how his gazing upon Beatrice causes him to rise up and to become aware of a new world around him:

> Beatrice tutta ne l'etterne rote
> fissa con li occhi stava; e io in lei
> le luci fissi, di là sù rimote.
>   Nel suo aspetto tal dentro mi fei,
> qual si fé Glauco nel gustar de l'erba
> che 'l fé consorto in mar de li altri dèi.

[Beatrice was standing with her eyes firmly fixed / Upon the eternal heavens; and I kept mine / Fixed upon her, and so away from them. / Looking at her I became such within / As Glaucus was when he tasted the grass / Which made him, in the sea, one with other gods.]

The pilgrim is empowered by the fullness of Beatrice's gaze, as we see from his reflection in the *Paradiso* on his journey through Hell and Purgatory:

> Giù per lo mondo sanza fine amaro,
> e per lo monte del cui bel cacume
> li occhi de la mia donna mi levaro . . .
> (17.112–14)

[Down in that world which is bitter without end / And up the mountain from whose lovely summit / The eyes of my lady raised me up . . .]

On another occasion Beatrice tells him not to look upon her and asks why he does not look directly at the heavenly realities around him:

> Perché la faccia mia sì t'innamora,
> che tu non ti rivolgi al bel giardino
> che sotto i raggi di Cristo s'infiora?
> (*Par.* 23.70–72)

[Why does my face so fascinate you / That you do not turn to the beautiful garden / Which, under Christ's rays, bursts into flower?]

While earlier we find:

> Vincendo me col lume d'un sorriso,
> ella mi disse: "Volgiti e ascolta;
> ché non pur ne' miei occhi è paradiso".
> (*Par.* 18.19–21)

[Conquering me with the light of a smile, / She said to me: 'Turn round and listen; / Paradise is not only in my eyes.']

There is a sense, then, in which the pilgrim's perception—as he gazes upon his "Lady"—is turned outwards: what he sees *within* her deflects his gaze *out* into the world. Beatrice's eyes, Dante repeatedly tells us, are radiant and smiling. They communicate the divine light. The light from her eyes purifies his, as we read in *Paradiso* 26.76–78:

> così de li occhi miei ogne quisquilia
> fugò Beatrice col raggio d'i suoi,
> che rifulgea da più di mille milia.

[So from my eyes did Beatrice chase away / Every speck with the beams of her eyes / Which would shine from a thousand miles away!]

Smiles too, like eyes, are frequently brilliant and radiant in the *Commedia*. Like eyes, smiles are also the communicative foci of a transfer and sanctifying communion between one sanctified human being and another, as we see in *Paradiso* 31.49–51, where Dante notes of the saints:

> Vedëa visi a carità süadi,
> d'altrui lume fregiati e di suo riso,
> e atti ornati di tutte onestadi.

[I saw faces full of charity, / Lit by another's light and their own smiles, / And gestures which bore all the marks of honour.]

The flash of the eyes and the smile are bodily gestures, and thus also maintain the particularity of human identity at the very moment when the body attains its highest semiotic and distinctively nonverbal—which is to say, nondiscursive or "angelic"—expression, itself signifying the light that fills the celestial cosmos and is "l'amor che move il sole e l'altre stelle" (*Par.* 33.145) [the love which moves the sun and the other stars].

As the reader follows the pilgrim on his ascent, we come vicariously, through the deixis and indexicality of the literary text, to share the transformation of his human body. There is also an important sense in which, for the medieval reader, the act of reading is internal to this vicarious sharing, since, in Dante's own time, texts display, with the truth of art, the character and destiny of the world. Here, Dante's own linking of "nature and art" (or perhaps "art and reality" would be a better way of putting it) is relevant. Art communicates nature and is a child of nature. Both issue from the supreme art of the divine creator:

> ... natura lo suo corso prende
>   dal divino 'ntelletto e da sua arte;
> e se tu ben la tua Fisica note,
> tu troverai, non dopo molte carte,
>   che l'arte vostra quella, quanto pote,
> segue, come 'l maestro fa 'l discente;
> sì che vostr' arte a Dio quasi è nepote.
>   (*Inf.* 11.99–105)

[... nature takes her direction from / The divine intellect and from its arts; / And if you pay attention to your *Physics*, / You will find there, somewhere near the beginning, / That your art follows nature, as far as it can, / Much in the way a student follows his master; / So that your art is the grandchild of God.]

The question of transformation inevitably takes the theologian into new areas of concern. While the literary critic can more easily rest content with transformation as such, as a discrete thematic, the systematic theologian must ask: what kind of transformation, transformed by what power? The next part of my essay will be concerned with the nature and ground of that transformation which Dante manifests in his own "work of language," in his "art," as a function of the deeper and greater transformation which he believes to be characteristic of the world and of humanity.

We can begin by reviewing briefly the possibilities. In the first place, it might be useful to point out that the pilgrim's journey cannot correspond to the typically "mystical" paradigm of *excessus*, or flight of the soul from the body. Thomas Aquinas identifies only Moses and St. Paul as having experienced this phenomenon.[8] Most importantly, *excessus* signals an entrance into Heaven and a vision of God that is essentially disembodied or detached from the senses.[9] Whatever else it may be, the pilgrim's ascent through the spheres is clearly an embodied one. We might then be able to understand the transformation not as an *excessus* but rather as a form of, or grounded in, the Transfiguration.[10] This happened before the death of Christ and so is consistent with the pilgrim's own premortem state. Transfiguration motifs are frequent in the *Vita nuova*.[11] Rather than reading the *Commedia* as narrating an ascent through the spheres of the Christian universe, perhaps we should read it rather as a fiction of cosmological display, whereby the Christian cosmos is dramatically and imaginatively performed around the pilgrim's own transfigured body. In other words, we might say that Dante's cosmic journey remains grounded in the "transfiguration" of his own body in the presence of the living, transformative body of Beatrice, thus giving a full Christian expression to the Platonic vision of his earlier years. The advantage of this reading is that it also gives full expression to the evident continuities between the *Vita nuova* and the *Commedia*; it proposes that the project of the *Commedia* remains in some sense within the structure of the vision of Beatrice in the *Vita nuova*, just as the latter finds its consummation in the *Commedia* in a new articulation of its meaning in Christian cosmological terms. And yet this reading quickly finds its limits. Dante is fundamentally concerned with those who have lived out their mortal lives and who now inhabit the cosmos differently (in Hell, Purgatory, or Heaven), *post mortem* and subjected to divine judgment. But transfiguration is paradigmatically the advent of glory in a *mortal* state. The body of Christ after his resurrection is understood not to be transfigured as such but to be glorified.

We may gain some help from a very striking passage (*Par.* 33.127–33) in which Dante seems to be telling us that he sees the *incarnate* Son in the Trinity, when he discerns, in that circle of the Trinity which appears to be a reflection, something that he describes as "nostra effige" (131) [our effigy]. Along with knowledge, the pilgrim becomes aware within the Trinity of the distinctly bodily act of smiling:

> O luce etterna che sola in te sidi,
> sola t'intendi, e da te intelletta
> e intendente te ami e arridi!
> (124–26)

[O eternal light, existing in yourself alone, / Alone knowing yourself; and who, known to yourself / And knowing, love and smile upon yourself!]

This is an intriguing crux within the work as a whole. Not only does it summarize the place of the smile for Dante throughout the *Commedia* as a uniquely human act; its occurrence in the Trinity, without any direct reference to the body of Christ which underlies this smiling, also points, for this systematic theologian, to a quite different, scriptural text. That text pervades premodern thinking about the cosmos and ultimate human destiny, although it is so fundamental that it is infrequently thematized as such.

The description of St. Paul's encounter on the road to Damascus with the risen and ascended Christ (Acts 9:3–19; 22:6–16; 26:12–18) is important for reading the *Commedia* for all kinds of reasons. In the first place, Dante is concerned with the triumphant Jesus in Heaven, "seated at the right hand of the Father" (to use the language of the Creeds and of Psalm 109). This embodiment of Christ "in glory" is not to be confused with the post-resurrection earthly embodiment, which, according to the post-resurrection appearances of the New Testament, involved some element of identifiable and objectifiable materiality (Thomas touches the risen Christ, for instance, who on other occasions eats fish).[12] To affirm this distinction does not undermine the continuity of the former with the latter. Following the deep cosmological changes of the sixteenth and later centuries, however, the Christian Church no longer really relates to the ascended or glorified Christ. The Heaven in which, for premodern readers, Christ continues to exist *in loco* (with a continuing human body now totally glorified and transformed) has for us almost wholly disappeared. Heaven is not a "place" for us, albeit an unusual one, as it was for Thomas or Dante, but is now a metaphor for spiritual exaltation. The medieval cosmological principle that physical height and spiritual exaltation are coterminous is utterly alien to us and as bizarre as the pre-heliocentric cosmology of Dante's day. We simply pass over comments such as that of Thomas Aquinas where he argues that the ascended body of Jesus must physically occupy the highest point in Heaven, since anything that is above it would be "more noble" than the body of Jesus.[13] Likewise, the extended discussions on the Eucharist at the time of the Reformation seem strange to us now in their insistence, across Luther, Zwingli, and Calvin (echoing the views of Thomas) that the body of Jesus still exists substantially, which means physically, in Heaven.[14]

The significance, then, of the account in Acts of St. Paul's encounter with the exalted Christ—an event occurring after the Ascension—is that it alone gives us an authoritative source for the way in which the exalted Christ—still wounded and embodied—might be perceived by human eyes. St. Paul's account is informative because, although he stresses that the same Jesus Christ was revealed to him as was revealed to the other Apostles, he nowhere fills in this humanity in sensible terms—quite unlike the content of the post-resurrection appearances. We are left with the theological mystery of a body which is still human (according to Christian orthodoxy) but also now radically transformed by the divinity that is part of Jesus Christ's nature. Dante's gesture towards the "smile" seems precisely to capture the "disembodied" embodiment, the radically transformed humanity (or what Luther thought of in terms of "ubiquity"), which is at the heart both of St Paul's paradoxical description and of the traditional Christian affirmation that Jesus still exists physically in Heaven, by virtue of the perfect *humanity* which—though transformed—remains fundamental to his nature.

The ascension of the glorified, victorious Christ sounds throughout Dante's *Commedia*:[15] Christ has gone before. This was not an insignificant proceeding for premodern Christians. Thomas states that the Ascension is "the cause of our salvation,"[16] and in the fourth century Leo the Great's sermon on the Ascension, on the occasion of the institution of that feast in Rome, points to the central importance of the Ascension for salvation and the possibility of eternal life:

> Et reuera magna et ineffabilis erat causa gaudendi, cum in conspectu sanctae multitudinis supra omnium creaturarum caelestium dignitatem humani generis natura conscenderet, supergressura angelicos ordines, et ultra archangelorum altitudines eleuanda, nec ullis sublimitatibus modum suae prouectionis habitura, nisi aeterni Patris recepta consessu, illius gloriae sociaretur in throno, cuius naturae copulabatur in Filio. Quia igitur Christi ascensio, nostra prouectio est, et quo praecessit gloria capitis, eo spes uocatur et corporis, dignis, dilectissimi, exultemus gaudiis et pia gratiarum actione laetemur.
>
> ---
>
> [There was great and indescribable cause for rejoicing when, in the sight of the holy multitude, above the dignity of all heavenly creatures, the nature of the human race went up, to surpass the ranks of Angels and to rise beyond the heights of the Archangels, to have its being uplifted limited by no sublimity until, received to sit with the eternal Father, it was associated on the throne of His glory, to whose nature it was joined in the Son. Since, therefore, Christ's Ascension is our uplifting, and the hope also of the Body is raised to where the glory of the Head has preceded it, let us exult, dearly beloved, with worthy joy, and be glad in a pious thanksgiving.][17]

The transformation of which Dante speaks and which he enacts cosmologically through his art is the primary transformation of the Christian Gospel: it is the glorification of Christ's humanity by which humanity was made perfect for Heaven and the cosmos was restored in a new creation. The loss of Heaven from our cosmos had the effect that the Christian community no longer related meaningfully to the concept of a truly human and therefore mysteriously embodied Christ, whose only possible site was Heaven itself.[18] Whatever the disagreements between Catholics and Reformers, and among the Reformers themselves with respect to the nature of the sacramental presence of Christ in the Eucharist, all were agreed that Jesus, in his continuing humanity, was in a state of glory in Heaven, to where we too, after judgment, might follow him.

But what have we learned from this necessarily brief theological reading of a premodern literary text?[19] We have inhabited a world as it existed before the occurrence of a deep cosmological shock, when the world, which at least from the point of view of ultimacy was widely believed to be much as Dante describes it, turned out not to be like that at all. It was not light, music, and warmth up there, but darkness, silence, and cold. The cosmos was not finite but infinite. The border between the spiritual reality and the earthly one was not located at the highest point of a finite universe. It was not located anywhere at all. What is interesting is that Dante has brought before us, through his literary medium, a foundational dimension of Christianity, which we have pretty much forgotten: namely, the ubiquity (to use Luther's word) of the exalted and glorified Christ. In its traditional form, that ubiquity was predicated upon the "overflow effect" of glory located at great height. Ephesians 4:7–10 is the governing text,[20] though its theme occurs on many occasions in the scriptures. The identification of physical height with spiritual exaltation is a quintessentially premodern commitment, which was utterly shattered by the scientific advances of the later sixteenth century. To read Dante is to be reminded of what a powerful image this is, but that it is an image. And once we have understood that, and read the text from the perspective both of the medieval and the modern reader, simultaneously or in dialogue with each other, we can begin to detach the image or cosmology from the Christology. We thus can begin the task of retrieving something that was fundamental for scriptural, patristic, medieval, and Reformation Christianity alike: the concept of the continuing, living, or ascended body of Christ as a matter of *doctrinal* rather than cosmological integrity. In other words, the reading of this literary text as both literature *and* theology has created a horizon of possibility for us today to think and to imagine the world that we share with Dante in ways that are new.

Notes

Translations of the *Commedia* are taken from Dante, *Divine Comedy*, tr. Sisson.

1. See, for instance, George Pattison's discussion of Kierkegaard in this light in his *Kierkegaard and the Crisis of Faith*. See also Günter Bader's masterly account of early Romantic views of language in his "Geist und Buchstabe."
2. We must remember that all this applies also to texts in which materiality is present to sight rather than hearing.
3. Botterill translates "sensuale" in *Dve* 1.3 as "perceptible" (or once, "perceptible to the senses"), showing a preference for pulling the word back towards cognition rather than allowing it its full, material resonance as being external to the human mind.
4. Heidegger's distinction between *Vorhandenheit* and *Zuhandenheit* is useful here; we only really look at the hammer when it breaks in our hand (*Sein und Zeit*, 75 and 106).
5. Merleau-Ponty, *The Visible and the Invisible*, 144: "Like crystal, like metal and many other substances, I am a sonorous being, but I hear my own vibration from within. . . ."
6. The prominence of this in Derrida's work is more generally known, but see Hartman, *Easy Pieces*, 194.
7. *ST* Ia.107.
8. *ST* IIaIIae.175.3.ad1.
9. St. Paul states that he did not know whether he was in the body or not when he was taken up to the "tertium caelum" (2 Cor 12:2–3) [third heaven]. Thomas argues that it is conceivable that St. Paul remained in his body as long as his intellect was withdrawn from his senses. In *Paradiso* 25.118–29, St. John points out that only two had entered the Empyrean in their resurrected bodies, Jesus and Mary (by participation). Dante would seem to be opposing the notion, therefore, that this had been the experience of either Enoch, Elijah, or St. John himself.
10. See Steven Botterill's reading of the pilgrim's ascent as a form of *raptus* (*Dante and the Mystical Tradition*, 194–241). This account, however, seems to underplay the pilgrim's continuing materiality. Peter Hawkins has an interesting approach in his discerning of the echoes of medieval pilgrimage in the pilgrim's

ascent. He asserts that "the whole of the *Commedia* can be said to represent a pilgrimage from the city of man to the city of God" (see *Dante's Testaments*, 247–64; quotation at 251).

11. I discuss this question in my "World and Body."
12. Jn 20:24–29; 21:4–14.
13. *ST* IIIa.57.4–5.
14. See my section on "Doctrine" in Davies, Janz, and Sedmak, *Transformation Theology*, 11–62, for further discussion of this point.
15. It does so with particular prominence, of course, from *Paradiso* 23.19 onwards. In this respect, I note that a full reading of the meaning of *Paradiso* 26.76–78, discussed earlier in this essay, should take into account how, earlier in the same canto (10–12), the transformative power of Beatrice's eyes is directly associated to the power that, through Ananias, transforms Paul following the vision on the road to Damascus.
16. *ST* IIIa.57.6.
17. Leo the Great, "Incipit de Ascensione Domini (I. VI. 444)," 4. Translation from Jurgens, *The Faith of the Early Fathers*, 3:279.
18. This is mapped in many texts, but see in particular Randles, *The Unmaking of the Medieval Christian Cosmos*, and Grant, *Planets, Stars and Orbs*. I have summarized some of this material in Davies, *The Creativity of God*, 16–21.
19. The interested reader can find a much more detailed exposition of this theology, with references, in Davies, Janz, and Sedmak, *Transformation Theology*.
20. "[U]nicuique autem nostrum data est gratia secundum mensuram donationis Christi. Propter quod dicit 'ascendens in altum captivam duxit captivitatem; dedit dona hominibus.' Quod autem ascendit quid est nisi quia et descendit primum in inferiores partes terrae? Qui descendit ipse est et qui ascendit super omnes caelos ut impleret omnia." [But to every one of us is given grace, according to the measure of the giving of Christ. Wherefore he saith: *Ascending on high, he led captivity captive, he gave gifts to men*. Now that he ascended, what is it, but because he also descended first into the lower parts of the earth? He that descended is the same also that ascended above all the heavens, that he might fill all things.] (Douay-Rheims translation.)

7

Dante's Davidic Journey
From Sinner to God's Scribe

THERESA FEDERICI

Dante's debt to the Psalms—the biblical book that, to many of its interpreters, contained the wisdom of the whole Bible in its words—is widely acknowledged, as is the influence of the biblical figure whom he believed to be its single author: King David.[1] In Dante's time, David was considered a sinner, a penitent, a just man, and an exemplary ruler. He was the psalmist, a divinely inspired *auctor*, a prophet, and a figure of Christ to come. The Book of Psalms was read as a compendium of precepts applicable to every aspect of the human condition. It functioned as a moral guide: in imitating the David of the Psalms, Christians could live a virtuous life. From Augustine onwards, the Book of Psalms was also seen as offering the most complete Christological prophecy of the Old Testament. The crucial importance of the Psalms to medieval society is clear from the attention given to this biblical book by commentators.[2] For the Church Fathers, for medieval monastic institutions, and for the devout laity, the Psalms of David played a fundamental role in both communal worship and private prayer.

Among his many biblical allusions and borrowings, Dante makes particular use of King David both as a character and as a poet.[3] On various occasions throughout the *Commedia*, Dante uses the figure of David in all his embodiments. This essay analyzes the ways in which Dante draws on established late medieval viewpoints about David and uses them for his own purposes. The breadth of Dante's biblical and classical borrowings and allusions is well known, as is the fact that Dante adopts no one biblical or classical author as his dominant literary model. Keeping this breadth and complexity in mind, however, I will argue for the importance of David and the Psalms in the construction of the *Commedia*. Images of David pervade the *Commedia* from beginning to end, and Dante's appropriation of Davidic characteristics both validates the intrinsic message of salvation found in the poetry of the *Commedia*—the work to which "ha posto mano e cielo e terra" (*Par.* 25.2) [both Heaven and earth have set their hand]—and also gives a divinely chosen precedent for the image of the pilgrim Dante as the archetypal penitent.

The image of David obviously most appropriate for Dante's use in *Inferno* and *Purgatorio* is that of the archetypal penitent. This image is almost exclusively connected with Psalm 50, the *Miserere*—a psalm that had a highly significant role in church ritual and penitential acts. This psalm is used or alluded to in each of Dante's *cantiche*, but is of particular importance in *Inferno* and *Purgatorio*, where the pilgrim learns about sin and penitence in general and about his own sin, resulting in his own crucial moment of penitence in the Earthly Paradise. For centuries, David the penitent had been perceived as an exemplary model of repentance, and in the *Commedia* Dante creates an analogous role for the pilgrim, presenting him as a "new David," a role model for his own times. As Robert Hollander has rightly noted, "the David who sinned in his love for Bathsheba and who for a time was denied his kingdom by his enemies was a natural figural precursor of Dante, a sinner in his false love and a political exile. The cry of the penitential psalmist found a ready way to the penitential Dante."[4] The medieval image of King David that is first appropriated by Dante for the pilgrim is that of sinner and penitent, and it is emblematically evoked by the first words of Psalm 50 in the pilgrim's first words to Virgil: "*Miserere* di me" (*Inf.* 1.65) [Have mercy on me].

Should David function in any way as a model for Dante in *Paradiso*, clearly it will not be in terms of sinner or penitent. The final citation of Psalm 50 in *Paradiso* 32, however, invites the reader to look back over the whole of the pilgrim's journey to the dark wood of sin and that first exclamation of *Miserere*. Dante's poetic abilities are of particular thematic importance in *Paradiso*, as he focuses on his mission to describe his journey as he saw it and to transcribe truthfully the words of the blessed, as he has been selected to do. In Dante's presentation of himself as God's vernacular poet we find the image of David as a literary forerunner. Dante is writing a "poema sacro" (*Par.* 25.1) [sacred poem], just as David is the "sommo cantor del sommo duce" (*Par.* 25.72) [highest singer of our Highest Lord] and the "cantor de lo spirito santo" (*Par.* 20.38) [he ... wrote songs inspired by the Holy Spirit]. Dante adopts the medieval image of David as psalmist and appropriates it to himself in order to enforce his self-presentation as a new, vernacular singer of God's message.

As a prelude to considering the significance of David and the Psalms in *Inferno* and *Purgatorio*, I provide a brief overview of notions of penitence and confession in the Middle Ages, in order to locate Dante's use of Davidic imagery within the religious practices and beliefs of his age. I then examine the uses of Psalm 50 throughout the *Commedia*. The analogous roles of David and the pilgrim, both in terms of sin and in terms of penitence, demonstrate that Dante aimed at presenting his contemporaries with a new model for repentance. In discussing Davidic imagery in *Paradiso*, I also assess the extent to which Dante presents himself as a divinely inspired poet following the Davidic model, and the degree to which this Davidic imitation allows him to make claims about his own authorial status and the status of his language.

The split between, on the one hand, Dante as David the sinner appropriated for *Inferno* and *Purgatorio* and, on the other hand, Dante as David the psalmist and divinely chosen poet found in *Paradiso* may seem irreconcilable. In late medieval exegesis, however, both facets of David's life were equally accepted and acknowledged. As Alistair Minnis puts it, "authors like David and Solomon had on occasion been divinely inspired, but they had sinned as well; yet respect for their authority had come to be regarded as perfectly compatible with recognition of their humanity. David was esteemed to be the greatest of the prophets: he was also a pattern of penitence, a man whom every sinner was urged to identify with and emulate."[5] By adopting characteristics that reflect both the sinful and the divinely inspired aspects of David, Dante echoed contemporary understandings of David.

The Psalms and Medieval Notions of Penitence

The pervading and enduring importance of the Psalms in medieval monastic and clerical life is clear. The Divine Office was based on the recitation of particular Psalms, and its form developed from the words of the Psalms themselves.[6] Many monastic houses required the weekly, or sometimes daily, recital of the entire book. The Psalms formed a crucial part of ecclesial worship not only for the clergy but also for the lay congregation. Psalms accompanied the faithful through all the major celebrations of the Christian calendar, and antiphons from the Psalms accompanied readings from other biblical books.[7] St. Paul urged his followers to praise God using the Psalms, and many of the Church Fathers describe the Book of Psalms as containing all aspects of the human condition.[8]

Psalm 50, one of the seven penitential psalms, held an important place within both monastic and secular Church ritual during the Middle Ages. In monastic services it was the second psalm to be sung every day during the dawn service of Lauds. In secular services it was the first psalm to be sung every weekday during Lauds, and, during the penitential season, that is, from Septuagesima (nine weeks before Easter) to the Triduum (Maundy Thursday, Good Friday, Holy Saturday), it was also sung on Sundays during Lauds. With its links to repentance and to God's capacity for forgiveness when confronted with a truly contrite heart, the nature of this particular psalm is clearly appropriate to the penitential periods in the Church calendar. Psalm 50 therefore had a strong affiliation with the Lenten period leading up to Easter. During the Triduum the first psalm to be sung at Lauds was an antiphon from the *Miserere*, and the service ended with the silent recital of the same psalm.[9] (In some churches the Maundy Thursday mass, which the whole community would attend, included a ceremony for the reception of penitents back into the community of the Church.) The daily singing of Psalm 50 and the general reception of the psalm as an ethical guide towards salvation would make this psalm a cultural commonplace, easily recognizable by Dante's contemporaries and known by heart by many. Although the word *miserere* can be found frequently in the Old Testament and in the liturgy (indeed two other Psalms—55 and 56—open with the words *Miserere mei*), in church services in the Middle Ages the term *Miserere* was used specifically to refer to Psalm 50.

During the Middle Ages the Psalms had a dual function. Not only were they considered the private, poetic expressions of David's sentiments, but they also had a public function as a work of reference for ethical issues and problems. The Book of Psalms could be seen as a moral guide, and King David as a moral authority. Many medieval secular authors and theologians believed that "imitating David could mean bringing together the private and public significances of psalm discourse, as a means of asserting the essential relationship between the renewal of the individual soul and the reform of society itself."[10] Psalm 50 played a significant role in the reception of the Book of Psalms as a source for guidance and as a model for repentance. For many commentators, including Augustine and Cassiodorus, the *Miserere* represents David's defining moment as a moral *exemplum*. As Cassiodorus puts it:

> Hinc est quod dam in hoc libro septem psalmi poenitentium esse doceantur, Ecclesiarum usu receptum est; ut quoties peccatorum venia petitur, per istum magis Domino supplicatur, non immerito. Primum quoniam in nullo psalmorum quae poenitentibus maxime necessaria est, tanta virtutis humilitas invenitur, ut rex potens et in porphetali cumine constitutus, tanquam extremus hominum sua festinaverit peccata deflere. Deinde quia post absolutionis promissionem tanta se constrinxit necessitate lacrymarum, quasi ei minime fuisset ignotum. . . . Nam potest hic et illud fortassis intelligi; idea eum in hoc psalmo dixisse: *Doceam iniquos vias tuas, et impii ad te convertentur:* quoniam praevidebat sequentes populos per istum psalmum copiosissimae poenitentiae munera petituros.[11]

> [This is the reason why, though seven Psalms of penitents are taught in the book, it has become customary in the Church that whenever pardon for sins is sought, the Lord is entreated through this one, and rightly. First, because in no psalm is such virtuous humility—an attitude particularly necessary for penitents—displayed, that a powerful king, set on a prophet's pedestal, hastened to lament his sins as the most abject of men; second, because after the promise of forgiveness he bound himself with such constraints of tears as if he had not been forgiven at all. . . . Perhaps a further meaning is to be grasped here: that the psalmist said in this psalm: Let me teach the unjust thy ways, and the wicked shall be converted to thee, because he foresaw that in the future people would through this psalm seek the gifts of most abundant repentance.]

Both in his deeds and in his words, David provides all Christians with a model of repentance that instructs others to imitate his example of true contrition. It is not surprising to find that the image of David as a penitent sinner is central to the medieval doctrine concerning penitence. Penitence was of fundamental importance to medieval life, and, as Gillian

Evans puts it, "almost every baptised person in the mediaeval West would accept that all human beings are sinners who *deserve* to be punished, by a God whose justice may express itself in mercy and prove to be full of surprises, but cannot compromise the divine and ultimate standard."[12]

The ritual action of the faithful asking forgiveness from God has taken place throughout the history of Christianity; but the precise form of the sacrament of confession took shape only at the end of the Middle Ages. During Dante's lifetime this doctrine was still evolving, and it contained aspects that could be found throughout Western Christendom alongside many regional idiosyncrasies. Thomas Tentler identifies the four consistent elements of the doctrine: "First, to be forgiven, sinners have always been required to feel sorrow at having lapsed. Second, they have consistently made some kind of explicit confession of their sins or sinfulness. Third, they have assumed, or had imposed on them, some kind of penitential exercises. And fourth, they have participated in an ecclesiastical ritual performed with the aid of priests who pronounce penitents absolved from sin or reconciled with the communion of believers."[13]

The doctrine of private penance and auricular confession that was predominent in the later Middle Ages represented a significant modification of previous systems. In this doctrine, "penances were made lighter and more arbitrary; contrition became the essential element for the penitent and pushed penitential exercises into a subservient position; private confession, already accepted as a necessary part of the forgiveness of sins, was declared universally obligatory by the Fourth Lateran Council of 1215; and the meaning of the priest's role was more carefully defined and its importance in the process of forgiveness radically enhanced."[14] *Omnes utriusque sexus*, canon 21 of the Fourth Lateran Council of 1215, came to be one of the most influential documents of church history. In this canon, the faithful are obliged by law to attend confession once a year at Easter. Confession to one's local parish priest became a legal requirement under pain of excommunication.

In the thirteenth century the doctrine of confession continued to be elaborated, as did the practice. The most important developments in penitential doctrine were articulated by St. Thomas Aquinas, who, following Peter Lombard, believed contrition to be the key act of repentance and the most important act in confession. Aquinas takes his doctrine further than that of his predecessors by clearly underlining the crucial importance of the (parish) priest in the sacrament of confession. Tentler summarizes Aquinas's doctrine thus: "Only the absolution of the priest . . . can apply the passion of Christ to the forgiveness of the guilt of sins. Thus, even though in the normal course of events the penitent becomes contrite and forgiven *before* he goes to confession and actually hears the words of absolution, that contrition is effective only by virtue of the power of the priest's absolution to relate the sinner's sorrow to the Atonement."[15] Aquinas's doctrine of absolution confirmed the fundamental importance of the priest in the act of confession and forgiveness of sins.

In Dante's time, "for the lay person confession was to be annual and to their own parish priest [and] the parish priest tending spiritual ills when hearing confession and imposing penance was compared to a physician tending wounds."[16] The varied nature of mid- to late-medieval confession, however, makes it very difficult to establish what actually took place between penitent and priest. As Alexander Murray states, "Confession, then, was individual, secret and unscripted."[17] That ritual acts of expulsion from the body of the faithful still took place in Dante's time may also be alluded to in the *Commedia*. In discussing the uses of penitential rituals in *Purgatorio,* John Barnes notes that "[p]ublic penance . . . was normal in Dante's day," and that "there seems to be a definite connection between public penance and Dante's encounter with the angel-doorkeeper [in *Purg.* 9], who, like the bishop, is sitting—this being a sign of authority and dignity."[18]

The centrality of penitence and confession was further enhanced, in Dante's time, by the Franciscan preachers, for whom penitence was an essential part of existence and "la 'penitenza' è lo 'stato' dell'uomo che riconosce Dio . . . l'unica possibile condizione per l'uomo davanti a Dio"[19] ["penitence" is the state of the man who recognizes God, . . . the only possible condition before God]. For Ida Magli, St. Francis "rappresenta la realizzazione totale della cultura penitenziale" [represents the total realization of the culture of penitence].[20] The place of penitence and confession within medieval society cannot be underestimated; in Dante's time, "confession is a part of, and penetrates deeply into, the lives of ordinary people."[21] The close associations between the exemplary nature of David's sin and repentance, the *Miserere,* and church ritual increase the significance of Dante's appropriation of these elements of Davidic imitation in the *Commedia*.

The *Miserere* in the *Commedia*

In the *Commedia*, Psalm 50 is referred to either directly or indirectly on six occasions. It is first alluded to in *Inferno* 1 when the pilgrim says "*Miserere* di me" (64) [Have mercy on me]. It then makes four appearances in *Purgatorio*, one in Ante-Purgatory (*Purg.* 5.24), one within the realms of Purgatory proper (*Purg.* 23.10–12), and two in the Earthly Paradise (*Purg.* 30.82–84, 31.98). Finally, the psalm is used in the Empyrean to refer to David himself (*Par.* 32.12).

The references to the psalm that occur in *Purgatorio* before the Earthly Paradise do not directly denote the strong penitential link between David and Dante that forms the most important role for this psalm in the *Commedia*. They are, however, significant and enrich our understanding of Dante's conception of penance. In Ante-Purgatory, the psalm is sung by the souls of the late-repentant, who are "cantando *Miserere*" (*Purg.* 5.24) [chanting *Miserere*]. The psalm is appropriate to the souls here and serves as a warning to others not to leave repentance to the last moment. Despite the predominance of auricular confession and inner contrition, clearly the notion of leaving repentance to the last moment was still common in Dante's time. These souls sing the *Miserere* while waiting. They should have sung it after they sinned, as Augustine, in his letter *De poenitentibus*, explains. Augustine expresses his doubts as to whether someone who leaves his confession to the last minute has a direct path to salvation. Using King David's repentant cry from Psalm 50 and from 2 Samuel 12:13 as a model of penitence, Augustine argues that in uttering the words "I have sinned," David opened the pathway to salvation.

> Si quis autem positus in ultima necessitate aegritudinis suae, voluerit accipere poenitentiam, et accipit, et mox reconciliatur, et hinc vadit; fateor vobis, non illi negamus quod petit, sed non praesumimus quia bene hinc exit.... Agens poenitentiam, et reconciliatus cum sanus est, et postea bene vivens, securus hinc exit. Agens poenitentiam ad ultimum et reconciliatus, si securus hinc exit, ego non sum securus.

> [But any who find themselves in the last throes of their illness, and wish to receive penance, and do receive it, and are straightaway reconciled, and so depart this life—I confess to you, we don't deny them what they ask for, but we cannot take for granted that they make a

good departure. Those who have done penance, and been reconciled while in good health, and after that lead good lives, can depart this life with nothing to worry about. But those who are doing penance to the very last moment, and are then reconciled, whether they have nothing to worry about as they depart this life, I myself cannot be so sure.]²²

The belief that deathbed penance, if genuine, opens the door to salvation but in a less sure way than the immediate confession of a sin, may be reflected in Dante's use of Psalm 50 here. Psalm 50 is used again by the gluttons on the sixth terrace of Purgatory (*Purg.* 23.10–12). They sing "*Labïa mëa, Domine*" (11) through their tears. This particular verse of the psalm is invoked here because the souls did not use their mouths in praise of God during their lifetime, but used them to gorge on food and drink. The reference is appropriate to the sin of gluttony, which is being purged here. Their mouths, the source of their sin, are now the source of their penance.

But the key use of Psalm 50 within the *Commedia* is based on its strong links with David's moment of repentance. Psalm 50 was the archetypal penitential psalm, and in his penitence, David was the archetypal model penitent. And in the *Commedia*, the pilgrim takes on the traditional role of David as model penitent. The first words the pilgrim speaks while lost in the dark wood of sin are "*Miserere* di me ... / qual che tu sii, od ombra od omo certo!" (*Inf.* 1.64–65) [Have pity on my soul, ... whichever you are, shade or living man!]. David, the penitential psalmist, prefigures Dante the penitent. Thus, from the outset the analogy between the two sinners is established. The link is reinforced in the penultimate canto of *Paradiso*, when David's great-grandmother, Ruth, is periphrastically introduced as "colei / che fu bisava al cantor che per la doglia / del fallo disse '*Miserere mei*'" (*Par.* 32.10–12) [she / who was the great-grandmother of the singer / who cried for his sin: '*Miserere mei*']. Dante and David, therefore, are the two figures in the *Commedia* who are reported as saying *Miserere* for their sins. Dante is presenting himself as a type for David in both the guilt of sin and the righteous act of contrition. To understand the links Dante creates between David and the pilgrim and their significance to the *Commedia* as a whole, we must look into the nature of David's sin and of his moment of repentance, as well as into the way in which Dante constructs similar circumstances for the pilgrim in his poem.

The Sins of David and the Sins of Dante-Pilgrim

The *Miserere* held particular significance within church ritual and biblical commentary because it describes the moment at which David repented of his horrendous sins of adultery and murder. The biblical account of David's sin and repentance is told in 2 Samuel. It refers to his sin of adultery with Bathsheba: "dum haec agerentur accidit ut surgeret David de stratu suo post meridiem et deambularet in solario domus regiae viditque mulierem se lavantem ex adverso super solarium suum erat autem mulier pulchra valde . . . missis itaque David nuntiis tulit eam quae cum ingressa esset ad illum dormivit cum ea" (2 Sam 11:2–4) [in the meantime it happened that David arose from his bed after noon, and walked upon the roof of the king's house: and he saw from the roof of his house a woman washing herself, over against him: and the woman was very beautiful. . . . And David sent messengers, and took her, and she came in to him, and he slept with her].

This sin is compounded by David's sin of indirect murder, in sending her husband, Uriah, into a battle from which David knew he would never return: "ponite Uriam ex adverso belli ubi fortissimum proelium est et derelinquite eum ut percussus intereat" (11:15) [Set ye Urias in the front of the battle, where the fight is strongest: and leave ye him, that he may be wounded and die]; "et mortuus est etiam Urias Hettheus" (11:17) [Urias the Hethite was killed also]. The prophet Nathan is sent by God to David in order to make him realize the nature of his sin. Nathan reveals David's sin to him through an allegorical story of a rich man who steals the only sheep belonging to a poor man. David, enraged by the rich man's behavior, is ready to exact moral judgment on this man: "Vivit Dominus, quoniam filius mortis est vir qui fecit hoc" (12:5) [As the Lord liveth, the man that hath done this is a child of death]. Nathan replies, "Tu es ille vir" (12:7) [Thou art the man]. In this moment David fully and consciously acknowledges his sin, saying, "Peccavi Domine" (12:13) [I have sinned against the Lord], and Nathan tells David, "Dominus quoque transtulit peccatum tuum: non morieris" (12:13) [The Lord also hath taken away thy sin: thou shalt not die]. In his contrition David is moved to write a psalm of penance—the *Miserere*. The sin for which he is repenting is disclosed in the title to the psalm: "Psalmus David cum venit ad eum Nathan propheta, quando intravit ad Bethsabee" (Ps 50:1) [Psalm of David when Nathan the prophet came to him, after he had sinned with Bethsabee]. In this psalm David prays for God's mercy and forgiveness: "Miserere mei Deus, secundum magnam misericordiam tuam: et secundum multitudinem miserationum tuarum, dele iniquitatem meam" (3) [Have mercy on me, O God, according to thy great mercy. And according to the multitude of thy tender mercies blot out my iniquity]; acknowledges his sin and repents of it: "Quoniam iniquitatem meam ego cognosco: et peccatum meum contra me est semper" (5) [For I know my iniquity, and my sin is always before me]; asks God to cleanse him from sin and from guilt: "Asperges me hyssopo, et mundabor: lavabis me, et super nivem dealbabor" (9) [Thou shalt sprinkle me with hyssop, and I shall be cleansed: thou shalt wash me, and I shall be made whiter than snow]; asks God to create in him a new heart and a new spirit: "Cor mundum crea in me Deus: et spiritum rectum innova in visceribus meis" (12) [Create a clean heart in me, O God: and renew a right spirit within my bowels]; and asks God to save him from death: "Libera me de sanguinibus Deus salutis meae" (16) [Deliver me from blood, O God, thou God of my salvation], so that he can proclaim God's righteousness: "et exsultabit lingua mea justitiam tuam / Domine, labia mea aperies: et os meum annuntiabit laudem tuam" (16–17) [and my tongue shall extol thy justice / O Lord, thou wilt open my lips: and my mouth shall declare thy praise] and teach sinners the way back to God: "Docebo iniquos vias tuas: et impii ad te convertentur" (15) [I will teach the unjust thy ways: and the wicked shall be converted to thee].

The pilgrim is, like David, also a sinner. Does Dante's Davidic imitation extend to an imitation of his sin? David's sins are those of adultery and, as a result, murder. The pilgrim knows himself to be guilty of the sin of pride (*Purg.* 13.136–38).[23] The sins for which he has to repent before ascending to Heaven, however, are not made known to him until he has reached the Earthly Paradise, when Beatrice confronts him in *Purgatorio* 30:

> Quando di carne a spirto era salita
> e bellezza e virtù cresciuta m'era,
> fu' io a lui men cara e men gradita;
>   e volse i passi suoi per via non vera,
> imagini di ben seguendo false,
> che nulla promession rendono intera.
>   (*Purg.* 30.127–32)

[When I had risen from the flesh to spirit, / become more beautiful, more virtuous, / he found less pleasure in me, loved me less, / and wandered from the path that leads to truth, / pursuing simulacra of the good, / which promise more than they can ever give.]

Beatrice charges him with having abandoned her in favor of a "cosa mortale" (*Purg.* 31.53) [mortal object], a "pargoletta / o altra novità con sí breve uso" (*Purg.* 31.59–60) [pretty girl / or ... other brief attraction]. Although the pilgrim's sin is left broadly undefined, it, like that of David, is linked with adultery. Beatrice, functioning as the pilgrim's personal guide to salvation, accuses Dante of a metaphorical form of adultery— in abandoning her, he loses sight of the true road to salvation. She continues to chastise him in *Purgatorio* 31 so that next time he hears "le serene" (*Purg.* 31.45) [the Sirens] he will be better able to resist.

It is worth noting here that in his *Vita di Dante*, Boccaccio, when listing Dante's defects, states that in his character "trovò ampissimo luogo la lussuria, e non solamente ne' giovani anni, ma ancora ne' maturi" [lust found a large place, and not only in his youth but also in his mature years].[24] After commenting on lust as a natural and common defect, Boccaccio proceeds to list others who have sinned in the same way. He rejects the classical predecessors as fictional and instead places Dante amongst the biblical lustful—Adam, Solomon, and, notably, David. "E David, non ostante che molte n'avesse, solamente veduta Bersabé, per lei dimenticò Iddio, il suo regno, sé e la sua onestà, e adultero prima e poi omicida" [And David, although he had many women, once he had seen Bathsheba, through her forgot God, his kingdom, himself, and his honour, and became first an adulterer and then a murderer].[25] Although David is guilty of both adultery and murder, clearly his defining sin is that of adultery— murder is a corollary effect of his desire for Bathsheba. Dante has never been accused of murder, yet Beatrice's words to the pilgrim indicate that the pilgrim's defining sin is also that of (a metaphorical) adultery. Augustine points out that David's fall took place in a time of stability, not adversity, in which "tumor excrevit" [his pride grew to excess], providing a further lesson that "timeamus felicitatem" [we must beware of complacency].[26]

Both David and Dante in their analogous sins of adultery can legitimately function as ethical *exempla* for all forms of sin, not just their specific instances of sinfulness. Concerning medieval notions of sin,

Michael Kuczynski states that "the particular sins of adultery and homicide were collapsed by Talmudic and Christian exegetes into the general sin of pride. And since pride, according to medieval hamartiology, is the root of sin, David can therefore function as an instance of human sinfulness in its most general sense." He adds that the sin of adultery "has a high if veiled moral use, in that it typifies the predicament of all who are 'conceived in iniquity'—all men and women."[27]

David's and the pilgrim's parallel sin of pride/adultery and parallel contrition when confronted with their sin allow both poets to become role models of repentance. Through David's humanity Dante can create the parallel between David the penitent sinner and Dante-pilgrim the penitent sinner, role models who are both effective and accessible to mankind precisely owing to their humanity. They are *like us*: conceived in iniquity and constantly carrying the "vinculum mortis" [chains of death] associated with sin; "nemo nascitur nisi trahens poenam, trahens meritum poenae" [each of us is born dragging punishment along with us, or at any rate dragging our liability to punishment].[28]

Model Penitents and Moral Prophets

Dante imitates David in the first two *cantiche* as a model of repentance. The sins of both men are so great that they have brought them close to death; in verse 16 of the *Miserere*, David prays to God to save him from death, and in *Inferno* 2, Lucia asks Beatrice if she can see how close the pilgrim is to death. The death that both David and the pilgrim face is a moral death resulting from the seriousness of their sins. The pilgrim, like David, is guilty of enormous sin, yet both are saved through repentance. Their salvation demonstrates God's benevolence and mercy when confronted with genuine contrition. In verse 16 of the *Miserere*, David also promises God that on his salvation he will use his voice to proclaim God's justice, a role that Dante takes upon himself. David proclaims God's justice through the example of his own experiences, just as Dante does in the *Commedia*. Dante is imitating David in becoming a contemporary *exemplum* in his righteous act of penitence. Through his example he hoped others would be moved to begin their own Davidic imitation.

At this point it is pertinent to recall another of David's incarnations in hagiographic traditions: that of *propheta*. This is perhaps one of the more unlikely titles applied to David. It is important to remember that he was a king, and, as James Kugel notes, "prophets, that is, messengers sent by the God of Israel with some divine commission, are dispatched *to* kings with words of divine reproach, encouragement, or advice."[29] David, therefore, has a prophet—Nathan. Yet even by the time of writing of the New Testament, David was himself considered a prophet and the Psalms were taken as a direct prophecy of the life of Christ. According to this view, David divinely foretells the coming of Christ, who would be born into his family line. Thus, from the early commentary tradition and certainly from Augustine onwards, the Psalms were interpreted in terms of this prophetic vision and their subject matter was Christ.[30]

David's sin, however, was problematic for many of the commentators, from the Church Fathers up to the twelfth century, who advocated a prophetic interpretation of the Psalms. Exegetes who adhered to a Christological view of the Psalms felt compelled to gloss over the nature of David's sins with elaborate allegory. There was a significant problem in the notion that a *scriba dei*, a vessel of the divine word, could be tainted with sin. In Dante's time, however, David's humanity was emphasized. The providential role previously accorded to David, within which he functions predominantly as a type for Christ, divests him of his humanity and lessens his impact as a *human* role model for mankind. Christ is simultaneously both human and divine. David, however, is man, not God made man, and as such, he does not take away the sins of the world as Christ does; human penitence, as exemplified by David, cannot absolve original sin. Yet the example set by David—a divinely selected human being—can provide the model of repentance for individual sins. David did commit terrible sins, but he truly repented from these and was therefore saved. He thus becomes an excellent model for humanity. As Alistair Minnis states, "In twelfth-century exegesis, what may be called David's personal 'good character' (as opposed to his divinely-ordained function as a *figura*) was established mainly by brief reference to his sin and repentance.... This interest in common humanity and common problems is a most striking development of the exemplary aspect of David's authorial role."[31]

Just as David had to acknowledge his own sins, the sins of David must be acknowledged by all, in order for others to learn from his example. When he is accredited with his own humanity, he can function both as a type for Christ and as King David in his own right, a human being, albeit selected by God for a specific function, who can sin but who can also repent and who—significantly—can write about his experience in his own way, through the poetry of the Psalms. Kuczynski states that "medieval writers insist that the Psalter only makes coherent literal and allegorical sense when grounded in the facts of Davidic history."[32] In fact, the title of prophet, when applied to David in the Middle Ages, had another very important meaning. David, the archetypal model of penitence, was considered a supreme example of a moral prophet. "According to Thomas Aquinas and others, one of the prophet's key functions is not to have visions of the future, but to teach common people by means of similitudes or figures—an essentially educative or didactic role."[33] To view David as a moral prophet reveals the importance of the Psalms as a work in which ethical solutions to individual problems and the problems of society could be sought.

The Psalms were never perceived on only one level: they were understood as the personal articulations of David's sentiments, but they also had a powerful social and moral function, speaking on behalf of everyone. His sins cannot and, indeed, must not be evaded or ignored; they are an important warning and example, one that is fundamental to becoming a good Christian. In his *Enarrationes in Psalmos* Augustine explains that "Deus noluit taceri quod uoluit scribi" [God wanted the matter to be written about].[34] David's transgression and subsequent composition of the *Miserere* were part of God's plan. The prophet Nathan is sent to David so that David may understand his sinful act and repent. David's destiny was to fall into sin so that others could learn from his example. It was, therefore, precisely his sin and his subsequent repentance that made David a powerful model for all Christians. As a king he is a model for all rulers; as a divinely inspired psalmist he is a model for all poets; but in his humanity, in his ability to forget his kingly status, acknowledge his sin, and repent of it, he is a model for all mankind.

Dante seeks to establish a similar role for the pilgrim. In the dark wood of *Inferno* 1, however, the pilgrim is even further ensconced in sin than David was, for he no longer knows to whom he should direct his repentant cry, nor indeed what it is that he needs to repent of. Hollander notices that "Dante, more lost than even David was, has forgotten to whom he should make his petition ('Dio' is replaced—at least it is so when we remember the words of the psalm which is in part the model for Dante's speech—by 'qual che tu sii')."[35] In the very first canto of *In*-

ferno, the pilgrim cries *Miserere* to the first human figure he sees, even before he knows it is Virgil. This is, however, neither the correct moment for confession nor the correct person to hear the confession. It could be argued that the function of Virgil in *Inferno* 1 is reminiscent of the role of Nathan to David, in that it is Virgil who extracts the word *Miserere* from the pilgrim—he becomes the pilgrim's confessor. Niccolò Mineo recognizes the correlation between the two: "Virgilio così sembra inserirsi nella catena delle tipologie ed assimilarsi a Natan, lui profeta pagano" [Thus, Virgil, the pagan prophet, seems to take his place in the typological chain and to assimilate himself to Nathan], and he concludes that "avremmo molti motivi per vedere nella figura apparsa a Dante misteriosamente, in Virgilio, un analogo di Natan" [we have many reasons to see, in the figure that mysteriously appears to Dante, in Virgil, a figure analogous to Nathan].[36]

In ascribing the role of Nathan to Virgil, however, caution is in order. There are many reasons why Virgil is not the correct person to hear the pilgrim's confession. For one, Virgil cannot grant the pilgrim absolution. The pagan poet, despite the blind prophecy of Christ in his fourth Eclogue, remains just that, a pagan poet. He neither knows nor understands God and will thus remain for eternity in Limbo. What is more, he is not aware of the pilgrim's sins; he is aware only of his own role in the pilgrim's journey. Unlike Nathan, Virgil is unable to confront the pilgrim with the sins that have brought him to the dark wood. Virgil can only elucidate on the special grace granted to the pilgrim so that he may be reunited with Beatrice. Virgil is merely obeying the request of another intermediary; he has been sent by Beatrice as a guide to take the pilgrim on a journey back to her—to Beatrice. Beatrice will lead the pilgrim to God and forgiveness, not Virgil. The pilgrim's true moment of contrition lies before him: in *Inferno* 1 he is not ready for it.[37]

Neither David nor the pilgrim were aware of their sin before it was revealed to them; both have to learn how to recognize sin in others before they are able to recognize it in themselves. David does not recognize himself in Nathan's story until the direct revelation, "Thou art the man." The poet explains that he is not aware of how he ended up in the dark wood: "Io non so ben ridir com' i' v'intrai" (*Inf.* 1.10) [How I entered there I cannot truly say]. In order fully to understand the severity of his sin, the pilgrim must first journey through Hell and Purgatory. The moment of revelation of the pilgrim's sins appears much later in the *Commedia*, when he has arrived at the Earthly Paradise. Here, the only thing left to purge is the memory of sin; and it is here that the pilgrim's sins are revealed to him.

Beatrice, I would argue, not Virgil, takes on the role of Nathan in extracting the pilgrim's confession. After her Christ-like apparition, the Beatrice in the Earthly Paradise is a fearsome judge, whose anger and scorn at the pilgrim's transgression invokes the pity of the angels and prompts them to sing up to verse 9 (in the Vulgate numbering) of Psalm 30. These verses underline the hope that a true believer has in God. The angels are rewarding the pilgrim for his hope and for his arrival at a state of grace. "Ella si tacque; e li angeli cantaro / di sùbito '*In te, Domine, speravi*'; / ma oltre '*pedes meos*' non passaro" (*Purg.* 30.82–84) [As she stopped speaking, all the angels rushed / into the psalm *In te, Domine, speravi*, / but did not sing beyond *pedes meos*].

Beatrice reprimands them for singing a song of hope at this time: her purpose is to make the pilgrim match his guilt with grief. The pilgrim must first repent of his sins with true and heartfelt contrition. The Anonimo Fiorentino explains in his commentary to these lines that the angels could not sing beyond that point because "quello che seguia del Salmo dice: *Miserere mei, quondam tribulor*; et l'Auttore era in punto di consolazione et non di tribulazione" [that which follows in the psalm says: *Have mercy on me, O Lord, for I am afflicted*; and the author was at a point of consolation not tribulation].[38] As this example illustrates, for many commentators only the first nine verses, those which concern hope and praise, were appropriate to the pilgrim's situation. There are, however, a great number of psalms of praise that Dante could have selected instead of Psalm 30.[39] Furthermore, Psalm 30 was used in an abridged form in church ritual, the first six verses being sung daily at Compline.[40] Making the angelic choir stop after the ninth verse instead of the sixth verse is, therefore, incongruous with the liturgical use of the psalm and draws the reader's attention to the part of the psalm the angels do not sing. Hollander has rightly concentrated on the notion that the next line is *in*appropriate, since the quotation of *Miserere mei* would immediately invoke Psalm 50 and David's act of contrition before Nathan.[41] Dante implicitly reintroduces the *Miserere* moments before the pilgrim's act of repentance. It would be entirely inappropriate to hear the word *Miserere* before the pilgrim's moment of full confession. The angels stop at *pedes meos* for that reason: Dante's moment of penitence still lies ahead of him.

The angels' song anticipates Dante's confession, and the reader is left waiting for the *Miserere mei*.

In the opening tercets of *Purgatorio* 31, we find Dante's true and heartfelt confession and penance. Beatrice forces him to answer to her charges, saying: "dì, dì se questo è vero: a tanta accusa / tua confession conviene esser congiunta" (*Purg.* 31.5–6) [Speak now, is this not true? Speak! You must seal / with your confession this grave charge I make!]. He breaks down and, wracked with guilt and shame, confesses to his sin, that of abandoning Beatrice and the *diritta via:* "Piangendo dissi: 'Le presenti cose / col falso lor piacer volser miei passi, / tosto che 'l vostro viso si nascose'" (34–36) [Weeping I said: 'Those things with their false joys, / offered me by the world, led me astray / when I no longer saw your countenance']. Beatrice, like Nathan, makes the sinner aware of his sin. Beatrice exposes the pilgrim's sin in a role analogous to that of Nathan, who "brought the sin out from behind David's back, and held it before his eyes."[42] Beatrice continues, emphasizing the pilgrim's humanity. He will return to earth and will once more have to be watchful for sin (43–45). Beatrice proceeds to present the pilgrim with his sins at great length so as to help him avoid any future transgressions on his return to earth.

The strength of the pilgrim's realization of his sin and his repentance of it is so overwhelming that it causes him to faint (*Purg.* 31.85–89). However, only after Dante's full confession and repentance can he be cleansed of sin. True to medieval doctrine on confession, only heartfelt contrition and repentance can lead to God's mercy. Beatrice acknowledges the pilgrim's genuine penitence, saying: "Se tacessi o se negassi / ciò che confessi, non fora men nota / la colpa tua: da tal giudice sassi!" (*Purg.* 31.37–39) [Had you kept silent or denied / what you have just confessed, your guilt would still / be clear to the great Judge who knows all things]. Just as Nathan is David's personal intercessor, both hearing David's confession and delivering the message of divine absolution, so too, Beatrice is the pilgrim's personal intercessor in his moment of contrition and confession, thus providing him with the divine message of absolution from his sins and permission to be carried through the waters of Lethe. As the pilgrim is being drawn through the river Lethe, the angels can then sing the words from Psalm 50, "*Asperges me*" (*Purg.* 31.98).

In this instance it appears that Dante intended the *Commedia* to function as a didactic guide for society that is consistent with the rites of the Church. Dante is creating links between his poem and church ritual in his use of Psalm 50. Beatrice, like Nathan, has heavenly approval to judge the sincerity of her charge's confession and absolve him of his sins. Beatrice, like the medieval priest, takes on the role of judge and representative of the heavenly court. Clearly, the pilgrim is unique in that his intercessor is at one and the same time both the aggrieved and the administrator of justice. In his use of an intercessor, in the form of Beatrice, Dante employs the Davidic model of contrition and repentance, with Beatrice in the role of Nathan, in combination with the medieval necessity for an intercessor. The link between the pilgrim's confession in Earthly Paradise, Psalm 50, and medieval doctrine is made explicit by some of the early commentators on the *Commedia*. The *Ottimo Commento*, for instance, indicates the important role of Psalm 50 within church ritual:

> *Asperges*, ch'è un verso del salmo penitenziale—*Miserere mei Deus, secundum magnam misericordiam tuam* etc., si dice quando per lo prete si gitta l'acqua benedetta sopra il confesso peccatore, il quale elli assolve, e dice: Signore, bagna me con isopo, e mondificami: laverai me, e sopra la neve diverrò bianco. Lo quale l'Autore bagnato in Lete introduce, per mostrare ch'egli è lavato di tutti suoi peccati, e massimamente qui di quello della lussuria.

> [*Asperges* is a line from the penitential psalm—*Have mercy on me, O God, according to thy great mercy* etc. that is said when the priest sprinkles holy water over the confessed sinner who is absolved by the priest and says *thou shalt wash me, and I shall be made whiter than snow*. The author, washed in the waters of the Lethe, introduces this psalm to show he has been washed of all his sins, and mainly here that of lust.][43]

Dante has now undergone his ultimate act of penitence, like David in the psalm. Both now have salvation in God, and both have been cleansed. With a clean heart and a new spirit, both are fitting vessels for the divine Word and can now use their voices in praise of God.

From the moment the pilgrim found himself in the dark wood of sin to the moment he is cleansed of all sin through his full confession and contrition, Dante is drawing a comparison between the pilgrim and David the Penitent. Using Davidic imitation, Dante has established for himself—through the experience of sin and repentance—the status of a role model for humanity. Like David, the poet is recording his own personal experience for the benefit of all, and again like David, God is presented as having chosen this role for him. Both poets have been saved by the direct intervention of Heaven due to the special grace they have both been accorded. Despite their transgressions and human weakness, they still hold privileged status with God. Once the pilgrim has passed through the waters of Lethe, however, he has been cleansed of all sin; and therefore the model of David the archetypal Penitent is no longer appropriate. This does not mean that Dante's Davidic imitation ceases. David has other characteristics that Dante is able to appropriate for himself; and in *Paradiso* David's role as a psalmist is of greatest importance.

God's Poets

Throughout *Paradiso*, Dante emphasizes David's role as the psalmist, the singer of God. When David is pointed out to the pilgrim in the eye of the eagle in the Heaven of Justice, where he is exalted for his virtue as a Just Ruler, he is described as "il cantor de lo Spirito Santo" (*Par.* 20.38) [he ... wrote songs inspired by the Holy Spirit]. From his place in Heaven, David now knows "il merto del suo canto" (*Par.* 20.40) [the value of his Psalms], that is, the extent to which the Psalms were his own work and the extent to which they were the work of the Holy Spirit. In this great celebration of David, Dante is also highlighting the point that, although David is responsible for the form of the Psalms, their content, God's message, is divine and from the Holy Spirit. David is God's highest poet and as such becomes a model for all poets. The figure of David the psalmist is a means for Dante to explore questions of authorship, self-definition, and literary genre. As many scholars have noted, these themes culminate in *Paradiso* 25, a canto of fundamental importance in understanding Dante's self-presentation as a *scriba Dei* in the *Commedia*.[44] One of the principal ways in which Dante alludes to his status as an *auctor* is through his own relationship with David the psalmist.

Paradiso 25 is set in the Heaven of the Fixed Stars, where the pilgrim undergoes an examination on the three theological virtues: faith, hope, and love. Before St. James begins to examine Dante on the virtue of hope, special attention is drawn to the exceptional nature of Dante's hope.

Beatrice announces that "[l]a Chiesa militante alcun figliuolo / non ha con più speranza" (52–53) [There is no son of the Church Militant / with greater hope than his]. As confirmation of this, Dante responds to St James: "'Spene,' diss'io, 'è uno attender certo / de la gloria futura, il qual produce / grazia divina e precedente merto'" (67–69) [I said "Hope / is sure expectancy of future bliss / to be inherited—the holy fruit / of God's own grace and man's precedent worth"]. The classical authors cannot bring hope to Dante. They do not know God, and they remain in Limbo, "sanza speme" (*Inf.* 4.42) [cut off from hope].[45] Virgil cannot function as a guide to spiritual salvation, just as he cannot function as a confessor—a Nathan figure—to Dante-pilgrim's David figure in *Inferno* and *Purgatorio*. Dante has to look to scripture to provide him with a model for the *Commedia*, his own song in praise of God: "Da molte stelle mi vien questa luce; / ma quei la distillò nel mio cor pria / che fu sommo cantor del sommo duce" (*Par.* 25.70–72) [From many stars this light comes to my mind, / but he who first instilled it in my heart / was highest singer of the Highest Lord]. So it was the Psalms that first brought hope to Dante; Dante finds his inspiration in David's song in praise of God—his *tëodia*, specifically Psalm 9: "'Sperino in te', ne la sua tëodia / dice, 'color che sanno il nome tuo': / e chi nol sa, s'elli ha la fede mia?" (73–75) ["Let them have hope in Thee who know Thy name," / so sings his sacred song. And who does not / know of That Name if he has faith like mine?].[46]

Here Dante is doing more than simply stating that his hope comes from reading the Psalms. He is establishing close ties between himself and David as an *auctor*. This correlation between David and Dante is strengthened by the first tercet of *Paradiso* 25. Dante's *Commedia* is a "poema sacro / al quale ha posto mano e cielo e terra" (1–2) [sacred poem / to which both Heaven and Earth have set their hand]. Both the Psalms and the *Commedia* are sacred poems in which a human author has chosen verse to communicate the divine message of salvation. Dante implicitly seems to be elevating his *poema sacro* to a status similar to that of the Psalms. As Teodolinda Barolini notes, "the term *tëodia*, 'divine song,' coined to describe the Psalms, is easily transferred to Dante's own *poema sacro*: needing a new descriptive term for his new genre, Dante invents it with the rest of the *Comedy*'s basic poetic baggage, its structure, form, and meter. True to his fundamental procedural principles of appropriation and revision, he first appropriates a standard rhetorical term, *comedìa*, and then—having redefined it from within as a *poema sacro*—replaces the original with a new one: *tëodia*." Dante is therefore "the author of the new *tëodia*."[47] It should also be noted, however, that Dante does not use this term for his poem.

Language and Authority

Dante is not, in fact, writing a second *tëodia*; he is doing something slightly different. In *Paradiso* 25, it appears that Dante puts his *comedía* in comparison with David's *tëodia* so as to suggest the literary superiority of his own genre. He is challenging David on a literary level. Dante does not claim superiority over the Psalms on a level of content; this is impossible since the message is from the Holy Spirit—divine, perfect, and unsurpassable. What Dante does suggest, however, is that his message is also in some way divinely inspired, and that his poetic talent is, on a strictly human level, in a sense superior to that of biblical authors.

Dante praises David's abilities—he *is* the "sommo cantor del sommo duce" [highest singer of the Highest Lord]—but at the same time suggests that David is limited to the genre of *tëodia* as his mode of expressing the divine Word. Dante, on the other hand, in his *comedía*, has created an all-encompassing, encyclopaedic, plurilingual work. Unlike the more restrictive genre of *tëodia*, Dante's *comedía* can talk about all things in all styles; in this sense, his literary talents are "greater" than David's. Dante can take his song in praise of God, his *poema sacro*, beyond the literary expectations and abilities of the psalmist. The implications of Dante's comparison between his own *comedía* and David's *tëodia* are, as Zygmunt Barański has argued, that "rather than just simply place himself on a par with David, Dante, as he did with secular authors, measures himself against him and suggests his own artistic superiority."[48]

As suggested by works of criticism such as those by Barolini and Barański quoted above, Dante attempts to create an identity for himself as a divinely inspired *auctor*, thus taking his place in a chain of *scribae Dei*. Dante presents himself as God's new author. In his answer to St. James, he states that he first gained hope through the Psalms and that his second source of hope was St. James himself: "Tu mi stillasti, con lo stillar suo, / ne la pistola poi; sì ch'io son pieno, / e in altrui vostra pioggia repluo" (*Par.* 25.76–78) [And in your own epistle you instilled / me with

his dew, till now I overflow / and pour again your shower upon others].
He has been filled with the hope that has been rained down on him by
these authors. It is now Dante's turn. As Hawkins puts it, "thus, when
St James asks in canto 25 how he learned to hope, Dante's answer is a
genealogy of authors and texts that culminate in himself."[49] Dante is creating a chain from the Old Testament to the New Testament to himself,
as the new bearer of God's message on earth.

With his reference to David the divine poet, Dante is also justifying his use of verse. The great importance of David as a literary model
is undeniable. Kugel states that "David the prophet had an afterlife. It
concretised the connection of poetry and prophecy for later ages as no
other biblical figure or theme did. Thenceforth, a poet, at least a divinely
inspired one, might *eo ipso* also be a prophet, and poetry itself (soon:
'verse') was thus at least one of the forms that prophecy might take....
This association of poetry and prophecy went on to play a major role
in the intellectual and, particularly, literary life of Europe for two millennia."[50] Poetry is a fitting vessel for the divine Word, so Dante's *poema*
can be *sacro*. In *Paradiso* 25, for the only time in the *Commedia*, Dante
explicitly presents himself as a *poeta*. Kevin Brownlee notes that "*Paradiso* XXV, 8 contains the last, and—significantly—the thirtieth appearance of the word *poeta* in the *Divine Comedy*."[51] Dante had previously employed this term in the *Commedia* to speak about the classical poets Virgil
and Statius.

The status of Dante as the vernacular *poeta* who claims to be on a
par with biblical authors implies that the *Commedia* surpasses secular and
pagan *auctores* not only in content but also in terms of language. Dante's
new Christian poetic vernacular becomes the new language of efficacious prayer. The vernacular *poeta*—God's new poet—provides an ethical example of how to repent and live a good life through his own experiences. The suitability of the Italian vernacular as a vessel for God's
message is underlined in *Paradiso*. In *Paradiso* 25, Dante quotes from scripture in Italian: "'Sperino in te'... 'color che sanno il nome tuo'" (*Par.*
25.73–74) translates Psalm 9:11. The Latin version of the psalm is sung
later on by the whole of Heaven, congratulating Dante on his answer:
"'*Sperent in te*' di sopr' a noi s'udì" (*Par.* 25.98) [*Sperent in te* was heard
above us].

Brownlee comments on the importance of the two citations of the
same psalm and the implications. "It is this *vernacular* citation of psalm

9:11 that seems to determine the Latin of the Heavenly chorus that celebrates Dante's successful completion of his examination on the second theological virtue. . . . Not only does the Italian citation of psalm 9:11 precede the Latin in Dante's text, but it also is given in its entirety—in contrast to the abbreviated (even fragmentary) Latin citation of the same verse. It is as if the Latin were (paradoxically) presented as a 'translation' of the Italian."[52] The use of this psalm in Italian is a literary device to demonstrate the superiority of the Italian vernacular over the traditional Latin. Brownlee concludes that the use of Italian here is "the programmatic Heavenly vernacularization of Latin sacred texts" found during Dante's theological examination and is "linked to Dante's explicit and definitive self-presentation as *theologus*."[53]

The issues of authorship, self-presentation, language, and literary genre that culminate in *Paradiso* 25 are fundamental not only to Dante's relationship with the psalmist but also to the way in which Dante intended the *Commedia* to be read. The meticulously assembled literary construct that is the *Commedia* allows Dante to make claims about his own *auctoritas*. As Hawkins states, "He wants to shine in the Christian firmament as the brightest poet of the faith, the newest star."[54] Dante becomes God's new *auctor*, whose vernacular language and style can most effectively transmit His Word, and Dante's use of the Psalms within the *Commedia* plays an important role in creating this identity.

Poetry and Humility

Dante presents himself as a type for David in his role as a divinely inspired poet and in his sin and repentance. David's humility in acknowledging and repenting of his sin is strictly linked to his role as archetypal penitent and moral prophet. Just as pride is the base of every sin, St. Thomas, in the *Summa Theologiae*, notes that among the virtues, "humilitas primum locus tenet, inquantum scilicet expellit superbiam" [humility holds the initial place in that it expels pride] and also that "humilitas dicitur spiritualis aedificii fundamentum" [humility is said to be the foundation of the spiritual edifice].[55] In Psalm 50 David says that "exultabunt ossa humiliata" (10) [the bones that have been humbled shall rejoice] and refers to a "cor contritum et humiliatum" (19) [contrite and humbled heart]. It is therefore no coincidence that Dante chooses David as an *exemplum* of humility in *Purgatorio* 10. The incident, described in "visibile parlare" (*Purg.* 10.95) [visible speech], precedes David's sin with Bathsheba in the biblical account, but the use of David as an example of humility is all the more potent if we bear in mind his repentance of the sin of pride as epitomized in his cry of *Miserere*.

Given Dante's presentation of himself as God's chosen (contemporary) poet, it is not obvious how Dante can extend his Davidic imitation to emulate the virtue that corresponds to the sin of pride, namely, humility. However, within the text of the *Commedia*, the pilgrim is humbled many times over the course of his journey, particularly in Purgatory and Paradise. His confession of his sins to Beatrice in the Earthly Paradise can be seen as his defining moment of contrition for his sins, akin to that of David. Here, the pilgrim takes on the humble attitude of small children: "fanciulli, vergognando, muti / con li occhi a terra stannosi, ascoltando / e sé riconoscendo e ripentuti" (*Purg.* 31.64–66) [children scolded into silence stand / ashamed, with head bowed staring at the ground, / acknowledging their fault and penitent].

Yet Dante's corresponding humility can also be seen in his poetry, in his proud yet humble admission that he is carrying out God's bidding in recounting the journey "ond' io son fatto scriba" (*Par.* 10.27) [which makes of me its scribe].[56] Throughout the journey described in the poem, the poet hints at the providential nature of the pilgrim's mission. From the outset, the pilgrim humbly protests his inability to carry out his mission: "Io non Enëa, io non Paulo sono" (*Inf.* 2.32) [I am not Aeneas, I am not Paul]. In citing his classical and biblical precursors in a journey through the afterlife, Dante is making an important statement. In his humble protestations, he is also suggesting again his literary superiority—neither Aeneas nor St. Paul wrote about their experiences in the afterlife. Unlike David and Dante, who write firsthand about their experience, Virgil tells Aeneas's story, and God forbade St. Paul to speak of what he had seen in the third sphere of Heaven (2 Cor 12:1–6).

Barolini has argued convincingly that the literary construct of Dante's humility is manifest in the very fabric of his poem. Commenting on *Purgatorio* 10, she notes: "the exaltation of divine art at the expense of human art paradoxically leads to the exaltation of that human artist who most closely imitates divine art, who writes a poem to which Heaven and earth contribute, and who by way of being only a scribe becomes the greatest of poets."[57] In his adoption of the "comic" style,

Dante creates a correlation between his poetry and the authors of scripture: between the *sermo humilis* of the Old Testament and the *sermo piscatorius* of the New Testament, and his own comic style.[58] Barolini also notes, with reference to David's dance before the ark that makes him "e più e men che re" (*Purg.* 10.66) [both more and less than king]: "Dante's *poema sacro*, his *comedìa*, is both more and less than the king of poems, the *tragedìa;* as David's humility makes him more glorious, so the *comedìa*'s lowly standing makes it more sublime."[59]

Through his use of the Psalms, Dante implicitly creates a bond between his *Commedia* and the Book of Psalms, and between Dante the author of the *Commedia* and David the author of the Psalms. Following the medieval image of David, Dante wanted to be perceived as a penitent, a prophet, and a psalmist. By analyzing Dante's use of the Psalms and of the images of David, the extent to which they have a pervading influence throughout the *Commedia* becomes apparent and can enrich our understanding of Dante's masterpiece as a work with theological aims.

Dante employs many biblical and classical texts within his poem, all of which are of fundamental importance in understanding the *Commedia*. Concentrating on his use of the Psalms and the characteristics of David is thus only a relatively small contribution to a much larger debate. However, David and the Psalms merit a special place within this debate. No other biblical author offers Dante such a complete role model or provides such an unimpeachable literary precedent. In adopting Davidic characteristics, Dante is presenting himself as a new and exemplary model of repentance. "Like the sinful David, who with the help of God's grace became the Bible's preeminent moral prophet, others through virtuous living can become authoritative moral teachers. As David's life was exemplary for them, their lives may serve as examples to others."[60] Kuczynski's description of Davidic imitation reflects Dante's aims within the *Commedia*. Imitating David adds to the credibility of Dante's claim to have undertaken the journey, and to have been chosen for the journey by virtue of his own literary abilities. Barolini refers to this as Dante's "daringly humble imitation"[61] of David. Dante states that his poetic authority is based not on self-promotion but on humility, since he is carrying out a heavenly mandate. It is difficult to doubt Hollander's suggestion that Dante "may have thought of his own poem as being like one of David's, a poem that reflects historical events and which at least claims to be similarly inspired."[62] In selecting David as his poetic model, Dante is surpassing the classical *poetae* and aligning himself with the *scribae Dei* of the Bible. In writing the *Commedia*, Dante is humbly doing God's bidding. This humble Davidic imitation enables us to read the *Commedia* as Dante wants—even demands—it to be read, that is, as a theological enterprise.

Notes

Translations of the *Commedia* are taken from Dante, *Divine Comedy*, tr. Musa. The translation adopted for Augustine's *Enarrationes in Psalmos* is by Boulding.

1. For Dante the term *salmista* is used to refer to King David alone and not to a composite authorship. In this belief, Dante is following the views of St. Augustine and of St. Thomas Aquinas. Other Church Fathers and commentators, St. Jerome, for example, believed that David was one of many authors of the Psalms. For the general influence of David on Dante, see Truijen, "David"; Penna, "Salmo"; Benfell, "David"; Beal, "Psalms." For the most sustained accounts of the influence of David on Dante, see Barolini, *Undivine Comedy*, esp. chapters 6 and 10; Hawkins, *Dante's Testaments*, esp. 19–95; Kuczynski, *Prophetic Song*.

2. See Minnis, *Medieval Theory of Authorship*, and Kuczynski, *Prophetic Song*, for a comprehensive review of medieval attitudes towards David.

3. The bibliography on Dante's use of biblical texts is vast. See, for example, Barański, *Dante e i segni*; Barbi, *Problemi fondamentali*; Barblan, *Dante e la Bibbia*; Battaglia Ricci, *Dante e la tradizione*; Brownlee, "Why the Angels Speak Italian"; Charity, *Events and Their Afterlife*; Chydenius, *The Typological Problem*; Curtius, *European Literature*, chapters 12 and 17; D'Alfonso, *Il dialogo con Dio*; Dronke, *Dante and Medieval Latin Traditions*; Esposito, *Memoria biblica nell'opera di Dante*; Fallani, *Dante, poeta, teologo*; Hawkins, *Dante's Testaments*; Higgins, *Dante and the Bible*; Kleinhenz, "Dante and the Bible"; Marzot, *Il linguaggio biblico*; Mazzeo, *Medieval Cultural Tradition*; Meersseman, "Penitenza e Penitenti"; Mineo, *Profetismo*; Paolini, *Confessions of Sin*; Pertile, *La Puttana e il gigante*; Rigo, *Memoria Classica*. The above list is in no way exhaustive on the subject. See also the following note for critics writing on Dante and David specifically.

4. Hollander, "Dante's Use of the Fiftieth Psalm," 110. For the comparison between David and Dante as penitents, see this essay in full and Hollander's "Dante as Uzzah?" In these articles, Hollander puts forward the principal ways in which Dante sets up a comparison between David and Dante as sinners and as poets. Barolini, *Dante's Poets*, 269–86, demonstrates the way in which Dante identifies the pilgrim with David as the author of humble poetics of praise.

5. Minnis, *Medieval Theory of Authorship*, 214.

6. Holladay, *Psalms*, 175.

7. See Harper, *Forms and Orders*, chapter 5.
8. See, for example, Cassiodorus, "Praefatio," *Expositio Psalmorum*.
9. Harper, *Forms and Orders*, 141.
10. Kuczynski, *Prophetic Song*, xvii.
11. Cassiodorus, *Expositio Psalmorum* 50.
12. Evans, *Law and Theology*, 11.
13. Tentler, *Sin and Confession*, 3.
14. Ibid., 16.
15. Ibid., 24.
16. Biller, "Confession in the Middle Ages," 5.
17. Murray, "Counselling," 67.
18. Barnes, "Vestiges of the Liturgy," 244–45.
19. Magli, *Gli uomini della penitenza*, 79. Translations are mine.
20. Ibid., 76. Magli notes that the sermons of the Franciscans evolved to become encyclopaedic in their content, containing elements of theology, science, history, local customs and gossip, folklore, and jokes (Magli provides an exhaustive list), and that "L'uso del volgare è certamente l'elemento di maggiore successo per la predicazione popolare" [The use of the vernacular was certainly the most successful element in popular preaching] (87–88).
21. Biller, "Confession in the Middle Ages," 5.
22. Augustine, *De poenitentibus*, 1714.
23. There is another explicit analogy between the two poets in the sin of pride. In his humanity, David has the potential to fall back into sin after having repented of his sin with Bathsheba and having written the *Miserere*. He sins once again later in life through pride, by presumptuously and impiously commissioning a census of the people of Israel. David realizes his sin himself, saying, "Peccavi valde in hoc facto" (2 Sam 24:10) [I have sinned very much in what I have done]. This time David has to choose between famine, flight from enemies, or pestilence to appease God.
24. Boccaccio, *Trattatello*, 44; tr. Nichols, 59. See also Minnis, *Medieval Theory of Authorship*, 211–17.
25. Boccaccio, *Trattatello*, 44 (tr. Nichols, 60).
26. Augustine, *Enarrationes in Psalmos* 35 (tr. Boulding, 413).
27. Kuczynski, *Prophetic Song*, 26. This view can be seen clearly in Augustine's commentary on Psalm 50, particularly in his comments on verse 7, "Ecce enim in iniquitatibus conceptus sum": "Suscepit personam generis humani David, et attendit omnium vincula, propaginem mortis consideravit, originem iniquitatis advertit.... Numquid David de adulterio natus erat, de Jesse viro justo et conjuge ipsius? Quid est quod se dicit in iniquitate conceptum, nisi quia trahitur iniquitas ex Adam?" [David spoke in the person of the whole human race, and had regard to the chains that bind us all. He had regard to the propagation of death and the origin of iniquity.... But surely David was not born of adultery? Was he not the son of Jesse, a righteous man, and his wife? How then can he say

he was conceived in iniquity, unless iniquity is derived from Adam?]. St. Augustine concludes that "merito ergo in Adam omnes moriuntur, in Christo autem omnes vivificabuntur" [all die in Adam, all shall be brought to life in Christ] and "in Adam ... omnes peccaverunt" [in Adam all have sinned]. Augustine, *Enarrationes in Psalmos* 50.

28. Augustine, *Enarrationes in Psalmos* 50.
29. Kugel, "David the Prophet," 45.
30. See, for example, "Prothemata in Psalterium," *Glossa Ordinaria*, PL 842B.
31. Minnis, *Medieval Theory of Authorship*, 109.
32. Kuczynski, *Prophetic Song*, xx.
33. Ibid., xxii.
34. Augustine, *Enarrationes in Psalmos* 50.
35. Hollander, "Dante's Use of the Fiftieth Psalm," 111.
36. Mineo, *Profetismo*, 178.
37. The analogy between Virgil and Nathan is further undermined when one looks at the *fabula* of the *Commedia*. In the narrative time neither the pilgrim (nor the first-time audience) knows who the figure is. The cry is uttered before Virgil's identity is disclosed. The *Miserere* here is, perhaps, more indicative of the fearful state of the pilgrim than the prophetic functions of Virgil.
38. Anonimo Fiorentino, *Commento*, 2:491.
39. The Book of Psalms was commonly divided into three sections: *in poenitentia, in justitia*, and *in laude*. This can be seen in Peter Lombard's "Praefatio" to his *Commentarium in Psalmos* (57B) and also in the "Prothemata in Psalterium" to the "Liber Psalmorum," *Glossa Ordinaria*, PL 843A. Kuczynski highlights the dual meaning of this division in the Psalms: "Part I (Psalms 1–50), ending in the *Miserere*, directs the soul in contrition; Part II (Psalms 51–100) guides it in its state of justification, through grace; Part III (Psalms 101–150) compels its imitation of David's joyous psalmody, in giving endless praise to God. This pattern traces David's own progress from sin through moral reform as it is reflected in the sentiments of his poems, and the potential progress of every Christian individual reading or listening to the Psalms" (*Prophetic Song*, 55). The division of the Psalms into three distinct sections is also mirrored in the structure of the *Commedia*. Dante would have been well aware of this exegetical commonplace when creating his tripartite division of the *Commedia* and when constructing the literary identity of the pilgrim. The progress of the pilgrim, as the individual writer whose experiences function as didactic lessons replete with universalizing values and moral messages, finds a parallel in the levels of meaning applied to the structure of the Psalms.
40. Psalm 30 was the second psalm to be sung every day at Compline; only the first six verses were sung. The complete psalm was sung during Matins on Mondays in the Ferial Psalter. See Harper, *Forms and Orders*, 244.
41. See Hollander, "Dante's Use of the Fiftieth Psalm."

42. "Abstulit a dorso peccatum, et ante oculos posuit" (Augustine, *Enarrationes in Psalmos* 50 (tr. Boulding, 415).

43. *Ottimo Commento*, quoted from The Dartmouth Dante Project (http://dartmouth.dante.edu; last accessed 24 January 2008). Francesco da Buti, writing towards the end of the fourteenth century, noted the ritual significance of this psalm, which is sung "la domenica mattina nel coro, quando lo sacerdote viene ad aspergere lo coro, per cacciare via l'immundi spiriti" [in the choir on Sunday mornings when the priest asperges the choir to drive out evil spirits]. Da Buti, *Commento*, 765–66; *Purgatorio*, 31.91–102.

44. See Hawkins, *Dante's Testaments*, chapter 4 for a lucid account of the importance of *Paradiso* 25 in Dante's self-presentation as an *auctor*.

45. Hawkins comments that "whereas no special claims are made for Dante's exceptional faith or remarkable charity, all the stops are pulled for hope.... Beatrice steps forward to protect Dante from the unbecoming charge of vainglory and boasting.... Because of the poet's superb control of his narrative throughout the *Commedia*, in which he is everywhere present but almost always concealed, it is easy to miss the cheek of this end run. But of course it is none other than Dante who makes all these moves himself" (ibid., 79).

46. On the specific relevance of Psalm 9: "Rather than simply offering a generic statement of confidence in God, such as one might find almost anywhere in the Psalter, Psalm 9 is striking in its particular relevance to Dante himself: it seems to describe both the existential situation of the exiled poet and the itinerary of the pilgrim in his journey from hell to Heaven.... It takes no great leap of interpretation to see why this text should so appeal to Dante. Like David surrounded by his foes, the exiled poet of the *Commedia* is beset by enemies; Dante's foes have banished him from Florence, doomed him to wander throughout Italy, and impugned his honor with false accusations" (Hawkins, *Dante's Testaments*, 83).

47. Barolini, *Dante's Poets*, 277.
48. Barański, "Poetics of Meter," 24.
49. Hawkins, *Dante's Testaments*, 90.
50. Kugel, "David the Prophet," 55.
51. Brownlee, "Why the Angels Speak Italian," 608.
52. Ibid., 599.
53. Ibid., 601.
54. Hawkins, *Dante's Testaments*, 91.
55. *ST* IIaIIae.161.5.
56. See Barolini, *Dante's Poets*, 269–86.
57. Ibid., 275.
58. See Auerbach, "Sacrae Scripturae."
59. Barolini, *Dante's Poets*, 276.
60. Kuczynski, *Prophetic Song*, 34.
61. Barolini, *Dante's Poets*, 275.
62. Hollander, "Dante *Theologus-Poeta*," 66.

8

Caritas and Ecclesiology in Dante's Heaven of the Sun

PAOLA NASTI

"Theologus Dantes, nullius dogmatis expers" [Dante theologian, stranger to no knowledge].[1] According to Boccaccio, this epitaph, composed by Giovanni del Virgilio, would have been inscribed on the tomb of Dante, had Guido Novello not died before he could "fare il sepolcro e li porvi li mandati versi" [make the tomb and inscribe the verses].[2] The image of Dante as *poeta-theologus* has always loomed large. Whether in awe of—or in some cases distressed by—his engagement with key theological debates and authorities, his readers have been ready to acknowledge his theoretical expertise and to scrutinize his texts in order to prove it. Since Dante's death, then, much has been written on his theology; much, it seems, has been understood. Yet even this dimension of the poet's work still holds some surprises for the modern reader, if they are prepared to reconsider the nature of medieval theology.[3] As numerous studies demonstrate, in the Middle Ages theology was not so much a scientific enterprise as an affective meditation on the word of God. The "figurative" language of the Bible was considered the receptacle of all divine mysteries and the only source of wisdom that man had to interrogate in order to achieve an understanding of the earthly and the divine. Medieval theology was therefore steeped in scriptural imagination and lived off the same language that it interpreted.[4] The images, the metaphors, and the parables of the Bible were not only the food that nurtured medieval theological thought; they were its very form. Words and theory were so closely intertwined that, from the twelfth century onwards, the understanding of the Bible as literature had become consolidated, so that the *scribae dei* were seen as the poets of God, and theology as the art of commenting on the poetic expression of the supreme artist.[5] Little wonder that Boccaccio should equate poetry with theology when defending those poets who, like Dante, express doctrine in the form of narrative: "Dico che la teologia e la poesia quasi una cosa si possono dire, dove uno medesimo sia il suggetto; anzi dico più, che la teologia niun'altra cosa è che una poesia di Dio.... Dunque bene appare, non solamente la poesì essere teologia, ma ancora la teologia essere poesia" [I say that theology and poetry can be considered almost identical when their subjects are identical. In fact, I will go even further and decree that theology is nothing less than the poetry of God.... And so it is clear not only that poetry is theology, but also that theology is poetry].[6]

The nature of medieval theology and its relationship with literature and rhetoric have several methodological and practical implications for those who intend to understand Dante's theological views. If medieval theology was considered a form of poetic expression, and metaphors and images were taken as signifiers of theological concepts, ideas, and theories, then our attempts at mapping the poet's uses and abuses of medieval theological discourse seem to open up infinite possibilities. The "technical" bearings and significance of key images, metaphors, and rhetorical uses can, however, be established through the careful study of theological, liturgical, and homiletical texts of the time. Once the theological "code" has been broken, its "translation" into secular poetry can be analyzed to shed light on the mysterious ways of poetical creation. In fact, the poet's rewriting of medieval theological discourse carries seeds of originality that occasionally transform his writings into daring theological statements. By examining these seeds of originality one can understand the complex philosophical, eschatological, and religious dimensions of a poem such as the *Commedia*.

This essay focuses on Dante's ecclesial theology as it emerges in his poetry. My intent is to illustrate the poet's awareness of, reliance upon, and also autonomy from medieval discourse on the most spiritual aspects of ecclesiology. Rather than looking for the direct sources of his representation, however, I aim to recreate a cross section of the ecclesiological discussion in which he participated, and to demonstrate the interdiscursive relationships that exist between his poetic articulation and medieval theological representations of the Church. Second, I wish to show that Dante deliberately reserved a prominent place in his prophetic poem for the treatment of the *ecclesia*, understood as a mystical body united with God both on earth and heaven. As I shall try to demonstrate, this place is the Heaven of the Sun, the heaven usually associated with the theme of wisdom.[7]

Of all the theological issues woven into the texture of the *Commedia*, ecclesiology is among the most debated among Dante scholars.[8] They have focused their attention primarily on Dante's perception of the institutional Church, on his treatment of the social aspects of Christ's redemptive work, and on his indignant denunciation of the popes' conduct, of their political maneuvers against the Empire, and of their alliances with the French monarchy. Conversely, theoretical issues concerning the poet's definition of the spiritual or intimate dimensions of the Church have generated less interest.[9] Even so, these apparently unequivocal issues are among the haziest aspects of both Dante's ecclesiology and medieval theology as a whole, and as such they require systematic investigation.

Ecclesiology is one of the most elusive aspects of medieval theological thought in general.[10] This is due in part to the ambiguity of the subject matter. The term *ecclesia* signified, often at the same time, a plethora of meanings, from a material edifice and place of worship to a hierarchical institution, a social body, and a communion of saints.[11] But the apparent elusiveness of medieval ecclesiological theory could also be attributed to the wide range of primary sources on the topic. The fathers of the Church and the medieval theologians frequently discussed ecclesiology in their writings, but systematic treatments did not appear until the beginning of the fourteenth century.[12] These, in turn, were limited to those apologetic or juridical aspects of ecclesiology that came under scrutiny in response to the polemical needs of the theologians, so much so that the majority of the fourteenth-century treatises on the Church were concerned almost exclusively with the long and intricate controversy between the Empire and the papacy over temporal power. If we attempt to map the medieval understanding of the Church as a mystical body in relation to the economy of salvation and thus focus on aspects of spiritual and moral theology, however, the corpus of texts for scrutiny becomes extremely difficult to contain. The best part of this textual mass consists of biblical commentaries, a favorite site for theological discussions in the Middle Ages. This returns us to our initial observations. The association between theological meditation on this matter and biblical interpretation brings us back to the question of the nature of medieval theological discourse: because of its ties with biblical exegesis, medieval writing on the Church rotates around a set of images and metaphors found in scripture and glossed by the exegetes. Medieval ecclesiology, in other words, must be understood less in terms of the theoretical concept of the Church and more in terms of the representation of the Church through multiple images inspired by the Bible. (To put it another way, we are dealing with *Kirchenbild* rather than *Kirchenbegriff*.)[13] These images, according to the seminal study of Yves Congar, ranged from that of the body of Christ to the lovely bride; from the temple to the city of Jerusalem. Less common, but nonetheless significant, were those scriptural images that seemed to bear some similarities with specific aspects of the Church and were therefore used as synonyms for it: Paradise, the moon, the ark, the daughter, the field, the vineyard. All of these symbols entered theological discourse to signify different facets and aspects of ecclesiology.

Most of these images were appropriated by Dante throughout the *Commedia* to refer to the Church Militant or the Church Triumphant; but, as many scholars have observed, the most frequently used simile is that of the Bride of God. Since images and language are the most appropriate point of departure for analyzing the poet's ecclesiology, it is fundamental to identify the theological and spiritual connotations associated with the lexical and rhetorical elaboration of this simile. Through such an approach, the theological and cultural layers of Dante's poetry will become clear and its poetic power will emerge more forcefully. In particular, this investigation examines the use of the image of the Bride of God, the *sponsa Dei*, in the Heaven of the Sun; through this analysis, it will be possible to assess Dante's take on the medieval *Kirchenbild*.

Medieval *Ecclesia*

The most influential meditations on the spiritual identity of the Church, understood as a communion of souls united in God, are found in the writings of St. Augustine. Augustine was first led to address the issue of how the Church should understand itself under the pressure of his controversy with the Donatists, who considered themselves the only real holy Church of God against the corrupt Church of Rome.[14] In the face of such attacks, Augustine's problem was to find a justification for the presence of evil faithful (the *mali*) in the community of the Church, without having to renounce the holiness of the community itself. His answer was ingenious. He formulated the idea of a mixed Church, described as a "place" on earth in which good and evil live together until the Last Judgment, when only the good will be recognized as the true Triumphant Church of God. The dilemma posed by the presence of evil within the body politic of the ecclesial community was thus settled eschatologically; the solution to the troubling moral implications of evil members of the Church was postponed to the afterlife. Nonetheless, even within this newly "devised" worldly mixed Church, Augustine distinguished the existence of a perfect minority: a mini-Church of what he called the *boni fideles*. To describe this superlative community of good Christians, Augustine employed a serious of metaphors drawn from the Song of Songs. First, he identified the mini-Church of the *boni* with the Virgin Bride, the enclosed garden of the biblical epithalamium (Song 4:12):[15]

> Et quod in Cantico canticorum Ecclesia sic describitur, "Hortus conclusus": hoc intelligere non audeo nisi in sanctis et iustis, non in avaris et fraudatoribus, et raptoribus, et feneratoribus, et ebriosis, et invidis, quos tamen cum iustis Baptismum habuisse comunenem.[16]

> [And in that the Church is described in the Song of Songs as an "enclosed garden"; I dare not understand this save of the holy and just—not of the covetous, and defrauders, and robbers, and usurers, and drunkards, and the envious, that they had baptism in common with the just.]

Augustine then addressed the mini-Church as the true pure and holy dove of God (Song 2:14; 5:2; 6:9), which shares the sacrament of baptism with the evil members of the Church, but has the gifts of love, peace, and humility that they lack:

> Ait tibi columba: "Et mali inter quos gemo, qui non pertinet ad membra mea, et necesse est ut inter illos gemam, nonne habent quod te habere gloriaris? Nonne multi ebriosi habent baptismum? Nonne multi avari? [...] Et isiti habent baptismum sed columba gemit inter

corvos. Quid ergo gaudes, quia habes? Hoc habes quid habet et malus. Habeto humilitatem, caritatem, pacem."[17]

[The dove says to you: "Even the wicked, among whom I groan, who belong not to my members, and it must needs be that I groan among them, have not they that which you boast of having? Have not many drunkards baptism? Have not many covetous? ... And yet these have baptism; but the dove groans among ravens. Why then do you boast in having it? What you have, the wicked man also has. Have humility, charity, peace."]

Augustine's preference for these biblical tropes was not coincidental. According to him, the characteristic which distinguished members of the mini-Church was the invisible unction of *caritas*. The good souls of the Church, in other words, were those united to God and to their neighbors by the bonds of love, because only *caritas*, the mark of Christ, is important in the history of salvation:

> Dilectio ergo sola discernit inter filio Dei et filios diaboli. Signent se omnes signo crucis Christi; respondeant omnes, Amen; cantent omnes, Alleluia; ... Qui habent caritatem, nati sunt ex Deo: qui non habent, non sunt nati ex Deo. ... Haec est margarita pretiosa, caritas, sine qua nihil tibi prodest quodcumque habueris: quam si solam habeas, sufficit tibi.[18]

[Therefore, love alone puts the difference between the children of God and the children of the devil. Let them all sign themselves with the sign of the cross of Christ; let them all respond, Amen; let all sing Alleluia ... They that have charity are born of God: they that have it not, are not born of God. ... This is the pearl of price, Charity, without which whatever you may have, brings you no profit: if you have it alone, it is sufficient for you.]

If, in Augustine's mind, love was at the heart of the true Church, there could be no better text then the Song of Songs to express this notion. This collection of amorous verses was considered the greatest celebration of divine love ever written, the holiest love song signed by the hand of God himself.[19] The image of the Bride united to God by an indissoluble bond of love is not unique to this holy book. As the bridal metaphors frequently used in the books of Hosea, Jeremiah, and the Psalms illustrate, it was a recurring image in the Old Testament, which signified one of the most important features of the teaching of the prophets: that the relationship between Yahweh and his chosen people is to be regarded as a matrimonial bond of fidelity, based on love.[20] Throughout the Middle Ages, however, the most frequently cited bridal figure of the scriptures remained that described in the Song of Songs. The poem's sexual imagery emphasizes love as desire and longing; and it does so to such an extent that, in order to justify the book's presence in the biblical canon, following the example set by Origen, Christian exegetes persistently read it as a prophecy, an allegory, or a figure of the salvific, God-given bond established between Christ and the newly formed Christian Church.[21] Augustine shared this interpretation and used it in his discussion of the fundamental role of *caritas* in the life of the Church.[22]

Needless to say, for medieval theologians approaching the question of the nature of the Church, Augustine's word carried considerable authority. Even when they broadened the idea of the *congregatio fidelium* to include the *mali* and eventually all the baptized, most medieval thinkers maintained Augustine's notion of the supremacy given to *caritas* over faith and the sacraments as a sign of positive integration in the Church.[23] The love of God and for God remained the mark of the miniature Church of the righteous and continued to predominate throughout the Middle Ages; no matter how the term *fideles* was employed, there remained a mini-Church of the good and the just, distinct because it chose to live with *caritas*.[24] Charity was "the supernatural love of fruition whereby the Christian loves God for his own sake and above all as his last end, thus entering the joy of the Lord";[25] this charity, mother of all virtues, was, for a theologian and mystic such as Bonaventure, "the root of that ecclesial unity which makes the Church what she is."[26]

Following the tradition established by Augustine and early scriptural commentators such as Origen and Cyprian, medieval theologians used the bridal language and images of the Song of Songs to show the bond of love at the heart of the *ecclesia universalis*; and commentaries to the Song of Songs became, alongside glosses to the Psalms, the privileged *loci* for ecclesiological discussions. Clearly, the Bride of the Song of Songs was not the only figure for the Church used in the Middle Ages; yet, compared with the images of the mystical body of Christ, the temple, or the city of God, the idea of the Bride played a primary role in medieval ecclesiological thought.[27] This bridal language was able to convey the idea of mutual love, the wine of charity that brings together God and his Church both on earth and in heaven. Images such as that of the temple, the body, or the *civitas* were not, on the other hand, closely associated to notions of love, and they play a relatively small part in the theology of *caritas-ecclesia*.

This brief overview of the medieval *Kirchenbild* and related biblical exegesis sets the scene for discussing Dante's interpretation and treatment of theological matters concerning the Church, intended as the intimate communion between God and his *fideles*. This is the scene against which we should try to understand Dante's use of the notion of the "Bride of God," the biblical correlative of the *caritas*-ecclesiology just outlined.

Dante's *Ecclesia*

The nuptial symbolism of the Song of Songs can be found in several places in Dante's works,[28] but wedding metaphors occur most frequently in the *Commedia* in the cantos of the Heaven of the Sun (*Paradiso* 10–14). In this cluster of cantos, bridal images are used to describe the different states of the Church Militant and Triumphant in such a consistent and coherent fashion that it would not be misleading to label this the "ecclesiological" section of the poem. This might seem a surprising claim: the idea that this episode sets forth Dante's views on the theological definition of the Church, its nature, and its role seems to clash with the usual characterization of the Heaven of the Sun as the abode of the wise.[29] For a poet like Dante, however, whose verse could open up to a plurality of motives and issues while preserving its formal cohesion, poetic structures and signification were never monolithic. On the contrary, in Dante a variety of principal "topics" can cohabit within the same enclosed structure when the logical and poetic links are strong enough to justify the risks related to multiple signification. In *Paradiso* 10–14, the coexistence of two subject matters, such as the Church and Wisdom, is underpinned by strong theoretical and theological similarities. As we shall see, for the poet, both the Church of the perfect and true wisdom could not exist unless marked by the seal of *caritas*.

The links drawn by the poet between wisdom and love had long been part of Dante's thought: in the *Convivio*, wisdom is described as a unitive experience with the divine mind, which discloses the mysteries of life and the creation to man. The role of *caritas* in the epistemological quest attempted in that earlier work is such that in many instances, the words chosen to describe wisdom are a fine blend of the erotic language of the book of Proverbs and that of the Song of Songs.[30] In the Heaven of the Sun, following the same logic, those souls of the Church Triumphant are wise who, through the flame of charity, have acquired erudition and knowledge of both the human and the divine.[31] Such is the bond between love and knowledge that the wisest soul of all, identified as Solomon, is also the most "loving," the one who is inspired and kept alive by the greatest "amor":

> La quinta luce, ch'è tra noi più bella,
> spira di tale amor, che tutto 'l mondo
> là giù ne gola di saper novella:
>   entro v'è l'alta mente u' sì profondo
> saver fu messo, che, se 'l vero è vero,
> a veder tanto non surse il secondo.
> (*Par.* 10.109–14)

[The fifth light, and the fairest light among us, / breathes forth such love that all the world below / hungers for tidings of it; in that flame / there is the lofty mind where such profound / wisdom was placed that, if the truth be true, / no other ever rose with so much vision.]

Dante therefore took an affective approach to knowledge, an approach that he shared with theologians and mystics of the caliber of Bernard of Clairvaux and Bonaventure of Bagnoregio.[32] It is no coincidence, in fact, that the words of Bernard's *Sermones super Cantica* seem to be the most appropriate gloss to accompany the characters found in the solar sphere imagined by Dante:

> Quid est venire ad animam Verbum? Erudire in sapientia. Quid est Patrem venire? Afficere ad amorem sapientiae, ut dicere posit, quia amatrix facta sum formae illius. Patris diligere est; et ideo Patris adventus ex infusa dilectione probatur. Quid faceret absque dilectione eruditio? Inflaret. Quid absque eruditione dilectio? Erraret.[33]

[What does it involve for the Word to come to the soul? This happens when the soul is taught wisdom. And how does the Father come to the soul? This happens when the Father touches the soul with the love of wisdom, so that it is able to say, "I was a lover of her beauty." To delight is of the Father, and therefore the coming of the Father is declared by the infusion of delight. What would be the effect of knowledge without delight? It would produce pride. And what of delight without knowledge? It would be the cause of error.]³⁴

But if delight, or *dilectio*, and therefore its cause, *amor*, is for Dante a prerequisite for the erudites' life, what about his idea of the Church? As I suggested earlier, and as the analysis of the rhetorical strata of this canto will show, it is intimately tied to love and the tradition of *caritas*-ecclesiology begun by Augustine. While appropriating the medieval *topoi* on the matter, however, the poet did not fail to experiment with the raw material and leave his own mark on it. To shed light on his representation of the Church and his elaboration of the medieval *Kirchenbild*, I turn in more detail to *Paradiso* 10–14.

The episode opens with a memorable representation of the Trinity:

> Guardando nel suo Figlio con l'Amore
> che l'uno e l'altro etternalmente spira,
> lo primo e ineffabile Valore
>   quanto per mente e per loco si gira
> con tant' ordine fé, ch'esser non puote
> sanza gustar di lui chi ciò rimira.
>   (*Par.* 10.1–6)

[Gazing upon His Son with that Love which / one and the Other breathe eternally, / the Power—first and inexpressible— / made everything that wheels through mind and space / so orderly that one who contemplates / that harmony cannot but taste of Him.]

This image is later reiterated in the same canto:

> Tal era quivi la quarta famiglia
> de l'alto Padre, che sempre la sazia,
> mostrando come spira e come figlia.
>   (*Par.* 10.49–51)

[Such was the sphere of His fourth family, / whom the High Father always satisfies, / showing how he engenders and breathes forth.]

The insistence on the mystery of the Trinity in this canto has been considered to be a homage to Bonaventure, through which Dante intentionally exposed his sympathy for the ideas of the seraphic doctor (whom Dante will meet later in canto 12).[35] The grand opening, nonetheless, could also be considered as a sort of Bonaventurian introduction to the ecclesiological preoccupation we find in this episode. To understand the bond that holds together the Church and God, according to the Franciscan theologian, one must think not of a natural, human, and therefore imperfect social order but of a social order that transcends the limitations of the world—an order as unique as the Trinity.[36] In other words, to find God as He is in Himself and to make possible the enjoyment of divine love as the very same three divine persons enjoy it,[37] the Church must have the imprint of the Trinity. But to imitate the Trinitarian model, *caritas* must become the cement that holds together the ecclesial community to her God. The originality of Bonaventure's ecclesiology was matched by an extraordinary ability to express it through simple yet vivid images. So, for example, if the Church is conventionally compared to a ship or an ark, what matters, for Bonaventure, is the glue (*glutino, bitumine*) that holds its parts together ("Navis est Ecclesia, quae iuncta est glutino caritatis").[38]

Parenthetically, in keeping with the Bonaventurian tenor of the episode of the Heaven of the Sun, these images and similes are also used by Dante in two sections of cantos 11 and 12, in which he deals with the Church and the salvific actions of Dominic and Francis:

> Pensa oramai qual fu colui che degno
> collega fu a mantener la barca
> di Pietro in alto mar per dritto segno
> (*Par.* 11.118–20)

[Consider now that man who was a colleague / worthy of Francis; with him, in high seas, / he kept the bark of Peter on true course.]

And,

> e tosto si vedrà de la ricolta
> de la mala coltura, quando il loglio
> si lagnerà che l'arca li sia tolta.
> (*Par.* 12.118–20)

[And soon we are to see, at harvest time, / the poor grain gathered, when the tares will be / denied a place within the bin—and weep]

Whether or not Dante had in mind the Bonaventurian *loci* quoted above, the important point is that the poet employs the language used by the theologians with competence. Moreover, the coincidence reveals a rather similar mindset, an analogous *modus operandi*, an equivalent cultural and ideological horizon.

In the opening lines of canto 10, the Bonaventurian reference to love between the three persons of the Trinity anticipates, in my opinion, the leitmotif of the episode as a whole: *caritas* as it is enjoyed by the Trinity, by the Church Militant, and by the communion of saints in Paradise. Echoes of the theme of charity are so frequent in these cantos that, as pointed out by Niccolò Mineo, the episode might be considered a variation on the "love note."[39] My aim here, however, is to focus only on those images of "love" that have a clear and specific ecclesiological significance. The numerous references to the Church as the Bride of God are unmistakably of this kind; this metaphor, as I hope to demonstrate, is used by Dante with the clear intention of emphasizing the theological meaning of the bond of charity that ties the community of the faithful to God.

The Bride

Dante refers to the *sponsa Dei* three times in the Heaven of the Sun; these three references constitute case studies, on which I focus for the remainder of this essay. The first reference is in the closing lines of *Paradiso* 10. Here, to describe the exultant joy of the glorified Church of God witnessed by the pilgrim, Dante recalls the devotional love of the militant community as shown in the hour of the morning liturgy. The worshipping community is described as the Bride of God, who awakens with the burning desire to love her groom:

> Indi, come orologio che ne chiami
> ne l'ora che la sposa di Dio surge
> a mattinar lo sposo perché l'ami,
>   che l'una parte e l'altra tira e urge,
> tin tin sonando con sì dolce nota,
> che 'l ben disposto spirto d'amor turge;

> così vid' ïo la gloriosa rota
> muoversi e render voce a voce in tempra
> e in dolcezza ch'esser non pò nota
> se non colà dove gioir s'insempra.
> (*Par.* 10.139–48)

[Then, like a clock that calls us at the hour / in which the bride of God, on waking, sings / matins to her Bridegroom, encouraging / His love (when each clock-part both drives and draws), / chiming the sounds with notes so sweet that those / with spirit well-disposed feel their love grow; / so did I see the wheel that moved in glory / go round and render voice to voice with such / sweetness and such accord that they can not / be known except where joy is everlasting.]

The second reference is in *Paradiso* 11, Thomas Aquinas, while commenting upon the life of St. Francis, describes the Church Militant as the Bride acquired by Christ through the sacrifice of his flesh on the cross:

> La provedenza, che governa il mondo
> con quel consiglio nel quale ogne aspetto
> creato è vinto pria che vada al fondo,
> però che andasse ver' lo suo diletto
> la sposa di colui ch'ad alte grida
> dispose lei col sangue benedetto,
> in sé sicura e anche a lui più fida,
> due principi ordinò in suo favore,
> che quinci e quindi le fosser per guida.
> (*Par.* 11.28–36)

[The Providence that rules the world with wisdom / so fathomless that creatures' intellects / are vanquished and can never probe its depth, / so that the Bride of Him who, with loud cries, / had wed her with His blessed blood, might meet / her Love with more fidelity and more / assurance in herself, on her behalf / commanded that there be two princes, one / on this side, one on that side, as her guides.]

Third, in *Paradiso* 12, Bonaventure retrieves the same image to present St. Dominic to the pilgrim:

> quando lo 'mperador che sempre regna
> provide a la milizia, ch'era in forse,
> per sola grazia, non per esser degna;

>   e, come è detto, a sua sposa soccorse
>   con due campioni, al cui fare, al cui dire
>   lo popol disvïato si raccorse.
>   (*Par.* 12.40–45)

[when the Emperor / who rules forever helped his ranks in danger— / only out of His grace and not their merits. / And, as was said, He then sustained His bride, / providing her with two who could revive / a straggling people: champions who would / by doing and by preaching bring new life.]

The bridal metaphor is such a well-known *topos* of medieval ecclesiology that its simple appropriation would not be sufficient to prove Dante's subtle understanding of *caritas*-ecclesiology, nor his wish to discuss it here. Yet we can say with confidence that all three images are embedded in the theological tradition that represented the Church in mystical union with God. Some details of the poetic diction, for instance, clearly show that Dante's knowledge of ecclesiological problems was broad, and that his intention here was to offer a competent representation of the intimate unitive experience that lies at the heart of the Church. As had become customary in theological discourse on *caritas*-ecclesiology, these details unmistakably pertain to the tradition of the glossed Song of Songs.[40] To see how, consider the second reference in *Paradiso* 11.28–36, quoted above. Two expressions fall under scrutiny: "però che andasse ver' lo suo diletto / la sposa . . . in sé sicura e anche a lui più fida" [so that the Bride . . . might meet / her Love with more fidelity and more / assurance in herself] and "ad alte grida / disposò lei col sangue benedetto" [with loud cries, / had wed her with His blessed blood]. The first set of lines obviously repeats the fundamental ecclesiological reading of the Bride of the Song of Songs inaugurated by Origen, Augustine, and Bede: the woman loved by the holy groom is the Christian Church. But if one looks at the lexical choices of Dante in "però ch'andasse ver' lo suo diletto . . . in sé sicura e anche a lui più fida," one finds that even this image of the Bride, who needs God's call so that she might follow him without getting lost, is, in fact, a *topos* of the exegesis of the Song of Songs that carried a clear theological meaning: the intervention of God is necessary for the Christian soul to keep on the path of love. Bernard, for example, in explaining to his monks the verse "Trahe me post te, in odore unguentorum tuorum curremus. Introduxit me rex in cellaria sua" (Song 1:3)

[Draw me: we will run after thee to the odour of thy ointments. The king hath brought me into his storerooms], wrote:

> Propterea opus habeo trahi, quoniam refriguit paulisper ignis in nobis amoris tui, nec valemus a facie frigoris huius currere modo, sicut heri et nudius tertius. Curremus autem postea, cum reddideris laetitiam salutis tuae, cum redierit melior temperies gratiae, cum sol iustitiae iterum incaluerit, et pertransierit tentationis nubes.[41]

> [I need to be drawn for this reason, because the fire of Your love has grown cold in us; and, because of that coldness, we are unable to run as we did yesterday and in past days. But we shall run when You will have restored us to the joy of your salvation, when the warmth of your grace shall have returned to us, when the sun of righteousness shall have warmed us once again, and when the cloud of temptation shall have passed away.]

The soul described by the theologian needs to be reminded of the benefits of the *sol iustitiae;* because she is frail and earth-bound, she must be pulled out of her inner inertia. In *Paradiso* 11.28–36, the "principi" sent by God warm the cooling heart of the Bride, so that she might follow her groom more confidently ("a lui più fida") and so that the clouds of temptations might be pushed away by the temperate wind of spiritual renewal. Perhaps not accidentally, therefore, Bernard's words remind us of the many similes employed by Dante later in canto 11 to portray the arrival of Saint Francis: the warmth of the sun and the beauty of a new spring, as well as the urge of the "fraticelli" to run after him and his Bride.[42]

The second set of lines highlighted in *Paradiso* 11.28–36, "ad alte grida / disposò lei col sangue benedetto" [with loud cries, / had wed her with His blessed blood], express a theological concept that was fundamental to the elaboration of *caritas*-ecclesiology, namely, that the Church was born on the cross through Christ's sacrifice of love.[43] According to medieval ecclesiology, the Church was the renewed Eve, the real Bride, born from Christ's bleeding wound. Such, for example, was Bernard's opinion:

> Denique non propter animam unam, sed propter multas in unam Ecclesiam colligendas, in unicam adstringendus sponsam, Deus tam multa et facit et pertulit . . . ? Quid non ab illo speret . . . ? Nec modo quaesivit, sed acquisivit. Adde et de modo acquisitionis in sanguine acquisitoris.[44]

[It was not on account of one soul alone that God has done and suffered so many things, ... but on account of a great number of souls which He would unite into one Church, and which would form one only Bride.... What may she not hope from Him ... ? Not only has He sought her, but he has found her and made her His own, through the price of the blood of the purchaser.]

Later, in *Paradiso* 12.40–45, Dante introduces another concept that is very common in medieval *caritas*-ecclesiology: the idea that God's deeds in favor of his real Church (especially the gift of his son's life) are gifts of his grace. To give an example: according to Bonaventure, for the Church "to be the likeness of God," and hence for her to love the Creator through the order of charity found in the Trinity, "implies a recreation through grace, i.e. first of all through an effective act of God's will."[45] The perfection of the ecclesial community achieved through charity, therefore, can be realized only thanks to the intervention of the divinity. Those who, granted this grace, are burning in charity can enjoy the attention of the lover and become, according to Bernard, worthy ("dignam") of his greatness: "Da mihi animam nihil amantem praeter Deum et quod propter Deum amandum est ... et ego non nego dignam Sponsi cura, maiestatis respectu"[46] [Give me a soul which loves God, and God only, and which deserves to be loved for God's sake ... and I do not deny that it is worthy of the care of the Bridegroom, of the regard of His majesty].

Read through the lens of such a topical text, the Church that Dante is imagining in *Paradiso* 12 appears unworthy ("non per esser degna") and "disviata" because it has, obviously, ignored *caritas*, the bond of love. We should not forget the words of Folquet at the close of canto 9, which describe Boniface VIII, the *malus par excellence*, as an adulterous lover who perverted *caritas* into prostitution:

> Ma Vaticano e l'altre parti elette
> di Roma che son state cimitero
> a la milizia che Pietro seguette,
>   tosto libere fien de l'avoltero.
>   (*Par.* 9.139–42)

[And yet the hill of Vatican as well / as other noble parts of Rome that were / the cemetery for Peter's soldiery / will soon be freed from priests' adultery.]

The second and third of our case studies (*Par.* 11.28–36 and 12.40–45), therefore, establish certain fundamental features of Dante's depiction of the Church Militant, all of which reflect medieval ecclesiological readings of the Song of Songs. The Church Militant should be rooted in *caritas*, born as she was out of the loving sacrifice of Christ's blood on the cross, and should aim at the same order of fruition as is found in the Trinity. Betraying her present corrupted nature, she is "disviata" and unworthy ("non degna") of God's grace and in need of guidance because of a lack of love. As Bonaventure puts it, the Church was *mala* because she only had the love of a *meretrix*.[47]

But this is not all Dante had to say on the role of charity in the Church. The richest image of the Bride of God is to be found in our first case study, *Paradiso* 10.139–48. Here, the Bride of God appears lovely and exultant, awaking to love her groom. This image, one of the most suggestive and daring comparisons of *Paradiso*, magistrally examined by Lino Pertile, rests upon the adoption of several words and images drawn from the Song of Songs.[48] As is widely recognized, Dante's similes and metaphors are rarely merely ornamental. The question, then, is why he needed to evoke the biblical text to describe the orderly, rhythmic, and circular movements of a clock, and why he found the simile between these movements and the dance of the blessed apt for the job. Why, moreover, did he use such explicitly sexual tones to characterize this heavenly dance? What, if any, are the theological principles upon which Dante established the equation between an image of the Church rising at the morning bells and the "festa di paradiso" he pictures here? The answer lies, in my opinion, in the complex exegetical texture woven around the biblical epithalamium echoed in these verses. By creating such an attention-grabbing vignette, Dante intended to make use of all the different meanings that medieval exegetes attributed to the Bride of the Song of Songs. The Bride of God of the Song of Songs was interpreted allegorically as the Church Militant, tropologically as the soul, and anagogically as the community of the blessed. At a first level of interpretation (allegorical), therefore, the Bride evoked by the poet can be read in full accordance with the exegetical tradition as the Church Militant, here seen as a congregation galvanized by their love for the Creator in the hours of the morning liturgy. From a tropological/moral perspective, the image is also meant to represent the soul united as a Bride to her loving God in the secrecy of the daily prayer. The anagogical senses associated with the bridal metaphor are activated, indirectly, by the context of the comparison. Dante compares the love-making of the Church to the celestial bliss enjoyed by the souls united to God in their final embrace. As we shall see, this system of *allegoresis* is supported by, and at the same time develops, a clear theological discourse on the Church, Militant and Triumphant.

The allegorical and moral meanings embedded in Dante's image of the Bride of God are fundamental to the understanding of his *Kirchenbild*. As Pertile hypothesized some years ago, a set of verbs used here by the poet, "surge" and "urge," seems to recall a famous scene of the Song of Songs. In one of his sudden visits to the Bride, the Bridegroom of the Canticle calls her with these words: "Surge, propera, amica mea, Columba mea, formosa mea, et veni" (Song 2:10) [Arise, make haste, my love, my dove, my beautiful one, and come]. In the exegetical tradition, this is interpreted as Christ's appeal to his Church to follow him on the path of salvation. Saint Ambrose considered these the words that God addresses to his Church to urge her to leave all worldly concerns and join him in higher thoughts and deeds. This is, he wrote, God's invitation to believe in the miracle of the resurrection and love him with confidence.[49]

The other reminder of the Song of Songs and its exegesis in Dante's lines is the use of the verb "tira." This, as noticed by Pertile, is an echo of the prayer that the Bride of the Song sends to her Bridegroom, one which we have already mentioned: "Trahe me post te ... curremus. Introduxit me rex in cellaria sua" (Song 1:3) [Draw me: we will run after thee. . . . The king hath brought me into his storerooms]. For the exegetes, with these words the Church, or the soul, prays to her Bridegroom to help her follow the example of Christ.[50] In the third of these case studies, *Paradiso* 12.40–45, Dante's rewriting of the language of the Canticle is meant to evoke this exegetical context in order to illustrate, in a few theologically dense lines, his ideal Church as a community of loving and devout souls, following the path of Christ, denying worldly pleasures, and waiting to be united to him after death. But it is above all the simile of *Paradiso* 10 that proclaims love as the driving force of the relationship between God and his people.

There is still more to this nuptial trope. The poet's actualization of the metaphor translates into imagery a concept that is fundamental to the triumph of *caritas*-ecclesiology. Dante's Bride is pictured in the hour of love-making, which in turn is identified with the time of worship. The Bride/Church Militant and her members are immortalized by Dante as a *congregatio*, as a community that prays together in charity. The Church is represented in her most social as well as spiritual practice because, as Bonaventure emphasized, "charity, or supernatural love, is inconceivable apart from a community of persons, i.e. an order in which the inner dynamic of a love which must give rather than receive can be realized."[51] "The nature of charity," in other words, "is communicative" and social.[52] The Song of Songs was a particularly apt text to represent these dimensions of *caritas*.

The passionate *amplexus* narrated by Solomon, according to most exegetes, symbolized the Church Militant retired in contemplation and prayer. William of Saint-Thierry's commentary on the Song describes most fully the importance of prayer to attain a state of grace and heavenly peace on earth, the *fruitio* described by Bonaventure as the closest thing to bliss. Commenting on the section of the Song that starts with the word "Surge," William observed that these lines recount the daily visitation of God to his people, when the promise of his royal bed lures the true Church into the contemplation of eternal happiness:

> Anxia pietate assidue eo cor dirigit suum, quo praemisit thesaurum suum, exspectans et accipiens cotidie induentem eam ex alto cotidianum virtutis divinae visitationem, donec soluta aliquando a vinculo carnis, recipi mereatur ad aeternum sponsi cohabitationem. Ibi ergo in ecclesia, in unitate fidei, quae sponsa est, saepe per internae visitationis gratiam illustratur; saepe per contemplationis virtutem usque ad visionem supernae pacis et regii thalami dignitatem, sponsum sponsa pio amore prosequitur.[53]

> [With anxious devotion the Bride constantly directs her heart to the place where she has already laid up her treasure; every day she expects and receives the daily visitation of the divine power, with which she is endowed from on high, until at length she is freed from the bond of the flesh and deserves to be permitted to dwell together with her Bridegroom eternally. Here therefore, in the Church, in the unity of faith, she who is a Bride is frequently enlightened by the grace of an interior visitation; often by the power of contemplation the Bride with devout love follows after the Bridegroom until she attains the vision of heavenly peace and is found worthy of the royal marriage chamber.]

Thus Dante's image of lovemaking could also refer to these aspects of the inward life of the ecclesiastic community, namely, devotion and contemplation, placing them at the heart of its *itinerarium in deum*. Through these means the return to God that the Church commences on earth effects a likeness to the Trinity that according to Bonaventure could be "expressed by the figure of the circle," with Christ as a center.[54] Within this circle, *caritas* flows from God to Son, from Son to Church, and from Church to God. This imagery suggests that Dante chose to encapsulate the trope of the Bride's love into a larger simile representing the circular movements of a clock because the Church's journey to God is a kind of circumincession that brings back the souls to the fruition of supernatural love—a circumincession that starts *in via* but is only perfected in the holy Jerusalem. This is why the circular movements of the Bride of God, the *sponsa Dei*, on earth can be compared by the poet to a wheel of dancing blessed souls;[55] this is why the circle of the wise souls best expresses the identity between love of God and knowledge of God. They, the Church Triumphant, have closed the circle, conquered supernatural love, and become godlike.

These observations lead to further anagogical meanings in *Paradiso* 10.139–48, where the image of the Church-Bride celebrating the morning liturgy is evoked in conjunction with the songs of praise that the pilgrim hears in Heaven.[56] The comparison thus established by Dante between the joy of heaven and the exultation of the *ecclesia in via* shows his awareness of an important theological concept. Theologians often maintained that the praise sung on earth is an echo of those sung in Heaven.[57] Such, for example, was Cassiodorus's position: "Unde hic profusa laetitia exsultat populus fidelis, quandam imaginem futuri saeculi designans, ubi voces istae continuae sunt et laudes Domini devota mente concelebrant"[58] [So here the faithful people exults in abundant joy, giving expression to some shape of the age to come, when these proclamations are uninterrupted, and they celebrate the Lord's praises together with devoted minds]. The continuity between the *laetitia* expressed by the Church Militant on earth and the *laetitia* of the Church Triumphant in Heaven exists because, as the theologians were keen to prove, the Church Militant should be modeled on the heavenly one.[59] Even though it is a community in the world, it transcends the world and history, because it is conceived on the ideal of the heavenly Jerusalem. In this sense, Augustine called blessed those souls who abide in the Church because they will possess the heavenly Jerusalem without worry or interruption: "Possident Ierusalem caelestem sine angustia, sine praessura sine diversitate et divisione limitum: omnes habeant eam, et singuli habeant totam" [They possess the heavenly Jerusalem, without constraint, without pressure, without difference and division of boundaries; all have it, and each have all].[60]

The list of theological authorities who make this point is long, and it includes Bernard: "Ipse igitur qui descendit ipse est et qui ascendit, ut nemo ascendat in caelum nisi qui de coelo descendit, unus idemque Deus, et sponsus in capite, et sponsa in corpor"[61] [He, therefore, who descended, is also He who ascended, for no one can ascend into Heaven but He who descended from Heaven, who is one and the same Lord]. The tradition is clear: because the mission of every pilgrim in the Church Militant is to reach the Church Triumphant, the two states of the Church are never far apart in the mind of the biblical exegetes. In fact, the very way in which they describe the Church Militant is influenced by the idea they have of the destination of the *fideles*, namely, the Church Triumphant. The actual link between the two Churches is the *iusti* themselves, those who will travel from earth to Heaven.[62] But what do the righteous of the Church Militant possess that will accompany them on their journey to the Church Triumphant and will remain with them there? Not hope, which will have no reason to perdure once the *iusti* are in Heaven, but *caritas*. *Caritas* is the bridge between earth and Heaven because it forms the bond between Christ and his members in both realms: "Per caritatem nobiscum est in terra; per caritatem cum illo sumus in coelo" [through love, he is with us on earth; through love, we are with him in heaven].[63] Dante was well aware of this idea, as he proves in the examination cantos, cantos that further develop his treatment of ecclesiological matters. As we know, *caritas* is described there as essential to faith and to the understanding of all the divine mysteries, from the Creation to the Incarnation to the final Resurrection:

> Lo ben che fa contenta questa corte,
> Alfa e O è di quanta scrittura
> mi legge Amore o lievemente o forte
> <div align="right">(<i>Par.</i> 26.16–18)</div>

> [The good with which this court is satisfied / is Alpha and Omega of all writings / that Love has—loud or low—read out to me.]

And further,

> Però ricominciai: "Tutti quei morsi
> che posson far lo cor volgere a Dio,
> a la mia caritate son concorsi:
> ché l'essere del mondo e l'esser mio,
> la morte ch'el sostenne perch' io viva,
> e quel che spera ogne fedel com' io
>   (*Par.* 26.55–60)

———

[Thus I began again: "My charity / results from all those things whose bite can bring / the heart to turn to God; the world's existence / and mine, the death that He sustained that I / might live, and that which is the hope of all / believers, as it is my hope]

Paradiso 10.139–48, therefore, translates in a beautiful image the continuity between the Church *in via* and in Heaven, and by relying on the tradition of the Song of Songs it places *caritas* at the heart of the spiritual life of both communities. The fruition of *caritas* is, in fact, the status of the Church Triumphant in Dante's *Paradiso*, which has been rightly described as the realm of desire: desire to be united to God, and desire to rejoice in him and in the other blessed souls.[64] Throughout the third *cantica*, the identification of bliss and *caritas* emerges linguistically and figuratively under different guises, but in the Heaven of the Sun the image most frequently used to translate it is that of the flower.[65] Dante compares the blessed to plants three times:

> Tu vuo' saper di quai piante s'infiora
> questa ghirlanda che 'ntorno vagheggia
> la bella donna ch'al ciel t'avvalora.
>   (*Par.* 10.91–93)

———

[You want to know what plants bloom in this garland / that, circling, contemplates with love the fair / lady who strengthens your ascent to heaven.]

> così di quelle sempiterne rose
> volgiensi circa noi le due ghirlande
>   (*Par.* 12.19–20)

———

[so the two garlands of those everlasting / roses circled around us]

> Diteli se la luce onde s'infiora
> vostra sustanza, rimarrà con voi
> etternalmente sì com' ell' è ora;
> > (*Par.* 14.13–15)

[Do tell him if that light with which your soul / blossoms will stay with you eternally / even as it is now]

This metaphorical texture relies on St. Bernard's use of images of the Song of Songs in his description of the triumph of the Church after the resurrection:

> Denique ait: *Ecce tu plcher es, dilecte mi et decorus! lectulus noster floridus* (Cant. I, 13). Quae lectulum monstrat, satis quid desideret aperit et cum floridum nuntiat, sati indicat, unde quod desiserat obtinere praesumant.... Porro autem Resurrectionis insigna, novos adverte flores sequentis temporis, in novam sub gratia revirescentis aestatem, quorum fructum generalis futura resurrectio in fine parturiet sine fine mansurum. *Jam*, inquit, *hiems transiit, imber abiit et recessit, flores apparuerunt in terra nostra* (Cant. II, 11–12): aestivum tempus advenisse cum illo significans, qui de mortis gelu in vernalem quamdam novae vitae temperiem resolutus, *Ecce*, ait, *nova facio omnia* (Apoc. XXI, 5): eujus caro seminata est in morte, refloruit in resurrectione; ad cujus mox odorem in campo convallis nostrae (Cant. II, 1) revirescunt arida, recalescunt frigida, mortua reviviscunt.[66]

[Then she says: "You are fair my Beloved, and handsome; our couch is strewn with flowers." By the couch she reveals clearly enough what she desires and by declaring that it is strewn with flowers, she indicates clearly whence she hopes to obtain what she wants.... But notice that the signs of the Resurrection are like this year's flowers, blossoming in a new summer under the power of grace. Their fruit will come forth in the end at the future general resurrection and it will last forever. As it is said: "Winter is over, the rain is past and gone. Flowers appear in our land," showing summer has come back with him who changed death's coldness into the spring of a new life, saying: "Behold I make all things new." His flesh was sown in death and rose again in the resurrection. By this fragrance the dry grass turns green again in the fields of the valley; what was cold grows warm again and what was dead comes back to life.]

This is merely one instance of a rich tradition. The point, however, is that the flower images used by Dante and inspired, once again, by the Solomonic tradition are effectively technical terms for the resurrected body of the Church, the last stage of the extraordinary *ascensus* of the *sponsa Dei* for which the poet reserved a solemn discussion at the close of the episode in *Paradiso* 14. That a theological lecture on the return of the flesh to its Creator occurs here is not a coincidence. If what I have argued so far is valid, Dante wanted to offer a glimpse of the real Church Triumphant, the Church that after the resurrection will finally enjoy God and his *caritas*, in order to conclude and complete his discussion in the Heaven of the Sun of *caritas*-ecclesiology. Moreover, Dante gave the honor of announcing the "good news" to Solomon. The choice could not have been more appropriate. As the language employed in these cantos shows, the biblical king is the *auctor* of *caritas*, the poet of the supernatural love to which the Christian soul and the Church aspire. Like his Song of Songs as viewed by the exegetes, Solomon's speech in canto 14 is a beautiful and highly poetic glorification of the resurrection as the final love union between the *ecclesia* and God.[67] However, things are not quite so simple. Dante chose the king as spokesman for such a topic in accord with a long and vibrant exegetical and theological tradition that linked the discussion on the resurrection and the Church Triumphant to his Song of Songs. This tradition was established by mystical writers and theologians such as St. Bonaventure, St. Bernard, and the Cistercians. For them, body and soul desire each other as a bride desires her bridegroom. The gifts of the soul at the resurrection were compared to a dowry, whereas the body was described as a tool of *spiritual dilectio*. For Bernard in particular, the union of soul and body after the Judgment generates a genuine state of intoxication or drunkenness. Similarly, Dante conceived the resurrection and the subsequent vision of God in terms of desire, a desire that lasts for eternity. His separated souls long for the return of their bodies to reach the fullness of knowledge and vision, but also to be able to love and desire the Trinity as the Trinity loves itself. Solomon declares that after the resurrection of the body, the blessed will be able to see deeper into the divine mind, and that this vision will increase the flame of charity that lightens the souls. The body will actually add light to light and love to love. The resurrection, therefore, is a union of charity that will become perfect at the end of time, when the Church Triumphant will expand the order of charity found in the Trinity.[68] If we understand Dante's "festa di paradiso" in such a way, the poet's words can be interpreted in Bonaventurian terms:

> Tanto mi parver sùbiti e accorti
> e l'uno e l'altro coro a dicer "Amme!,"
> che ben mostrar disio d'i corpi morti:
>   forse non pur per lor, ma per le mamme,
> per li padri e per li altri che fuor cari
> anzi che fosser sempiterne fiamme.
>   (*Par.* 14.61–66)

[One and the other choir seemed to me / so quick and keen to say "Amen" that they / showed clearly how they longed for their dead bodies— / not only for themselves, perhaps, but for / their mothers, fathers, and for others dear / to them before they were eternal flames.]

For Bonaventure, if the resurrected Church is an expansion of the Trinity, it follows that, just as in the Godhead the "plurality of really distinct persons is necessary"[69] for the flow of charity to happen, so too, the plurality of the Church is necessary for the Church Triumphant to love as God loves himself. The resurrected soul could not come to fruition in isolation: mothers, fathers, sons, and daughters are necessary for that joy to be complete. Perfect charity is a communicative, social virtue; hence Dante represented both the Church *in via* (*Par.* 10.139–48) and the Church Triumphant as communities, the latter of which is perfect, the former stained by the *mali*.

Before concluding my overview of Dante's *Kirchenbild* in the Heaven of the Sun, I would like to return from images of the Church Triumphant to those of the Church Militant. In *Paradiso* 10–14, Dante offers two clear examples of how the Church on earth can act to resemble as much as possible the Church Triumphant, the perfect Bride described by Solomon's speech. This perfect spiritual Church Militant, which will become the glorious lover of God after the Last Judgment, finds blood and flesh in the lives of the two "champions" chosen, according to Dante, by God to save his Bride: Saints Dominic and Francis. Dante presents these two *iusti* here because, as the theologians thought, the *iusti* cannot exist outside the community: sanctity does not concern only the relationship between the individual and his God, but must be realized in and through a community, and, vice versa, the community cannot prosper without the deeds of men of *caritas*.[70] The poet, in other words, would not have offered a comprehensive representation of his *caritas*-ecclesiology without presenting the greatest examples of holiness known to him. The presence of these two champions in the heaven dedicated to the wise can therefore be explained partly in relation to the ecclesiological preoccupations of these cantos, and the discourse on the Church sustained here by Dante could also explain (at least in part) the form given by the poet to the *vitae* of his spiritual heroes.

The modes of narration of the two cantos dedicated to the saints whose historical existences have been transformed into allegorical erotic narratives has often puzzled scholars.[71] Nevertheless, in the light of what has been said so far, Dante's rhetorical choices appear theologically determined. We have seen above that for the bridal similes examined in this study (*Par.* 10.139–48; 11.28–36; 12.40–45), the archetype followed by the poet is the mystical tradition of the Song of Songs. The same rhetorical and thematic patterns tie together the representation of Francis, Dominic, and the loving Church because the two saints are the new perfect lovers, fulfilling the eternal love story between the community and her God prophesied by the Song of Solomon. In *Paradiso* 11 and 12, furthermore, the biblical trope is activated to prove what is made clear in our second case study, *Paradiso* 11.28–36: that the gifts of grace are gifts of *caritas* and that therefore God can love some of his creatures with a special love that infuses them with the greatest capacity to love him and creation.[72] Francis's and Dominic's lives were dominated by *caritas* because they were the objects of God's special affection, and as such they had become his likeness, loving him for his own sake with supernatural love. This, of course, was a *topos* of Franciscan and Dominican hagiography, but in order to signify the profundity of the saints' fruition of God's love, Dante was ready to say what others had not: he summed up the account of their rich and eventful lives, on which a huge tradition had been built, as love affairs. Significantly (with the exception, perhaps, of Dante and Beatrice), these are the only love affairs accepted in the *Paradiso*. Moreover, the poet colored these romances with a language that is often explicit and erotic. One example makes the point. In his retelling of the inspired life of St. Francis, we read:

> ché per tal donna, giovinetto, in guerra
> del padre corse, a cui, come a la morte,
> la porta del piacer nessun diserra;
>   e dinanzi a la sua spiritual corte
> et coram patre le si fece unito;
> poscia di dì in dì l'amò più forte.
> (Par. 11.58–63)

[or even as a youth, he ran to war / against his father, on behalf of her— / the lady unto whom, just as to death, / none willingly unlocks the door; before / his spiritual court *et coram patre*, / he wed her; day by day he loved her more.]

The charm of the "porta del piacer" opened by Francis is by now a familiar theme in the critical literature. Readers are generally shocked by the intrusion of the sensual and sexual allusions of this image. Yet even on this occasion, the paradoxical and conflicting presence of the corporeal alongside the spiritual can be understood in terms of the exegetical tradition of the Song of Songs. Francis's door of pleasure recalls the more "notorious" door of the Song of Songs. According to the biblical story, after a long and painful absence, the Bridegroom finally returns to his lover and awaits at her door. The woman opens it and is overwhelmed by his presence:

> Vox dilecti mei pulsantis, aperi mihi, soror mea, amica mea, columba mea . . . / Dilectus meus misit manum suam per foramen et venter meus intremuit ad tactum eius. / Surrexi ut aperirem dilecto meo manus meae stillaverunt murra digiti mei pleni murra probatissima. / Pessulum ostii aperui dilecto meo at ille declinaverat atque transierat anima mea liquefacta est ut locutus est. (Song 5:2–6)

[the voice of my beloved knocking: Open to me, my sister, my love, my dove . . . / My beloved put his hand through the key hole, and my bowels were moved at his touch. / I arose up to open to my beloved: my hands dropped with myrrh, and my fingers were full of the choicest myrrh. / I opened the bolt of my door to my beloved: but he had turned aside, and was gone. My soul melted when he spoke.]

This image is one of the most suggestive of the Song and has appealed to the imagination of artists and commentators for centuries. In the Middle

Ages it was interpreted both from an ecclesiological and from a tropological point of view. On the ecclesiological interpretation, the image of the Bridegroom standing at the door was the moment of the liberation of the Synagogue, the moment of call for the community, when God appears to his new Church to illuminate and liberate her from the powers of evil. The moral, or tropological, exegesis of this passage emphasized the individual *katarsis* and the emancipation of the soul from sin. Against this background, Dante's words appear clear. Francis, as *figura Christi*, gave to the loving Church the (spiritual) freedom that had long been forgotten by her members. On the other hand, Francis, considered as a soul and therefore as a Bride, was liberated by the grace of his lady, the divine figure of God. In other words, Dante's appropriation of the famous erotic image carries all the spiritual senses that it had acquired in the exegetical and iconographical tradition. But the sensual connotations, which are increased by the nudity of the two characters of *Paradiso*'s narrative, are also Dante's original sign for a person's full enjoyment of God, for a life spent in the likeness of God. As in the image of the Bride in *Paradiso* 10, the erotic language of Dante's account of the life of Francis is the epiphany of Dante's belief in the supremacy of *caritas* as the principle that holds together the Church in this world and the other.

Dante, as we have seen, had a sharp and extensive understanding of the ecclesiological questions addressed by contemporary theologians. This is revealed by his precise mastery of a language that is both technical and scriptural, a figurative language employed by theologians to signify the great mystery of the bond of *caritas* that brings together earth and Heaven. Dante's understanding of the nature of the Church was deeply rooted in the *caritas* ecclesiology elaborated by Augustine and developed by Bernard and Bonaventure. His positions, in fact, in a number of ways seem to follow closely Bonaventure's theory on the role of *caritas* within the economy of the Church and in the history of salvation as a whole. Yet as much as one has to recognize the voice of the times in the *Commedia*, one should also emphasize the originality of Dante's *Kirchenbild*. The ecclesiological representation set up in the Heaven of the Sun, based on medieval ideas of *caritas* and on the language of the glossed Song of Songs, shows that Dante was ready to push the boundaries of theological discourse. Quite surprisingly, especially if one considers the spiritual atmosphere of *Paradiso*, the poet's language swings towards strong and obvious sexual connotations on many occasions (the Bride's lovemaking, the door of pleasure—images striking for their sensuality in the context of the *Paradiso*). From Augustine and Bede onwards, the sensuality of the Song of Songs had been heavily censured in the tradition. Was Dante alone, then, on such risky grounds? Not completely. To a certain extent, his position is not far from that of the mystical theologians who put the experience of *caritas* at the center of the spiritual life of a Christian and who employed the sexual metaphor of the Song of Songs as correlative of this principle. Gregory the Great and Bernard of Clairvaux, for example, read the Song in such a way as to suggest that, although all the sensual images had to be taken spiritually, the language of bodily love was actually the most appropriate and holy means to communicate the spiritual enjoyment involved in the relationship between God and his Church, between the human soul and the divine.[73] Nonetheless, Dante's sensualism appears more explicit. It is closer to that of the Song of Songs than to the explanatory prose of the commentators. Dante, in other words, is closer to Solomon the *scriba Dei* than to the theologians.

In conclusion, I offer a final observation on the theological value of poetry. It has frequently been noted that the language of the Heaven of the Sun is a brilliant exercise in different narrative techniques, as well as in the dense use of rhetoric *colores*. This technical virtuosity is a clear sign of Dante's keenness to show that poetry at its best has great epistemological value, and that figurative language, as the Bible and its exegesis clearly demonstrate, is the most truthful way to speak about God. Like the *scribae* of God, Dante is a writer whose subject transcends the human mind and can therefore be expressed only *per aenigmata*. In this context, the Song of Songs revealed to Dante the ways through which the language of human desire could signify the supreme love that brings the *congregatio fidelium* back to their only true love: God.

Notes

I thank Zygmunt Barański and Claudia Rossignoli for their comments on a previous version of this work. Translations of the *Commedia* are taken from Dante, *Divine Comedy*, tr. Mandelbaum.

1. Boccaccio, *Trattatello*, 47.
2. Ibid.
3. See, for example, Mazzotta, *Dante's Vision*, and the studies gathered in Barański, *Dante e i segni*.

4. On medieval theology as *scientia affectiva*, see Chenu, *La théologie*; Leclercq, *L'amour des lettres*. On the study of the Bible, see Smalley, *Study of the Bible*; de Lubac, *Medieval Exegesis*; Evans, *Language and Logic*. On medieval theology in general, see Evans, *Philosophy and Theology*.

5. On this topic see Minnis, *Medieval Theory of Authorship*.

6. Boccaccio, *Trattatello*, 64–65. This translation is by Bollettino (41).

7. This idea is also suggested by Trovato, "Canto XI," 157.

8. The bibliography on Dante and the Church is vast. See, for example, Botterill, "'Not of This World'"; Brezzi, "Dante e la Chiesa" and "Chiesa"; Comollo, *Il dissenso religioso*; C. Davis, *Dante and the Idea of Rome*, "Dante and the Empire," and "Roma e Babilonia"; D'Entrèves, *Dante as a Political Thinker*; Ferrante, *The Political Vision*; Kantorowicz, *The King's Two Bodies* and "Dante's Two Suns"; Manselli, "Dante e l'*ecclesia spiritualis*." For *lecturae* of *Inferno* 19, see Foster, "The Canto of the Damned Popes"; Kay, "The Pope's Wife"; Scott, "The Rock of Peter." On the last cantos of *Purgatorio*, see Armour, *Dante's Griffin*; Friedman, "La processione mistica"; Kaske, "Dante's *Purgatorio* XXXII and XXXIII"; Lansing, "Narrative Design."

9. The majority of work has focused on the influence of Franciscan and Joachimite thought on Dante. See Manselli, "Dante e l'*ecclesia spiritualis*"; but also C. Davis, "Dante and Ecclesiastical Property" and "Poverty and Eschatology."

10. Hendrix, "*Ecclesia in via*," 2. On medieval ecclesiology, see Herrin, *The Formation of Christendom*; Tellenbach, *The Church*; Thomson, *The Western Church*. On the medieval Church in general, see also Southern, *Western Society*.

11. See the relevant entries in *Dictionnaire de théologie catholique* and *The Catholic Encyclopaedia*. See also Congar, "L'ecclésiologie de S. Bernard."

12. See Hendrix, "*Ecclesia in via*," 6 ff.

13. See Congar, "L'ecclésiologie de S. Bernard," 136–47.

14. *De baptismo* is certainly his most comprehensive piece of polemical writing on ecclesiology, but Augustine further developed his ecclesiological thought in his *Enarrationes in Psalmos*, *De civitate Dei*, and the *De doctrina Christiana*. On Augustine's view of the Church, see Hendrix, "*Ecclesia in via*," esp. 15 ff.

15. On Augustine and his exegesis of the Song of Songs in relation to the Donatist controversy, see Cameron, "Augustine's Use of the Song of Songs"; N. Henry, "The Lily and the Thorns."

16. Augustine, *De baptismo* 5.27–28.

17. Augustine, *In Iohannis* 6.14.

18. Augustine, *In epistolam Iohannis* 5.3; on this see Hendrix, "*Ecclesia in via*," 19.

19. Augustine's use of the Song of Songs was also triggered by the controversy with the Donatists, who had used the biblical text to support their view of the true Church of God.

20. See the relevant entries in Metzger and Coogan, *The Oxford Companion to the Bible*.

21. On the medieval commentaries to the Song of Songs, see Ohly, *Hohelied-Studien*; Astell, *The Song of Songs in the Middle Ages*; Matter, *The Voice of My Beloved*; Pope, *Song of Songs*; Ravasi, *Il Cantico dei cantici*; Turner, *Eros and Allegory*.

22. See Hendrix, "*Ecclesia in via*," 15–74.

23. For them, "*caritas* is the mark of the true *fideles* who dwell in the Church, *numero et merito*" (Hendrix, "*Ecclesia in via*," 72).

24. See, for example, Bede, *In cantica canticorum* 1.2.4.

25. Fehlner, *The Role of Charity*, 143.

26. Ibid., 145. On Bonaventure's idea of the Church, see also Blasucci, "La costituzione gerarchica."

27. Congar, "L'ecclésiologie de S. Bernard," 136–90.

28. In the *Letters* (*Ep.* 11.6.26); in *Monarchia* (3.3.12); in the *Convivio* (2.5.5); and in the *Commedia* (above all in *Par.* 10.140; 11.32; 12.43; 27.40; 32.128).

29. On the Heaven of the Sun, see some of the existing *lecturae* on *Paradiso* 10: Cestaro, "Canto X"; Foster, "The Celebration of Order"; Freccero, "Paradiso X"; Nardi, "Il canto di s. Francesco." On *Paradiso* 11, see Auerbach, "Il canto XI"; Baldelli, "Il Canto XI del *Paradiso*"; Bosco, "Canto XI"; Mineo, "Il canto XI." On *Paradiso* 12, see Botterill, "Canto XII"; Manselli, "Il canto XII"; Ulivi, "San Francesco e Dante." On *Paradiso* 13, see Took, "Canto XIII"; Vandelli, "Il canto XIII del *Paradiso*." On *Paradiso* 14, see Bosco, "Domesticità"; Fallani, "Il canto XIV." See also some general studies on the episode: Cornish, *Reading Dante's Stars*, 93–107; Dronke, *Dante and Medieval Latin Traditions*, 82–102; Girardi, "La struttura del *Paradiso*"; Marietti, "Au Ciel du Soleil"; Meekins, "Reflecting on the Divine"; Mazzotta, "The Heaven of the Sun."

30. Dronke, *Dante's Second Love*; Vasoli, "La Bibbia." See also my observations on the *Convivio* in *Favole d'amore*.

31. See especially Dronke, *Dante and Medieval Latin Traditions*.

32. See, for example, Barański, *I segni di Dante*; Meekins, "Reflecting on the Divine"; Nasti, "The Wise Poet." For Bonaventure, "[t]he desire of God and the knowledge of God are not consummated, unless informed by charity, i.e. conjoined with it. Thus, fruition of God includes desire and knowledge and possession as necessary dispositions to the enjoyment of God in charity" (Fehlner, *The Role of Charity*, 116).

33. Bernard of Clairvaux, *Sermones super Cantica Canticorum* 69.2.2.

34. Translation by volume editors.

35. On this, see Meekins, "Reflecting on the Divine."

36. This is the theory supported throughout by Fehlner, *The Role of Charity* (for example, 17 and 24).

37. "Solus enim Deus est summum bonum et diligit se fruendo se, diligit etiam alia fruendo se" [For God alone is the Most High Good and He loves Himself by enjoying Himself, (and) He also loves others by enjoying Himself]. Bonaventure, *Sententiarum*, dub. 12, I, 44b.

38. Bonaventure, *Sententiarum*, dub. 1, IV, 328a; see also *Commentarius in Evangelium Lucae*, c. 17, 440.

39. According to Mineo's reading of cantos 10–14 of *Paradiso*, love is one of the metaphors and themes that unify the complex structure of the solar episodes. The cantos are dominated by two distinct semantic fields: on the one hand, reflection on the creative wisdom and power of God; on the other hand, joy and love, expressed in the song and the dance of the canto ("Il canto XI," 255). Within this division, Mineo finds a second pair of all-encompassing metaphors: military and marital (257). See the *loci* pertaining to the semantic field of love: "e lì comincia a vagheggiar ne l'arte / di quel maestro che dentro a sé l'ama, / tanto che mai da lei l'occhio non parte" (*Par.* 10.10–12) [and there begin to look with longing at / that Master's art, which in Himself he loves / so much that his eye never parts from it]; "Cor di mortal non fu mai sì digesto / a divozione e a rendersi a Dio / con tutto 'l suo gradir cotanto presto, / come a quelle parole mi fec' io; / e sì tutto 'l mio amore in lui si mise" (*Par.* 10.55–59) [No mortal heart was ever so disposed / to worship, or so quick to yield itself / to God with all its gratefulness, as I / was when I heard those words, and all my love / was so intent on Him]; "E dentro a l'un sentì cominciar: "Quando / lo raggio de la grazia, onde s'accende / verace amore e che poi cresce amando, / multiplicato in te tanto risplende" (*Par.* 10.82–85) [and from within one light I heard begin: / "Because the ray of grace, from which true love / is kindled first and then, in loving, grows, / shines with such splendor]; "qual ti negasse il vin de la sua fiala / per la tua sete, in libertà non fora / se non com' acqua ch'al mar non si cala" (*Par.* 10.88–90) [whoever would refuse to quench your thirst / with wine from his flask, would be no more free / than water that does not flow toward the sea].

40. On Dante and the Song of Songs, see Auerbach, *Studi su Dante*, 248–56 and 261–68; Chydenius, *The Typological Problem*; Leclercq, *Monks and Love*, 137–44; Priest, "Dante and the *Song of Songs*." On the relationship with the *Convivio* in particular, see Dronke, *Dante's Second Love*. On the *Vita Nuova* and the Song of Songs, see Nasti, "La memoria del *Canticum*." See also Sarolli, "Salomone." The most thorough and recent studies on the subject are those conducted by Pertile: "'La punta del disio'"; "*Cantica*"; "'Così si fa'"; "'Canto'—'Cantica'—'Comedìa'"; "*Paradiso*: A Drama of Desire"; and *La puttana e il gigante*.

41. Bernard, *Sermones super Cantica Canticorum* 21.4.

42. See for example: "La lor concordia e i lor lieti sembianti, / amore e maraviglia e dolce sguardo / facieno esser cagion di pensier santi; / tanto che 'l venerabile Bernardo / si scalzò prima, e dietro a tanta pace / corse e, correndo, li parve esser tardo" (*Par.* 11.76–81) [Their harmony and their glad looks, their love / and wonder and their gentle contemplation, / served others as a source of holy thoughts; / so much so, that the venerable Bernard / went barefoot first; he hurried toward such peace; / and though he ran, he thought his pace too slow].

43. Hendrix, "*Ecclesia in via*," 2–74.

44. Bernard, *Sermones super Cantica Canticorum* 68.2.4. See also Bede, *Hexameron*, 51.
45. Fehlner, *The Role of Charity*, 121.
46. Bernard, *Sermones super Cantica Canticorum* 69.1.
47. Fehlner, *The Role of Charity*, 21.
48. Pertile, "'La punta del desio.'" See also Chiarenza, "Dante's Lady Poverty."
49. Ambrose, *Commentarius in Cantica Canticorum* 2.57–59.
50. See, for instance, Ambrose, *Commentarius in Cantica Canticorum* 1.14.
51. Fehlner, *The Role of Charity*, 147.
52. Ibid., 160.
53. William of Saint-Thierry, *Expositio super Cantica Canticorum*, c. 30, 141–42.
54. Fehlner, *The Role of Charity*, 153.
55. For other observations on the circular movements of the blessed, see Dronke, *Dante and Medieval Latin Traditions*.
56. We find at least five explicit examples of these songs in cantos 10, 12, and 14: "Io vidi più folgór vivi e vincenti / far di noi centro e di sé far corona, / più dolci in voce che in vista lucenti" (*Par.* 10.64–66) [I saw many lights, alive, most bright; / we formed the center, they became a crown, / their voices even sweeter than their splendor]; "e 'l canto di quei lumi era di quelle; / chi non s'impenna sì che là sù voli, / dal muto aspetti quindi le novelle" (*Par.* 10.73–77) [the song those splendors sang. / He who does not take wings to reach that realm, / may wait for tidings of it from the mute]; "e moto a moto e canto a canto colse; / canto che tanto vince nostre muse, / nostre serene in quelle dolci tube, / quanto primo splendor quel ch'e' refuse" (*Par.* 12.6–9) [and motion matched with motion, song with song— / a song that, sung by those sweet instruments, / surpasses so our Muses and our Sirens / as firstlight does the light that is reflected]; "Poi che 'l tripudio e l'altra festa grande, / sì del cantare e sì del fiammeggiarsi / luce con luce gaudïose e blande, / insieme a punto e a voler quetarsi" (*Par.* 12.22–25) [When dance and jubilation, festival / of song and flame that answered flame, of light / with light, of gladness and benevolence, / in one same instant, with one will, fell still]; "Quell 'uno e due e tre che sempre vive / e regna sempre in tre e 'n due e 'n uno, / non circunscritto, e tutto circunscrive, / tre volte era cantato da ciascuno / di quelli spirti con tal melodia, / ch'ad ogne merto saria giusto muno" (*Par.* 14.28–33) [That One and Two and Three who ever lives / and ever reigns in Three and Two and One, / not circumscribed and circumscribing all, / was sung three times by each and all those souls / with such a melody that it would be / appropriate reward for every merit]. Interestingly, the melody is often connected to the image of the circle or to circular movements, because, as we said, in Bonaventurian terms the flow of love, here expressed vocally in songs of praise, is best represented by the circle, image of the Trinity.
57. Hendrix, "*Ecclesia in via*," 75 ff., and Fehlner, *The Role of Charity*, 16.

58. Cassiodorus, *Expositio Psalmorum* 110.1.
59. Hendrix, "*Ecclesia in via*," 75.
60. Augustine, *Enarrationes in Psalmos* 83.8. On this, see Hendrix, "*Ecclesia in via*," 78.
61. Bernard, *Sermones super Cantica Canticorum* 27.7.
62. Hendrix, "*Ecclesia in via*," 75–85.
63. Augustine, *Enarrationes in Psalmos* 122.1.
64. On the theme of desire in *Paradiso*, see Pertile, "*Paradiso*: A Drama of Desire," and Chiavacci Leonardi, "Il *Paradiso* di Dante."
65. Flowers are a recurring image in these cantos, and given the fact that Paradise as a whole is depicted as a mystic rose, this metaphor has considerable significance.
66. Bernard, *De diligendo Deo* 3.8. See Petrocchi, *L'ultima dea*, 141.
67. Nasti, "The Wise Poet," and *Favole d'amore*, 119–228.
68. Fehlner, *The Role of Charity*, 159.
69. Ibid.
70. On this, see ibid., 93.
71. The existing bibliography is vast. Here I note only some of the most significant studies: Auerbach, "Francesco d'Assisi"; Battaglia Ricci, "Figure di contraddizione" and "Scrittura e riscrittura"; Bosco, "San Francesco"; Chiari, "San Francesco cantato da Dante"; Cosmo, "Le mistiche nozze"; da Campagnola, "Francesco di Assisi"; Delcorno, "Cadenze e figure"; Fleming, *An Introduction to Franciscan Literature*; Foster, "Gli elogi danteschi"; Manselli, "San Francesco e San Domenico"; Pasquazi, "San Francesco"; Ulivi, "Il 'magnanimo' S. Francesco." The representation of the marriage between Francis and Poverty is not foreign to St. Bonaventure, the official biographer of Francis. Bonaventure mentions the "marriage" between Francis and Poverty, even though only in passing: "Inter cetera charismatum dona, quae a largo Doctore Franciscus obtinuit, prerogativa quadam speciali promeruit in divitias simplicitatis excrescere per altissimae paupertatis amorem. Hanc Filio Dei vir sanctus familiarem attenens et iam quasi tot orbe repulsam, caritate sic studuit desponsare perpetua, quod non solum pro ea patrem matremque reliquit, verum etiam quae habere potuit universa dispersit" (Bonaventure, *Legenda maior* 7.1) [Among the many gifts of spiritual graces, which holy St Francis obtained, he merited by a certain special prerogative to abound in the riches of simplicity, by the love of most perfect poverty. This virtue, the holy man considering to have been familiar to the son of God, and weighing also the same to be now abandoned throughout the world, did so efficaciously endeavour to espouse the same unto himself by perpetual charity, for the love of which he not only forsook both Father and Mother, but also freely distributed whatever he had]. For an excellent summary of the differences and similarities between the *Legenda maior* and the canto of St. Francis, see Battaglia Ricci, "Scrittura e riscrittura," 148–65. For the occurrence of this *topos* in other Franciscan texts, see Cosmo, "Il primo libro francescano,"

especially 36–38 and 56–57; da Campagnola, "Le prime biografie del Santo," especially 40; C. Davis, "Poverty and Eschatology"; Havely, "Poverty in Purgatory." Following Cosmo, Havely notes that even Tommaso of Celano in his *Vita Prima* represented the marriage of the saint with Faith and Poverty (242, n. 23). See also Zino, "Liturgia e musica."

72. This is the line of thought found in Bonaventure according to Fehlner, *The Role of Charity*, 118–22.

73. This is Gregory's explanation of the sensuality of the Song: "Hinc est enim, quod in hoc libro amoris quasi corporei verba ponuntur: ut a torpore suo anima per sermones suae consuetudinis refricata recalescat et per verba amoris, qui infra est, excitetur ad amorem, qui supra est. Nominantur enim in hoc libro oscula, nominantur ubera, nominantur genae, nominatur femora; in quibus verbis non irridenda est sacra descriptio, sed maior dei misericordia consideranda est: quia, dum membra corporis nominat et sic ad amorem vocat, notandum est quam mirabiliter nobiscum et misericorditer operatur, qui, ut cor nostrum ad investigationem sacri amoris accenderet, usque ad turpis amoris nostra verba discendit. Sed, unde se loquendo humiliat, inde nos intellectu exaltat: quia ex sermonibus huius amoris discimus, qua virtute in divinitatis amore ferveamus" (Gregory the Great, *Expositio in Canticum Canticorum*, 23–37) [This is why in this book the terms of a love which appears carnal are employed: it is so that the soul, leaving its torpor, is heated under the friction of subject matter which is familiar to it, and, thanks to the language of love contained therein, it might be stimulated to the love which is above it. Indeed in this book, kisses, breasts, cheeks, and thighs are mentioned; these words should not provoke irreverence towards the sacred text, but should make even clearer than before the mercy of God: for, when it names the parts of the body, and thus incites us to love, we must recognize in what a marvellous and merciful way He is acting towards us—He who, in order to set our hearts aflame and to lead them to sacred love, goes so far as to employ the language of our crude love. However, in the same way that He humbles himself in words, He raises us in comprehension; for it is from the language of that love that we learn with what strength we must burn with divine love.]

9

Neoplatonic Metaphysics and Imagination in Dante's *Commedia*

DOUGLAS HEDLEY

> It must puzzle us to know what thinking is
> if Shakespeare and Dante did not do it.
> —Lionel Trilling, *The Liberal Imagination*

Readers often find an image of their own longings in the works of great poets. Dante, for example, exerts considerable sway over those, like T. S. Eliot and Dorothy Sayers, who see him as a representative of a lost Christendom—the Catholic poet par excellence. Others, like Benedetto Croce, have played down the theology and exalted the aesthetic component of Dante's achievement. My aim in the present essay is to highlight the Neoplatonic aspect of Dante's aesthetics, which later flourished in the Romantic period, one of the two modern periods in which Neoplatonism was an intellectually dominant force in the West.[1] I further suggest that this aesthetics is linked to a rather surprising aspect of Neoplatonism: its emphasis on the indwelling divine spirit.

My starting point is that Dante gives us an astonishingly articulate account of his own creative imagination, located within a particular relation between prophecy and art, and deeply indebted to Neoplatonic metaphysics. This is an ontology of the "image" or "icon," in which the sensible cosmos is viewed as a *likeness* of the intelligible reality that is its source. The imagination itself is an instance of that force of the divine within humanity, awoken by heavenly *eros*, which arouses the longing to return to the divine origin:

> Non dei più ammirar, se bene stimo,
> lo tuo salir, se non come d'un rivo
> se d'alto monte scende giuso ad imo.
>   Maraviglia sarebbe in te se, privo
> d'impedimento, giù ti fossi assiso,
> com' a terra quïete in foco vivo.
>   (*Par.* 1.136–41)

[If I am right, thou shouldst no more wonder at thy ascent than at a stream falling from a mountain-height to the foot; it would be a wonder in thee if, freed from hindrance, thou hadst remained below, as on earth would be stillness in living flame.]

We find here the Neoplatonic tenet that when the soul is liberated from evil, it ascends quite naturally to the Good: *omnia in deum tendunt et recurrunt*. This metaphor of the natural place of the soul in God or its gravitation towards the One is employed by Christian theologians of Neoplatonic provenance, such as Eriugena and Eckhart.[2] This doctrine of the indwelling divine power was not a gloomy determinism. Precisely on account of their conviction that the divine was immanent in the human soul, for instance, the Neoplatonists of Renaissance Florence believed that the *artes liberales* are properly so called because they *free* and thereby enlarge the mind through the awakening and inspiring light of divine presence. A Neoplatonic construal of Dante is not a cultural oddity but based upon an elective affinity. Romantic Neoplatonists such as Coleridge or Schelling saw, I believe, a congenial spirit in Dante—and in this essay I will suggest why they were correct.[3] At the core of such a belief in a genial coincidence is a paradoxical insistence on the transcendence *and* the immanence of the divine, on estrangement from *and* intimacy with God. The crucial verb, in Dantean terms, is "trasumanar" (*Par.* 1.70): to transhumanize. The *Commedia* has a triadic structure expressive of the transformation, purification, and spiritualization of love as the soul ascends to God through the three stages of alienation, purgation, and contemplative union.

This might well strike one as being in contrast with a common image of "Platonism," often attributed to Dante. Emphasis upon the "presence" of the divine contrasts with the widely diffused image of the "great chain of being," where the emphasis lies rather upon the immeasurable dignity and transcendence of the divine source. Yet such a powerful sense of divine *immanence* as opposed to some radical and inaccessible transcendence is central to Neoplatonic thought. As beautifully expressed by Coleridge, "Dante does not so much elevate your thoughts as send them down deeper. In this canto all images are distinct, and even vividly distinct; but there is a total impression of infinity; the wholeness is not in vision or conception, but in an inner feeling of totality, and absolute being."[4]

Modern scholars of Dante have shared this sentiment. Christopher Ryan observes that "the central quest of Dante's understanding in the poem, and indeed in his *oeuvre* as a whole, was to grasp how the divine is present in the human. Behind the thirst for that knowledge lay the conviction, permeating all his works, that God is supremely to be discovered in human nature."[5] I will argue that it is the presence of God *in* man that enables Dante to maintain the conviction that the long and painful ascent of the soul *to* God is at the same time a journey *within* the divine sphere. Here we encounter the Neoplatonic absolute or One, whose center is everywhere and circumference nowhere. The goal of the *Commedia*, on this interpretation, is the vision of the invisible, that immaterial principle which is the transcendent source of all being. The light that dominates Dante's poem is intellectual, not physical.

THE ROMANTIC REVIVAL OF DANTE

The German philosopher Friedrich Wilhelm Joseph von Schelling enjoys a decisive position in the Romantic evaluation of Dante's *Commedia* as the "archetype of all modern poetry" that produces "a world by itself and wholly characteristic."[6] Schelling has a thoroughly Neoplatonic view of art, one which identifies beauty with truth and in which human art is analogous to divine creativity. The world is a theophany, and through symbolic representations of the intelligible order the artist can facilitate the transcendence of the sensible appearance back to the unitary source of the cosmos.[7]

Schelling stresses the medieval context of Dante's thought and creative genius, as well as his capacity to hold together the history and ideas of his age. Dante, for Schelling, is no mere craftsman arranging preexisting materials, but a genius who was miraculously attuned to his own culture. Furthermore, in Dante's work the subject matter becomes the feeling subject. In his *Vorlesungen zur Philosophie der Kunst*, Schelling discusses the mythological component of Christianity as lying in its history—from Christ, the apostles and saints, to medieval knights. The unity of finite and infinite is to be found in historical individuals and events. Schelling states: "In as much as Dante himself is viewed as the main protagonist, one who serves as the link between the immeasurable series of visions and portraits, and who behaves passively rather than actively, . . . [the Christian mythology of Dante] is an absolutely individual thing, not comparable to anything outside itself."[8] From this perspective, the *Commedia* is not an epic, comedy, or drama but a fusion of all of these genres, which, through its particular focus on the individual historical subject, is of great philosophical value.

One of the most important contemporary readers of Schelling was the English poet-philosopher Samuel Taylor Coleridge, a figure of considerable significance for the reception of Dante, both in his mediation of the German Romantic-Idealistic revival of interest in Dante and in his relationship with Reverend Francis Cary's translation of the *Commedia*.[9] Coleridge stresses the importance of philosophy in Dante, "for Dante was the living link between religion and philosophy, he philosophized the religion and christianized the philosophy of Italy; and in this poetic union of religion and philosophy, he became the ground of transition into the mixed Platonism and Aristotelianism of the schools."[10] The *Commedia*, according to Coleridge, is a "system of moral, political and theological truths."[11] Further,

> In studying Dante, therefore, we must consider carefully the differences produced, first, by allegory being substituted for polytheism; and secondly and mainly, by the opposition of Christianity to the spirit of pagan Greece, which receiving the very names of its gods from Egypt, soon deprived them of all that was universal. The Greeks changed the ideas into finites, and these finites into *anthropomorphi*, or forms of men. . . . The reverse of this was the natural effect of Christianity; in which finites, even the human form, must, in order to satisfy the mind, be brought into connexion with, and be in fact symbolical of, the infinite; and must be considered in some ending, however

shadowy and indistinct, point of view, as the vehicle or representative of moral truth.[12]

Here Coleridge is presenting Dante in the context of an overarching theory regarding the difference between the Hellenic and the Christian traditions, and according to which Christianity was able to unite properly the manifold of finite symbols with the universal source. Whereas the myths of the Greek gods present a random assortment of morally opaque or disreputable tales, Christianity is able through allegory to forge a link between symbolic representation and a properly monotheistic conception of providence. As Dante writes:

> ... Le cose tutte quante
> hanno ordine tra loro, e questo è forma
> che l'universo a Dio fa simigliante.
>   Qui veggion l'alte creature l'orma
> de l'eterno valore, il quale è fine
> al quale è fatta la toccata norma.
> (*Par.* 1.103–8)

[All things whatsoever have order among themselves, and this is the form that makes the universe resemble God; here the higher creatures see the impress of the Eternal Excellence, which is the end for which that system itself is made.]

Coleridge observes that the allegorizing monotheistic poetry of Christianity embodied in Dante resulted in "two great effects; a combination of poetry with doctrine, and, by turning the mind inward on its own essence instead of letting it act only on its outward circumstances and communities, a combination of poetry with sentiment. And it is this inwardness or subjectivity, which principally and most fundamentally distinguished all the classic from all the modern poetry."[13]

Coleridge is claiming—I think plausibly—that religion is not, for Dante, a set of facts *extra nos* but rather is inextricably linked to the inner life: it is "La concreata e perpetüa sete / del deïforme regno" (*Par.* 2.19–20) [The inborn and perpetual thirst for the godlike kingdom]. And morality is not a matter of external observance or effects but a matter of *intention*. Sins of weakness are punished in upper Hell, and deliberate sin is punished in lower Hell, forming a descending hierarchy from incontinence to treachery. The path back to the good, moreover, requires recognition of the disorder of the soul. The terraces of Purgatory demand a gradual purification of the will. As Sordello explains to Virgil in *Purgatorio* 7, it is not possible to ascend the Mountain of Purgatory after the setting of the sun (43–45). The sun, for Dante, is an image of divine truth (e.g., *Inf.* 1.13–18; see also *Conv.* 3.12.7), and in the *Commedia* he presents us with a picture of the spiritual necessity for clear vision as a precondition for the ascent of the soul.[14]

Dante clearly believed in an eternal and immutable morality: "lume v'è dato a bene e a malizia" (*Purg.* 16.75) [light (is) given (to you) on good and evil]. The figure of Beatrice illuminates this principle (*Purg.* 18.46–75). As she says, in reproaching Dante upon meeting him in the Earthly Paradise,

> Sì tosto come in su la soglia fui
> di mia seconda etade e mutai vita,
> questi si tolse a me, e diesse altrui.
>
> Quando di carne a spirto era salita,
> e bellezza e virtù cresciuta m'era,
> fu' io a lui men cara e men gradita;
>
> e volse i passi suoi per via non vera,
> imagini di ben seguendo false,
> che nulla promission rendono intera.
>
> Né l'impetrare ispirazion mi valse,
> con le quali e in sogno e altrimenti
> lo rivocai: sì poco a lui ne calse!
>
> (*Purg.* 30.124–35)

[As soon as I was on the threshold of my second age and I changed life he took himself from me and gave himself to another. When I had risen from the flesh to spirit and beauty and virtue had increased in me I was less dear to him and less welcome and he bent his steps in a way not true, following after false images of good which fulfil no promise; nor did it avail me to gain inspirations for him with which both in dream and in other ways I called him back, so little did he heed them.]

The Florentine woman Beatrice can point Dante beyond herself to the divine beauty of the Godhead. The Neoplatonic emphasis is striking.

She has risen from flesh to spirit, and he is immersed in false images and the "shame of his wandering." Dante's remorse and humiliation are contrasted with the spiritual love of Beatrice transformed:

> Sotto 'l suo velo e oltre la rivera
> vincer pariemi più sé stessa antica,
> vincer che l'altre qui, quand' ella c'era.
> Di penter sì mi punse ivi l'ortica,
> che di tutte altre cose qual mi torse
> più nel suo amor, più mi si fé nemica.
> Tanta riconoscenza il cor mi morse,
> ch'io caddi vinto; e quale allora femmi,
> salsi colei che la cagion mi porse.
> (*Purg.* 31.82–90)

[Beneath her veil and beyond the stream, she seemed to surpass her former self more than she surpassed the others here when she was with us. The nettle of remorse so stung me there that of all other things that which had most bent me to the love of it became for me the most hateful; such self-conviction bit me at the heart and what I became then she knows who was the cause of it.]

Dante's own spiritual experience is a mirror of an eternal and immutable reality, to which—as indicated by Beatrice—he can conform, in repentance and confession, by turning to a correct understanding of the world's manifestation of the divine, and to a correct understanding of the presence of the divine within him. Following Hegel, we might see the lasting value of Dante's work as lying precisely in his expression of the Christian faith in the infinite value of the individual.

A Phenomenology of Spirit

The *Commedia* is a first-person ascent. The poem is about the journey of Dante's soul to God: it is a spiritual autobiography akin to those of Augustine and Boethius.[15] This is not simply a religion of the genial layperson addressed to his muse, Beatrice. The protagonist is also the visionary, who, like Adonis, Osiris, Ulysses, or Aeneas, must confront and enter the realm of death; and who, like Ezekiel, St. John, or St. Paul, is called to penetrate the heavenly mysteries.[16] (Thomas Carlyle or Henri Bergson would have appreciated this aspect of Dante's work.) As Peter Hawkins remarks, the *Commedia* can be viewed "as an extended call narrative, a story about the making of a prophet."[17] The *Commedia* thus presents us with the idea that prophecy and poetry are intimately linked, an idea that, especially in the light of texts such as the *Phaedrus*, we can once again characterize, at least in one of its aspects, as Platonic. On this view, the "strangeness" of Dante's journey does not lie primarily in the fact that he is accompanied by the greatest poet of Latin antiquity, or that he meets contemporary Florentines and mythical figures of antiquity, or that he is reunited to Beatrice in the Earthly Paradise. It lies in the parallels between the *Commedia* and apocalyptic visions like that of Enoch and, most importantly, in Dante's comparison of his journey with the rapture of St. Paul (*Inf.* 2.28–36; *Par.* 1.4–6, 73–75; 2.37–42). It would appear, moreover, that Dante thought that the theory of the four senses, which he felt appropriate for the interpretation of scripture, could also apply to his poetry.[18]

Throughout the *Commedia*, Dante (who of course, like Ovid, was a banished poet) uses the biblical motif of exile. This motif has both a physical and a spiritual dimension for Dante and, in relation to both of these, bestows urgency upon the poem. The shocking Ovidian image of Marsyas at the beginning of the *Paradiso* (1.13–21) is highly appropriate, for the journey of return to the divine source of being requires a descent into Hell.[19] At the beginning of the *Commedia* we are famously informed that the protagonist tries to escape from the dark wood on the edge of Hell, but three beasts prevent this (*Inf.* 1.28–60). And, as Virgil explains in rescuing Dante, if Dante is to be able to journey towards salvation without the impediment of the beasts, his journey must begin with an exploration of Hell (1.82–129). The providential helper thus guides Dante through the realm of unrelenting and willful sin, and then, as the second stage on Dante's journey, through the mountain of Purgatory on a path of ever increasing illumination and purification. The protagonist finally encounters Beatrice, through whom he had the first intimations of truth, and with whom he will now ascend into Heaven. The basic pattern of the tale is death and rebirth.[20]

The path towards this "emptying" of the self is initiated by the experience of restlessness, the mood of foreboding, and homesickness for the spiritual homeland. Thomas Finan draws an instructive parallel between the terror of St. Paul's experience on the road to Damascus ("tremens ac stupens" [Acts 9:6]), the numinous fear and trembling of Christian mystical experience, and Dante's state, "filled with fear," in the *Vita nuova*.[21] And at the very opening of the *Inferno* we find precisely the Platonic-Pauline-Augustinian anxiety that finds its way into Pascal, Kierkegaard, and Heidegger: "Nel mezzo del cammin di nostra vita" (*Inf.* 1.1) [In the middle of the journey of our life]. This is the "sickness unto death" of life alienated from God. This is the beginning of the journey of the soul, a phenomenology of spirit—from the abyss of living death to divine life and truth. Or, to borrow the Neoplatonic terminology of Cristoforo Landino, the plan of the *Commedia* might be understood in terms of the "amor caelestis," which impels the soul by a "furor divinus" towards its transcendent telos.[22]

The significance of all this is enhanced by the way in which Dante employs the language of wonder and amazement to express a sense of the sublime. This is a *mood* rather than an emotion, and is related to Dante's conception of the nature of reality. For Dante, an experiential element in the comprehension of reality is "stupore."[23] Such wonder punctuates Dante's journey towards God. We find it, for example, at the moment in which Dante tells us he is once again able to travel on that road that had been lost at the beginning of the *Inferno*:

> Noi andavam per lo solingo piano,
> com' om che torna a la perduta strada,
> che 'nfino ad essa gli pare ire in vano.
> (*Purg.* 1.118–20)

[We made our way over the lonely plain, like one who returns to the road he has lost and, till he finds it, seems to himself to go in vain.]

We also find such wonder inaugurating the *Paradiso*:

> La gloria di colui che tutto move
> per l'universo penetra, e risplende
> in una parte più e meno altrove.
> Nel ciel che più de la sua luce prende
> fu' io, e vidi cose che ridire
> né sa né può chi di là sù discende;

>   perché appressando sé al suo disire,
> nostro intelletto si profonda tanto,
> che dietro la memoria non può ire.
>   Veramente quant' io del regno santo
> ne la mia mente potei far tesoro,
> sarà ora materia del mio canto.
>
> (1.1–12)

[The glory of Him who moves all things penetrates the universe and shines in one part more and in another less. I was in the heaven that most receives His light and I saw things which he that descends from it has not the knowledge or the power to tell again; for our intellect, drawing near to its desire, sinks so deep that memory cannot follow it. Nevertheless, so much of the holy kingdom as I was able to treasure in my mind shall now be matter of my song.]

A*mor caelestis*

One of the boldest components of Dante's theological vision is the figure of Beatrice, and especially the way that she manifests and embodies the ultimate principle of the poem—"l'amor che move il sole e l'altre stelle" (*Par.* 33.145) [the Love that moves the sun and the other stars]. The role of Beatrice has roots in Wisdom literature and in Boethius's Lady Philosophy. Consider, for example, Boethius's "O felix hominum genus, / Si vestros animos amor / Quo caelum regitur regat" (*Consolation* 2.8.28–30)[24] [O happy race of men, / If the love that rules the stars / May also rule your hearts!]. The ascent of the soul to God, for Dante, is at the same time a profound vision of the nature of Beatrice. Speaking to Beatrice, Dante says: "di tante cose quant' i' ho vedute, / dal tuo podere e da la tua bontate / riconosco la grazia e la virtute" (*Par.* 31.82–84) [of all the things that I have seen I acknowledge the grace and virtue to be from thy power and from thy goodness]. In the *Commedia*, love is presented to us as a metaphysical and theological force within the context of a specifically Christian vision of the soul's journey to God. Dante puts much greater stress upon sorrow and grief than a Stoic or a Neoplatonist would, and he does so in large part through the figure of Beatrice and through the narrative of the protagonist's relationship with her. Love, for Dante, is a mystery, which means not that it is incomprehensible but that it is a higher truth that can be revealed through its manifestation in a lower reality, especially—as with Beatrice—through its embodiment in individual persons.

For Aristotle, God is the unmoved mover which moves all things, as a lover is moved toward the beloved. Aristotle, however, does not identify God with love. That said, we should be wary of treating the identification of love with the divine ground of the cosmos, which we find in authors such as Dante and Boethius, simply as a fusion of Aristotle with John's Gospel. As Cornelia de Vogel argues persuasively in relation to Boethius, the formulation of *Consolatio philosophiae* 2.8.28–30, cited above, is Neoplatonic in character, with Proclus as a specific source. For Plato, *eros* is typically a phenomenon of human life—a demon that involves a sense of inadequacy. Hence it can stand for the longing for perfection in the midst of imperfection. Proclus, however, refers more specifically to a "*Divine descending Love*, stretching from the transcendental level of Nous down to the souls of human beings living on earth."[25]

An interpretation such as that just outlined can enhance our sense of the audacity of Dante's spirit, which in this respect is reminiscent of Eckhart. Hegel, for example, insists that "[t]heology is not just religious piety . . . but rather the *comprehension* of religious content." He comments that "[e]arlier Theologians saw to the very bottom of this depth, especially Catholic theologians," and notes Meister Eckhart's astonishing claim that "'the eye with which God sees me is the eye with which I see him.'"[26] Behind Eckhart's image of the eye is the mystical-Neoplatonic conception of the transformation of the self into the Divine, to which one could usefully apply Jean Trouillard's description of Platonism as "une doctrine et une méthode des métamorphoses du moi"[27] [a doctrine and a method of the metamorphoses of the "me"]. To begin to see the specifically Dantean implications, one could turn again to Coleridge, who interprets the image of Marsyas in *Paradiso* 1 in a Neoplatonic fashion: "Dante did not mean to speak of Apollo's *own* Song in his strife with Marsyas; but asks for an evacuation and exinanition of all *Self* in *him* (Dante) like the unsheathing of Marsyas that so he (Dante) might become a mere vessel, or Wine skin of the Deity."[28]

Coleridge picks up on the Ovidian story of the metamorphosis of Marysas to illustrate Dante's poetic vocation in explicitly mystical terms. This is an intriguing construal of a story that might be more naturally interpreted in terms of the opposition of theology and poetry.[29] The rare word "exinanition" means the "process of emptying or exhausting, whether in a material or immaterial sense; emptied or exhausted condition," and the "action or process of emptying of pride, self-will, or dignity; abasement, humiliation."[30] Thus, John Donne states that "[t]his exinanition of ourselves is acceptable in the sight of God."[31] In one of its recorded meanings, moreover, the word specifically refers to Christ, as in St. Paul's Christological hymn of Philippians 2:8: "humiliavit semet ipsum factus oboediens usque ad mortem, mortem autem crucis" [He humbled himself, becoming obedient unto death, even to the death of the cross]. Jeremy Taylor, for example, speaks of how Christ was "to take upon him all the affronts, miseries and exinanitions of the most miserable."[32]

Coleridge's reading of *Paradiso* 1 thus foregrounds the boldness of Dante's conception of the relationship and union between the human and the divine. Dante's word "trasumanar" should clearly be read in the light of such audacity. And the full significance of the figure of Beatrice in the poetic narrative of the *Commedia* can only be appreciated in the light of this audacity.

The Vision and Experience of God

Dante, like Plato, Aristotle, and Plotinus, thought that contemplation was the highest activity of humanity. As Cacciaguida tells Dante in the Heaven of Mars, "Tu credi 'l vero; ché i minori e ' grandi / di questa vita miran ne lo speglio / in che, prima che pensi, il pensier pandi" (*Par.* 15.61–63) [Thou believest rightly, for small and great in this life gaze into the mirror in which, before thou thinkest, thou makest plain the thought]. Each rational being is a mirror of the divine light. But there is also a contemplation of God that surpasses images:

> . . . la mia vista, venendo sincera,
> e più e più intrava per lo raggio
> de l'alta luce che da sé è vera.
>   Da quinci innanzi il mio veder fu maggio
> che 'l parlar mostra, ch'a tal vista cede,
> e cede la memoria a tanto oltraggio.
>   Qual è colüi che sognando vede,
> che dopo 'l sogno la passione impressa
> rimane, e l'altro alla mente non riede,

> cotal son io, ché quasi tutta cessa
> mia visïone, e ancor mi distilla
> nel core il dolce che nacque da essa.
>   Così la neve al sol si disigilla;
> così al vento ne le foglie levi
> si perdea la sentenza di Sibilla.
>   (*Par.* 33.52–66)

[... for my sight, becoming pure, was entering more and more through the beam of the lofty light which in itself is true.
  From that moment my vision was greater than our speech, which fails at such a sight, and memory too fails at such excess. Like him that sees in a dream and after the dream the passion wrought by it remains and the rest returns not to his mind, such am I; for my vision almost wholly fades, and still there drops within my heart the sweetness that was born of it. Thus the snow loses its imprint in the sun; thus in the wind on the light leaves the Sibyl's oracles was lost.]

Within the Aristotelian tradition one generally finds the desire to identify language with the world. For Platonists, on the other hand, exalted experiences of ecstasy and also certain moods or feelings resist conceptual definition. As Ernst Gombrich observes, "It was the Platonists who made man feel the inadequacy of 'discursive speech' for conveying the experience of a direct apprehension of truth and the 'ineffable' intensity of the mystic vision."[33] The Platonic tradition stresses the inadequacy of language, especially discursive language. In the same tradition one also finds a preference for images that approximate the experiential immediacy of union with the Divine, which for the Platonist is the end-goal of philosophy.[34] For Dante, the point at which imagination breaks down is that of ecstatic or *sit venia verbo* "mystical" experience:

> A l'alta fantasia qui mancò possa;
> ma già volgeva il mio disio e 'l *velle*,
> sì come rota ch'igualmente è mossa,
>   l'amor che move il sole e l'altre stelle.
>   (*Par.* 33.142–45)

[Here power failed the high phantasy; but now my desire and will, like a wheel that spins with even motion, were revolved by the Love that moves the sun and other stars.]

Triadic Spheres of Light

It is not surprising that at the climax of the *Commedia* Dante employs images of triadic spheres of light. It also should not be surprising that these images are deeply Platonic.

In *Paradiso* 28 we are told about Dante's vision of the nine fiery circles of the angelic hierarchies, and at the end of the canto Beatrice says:

> E Dïonisio con tanto disio
> a contemplar questi ordini si mise,
> che li nomò e distinse com' io.
>   Ma Gregorio da lui poi si divise;
> onde, sì tosto come li occhi aperse
> in questo ciel, di sé medesmo rise.
>   E se tanto secreto ver proferse
> mortale in terra, non voglio ch'ammiri:
> ché chi 'l vide qua sù gliel discoperse
>   con altro assai del ver di questi giri.
>   (130–39)

[And Dionysius set himself with such zeal to contemplate these orders that he named and distributed them as I do; but later Gregory differed from him, so that as soon as he opened his eyes in this heaven he smiled at himself. And if a mortal on earth set forth truth so secret thou needst not marvel, for he that saw it here above revealed it to him, with much more of the truth of these circles.]

These lines contain an appeal to immediate and certain knowledge, based, like that of Dionysius, on *experience* (in Dionysius's case, the experience of Paul) rather than on tradition, as in the case of Gregory. Yet what is the truth of the fiery circles? How, for Dante, is the image of the circle related to divine truth and to the relationship between divine truth and the human mind?

Plato presents the reflection of the soul as circular in the *Timaeus*. This model is criticized by Aristotle in *De anima* for implying redundancy. Productive reasoning is linear rather than circular; reflection pursues specific goals through premises to conclusions. A circular model of thought denies real progress. Only at the level of divine thought, for Aristotle, is the circular model appropriate.[35] Plotinus, however, typically brings together the two ideas of the circle as a paradigm of both the finite soul and the supreme principle. In the context of this aspect of his metaphysics, he systematically employs the image of the sphere.[36] The spheres of the intellect and the soul are circles that spring from the One. The cosmos is the unfolding of the enclosed reality of the One, conceived as the center from which spheres or circles proceed, and is the point of initiation for the return of the intellect to its source. De Vogel helpfully describes Plotinus's image as one of "*circum-radiation*, encircling light."[37] Just as the radii of the circles are related to a central point, and the periphery can be understood only in relation to the center, the circumference and center form a unity. As Plotinus writes, "what are we to think of as surrounding the One in its repose? It must be a radiation from it while it remains unchanged, like the bright light of the sun which, so to speak, runs round it, springing from it continually while it remains unchanged."[38]

In this image of Plotinus, the transcendent source of reality, which is also the ultimate ground of the return of the spirit to its source, is best understood as a circle whose center is everywhere and circumference nowhere.[39] Or, as Dante puts it in the prayer that opens *Purgatorio* 11: "O Padre nostro, che ne' cieli stai, / non circunscritto, ma per più amore / ch'ai primi effetti di là sù tu hai" (1–3) [Our Father which art in heaven, not circumscribed but by the greater love Thou hast for Thy first works on high].

As Irma Brandeis observes, Dante's Hell might be seen as "a concrete projection of the spiritual condition of its inmates."[40] The circular movement in Hell reflects the contraction of the sinful will on the ego's own center rather than, as in the spiral motion of Purgatory, the gradual expansion of the self desiring the circle whose circumference is nowhere and center everywhere. The circles of Hell are not outside the divine influence, but they are far removed from the transcendent source depicted by Beatrice in the *Paradiso*:

> La natura del mondo, che quïeta
> il mezzo e tutto l'altro intorno move,
> quinci comincia come da sua meta;
>   e questo cielo non ha altro dove
> che la mente divina, in che s'accende
> l'amor che 'l volge e la virtù ch'ei piove.

Luce e amor d'un cerchio lui comprende,
sì come questo li altri; e quel precinto
colui che 'l cinge solamente intende.
                    (27.106–14)

[The nature of the universe, which holds the centre still and moves all else round it, begins here as from its starting-point, and this heaven has no other *where* but the Divine Mind, in which is kindled the love that turns it and the virtue which it rains down. Light and love enclose it in a circle, as it does the others, and of that girding He that girds it is the sole Intelligence.]

Here we find an image of the sphere or circle of the intelligible cosmos as the translucent unfolding of the center or point (*Par.* 28.41–42) from which the One bodies forth itself, while remaining undiminished by its irradiation. Light is thus an image which expresses the translucence and interpenetration of the levels of reality; an image which expresses the immediacy of the *presence* of the spiritual or intelligible in the domain of sense perception. Dante also employs such Neoplatonic metaphysics when he writes about his final vision of, and union with, God:

Omai sarà più corta mia favella,
pur a quel ch'io ricordo, che d'un fante
che bagni ancor la lingua a la mammella.
    Non perché più ch'un semplice sembiante
fosse nel vivo lume ch'io mirava,
che tal è sempre qual s'era davante;
    ma per la vista che s'avvalorava
in me guardando, una sola parvenza,
mutandom' io, a me si travagliava.
    Ne la profonda e chiara sussistenza
de l'alto lume parvermi tre giri
di tre colori e d'una contenenza;
    e l'un da l'altro come iri da iri
parea reflesso, e 'l terzo parea foco
che quinci e quindi igualmente si spiri.
                    (*Par.* 33.106–20)

[Now my speech will come more short even of what I remember than an infant's who yet bathes his tongue at the breast. Not that the living light at which I gazed had more than a single aspect—

for it is ever the same as it was before—, but by my sight gaining strength as I looked, the one sole appearance, I myself changing, was, for me, transformed. In the profound and clear ground of the lofty light appeared to me three circles of three colours and of the same extent, and the one seemed reflected by the other as rainbow by rainbow, and the third seemed fire breathed forth equally from the one and the other.]

Light is an image of the intelligibility of the universe—both in the projection of light from the transcendent source and in the ascent towards that source, which, through the exercise of thought and the purification of the soul, culminates in the sudden ineffable vision of the source itself. It is also an image of human community properly conceived in its relationship to the divine. The image of the white rose of the blessed in *Paradiso* 31—which is perfectly illuminated by the triune light that God is (28–29), insofar as such "luce divina è penetrante / per l'universo secondo ch'è degno, / sì che nulla le puote essere ostante" (22–23) [divine light penetrates the universe according to the fitness of its parts so that nothing can hinder it]—is clearly indebted to the same Neoplatonic metaphysics.

DANTE'S PLATONIC THEOLOGICAL AESTHETIC

In *Inferno* 9.61–63 and *Purgatorio* 8.19–21 we read that poetry is a veil, through which we must see; and the Letter to Can Grande claims that the purpose of the *Commedia* is moral or ethical: "finis totius . . . est removere viventes in hac vita de statu miserie et perducere ad statum felicitatis" (*EC* 15) [the aim of the whole . . . is to remove those living in this life from a state of misery, and bring them to a state of happiness]. When Beatrice says, "riguarda qual son io" (*Par.* 23.46) [look at me as I am], Dante is presenting her as a legitimate image both for his poetic imagination and for his divine revelation. This dual function can fruitfully be linked both to the theory in Plato's *Symposium* and *Phaedrus* that the love of sensible beauty can inspire the mind to ascend to spiritual realities, and to Plotinus's theory (contra Plato) that the artist can point the mind to spiritual realities more effectively than mere exposure to nature. Coleridge writes: "The Images in Dante are not only taken from obvious nature, and are all intelligible to all, but are ever conjoined with the universal feeling received from nature, and therefore affect the general feelings of all men."[41]

From this perspective, we find a congruence between Dante's theory of his own expression and the Renaissance theory that the true poet is a maker of images, not idols, and that the enigmatic image contains a surfeit of meaning. The interpretation of symbols incites and ignites contemplation of invisible realities; the realm of symbols is thus akin to divine communication. Furthermore, insofar as the symbol is intuited in its meaning, such intuition provides an analogy of the superior, nondiscursive awareness that is proper to the noetic realm or the divine mind.[42]

As Beatrice puts it:

> Così parlar conviensi al vostro ingegno,
> però che solo da sensato apprende
> ciò che fa poscia d'intelletto degno.
>   Per questo la Scrittura condescende
> a vostra facultate, e piedi e mano
> attribuisce a Dio e altro intende;
>   e Santa Chiesa con aspetto umano
> Gabrïel e Michel vi rappresenta,
> e l'altro che Tobia rifece sano.
> <div align="right">(<i>Par.</i> 4.40–48)</div>

[It is necessary to speak thus to your faculty, since only from sense perception does it grasp that which it then makes fit for the intellect. For this reason Scripture condescends to your capacity and attributes hands and feet to God, having another meaning, and Holy Church represents to you with human aspect Gabriel and Michael and the other who made Tobit whole again.]

Alongside a distinctly Aristotelian epistemology, this passage presents a Neoplatonic view of symbols as preserving both aspects of the human relationship with the divine; that is, of symbols as representations of the divine that are truthful and therefore not merely fanciful, but that are also not fully adequate to their object given the latter's transcendence and the nature and limitations of the human mind.

In the *Commedia*, the passage of the soul to God is reflected in the nature of Dante's imagination of the divine. Murray Bundy remarks that the dream visions of *Purgatorio* 9, 19, and 27, occurring on successive mornings, "record dreams whereby the imaginative activity is stimulated, corrected and strengthened, that it may have the capacity to receive the more intense light."[43] Dreams can serve to convey a sense of a hierarchy of being, in which levels of reality are dimly perceived. This immanent drive manifest in the imagination makes possible the vision of God.

After being swept up by the eagle, like Ganymede, Dante states: "Lettor, tu vedi ben com' io innalzo / la mia matera, e però con più arte / non ti maravagliar s'io la rincalzo" (*Purg.* 9.70–72) [Thou seest well, reader, that I rise to a higher theme; do not wonder, therefore if I sustain it with greater art]. The higher imagination, according to Dante, is an index of the presence of the divine:

> O imaginativa che ne rube
> talvolta sì di fuor, ch'om non s'accorge
> perché dintorno suonin mille tube,
>   chi move te, se 'l senso non ti porge?
> Moveti lume che nel ciel s'informa,
> per sé o per voler che giù lo scorge.
>   (*Purg.* 17.13–18)

[O imagination, which so steals us at times from outward things that we pay no heed though a thousand trumpets sound about us, who moves thee if the senses offer thee nothing? A light moves thee which takes form in the heavens, either of itself or by a will which directs it downwards.]

The "masters of suspicion" insist on finding the true basis of religion in the struggle for power. Can Dante really guide us to hitherto unexplored regions of truth, as is his bold claim? The answer depends upon the metaphysics. If we accept the credo of Lucretius, Spinoza, Schopenhauer, Nietzsche, the Postmodernists, and Neo-Darwinians, and accept that beauty is a mere ruse of nature, then visionaries like Dante are victims of a delusion. But if, on the basis of the Christianized Neoplatonic metaphysics briefly outlined in this essay, there is an ontological bond between the "images" of the mind's imagination and "Being" in the most exalted sense of that word, then the poet can indeed be a vehicle of truth.

Notes

An earlier version of this essay has appeared as "Dante's Romantic Imagination: A Neoplatonic Fantasy?" in Gatti and Zanardi, *Filosofia, scienza, storia*. Translations from the *Commedia* are taken from Dante, *Divine Comedy*, tr. Sinclair. I am grateful for the help, learning, and support of my erstwhile colleague Vittorio Montemaggi. Thanks are also due to Werner Beierwaltes, Helena Sanson, Jan Rohls, James Vigus, and George Watson.

1. The other such period was, of course, the Florentine Renaissance, during which thinkers such as Ficino and Landino read Dante both in the light of a fusion of Platonic and Christian conceptions of the intellect's relationship to truth and in the light of a synthesis of Platonic *eros* and Christian *caritas*. The influence of this Florentine Neoplatonism on subsequent centuries of interpretation of the philosophical tradition, from the early modern period to Romanticism, was momentous. It gave a Christian shape to resolutely pagan antique sources and a bold pattern of theological apologetics of a broadly Platonic stamp. While often attacked and sometimes discredited, this Florentine legacy is the most decisive factor in the history of Christian Platonism between the early Christian humanism of Alexandria and the historical critical work of nineteenth-century German scholarship. The University of Tübingen (the alma mater of the great German Idealists), for example, was a humanistic foundation (1477) and bore the stamp of Ficino and Neoplatonic humanism well into the eighteenth century. See Franz, *Schellings Tübinger Platon-Studien*, 99 ff. See also Gilson, *Dante and Renaissance Florence*, and Parker, *Commentary and Ideology*.

2. Beierwaltes, *Platonismus und Idealismus*, 63.

3. My aim here is not to trace specific Neoplatonic sources for the *Commedia*, nor to propose specific historical connections between Dante's work and that of earlier or later Platonic authors. Rather, I suggest possible philosophical and theological connections between important aspects of the *Commedia* and some central features of Neoplatonic thought, thereby enhancing our sense of the value of reading Dante's poem with an eye to how such an exercise might enrich our thinking about the divine. My emphasis on the Neoplatonic aspect of Dante's aesthetics clearly should not be interpreted as a denial of the significance of other aspects of and influences on Dante's work—including, most importantly, those relating to Aristotelian thought. The term "aesthetics" is an anachronistic but useful one.

4. Coleridge, "Lecture on Dante," 445.

5. Ryan, "The Theology of Dante," 136.

6. See Pite, *The Circle of Our Vision*, 22.

7. See Barth, *Schellings Philosophie der Kunst*.

8. Schelling, "On Dante," 140 ff.

9. Cary's translation was first published in 1814 but was not successful. After Coleridge praised it in 1817, it received good reports that year in the *Edinburgh Review* and the *Quarterly Review*. For a general study of Dante's reception by the English Romantics, see Braida, *Dante and the Romantics*.

10. Coleridge, "Lecture on Dante," 441.

11. Ibid., 442.

12. Ibid.

13. Ibid.

14. See Brandeis, *The Ladder of Vision*, 184 ff.

15. Compare *Conv.* 1.2.

16. See also Barolini, *Undivine Comedy*.

17. Hawkins, "Dante and the Bible," 131.

18. See *Conv.* 2.1 and *EC*. See also Hawkins, "Dante and the Bible," 133.

19. "O buono Appollo, a l'ultimo lavoro / fammi del tuo valor sì fatto vaso / come dimandi a dar l'amato alloro. / Infino a qui l'un giogo di Parnaso / assai mi fu; ma or con amendue / m'è uopo intrar ne l'aringo rimaso. / Entra nel petto mio, e spira tue / sì come quando Marsïa traesti / de la vagina de le membra sue." [O good Apollo, for the last labour make me such a vessel of thy power as thou requirest for the gift of thy loved laurel. Thus far the one peak of Parnassus has sufficed me, but now I have need of both, entering on the arena that remains. Come into my breast and breathe there as when thou drewest Marsyas from the scabbard of his limbs.]

20. Brandeis, *The Ladder of Vision*.

21. Finan, "Dante and the Religious Imagination," 78 ff.

22. Lentzen, *Studien zur Dante-Exegese Christoforo Landinos*, 123–31.

23. Finan, "Dante and the Religious Imagination," 74 ff.

24. de Vogel, "Amor quo caelum regitur," provides an extremely important analysis of *Consolation* 2.8.

25. Ibid., 31.

26. Hegel, *Lectures*, 347.

27. Trouillard, *La purification plotinienne*, 208.

28. Coleridge, *Marginalia*, 135.

29. Bundy suggests that the appeal to Apollo expresses Dante's (unrealizable) wish to be freed from the limits of bodily existence, while maintaining his poetic creativity. Bundy, *Theory of the Imagination*, 250.

30. S.v. "exinanition" (Oxford English Dictionary). I owe this reference to James Vigus.

31. Ibid.

32. Ibid.

33. Gombrich, *Symbolic Images*, 190.

34. Robb, *Neoplatonism*, 37.

35. Beierwaltes, *Proklos*, 384 ff.
36. For instance, *Enneads* 2.9(33).17.
37. de Vogel, "Amor quo caelum regitur," 19.
38. *Enneads* 5.1(10).6.27–30.
39. See Mahnke, *Unendliche Sphäre und Allmittelpunkt*. Although the basic metaphysical image is that of Plotinus, the model of triadic spheres of light is pervasive in the great philosopher of the Athenian Neoplatonic school, Proclus. See Beierwaltes, *Proklos*, 188 ff.
40. Brandeis, *The Ladder of Vision*, 173.
41. Coleridge, "Lecture on Dante," 444.
42. Gombrich, *Symbolic Images*.
43. Bundy, *Theory of the Imagination*, 241.

10

"Il punto che mi vinse"
Incarnation, Revelation, and Self-Knowledge in Dante's *Commedia*

CHRISTIAN MOEVS

Dante often speaks of God as a point. The thrust of the term *punto*, as Dante explains in the *Convivio*, is indivisible irreducible unity, a measure of space or time reduced to infinity, to the dimensionless ("lo punto per la sua indivisibilitade è immensurabile" [*Conv.* 2.13.27] [the point cannot be measured at all, since it cannot be divided]). The *punto* thus becomes a reference to God as the ultimate unity and simplicity, since it is analogous to God in its lack of attributes or determining characteristics. The *punto* also conjures the apparent paradox that God, who encompasses all space and time, has no extension in either space or time: God is the extensionless source, the substance and being of all spatiotemporal extension ("il punto / a cui tutti li tempi son presenti" [*Par.* 17.17–18] [the point to which all times are present]). The point is the timeless now, the ubiquitous here, which constitutes eternity and omnipresence, like the center of an infinite circle or sphere with no circumference.[1]

In the *Commedia*, the image of the *punto* culminates in the *Primo Mobile* or ninth sphere, which corresponds to cantos 27 through 29 of the *Paradiso*. The *Primo Mobile* is the nexus, or threshold, between the manifest universe and the Empyrean. In fact, the visible universe (all determinate form in space and time) begins from the eighth sphere, that of the constellations. The Empyrean for Dante is God: it is the self-subsistent, uncreated, Awareness-Light-Love-Bliss that projects or gives being to the world, and in which the being of the world ultimately consists.[2] In the *Primo Mobile*, at the beginning of *Paradiso* 28, the pilgrim Dante turns, so that instead of looking at a reflection in Beatrice's eyes, he sees instead as Beatrice sees: he aligns his sight with hers. He thus has his first direct glimpse of the Empyrean, the ultimate, all-encompassing, self-subsistent, ontological principle or reality. But that reality appears to him as a burning infinitesimal point. Instead of encompassing the universe, that point radiates or projects the concentric rings of creation around itself as a light paints a halo onto mist. Beatrice explains to Dante, "Da quel punto / depende il cielo e tutta la natura" (*Par.* 28.41–42) [From that point depend the heavens and all of nature]. Beatrice is quoting Aristotle's *Metaphysics*, where Aristotle speaks of the Unmoved Mover as the ultimate cause that lies beyond space and time, the reality that "contains" or grounds the manifest universe. Aristotle says of the Unmoved Mover what Beatrice says of the point: "On such a principle depend the heavens and the world of nature" (12.7.1072b14).

That ultimate ontological principle, Aristotle explains, is the reflexivity or self-awareness of pure intellect, the "thought that thinks itself" or "thinking thinking thinking" (*noesis noeseos noesis*).[3] In other words, for Aristotle, divinity, conceived in itself, is the perfect reflexive actuality (self-awareness) of pure awareness. Pure awareness or intellect (consciousness) in itself is nothing at all: it is the power to be everything and nothing. This is because for Aristotle, and for the whole Aristotelian-Thomistic tradition following him, awareness or consciousness (intellect) is nothing (not a thing) until it thinks, and when it thinks, it is what it thinks.[4] This is how the sensible spatiotemporal world depends on consciousness or intellect, which is the ultimate, and only, self-subsistent ontological principle. It is a dependence perfectly visualized in Dante's *Primo Mobile* by the simultaneous and equivalent, but inverted, cosmological pictures of *Paradiso* 28. One picture is of a manifest universe of concentric spheres entirely contained within the realm of Awareness-Light-Love that gives it being, and in which it alone consists. The other picture is of a dimensionless burning point of Awareness-Love-Being radiating or projecting the spheres of creation around itself as concentric rings of reflected light. In the first picture, the ephemeral flux and potentiality of the earth is at the center and the Empyrean is the encompassing limit of pure being. In the second picture, the Empyrean is the central dimensionless point of pure being, and the earth is the outer limit of unstable projected existence, verging on nonbeing. The two pictures, Beatrice explains, are perfectly equivalent, once one gives up the false notion that space is a self-subsistent principle. In reality space is only "parvenza" (*Par.* 28.74), a visual manifestation of the different degrees to which intellect, the only self-subsistent reality, enters into or knows itself.[5] (She had made an equivalent demonstration for time as not consisting in anything, in any irreducible units, upon first entering the *Primo Mobile* in the preceding canto, *Paradiso* 27. Beatrice's task in the *Primo Mobile*, on the threshold between the universe and the ultimate reality in which it consists, is to deconstruct, so to speak, the notions of time and space. She is showing that the constituent principles of the universe, of matter, are not self-subsistent things.) In either spatial picture presented in *Paradiso* 28, the underlying axiom is the utter contingency and non-self-sufficiency of the sensible world: if one were to remove the Empyrean (the burning point), the entire manifest universe would instantly vanish. The world has no being apart from the Empyrean, from the burning point of consciousness or self-awareness.

How does the human intellect assimilate itself to, or approach, this burning point of pure self-awareness, which, as we have seen, can also be described as an unlimited expansion of consciousness? In other words, how does it come to know itself as (one with) pure intellect or being, the reality that contains, sustains, and creates all things? The answer is by gradually detaching itself from the manifest world in order to focus itself on itself in pure contemplation. This is in fact the pilgrim's progress from the center of the manifest universe (the center of the earth) outward through the spheres of creation toward the Empyrean. The analogue of this progress in the inverted image of *Paradiso* 28 is the approach from the outer limit of projected being inward to the burning point that sustains and projects all creation. In *Paradiso* 28, the pilgrim has reached the *Primo Mobile*, or last spatiotemporal sphere, bordering on the Empyrean, so his position corresponds to the ring closest to the point: he is so *punto* by the *punto* as to have almost become (one with) the *punto*.[6] Indeed, once Beatrice's explanation about the perfect equivalence of the two images of creation reveals space-time to be *parvenza* (in relation to the self-subsistent reality that gives them being), Dante's understanding is swept clear like the sky after a north wind, and in that perfect transparency of awareness, Dante says, truth (awareness or conscious being) saw itself ("come stella in cielo il ver si vide" [*Par.* 28.87] [like a star in heaven the truth was seen]).[7] This is to have reached the reflexivity or self-awareness of pure awareness, which is the definition of the Empyrean: in fact, that is where Dante will find himself one canto later. He has only to see clearly how all creation depends on the reflexivity of intellect/love. That is the work of the first thirty-six lines of *Paradiso* 29.

Dante is drawing on a long tradition of contemplative literature, which was built on Aristotelian noetics and on the great Neoplatonic tradition founded on those noetics. In essence, that tradition explained that the mind ascends toward the divine by focusing itself on itself (entering into itself) through single-pointed concentration. The tradition heavily informs the thought of Augustine, who advises us to enter into ourselves and to "sharpen our minds to a point" in order to find the Truth that dwells within us.[8] For Pseudo-Dionysius, the soul is divinized by emptying itself, turning "within itself and away from what is outside" to reach "a godlike oneness . . . a unity reflecting God."[9] Richard of St. Victor tells us that the mind, forgetting the body and the world and turning inward, is "ravished into the abyss of divine light," ultimately to pass into God on the mountain of self-knowledge, where the mind comes to a supreme point, in the *sanctum sanctorum* of the innermost recess of the mind. Reaching this point, the mind is transfigured from the human into the divine, through a dawning of divine light.[10] Saint Bonaventure calls the focal point of the mind turned on itself the *apex mentis* or *synderesis scintilla*. Through that point the mind enters itself, turning away from creatures and leaving behind "everything sensible, imaginable, and intelligible," in order to focus on the eternal Light that formed the mind itself, until as pure intelligence it passes beyond itself into that source; this is for the mind or love to pass over (*transire*) into Truth, pure Being, "totally transferred and transformed into God."[11] Meister Eckhart, Dante's exact contemporary north of the Alps, goes so far as to say that the "spark" or ground of the soul, pure Intellect, is identical with God; through that spark, turning away from things and diving into the infinite well within our being, we come to know ourselves as God, or rather, God (pure conscious being) contemplates itself through us.[12]

The *punto* can thus also be seen as the nexus between the world and the ground of its being, between the multiplicity of the created world and the unity in which all things ultimately consist. That is why it appears in the *Primo Mobile*, which is itself the threshold or nexus between the multiplicity of creation and the self-subsistent reality in which it consists. We have seen that by gazing on that burning point, which corresponds to the all-encompassing Empyrean, Dante will pass over from the *Primo Mobile*, from the limit of the world, into the Empyrean itself. This is to know all things as "not other" than oneself, that is, as a projection or reflection of Being itself. This awakening can also be described (in the equivalent picture) as coming to know oneself as (one with) the self-subsistent reality that "contains" all things. In perfect self-knowledge, the intellect knows itself as a dimensionless point of awareness spawning all experience, which is to know itself as an infinite, spaceless, timeless reality encompassing all space and time. As the reality in and through which all things exist, consciousness or intellect alone is in some sense both one and many: it is nothing in itself, and hence it is the ultimate unity, and yet it gives being to all things by becoming those things in an act of intellection.[13] That is, the One and the Many, the Creator and creation, while radically distinct, are not ultimately two: they coincide, as the intelligence that comes to know itself discovers. In the Christian religion this nondualistic principle, that the world and the ground of its being are not two, though not the same, is named "logos" or "Christ." For the Christian faith it is not a concept, not an idea: it is truth, history, experience, oneself. To know Christ, to know God, can only be to know oneself *as* Christ, as God. It is to know oneself as not other than the one ultimate subject of experience. If it were otherwise, there would be at least two self-subsistent principles in the world, not one. Dante captures this nexus, or nonduality, between the world of ephemeral multiplicity and the self-subsistent, unitary ground of its being in the image of the *punto*. This is why, as we shall see, he also associates the *punto* with Christ and the Incarnation.[14]

For Dante, the true goal and fruition of every human life is to come to this awakening to the divine, which is really the awakening of divine, self-subsistent Intellect to itself as or through each human being. It is to experience oneself as Christ, as both God and nature, thus bridging the infinite and the finite. It is to experience a fullness or sweetness that eclipses the lure of the senses and reverses the natural orientation of the mind from outward to inward, resulting in spontaneous renunciation, detachment, and selfless love. It is a feeding on the source of all being within oneself. To reverse the natural orientation of the mind from outward to inward—from identifying itself with the earth as the center to focusing itself on itself (the focal point of pure awareness) as the center—is for the human soul to witness the sunset of greed (*cupidigia*), ignorance, and desire, and the dawn of understanding, freedom, and immortality.[15] The soul, like the *Primo Mobile*, is thus a horizon (as *Monarchia* 3.16.3 and a long medieval tradition call it). The soul is the horizon between the One and the Many, between the eternal and the corruptible, between the spiritual and the material, and between the divine and the mortal.

Elsewhere in the *Commedia*, Dante uses the word *punto* to represent the nexus between the mortal body and the immortal soul, between the natural and the divine. Let us briefly look at two instances before we turn to *Paradiso* 29.[16] The first is in *Purgatorio* 25, where Statius explains the generation of the human animal organism (37–60). The active power of the semen first informs menstrual matter with a nutritive life-principle corresponding to that of a plant; continuing its work, it becomes a sensitive life-principle with powers of movement and sensation, and as such produces, through the processes of nature ("tant' arte di natura" [71]), all the members and organs of the fetus. The so-called sensitive soul, or living human organism, is the "greatest work" that nature (things) can produce. Now, says Statius, comes the critical point or nexus ("tal punto" [62]), which has misled even the wise, namely, Averroës: how the fetus is transformed from a mere living thing or animal ("animal") into a "speaker" or human child ("fante"), that is, a rational soul, a user of language, and a being aware of itself (61–66). Why is this "point" so critical? Because not to see it is to be blind to the Christic nexus between the natural and the transcendent, between the human and the divine. It is either to "disjoin" (compare "disgiunto" [64]) the possible intellect from the living organism (like Averroës) or else to conflate the two by thinking that natural processes could generate the intellect. Since the human potential intellect, or rational soul, is a power to take on or encompass the forms of all things, it cannot be any of those things or be produced by any thing: it radically transcends the order of nature. As Aristotle explained, it comes "from outside" and is immune to all natural processes; as Dante says, it "breathes" only from God, in whose unqualified existence it shares. To miss this *punto* or nexus is to consider oneself simply an ephemeral product of nature. This is to eclipse the light of being in oneself, which is to crucify Christ (to fail to recognize Christ).

Note that when God breathes into the fetus the rational soul, which is created directly by God and dependent on nothing, that soul subsumes into itself the life-principles generated by nature, so that the complete soul "vive e sente e sé in sé rigira" (*Purg.* 25.75). Thus this soul not only "lives and feels" ("vive e sente"), through the natural powers of nutrition and sensation it has subsumed; it also "turns itself upon itself" ("sé in sé rigira"). Like the angels, and like the ultimate ontological principle itself, the soul is a power of self-awareness or consciousness or self-knowledge, a power to know all things as itself and to know itself as (one with) the ground of all things.[17]

The second loaded use of the term *punto* comes in *Paradiso* 13. There Dante observes that the compounds of elements (the "cera" or "wax" of matter) from which the turning heavens ("il ciel movendo") generate "brief contingencies" (the ephemeral forms of the sublunar world) may be better or worse suited to receive that heavenly influence, which is why one tree gives more fruit than another, and why humans are born with different dispositions ("con diverso ingegno") (63–72). If those compounds were worked to the perfect point ("Se fosse a punto la cera dedutta" [73]) and the heavens aligned to exert their greatest power, the light of the imprinting seal would be completely manifest ("la luce del suggel parrebbe tutta" [75]). In that case the Trinity or ground of being would be fully revealed in human form, as in another incarnation of God (*Conv.* 4.21.10). Dante tells us that this was the case at the creation of Adam, the Incarnation of Christ, and (if we are to believe the *Vita nuova*) at the birth of Beatrice. Yet again, a "point" designates the nexus of human and divine, at the limit of nature.

Dante's meditation on the *punto* climaxes in the first twelve lines of *Paradiso* 29.[18] These lines constitute the exact midpoint of Dante's sojourn in the *Primo Mobile* (27.100–30.54). Since the *Primo Mobile* is the nexus between Creator and creation, between the divine and the natural, these lines constitute the nexus of the nexus, so to speak. They serve to introduce the *Commedia*'s culminating account of the act of creation, or more precisely, the account of "how" the world arises from the reflexivity of consciousness. (The answer, of course, will be that there is no how, or when, or where, in the act of creation: all how and when and where are part of nature, and have nothing to do with the relation between the world and the ground of its being.) These twelve lines also separate the treatment of time and space in *Paradiso* 27 and 28 from this final metaphysical clarification in *Paradiso* 29 (after which, in *Paradiso* 30, Dante will find himself in the Empyrean).

> Quando ambedue li figli di Latona,
> coperti del Montone e de la Libra,
> fanno de l'orizzonte insieme zona,
>
>   quant' è dal punto che 'l cenìt inlibra
> infin che l'uno e l'altro da quel cinto,
> cambiando l'emisperio, si dilibra,
>
>   tanto, col volto di riso dipinto,
> si tacque Bëatrice, riguardando
> fiso nel punto che m'avëa vinto.
>
>   Poi cominciò: "Io dico, e non dimando,
> quel che tu vuoli udir, perch' io l'ho visto
> là 've s'appunta ogne *ubi* e ogne *quando*."
>   (*Par.* 29.1–12)

[When both the children of Latona, covered by the Ram and by the Scales, make the horizon their belt at one same moment, as long as from the instant when the zenith holds them balanced till one and the other, changing hemispheres, are unbalanced from that belt, for so long, her face painted with a smile, was Beatrice silent, looking fixedly at the point which had overcome me. Then she began, "I tell, not ask, what you wish to hear, for I have seen it there where every *ubi* and every *quando* comes to a point."]

We might note, first, that these twelve lines, which seem arbitrarily to interrupt Beatrice's continuing lecture on the angels, make four tercets. This is probably not by chance. Four is the number of matter (which is made of the four corruptible elements); three is the number of the Trinity, or of the incorruptible intellect, will, and memory (the rational soul). (Dante will make the same play on four and three in the "squaderna" and "interna" of *Paradiso* 33, where they are again associated with the *punto*.) Four and three make seven, which in the medieval tradition represents the Neoplatonic world soul, the nexus between the One and the Many; the Holy Spirit, the completion of the work of creation, "the knot of almost everything," as Cicero said.[19] Seven is also the number of man, who, by fusing matter (a four) and intellect or spirit (a three), is the bridge or nexus between the corruptible and the incorruptible, between the spatiotemporal world and the Creator.

We should also note that these lines, which divide the pilgrim's sojourn in the *Primo Mobile* into equal halves, also divide into equal halves with perfect symmetry. As Robert Durling and Ronald Martinez have observed, these lines begin and end with the word "quando" [when]; the center of the twelve lines, or threshold to the second half of the simile, is marked by the words "emisperio" [hemisphere] and "dilibra" [unbalances]; the word "punto" [point] is balanced around this midpoint in the fourth and ninth lines, occupying the same metrical position in both; the tercets bracketing the midpoint are symmetrically balanced by "quanto" [as long] and "tanto" [so long], both in initial position; multiplicity ("ambedue" [both]) in the first line is balanced by unity ("s'appunta" [comes to a point]) in the last.[20]

Both in its structure and in its meaning, the simile enacts and describes a balance, which Durling and Martinez call "an instant of cosmic equilibrium."[21] "Both Latona's children" are Apollo and Diana, the sun and the moon. When the plane of the horizon bisects ("makes a *zona* [girdle] or *cinto* [belt] for") both at once, they are on opposite sides of the earth, under the opposing constellations of Aries and Libra: the moon is setting at the instant the sun is rising, or vice versa. Dante pictures the sun and moon as hanging like the pans of a balance from a point directly above wherever the observer happens to be—the zenith. At the mathematical instant ("punto") that the "pans" of the scale are both bisected by the horizon, they are in balance ("'l cenìt inlibra"); by the "next" mathematical instant (i.e., in no time at all, since time is infinitely divisible and continuous), they are out of balance ("si dilibra"): they have switched hemispheres. Whether it is the sun which is rising and the moon which is setting, or vice versa, depends upon whether the sun "is covered by" Aries and the moon by Libra, or vice versa. As Alison Cornish has pointed out—and it is a fundamental observation—this is precisely what the text does not tell us. We know we are in an equinox, in a perfect balance between day and night, light and darkness, summer and winter, but we do not know which way the balance is tipping. If the sun is in Aries, then we are in the vernal equinox, and the sun is rising: we are on the threshold of day, summer, light, and life. If the sun is in Libra, then we are in the autumnal equinox, and it is evening: we are going into night, winter, darkness, and death.[22]

So how long is Beatrice silent? As long as the sun and moon, in their revolution, are perfectly bisected by the plane of the horizon. In other words, for an extensionless instant in time, or *punto*; as we have seen, a *punto* according to Dante is unmeasurable, infinitely small (*Conv.* 2.13.26–27). Beatrice is silent for no time at all. Dante emphasizes the importance of the simile, and sets it off as the fulcrum of the *Primo Mobile*, which is the fulcrum of all reality, by its apparent gratuitousness: it seems simply to interrupt a discourse on angels which began in *Paradiso* 28, and the pause it designates is no pause at all. Yet that no-pause, that nothingness in time of the present instant, is made to seem a cosmic expanse by the simile itself. What is Beatrice looking at in an extensionless point of time? "Il punto che m'avëa vinto" [the point which conquered me]: the infinitesimal burning point Dante saw in *Paradiso* 28. That point, as we saw, is the all-encompassing Empyrean, infinite Being-Light-Love-Bliss, as the dimensionless, all-projecting focal point of pure self-awareness. In gazing "where all *where* and *when* come to a point," Beatrice is seeing nothing, that is, no thing, but the source of all things. More precisely, she is seeing the nexus between God and creation, "where, when, and how" space and time arise from, or within, Intellect-Being itself.

So where and when is it that all *where* and *when* come to a point? We have already seen that space-time comes to a point when or where the finite human intellect enters itself, focusing itself in a dimensionless point of self-awareness, through which it passes over into pure Intellect-Being-Truth. *Where* and *when* come to a point when consciousness experiences itself as the ground of all being, the ground of all being as itself. This is the point from which depend "heaven and all nature."

The balance the simile describes is between the sun and the moon in opposition, between Apollo and Diana. As the invariant and unfailing source and sustainer of cosmic light and life, the sun, Dante says in the *Convivio*, is the most worthy exemplar of God (3.12.7). The sungod Apollo is the god of light, understanding, pure intellect, revelation, prophecy, divine inspiration, and salvation, attributes which make him an image of Christ as well as the presiding deity of the *Paradiso*, which opens by invoking him. The realm of the inconstant moon, of its contingent re-reflection of the light of the sun, is Diana's or Persephone's kingdom: it represents finite being, memory, mind, nature, change, ephemerality, temporality, shadow, and mortality. The balance between the moon and the sun, belted together ("cinto") by the horizon, is the balance or nexus between the contingent world and the ground of its being. It is thus also the yoking together of the mortal and the divine in the human being, a "yoking" perfectly revealed in Christ. This balance or nexus thus has a moral dimension: it is also, in every finite (created) intellect, the ambiguous or undecided balance between day and night, between the eternal and the temporal, between the self-subsistent and the contingent, and between self-knowledge and the hypnosis of finite being. That moral dimension or tension, in both angels and humans, will occupy Beatrice later in *Paradiso* 29, from line 49 to the end of the canto.[23]

Alison Cornish has shown that this poised instant of cosmic balance, which is either a sunrise or sunset, represents the *cognitio vespertina* ("twilight knowledge") of the angels at the moment of their creation. At the same instant (logically but not temporally distinct), they "chose sides": they either recognized themselves as dependent upon (reflections of) one self-subsistent reality, as "one with" the ground of all finite being, or they did not. As Beatrice puts it, they either remained in the Empyrean, or else they precipitated from it into Hell. The former enjoy *cognitio matutina*, an eternal spring or morning undespoiled by an autumnal equinox (as Beatrice says); the latter pass into night (*facti sunt nox*, says Augustine).[24]

To know that the opening simile of *Paradiso* 29 applies not only to angelic intelligence but equally, or perhaps principally, to human intellect, we need only remember the age-old metaphor that the human being is the horizon between eternity and time, between God and creation, between the self-subsistent and the contingent. To use Dante's words in the *Monarchia*: "homo solus in entibus tenet medium corruptibilium et incorruptibilium; propter quod recte a phylosophis assimilatur orizonti, qui est medium duorum emisperiorum" (3.16.3–4) [man alone among created beings is the link (*medium*) between corruptible and incorruptible things; and thus he is rightly compared ("assimilated") by philosophers to the horizon, which is the link (*medium*) between two hemispheres]. As the belt or girdle balancing and yoking the sun and moon, the horizon of the simile, and indeed the *Primo Mobile* as a whole, is the human soul or intelligence itself, the dimensionless point or nexus or bridge between Intellect-Being and space-time. The horizon linking sun and moon is the boundary between the inward and outward orientation of the mind: between, on the one hand, feeding on the ground of being within oneself through self-knowledge and Christic awakening (the sun rises, and the moon sets); and, on the other hand, the insatiable desire or *cupidigia* of the mind that—petrified through its self-identification as this-or-that and thus tinted with death—seeks to feed on ephemeral finite being through the senses, like Ulysses or Francesca (the moon rises, and the sun sets). The boundary is one between life and death, light and darkness, day and night, self-knowledge and self-alienation, and salvation and damnation.

We have said that the image of the sun and moon, the divine and the natural, yoked together, is an image of Christ as well as of man. In particular, the image fuses the Incarnation and the Crucifixion. A pervasive medieval tradition links the Incarnation and Crucifixion by portraying Christ as both the rising sun (*sol oriens*) and the setting sun (*sol occidens*). This idea has never been more profoundly and perfectly expressed than in the dimensionless point or instant of *Paradiso* 29's exordium, a nexus-balance-knot-yoking of Creator and creation, which is simultaneously and undecidably a sunrise and a sunset. Incarnation and Crucifixion are one. What is eclipses itself by revealing itself as or through finite form; at the same time, it reveals itself by eclipsing itself as (sacrificing) finite form.

As a point of conversion or turning or awakening, the "punto che m'avëa vinto," the point which conquered Dante in *Paradiso* 28 and which Beatrice is gazing upon in *Paradiso* 29, explicitly conjures, symmetrically balances (the phrase occurs five cantos from either end of the poem), and ironically contrasts with Francesca's "solo un punto fu quel che ci vinse" (*Inf.* 5.132) [one point alone it was that conquered us]. To make sure we don't miss the point, so to speak, Dante repeats the phrase again in *Paradiso* 30.11–12: the "point which seems encompassed by what it encompasses" is the "point which conquered me" ("al punto che mi vinse, / parendo inchiuso da quel ch'elli 'nchiude"). The point which conquered Francesca, interrupting her reading so that she and Paolo "quel giorno più non vi leggemmo avante" (*Inf.* 5.138) [that day read no further], was an eclipse of the light of intellect in her by the body, a failure of self-knowledge and love, and a failure to recognize Paolo *as herself.* That point of eclipse and sensuality is in ironic contrast to the moment of Augustine's conversion in the *Confessions* (8.12) where, weeping in agony and doubt, Augustine hears a voice chanting "Pick up and read" ("tolle lege"). Seizing the book of the apostle Paul, he reads: "sicut in die honeste ambulemus non in comesationibus et ebrietatibus non in cubilibus et inpudicitiis non in contentione et aemulatione sed induite Dominum

Iesum Christum et carnis curam ne feceritis in desideriis" (Rom 13:13–14) [Let us walk honestly as in the day: not in rioting and drunkenness, not in chambering and impurities, not in contention and envy: But put ye on the Lord Jesus Christ, and make not provision for the flesh in its concupiscences]. Augustine too stops reading, but because of a sunrise, not a sunset: "nec ultra volui legere, nec opus erat" [I neither wished nor needed to read further]. Light dawned instantly, Augustine says, all shadows of doubt were expelled, and he found peace (contrast Francesca's "dubbiosi disiri" and thirst for peace [*Inf.* 5.120, 92, 99]).

Although there is not enough space to pursue the topic here,[25] the blocking of the light by sublunar form is built into Dante's sun-moon image in *Paradiso* 29: he has described a lunar eclipse. Eclipse in the *Paradiso* unfailingly denotes the Crucifixion and the failure to recognize Christ, and *Paradiso* 29 presents a Trinity of eclipses. But we can take heart: the instantaneous now, our moment of reading, must be a sunrise. It must be the vernal, not autumnal equinox, because we are in the *Primo Mobile*, the nexus or point or instant (the eternal now) through which creation arises from Intellect-Being. At the instant of first creation, as the Christian tradition and Dante tell us, the cosmos was ordered in a vernal equinox. That nexus or point or instant of creation is also the dimensionless point through which created intelligence, focused upon itself, sacrifices all finite form and returns to its source. This is the crucifixion of self, and at the moment of Crucifixion, too, as the Christian tradition tells us and the evocations of eclipse and crucifixion in *Paradiso* 29 remind us, the cosmos was ordered in a vernal equinox. This means that Dante's own journey from the earth to the Empyrean, from spacetime to its source—a journey or self-crucifixion which balances and reverses, so to speak, the act of creation, and which is the now or present moment of the poem's narrative—occurs on the vernal equinox, as we know also from the opening of the poem (*Inf.* 1.38–40), as well as the opening of the *Purgatorio* (2.1–6) and the *Paradiso* (1.37–45). The "act" of creation, the Crucifixion, the pilgrim's journey, and (in the terms Dante has set) our present act of reading the poem are all a timeless instant of revelation-salvation, in which the ground of being manifests or awakens to itself within and as the finite, that is, in and as ourselves.

The final occurrence of the word *punto* in the poem is the famous Argo simile of *Paradiso* 33. Dante is gazing into the divine light and trying to describe the experience. This is to try to make the power to see (the subject of experience) into something seen (an object of experience). Dante sums up his defeat in the lines: "Un punto solo m'è maggior letargo / che venticinque secoli a la 'mpresa / che fé Nettuno ammirar l'ombra d'Argo" (*Par.* 33.94–96) [One moment alone brings more forgetfulness to me than twenty-five centuries have brought to the endeavor that startled Neptune with Argo's shadow]. There is not space to pursue the riches of this simile here,[26] except to observe that the Argo is emblematically the first ship and the first human quest: Dante is conjuring the sum of all human aspiration and exploration in history. Like the exordium of *Paradiso* 29, the Argo simile balances the *punto* of divine self-awareness against the gigantic scope of its quest, in that this divine self-awareness has reflected itself as a finite human intelligence in order to seek itself and reawaken to itself. The balance between human aspiration and self-knowledge evoked by the simile is reflected in the equilibrium of the *Commedia* itself, which balances the dimensionless Empyrean (the concluding cantos of the *Paradiso*) against the rest of the *Commedia* and against the entirety of human experience. This *punto* of spiritual self-knowledge, in the last canto of the *Paradiso*, also symmetrically balances the *punto* of self-alienation, the *punto* of matter, weight, and blindness that is both the center of the earth and the center of Satan's body through which the pilgrim passes in the last canto of the *Inferno* ("il punto / al quale si traggon d'ogni parte i pesi" [*Inf.* 34.110–11] [the point to which weights are drawn from every part]; "il punto ch'io avea passato" [93] [the point that I had passed]; see also *Inf.* 10.64).[27]

Perhaps the symmetry is even stronger. The point of sleep at which the pilgrim wanders from the true path in the first lines of the poem ("Tant' era pieno di sonno a quel punto / che la verace via abbandonai" [*Inf.* 1.11–12] [I was so full of sleep at that moment when I left the true way]) balances the point of "forgetfulness" or divine union in the last lines ("Un punto solo m'è maggior letargo / che venticinque secoli" [One moment alone brings more forgetfulness to me than twenty-five centuries]), just as five cantos in from each end of the poem, the point of sensual delusion that conquered Francesca balances the point of divine self-revelation that conquered Dante. Again, one point, this point or the now of the eternal present, the present moment of reading this poem, is the point of our damnation or our salvation, of slumber or awakening, and the moment of creation, Incarnation, and Crucifixion together.

Notes

The main ideas of this essay are developed at greater length in my *Metaphysics of Dante's "Comedy."* The concluding portion is an abridged version of the sections "Latona's Children" and "Argo" now in that book. Translations from the *Commedia* are taken from Dante, *Divine Comedy*, tr. Sinclair.

1. For a survey of the center-circumference imagery associated with the divine, see the introduction to Poulet, *Metamorphoses of the Circle*, xi–xxvii.
2. See *Par.* 27.106–14: "La natura del mondo, che quïeta / il mezzo e tutto l'altro intorno move, / quinci [from the Primo Mobile] comincia come da sua meta; / e questo cielo non ha altro dove / che la mente divina [the Empyrean], in che s'accende / l'amor che 'l volge e la virtù ch'ei piove. / Luce e amor d'un cerchio lui comprende, / sì come questo li altri; e quel precinto / colui che 'l cinge solamente intende" [the nature of the universe that holds the center still and moves all the rest around it begins here as from its starting point; and this Heaven has no other *where* than the divine mind, in which are kindled the love that turns it and the formative influence it rains down. Light and love enclose it in a circle, as it does the others, and this enclosing, he alone who girds it understands]; 28.52–54: "Onde, se 'l mio disir dee aver fine / in questo miro e angelico templo [the Primo Mobile] / che solo amore e luce ha per confine" [Thus if my desire is to attain its end in this wondrous and angelic temple, which has only love and light for its confine]; 30.38–42 (entering the Empyrean from the *Primo Mobile*): "Noi siamo usciti fore / del maggior corpo al ciel ch'è pura luce: / luce intellettüal, piena d'amore; / amor di vero ben, pien di letizia; / letizia che trascende ogne dolzore" [We have issued forth from the greatest body to the heaven that is pure light: light of the intellect, full of love, love of the true good, full of joy, joy that transcends every sweetness].
3. "The nature of the divine thought involves certain problems; for while thought is held to be the most divine of phenomena, the question what it must be in order to have that character involves difficulties. For if it thinks nothing what is there here of dignity? . . . And if it thinks, but this depends on something else, then . . . it cannot be the best substance. . . . Evidently, then, it thinks that which is most divine and precious, and it does not change. . . . Therefore it must be itself that thought thinks (since it is the most excellent of things), and its thinking is a thinking on thinking [*noesis noeseos noesis*]" (1074b15–34). See also *Metaphysics* 12.7.1072b14–30.
4. *De anima* 3.4.429a24, 429b32; see also 3.4.429a17, 3.5.430a20, 3.7.431a1; *Metaphysics* 12.7.1072b17–25.
5. "Li cerchi corporai sono ampi e arti / secondo il più e 'l men de la virtute / che si distende per tutte lor parti. / Maggior bontà vuol far maggior salute; / maggior salute maggior corpo cape, / s'elli ha le parti igualmente compiute. /

Dunque costui [the *Primo Mobile*] che tutto quanto rape / l'altro universo seco, corrisponde / al cerchio che più ama e che più sape [the smallest ring]: / per che, se tu a la virtù circonde / la tua misura, non a la parvenza / de le sustanze che t'appaion tonde, / tu vederai mirabil consequenza / di maggio a più e di minore a meno, / in ciascun cielo, a süa intelligenza" (*Par.* 28.64–78) [the material spheres are wide or narrow according to the more or less of causal-formative power that is diffused through all their parts. Greater goodness must needs work greater weal (health, blessedness); and the greater body, if its parts are equally complete, contains the greater weal. Hence this sphere, which sweeps along with it all the rest of the universe, corresponds to the circle which loves most and knows most. Wherefore, if you draw your measure round the power, not the semblance, of the substances which appear to you as circles, you will see a wondrous correspondence of greater to more and of smaller to less, in each heaven with respect to its intelligence].

6. Beatrice says to him: "Mira quel cerchio che più li [to the *punto*] è congiunto; / e sappi che 'l suo muovere è sì tosto / per l'affocato amore ond' elli è punto" (*Par.* 28.43–45) [See that circle that is closest to it, and know that its motion is thus swift from the burning love by which it is impelled]. See also 100–103 on the angelic intelligences corresponding to the rings closest to the point: "Così veloci seguono i suoi vimi, / per somigliarsi al punto quanto ponno; / e posson quanto a veder son soblimi" [They follow their bonds thus swiftly to gain all they may of likeness to the point, and this they may in so far as they are exalted in vision]; in *Par.* 30.11–12, Dante refers to the burning point as the "punto che mi vinse, / parendo inchiuso da quel ch'elli 'nchiude" [the point that conquered me, seeming encompassed by what it encompassed].

7. "Come rimane splendido e sereno / l'emisperio de l'aere, quando soffia / Borea da quella guancia ond' è più leno, / per che si purga e risolve la roffia / che pria turbava, sì che 'l ciel ne ride / con le bellezze d'ogne sua paroffia; / così fec'ïo, poi che mi provide / la donna mia del suo risponder chiaro, / e come stella in cielo il ver si vide" (*Par.* 28.79–87) [Just as the hemisphere of the air remains splendid and serene when Boreas blows from his milder cheek, purging and dissolving the refuse that had obscured it, so that Heaven smiles to us with the beauties of its every region, so I became after my lady had provided me with her clear answer, and like a star in heaven the truth was seen (saw itself)].

8. "Et inde admonitus redire ad memet ipsum, intravi in intima mea" (Augustine, *Confessions* 7.10.16) [By the Platonic books I was admonished to return into myself]; "et ecce intus eras et ego foris, et ibi te quaerebam" (10.27.38) [see, You were within and I was in the external world and sought You there]; "Noli foras ire; in teipsum redi" (*De vera religione* 72). The notion of sharpening the mind occurs in Augustine's *Enarrationes Psalmorum* 41.10, *Confessions* 7.17 and 9.10, and *De Genesi ad litteram* 54–56. See Cousins, "'*Intravi in intima mea*'"; Lloyd, "*Nosce Teipsum* and *Conscientia*."

9. Pseudo-Dionysius, *Divine Names*, 4.9.705A; 1.4.589D.
10. Richard of St. Victor, *Mystical Ark (Benjamin Major)* 5.5, 3.6, 4.16, 4.22–23, 5.2, 5.9.
11. See, for example, Bonaventure, *Itinerarium mentis in Deum* 1.6, 7.4, 1.2, 1.4, 5–7.
12. See especially Eckhart, *German Sermons* 2, 5b, 6, 12, 40, 48.
13. "Vedi l'eccelso omai e la larghezza / de l'etterno valor, poscia che tanti / speculi fatti s'ha in che si spezza, / uno manendo in sé come davanti" (*Par.* 29.142–45) [Behold now the height and breadth of the Eternal Goodness, since it has made itself so many mirrors wherein it is reflected, remaining in itself One as before]; "Non per aver a sé di bene acquisto / ch'esser non può, ma perché suo splendore / potesse, risplendendo, dir *"Subsisto"* / in sua etternità di tempo fore, / fuor d'ogne altro comprender, come i piacque, / s'aperse in nuovi amor l'etterno amore" (*Par.* 29.13–18) [Not to acquire good for Himself, which cannot be, but in order that his reflected light might, by re-reflecting, say "I subsist," in His eternity out of time, beyond all other encompassing, as it pleased Him, the Eternal Love opened Itself into new loves]; "così l'intelligenza sua bontate / multiplicata per le stelle spiega, / girando sé sovra sua unitate" (*Par.* 2.136–38) [so the intelligence deploys its goodness multiplied among the stars, while revolving upon its own unity]; "quella viva luce che sì mea / dal suo lucente, che non si disuna / da lui né da l'amor ch'a lor s'intrea, / per sua bontate il suo raggiare aduna, / quasi specchiato, in nove sussistenze, / etternalmente rimanendosi una" (*Par.* 13.55–60) [that Living Light which so streams from its lucent source that it is not disunited from it nor from the Love which is intrined with them, through its own goodness gathers its rays, as though reflected, in nine subsistences, itself eternally remaining one].
14. For a reading of the opening simile of *Paradiso* 29 as linking the *punto* to the Incarnation and Crucifixion, see further in this essay and, more extensively, my *Metaphysics of Dante's "Comedy,"* 158–60. Other relevant passages include *Par.* 13.73–75: "Se fosse a punto la cera dedutta / e fosse il cielo in sua virtù suprema, / la luce del suggel parrebbe tutta [resulting in another divine Incarnation]" [If the wax were moulded perfectly and the heavens were at the height of their power, all the brightness of the seal would be seen]; *Purg.* 25.61–65: "Ma come d'animal divegna fante, / non vedi tu ancor: quest' è tal punto, / che più savio di te fé già errante, / sì che per sua dottrina fé disgiunto / da l'anima il possibile intelletto" [But how from animal it becomes a child thou seest not yet; this is the point which once made one wiser than thou to err, so that in his teaching he made the possible intellect separate from the soul]; also of course the opposition between, on the one hand, "il punto che mi vinse" (*Par.* 30.11) [the point which conquered me] and "il punto che m'avëa vinto" (29.9) [the point which had conquered me], and, on the other hand, Francesca's "solo un punto fu quel che ci vinse" (*Inf.* 5.132) [one point alone it was that conquered us].

15. For the sunrise/sunset image of *Par.* 29.1–12 as an image of the soul on the horizon between Creator and creation, see further in this essay and, more extensively, my analysis in *Metaphysics of Dante's "Comedy,"* 156–57.

16. Some of the material in this and the next two paragraphs reproduces material found in my *Metaphysics of Dante's "Comedy,"* 126–28.

17. The same process is described in *Convivio* 4.21.4–5, laying more stress, however, on the role of the spheres ("vertù del cielo," "vertù celestiale") in the production of the human animal organism ("anima in vita"). For a particularly lucid overview of the issues involved in Statius's speech, see Boyde, *Dante Philomythes and Philosopher,* 270–79; for the vexed details, see Nardi, "Sull'origine dell'anima umana"; Busnelli, *Cosmogonia e antropogenesi* and *L'origine dell'anima;* also Trovato, "Due elementi." For a detailed overview of the Aristotelian understanding of soul, see Boyde, *Perception and Passion;* for a lucid introduction to the concept of soul in Aquinas, see Kretzmann, "Philosophy of Mind." For the phrase "Sé in sé rigira," compare *Conv.* 2.4.18; for the idea of "a power to know all things," see *Conv.* 4.21.5; 1.3.8–9. For the relation of the human being to nature, see also *Mon.* 1.3 and 1.11; *Conv.* 3.6.4–6 (what "the angelic intelligences fabricate with the heavens" is not the rational soul, but the *anima in vita* or human organism: compare 3.6.11–12; 3.2.14, 17–19; 4.21.4–10) and 4.23.6; also Nardi, "L'arco della vita" and "L'immortalità dell'anima."

18. This discussion of "Latona's Children" is an abridged version of my *Metaphysics of Dante's "Comedy,"* 147–60.

19. Cicero, *De re publica* 6.18 ("rerum omnium fere nodus est").

20. Durling and Martinez, *Time and the Crystal,* 208–9.

21. Ibid., 209.

22. Cornish, *Reading Dante's Stars,* 119–20. Porena interpreted "si dilibra" as "frees itself" ("Noterelle Dantesche," 203); in response, see Boyde, *Dante Philomythes and Philosopher,* 239–40, and Cornish, *Reading Dante's Stars,* 124–25.

23. On the idea of Apollo as revelation, see *Par.* 1.13–33; 2.8–9; 13.25; *Conv.* 4.25.6; see also Padoan, "Apollo"; Castellani, "Heliocentricity," 211–23; for the *Paradiso*'s invocation of a "Christlike" Apollo, see Hollander, *Allegory in Dante's "Commedia,"* 204–16; on the notion of Christ as sun, see, for example, *Par.* 23.29; 23.79–84; 25.54; for the relation between God and sun, see Mazzeo, *Structure and Thought,* 141–66. The Proserpinan associations of the moon are thoroughly treated in Kerr, "Proserpinan Memory"; for the contrast between sun and moon, see *Mon.* 3.4 and the relevant articles in *ED.* On the idea of the sun and the moon being belted together, Cornish observes that Dante's "cinto" renders "syzygy," which means "yoked together," and is the technical term for an "oppositional alignment of sun, moon, and earth" (*Reading Dante's Stars,* 122–23). Durling and Martinez acutely realize that in the simile "the metaphysical relation of God and nature is mirrored in the astronomical relation of sun and moon," but do not develop the suggestion (*Time and the Crystal,* 209). Von Richthofen

interprets the perfect balance between sun and moon as the perfect equilibrium between papal and imperial power, which is to balance the scales of justice ("The Twins of Latona").

24. Cornish, *Reading Dante's Stars*; Augustine, *De Genesi ad litteram* 4.22–32, 11.16–30; *De civitate Dei* 11.13–22.

25. See my *Metaphysics of Dante's "Comedy,"* 158–60.

26. See ibid., 165–67.

27. For the *punto* as the center of earth and weight, see Gilson, "'Rimaneggiamenti danteschi,'" n. 45. Gilson cites Restoro d'Arezzo, *La composizione del Mondo colle sue cascioni* 1.xx, and Sacrobosco, *De spera* c. 1.

11

How to Do Things with Words
Poetry as Sacrament in Dante's *Commedia*

DENYS TURNER

In this essay I propose to conduct two lines of conversation of different sorts. The first, which forms the substance of my essay, is a sort of trialogue—constructed more or less hypothetically (you might say that I invent it)—between three near contemporary theologians: Dante, Thomas Aquinas, and Meister Eckhart.[1] The second forms the point of my doing the first, and is an actual and continuing dialogue with some propositions about Dante as theological poet that I derive primarily from the work of Vittorio Montemaggi.[2] Not all of these propositions are his alone, of course, though it is through his work that I have learned to be convinced of them.

The propositions in question are four. The first is that the theological significance of the *Commedia* is to be found at least as much in Dante's *poeticization* of the theological act itself as in any theology which is done, or referred to, in the poem. The second concerns the nature of Dante's apophaticism. That apophaticism pervades so much of the *Commedia* as to constitute its very nature *as* poetry, and the proposition is that in the *Commedia*, the ultimacy of the divine mystery, its unknowability, is to be found only in its conjunction with Dante's more widely acknowledged cataphatic impulses; and that both—the apophatic and the cataphatic—play out their interactions across the whole extent of the *Commedia*'s range, across its epistemology, its ethics, its cosmology, and, most importantly, its theology. The third proposition is that this interplay of the cataphatic and the apophatic is to be found primarily in the manner in which human language—the phrase is a pleonasm for Dante—reflects and at every juncture is formed and shaped by the incorrigibly mysterious interactiveness of human persons. In this sense, Dante's apophaticism is a discovery of God's unknowability within the unknowability of the human other. Dante's apophaticism is, in short, an ethical apophaticism. Rooted in the principle enunciated in *De vulgari eloquentia* that "in homine sentiri humanius ... quam sentire" (1.5.1) [it is more truly human for a human being to be perceived than to perceive], this third proposition is best expressed in Dante's own words: "nulla vedere e amor mi costrinse" (*Par.* 30.15) [seeing nothing and love constrained me], a text Montemaggi interprets as meaning that in the love transacted between self and other, our perception of God is made vulnerable to constant redefinition and modification.

The fourth proposition brings the first three together: if the *Commedia* is to be seen as a conscious "poeticization" of the theological act, then it is also to be seen, whether as poetry or as theology, both as an account of and as in its own way an instance of language as rhetorically "performative" in character, as possessing in its own terms that same character of "interactiveness." The language of the *Commedia*, precisely as poetic, creates and transforms the realities of interaction of which it speaks—it enacts that of which it speaks. And this character of the sign, which somehow makes to be that which it discloses, is, I argue, "quasi-sacramental"—for, as Thomas Aquinas says, following a tradition through Hugh of St. Victor back to Augustine, it is in the nature of a sacrament that it "efficit quod figurat," it "effects what it signifies."[3]

I do not propose to defend these propositions by a detailed exegesis of the text of the *Commedia*. Rather, coming at them from a more theoretical height, I will attempt to show that they follow consistently from certain general principles of theological method, which appear to be shared by Thomas Aquinas and by Meister Eckhart. This, of course, will *prove* nothing about how to read Dante theologically. But, if these principles are convincing as general considerations, they might add some degree of antecedent plausibility to the four propositions outlined above. They might also contribute to the removal of certain frequently encountered assumptions about the nature of Dante's theological indebtednesses, which, it seems to me, are unwarranted. But first, some general remarks about the nature of theological rhetoric in Dante, Thomas Aquinas, and Meister Eckhart.

Theological Rhetoric

Anyone who has had the least acquaintance with the work of Thomas Aquinas and of Meister Eckhart will be struck by the fact that the writings of these two Dominicans, both educated in the same priory at Cologne and possibly both taught by Albert the Great (albeit some forty years apart), differ starkly in rhetorical "feel." And for this reason they are likely to be the more surprised that I should consider reading Thomas in conjunction with Meister Eckhart in support of a proposition about theology *as poetry*, particularly in view of what are often taken to be Thomas's evaluations of the epistemological standing of poetry. I shall have something to say shortly about how that evaluation of poetry in Thomas is importantly misconceived in some contemporary scholarship, and not only among *dantisti*. But let me begin with a comparison between Thomas and Eckhart and push the differences between them as far as they can be fairly made to go.

It is possible to think these differences to be of little substantive theological significance, as being but a relatively superficial matter of style and imagery, dictated by differences of intellectual temperament. But I think there is more to it than that, and that those differences of style and imagery derive from a difference of a more fundamental kind, and are symptomatic of a difference in theological strategy of historical and more than merely personal significance. Eckhart—and in his own way Dante shares in this—exhibits an important development in late-thirteenth- and early-fourteenth-century theology, namely, a marked shift towards a more self-conscious cultivation of a distinctive theological rhetoric. It is possible that this explicit cultivation of new rhetorical techniques at the service of theology is connected, in turn, with the emergence throughout most of Europe of vernacularity as a major theological medium. At any rate, we need some explanation of the fact that from the late thirteenth century onwards there emerges a large number of theological writings whose vernacularity stimulated the development of new theological strategies, one of which Eckhart's German *Sermons* so strikingly represents. What one can say with some measure of certainty is that all of those emergent theological strategies in the early fourteenth century involve poetry, or at least a new awareness of the theological potential of the "poetic." This holds whether one is considering the formal stanzaic poetry of Hadewijch of Brabant, the poetic prose of Marguerite Porete and of Mechtild of Magdeburg, or (this being the only example apart from the *Commedia* that I shall consider here) the homiletic exploitation of the "poetic" in Eckhart's vernacular sermons.

Whatever accounts for them, the superficial differences between Thomas and Eckhart in style and imagery are all too obvious. Oliver Davies has pointed to the significance of rhetorical features of Eckhart's theology, features which are, of course, more prominent in the vernacular sermons—naturally enough, since they are sermons—but by no means absent from his more technical, Latin treatises. As Davies says, Eckhart's theology is a sort of "poetic metaphysics," in which, as in all poetry, there is a certain "foregrounding" of the language itself, of the signifier, so that the language itself is thrust forward in its sensuous physicality;[4] and, one might add, linking back to the fourth of the propositions from which we started, this "poeticization" of theological discourse in Eckhart goes along with a certain rhetorical "performativeness," with a quasi-sacramental character. A characteristic of Eckhart's language is that it does not merely say something: it is intended to do something by means of saying. Nor is this to be accounted for only by the fact that Eckhart is composing sermons, which have an explicitly transformative purpose. As with Dante, it has to do with a very distinctive view of how human language can, in the medium precisely of its sensuous physicality, be made to express the unsayable otherness of God.

Performative Utterances and Uttering Performances

The above considerations bring us to the more general, and partly philosophical, matter of linguistic "performativeness" as such, on the philosophical aspects of which I will be brief and excessively compressed. Today we are familiar, since J. L. Austin's famous essay on how to do things with words,[5] with the idea of the performative utterance, the utterance that *in* saying something, *does* what it says. The uttered words "I promise" are such that under certain conditions their utterance *is* to promise; to say "I love you" is not a way of providing information about my states of mind, it *is* how I make love to you, and so forth. But if we are familiar since Austin with the notion of performative utterance, we ought to be as familiar since Wittgenstein with the notion of an "uttering performance," with the fact, that is to say, that actions speak as gestures do. But if actions speak, then verbal utterances are actions too, and so "utter" as actions and not just as words uttered. And these conjunctions of performative utterance and uttering performance allow for the analysis of complex interactions between them within speech-acts themselves, insofar as we may distinguish within speech-acts between what is said *in* saying the words, and *the meaning that the action of saying them* bears. This is just as true of gestures as it is of verbal speech. Judas greets Jesus with a kiss. But there is irony in the kiss, because what the kiss says as a gesture of greeting between friends is subverted by what Judas's action of betraying Jesus by means of it says. One and the same gesture has a double meaning, therefore, because of the distinction between what is said by an utterance, and what the action of uttering it says. And as with gestures, so with words; as with words, so with gestures. Thus far, at any rate, there are no differences between them. Moreover, in either case these two ways in which a communicative act can "mean" may stand in many different kinds of relationship with one another.

They may, of course, ironically contradict each other, as with Judas's kiss; or they may complement one another, as when a beautiful poem is complemented by the beauty of its typography, or when its beauty is doubly enacted by the beauty of its being uttered. In that case, from one point of view the shapes of the squiggles on the page or the musicality of the speech are that which we read or hear, the words; from another point of view, those same shapes or sounds seduce by their typographical or tonal beauty; thus the same shapes or sounds speak twice and do not twice "say" the same. Sometimes the relationship is "hermeneutical"; for the thing said is interpreted in a particular way by the material qualities of its being said, as when in poetry, rhythmic speech-patterns read a layer of significance into what the words themselves say. "Thou mastering me God" are the opening words of Hopkins's *The Wreck of the Deutschland*, and the combined effect of alliteration and of natural inflection, which is to pile the first three words up on one another and to cause a caesura before the fourth, alerts us to the fact that the line is invocative, and an exclamatory prayer, and that the first three words form a single compound adjective qualifying the fourth, the God addressed: "Thou-mastering-me / God!" (hyphenation mine). The rhythm reads the sense.

So far, I think, Dante is with us. Certainly it is Dante's view in *De vulgari eloquentia* that human beings are animals whose distinctiveness as rational consists principally in their being "linguistic." For Dante, human beings are animals, as we might say, "inserted" into language. If we were not the kind of rational creatures that we are, then either we would not need to speak, as angels do not need to speak, or else we would not be able to speak, as brute animals cannot speak (*Dve* 1.2). But what makes an animal *human* is both the ability and the need to speak, which is why it matters to Dante so much *how* we speak, the quality of our language: it has everything to do with how *human* we are. At all events, human beings are for Dante speech-making and speech-receptive *bodies*. For that reason it is not just the case that language has a "perceptible" and a "rational" component, as Dante puts it in *De vulgari eloquentia* 1.3; it is also true that only in the human animal is the perceptible, the bodily, also properly, that is to say "rationally," communicative. Hence, to say that human beings are "rational" is to say that human beings cannot help but that their grossest actions should speak: they cannot do anything meaninglessly. Bodily actions cannot help but be *gestures*. Our bodies are caught up into language whether we like it or not, which is why bodies are something we have to read. Smiles, we may say, are texts. They are as vulnerable to as many readings and misreadings as are words.

On this account, therefore, one can say that human beings cannot speak but that their action of speaking also says something. We may be able to choose to say something or not. But even the avoidance of speech, being an action, can say something, as when we grasp the significance of a silence, such as the terrible, frozen, silence of Ugolino in Hell (*Inf.* 33.64 ff.) or, more trivially, when someone noticeably fails to say "thank you." And this is what is meant when we say that human animality is rational: all human action is speech, including the speech-acts themselves. All human "performances" utter.[6] For these reasons I shall say, simply to stipulate a terminology, that everything to do with how the *actions of human communication* interact with *what they formally communicate* is the domain of "rhetoric."[7] In this sense, therefore, the "rhetorical" refers to those features of human speech-performance which are themselves meaningful *qua* performed, as distinct from what the speech itself means, taken on its own and however enacted. And I shall say that the purposeful construction of such interactions within a discourse is a, or even perhaps a central, characteristic of the "poetic."

Doing Theology by Means of Poetry

Leaving for the moment the very general question of "how to do things with words," let us next consider the more particular question of how to do theology by means of poetry, and so to the matter of Eckhart's "poeticizing" of theological and metaphysical language. I think that it is important here to distinguish this conception of the "rhetorical," as the poeticization of theology, from a more casual sense of the "rhetorical," as referring to the employment of a particular style of imagery, or just to the employment of metaphor as such. The importance of this distinction comes out when we observe how the apophatic finds its way into Eckhart's homiletic rhetoric. We can hardly miss the extreme negativity of Eckhart's theological language; it is saturated with images of "nothingnesses" and "abysses," by the featurelessness of "deserts" and "ground," and by "nakedness" and "emptiness." We all know that Eckhart's theology is emphatically "apophatic" in character. But it is all too easy to be misled as to what that apophaticism consists in, if one supposes that it is embodied principally in his employment of such metaphors of bleak negativity.

Listen to this typical passage (it is essential to listen, even in modern English translation):

> Then how should I love God? You should love God unspiritually, that is, your soul should be unspiritual and stripped of all spirituality, for so long as your soul has a spirit's form, it has images, and so long as it has images, it has a medium, and so long as it has a medium, it is not unity or simplicity. Therefore your soul must be unspiritual, free of all spirit, and must remain spiritless; for if you love God as he is God, as he is spirit, as he is person and as he is image—all this must go! 'Then how should I love him?' You should love him as he is non-God, a nonspirit, a nonperson, a nonimage, but as he is pure, unmixed, bright 'One', separated from all duality; and in that One we should eternally sink down, out of 'something' into 'nothing'.[8]

From the standpoint of its imagery, the negativity of Eckhart's language is striking. But it is also true that, looked at from the standpoint of the formal articulation of his negative theology, the negative imagery is almost entirely incidental. This is important because so often the negativity of the metaphors is taken to be indicative of Eckhart's apophaticism. It cannot be emphasized enough that negative imagery is, for all its negativity, still imagery; negative language is still language; and if the "apophatic" is properly understood, as in the classical theological traditions on which Eckhart explicitly draws, as that which surpasses *all* language, then, as the pseudo-Dionysius says, it lies beyond both "affirmation" and "denial."[9] *Eadem est scientia oppositorum*, as Aristotle said;[10] what is sauce for the affirmative goose is sauce for the negative gander. Not incidentally, connected with this fundamental failure to understand medieval forms of apophaticism are all sorts of misunderstandings, still unfortunately to be heard and read these days, about "apophatic language," and worse, about an apophatic language that "transcends Aristotelian logic." So let me just say dogmatically, for want of time for nuance: insofar as language is in question, theology cannot transcend Aristotelian logic; insofar as the "apophatic" is in question, it is not a particular metaphoric repertoire to which one refers but the failure of language as such, the failure of *all* metaphor, whether negative or affirmative. Eckhart's explosive theological rhetoric is far from a mere metaphoric preference for the negative. And as to Dante, one will entirely miss the point of *his* apophaticism—indeed one will miss his apophaticism altogether—if one searches the *Commedia* for instances of an "Eckhartian" negativity of *metaphor*. One will find little enough corresponding to it at *that* level in the *Commedia*. For this reason many readers, quite mistakenly, neglect the importance in Dante of the apophatic. They necessarily miss it, for they are looking for it in the wrong place.

Eckhart is clear about the distinction between the theologically apophatic and a merely literary partiality for negative trope. And it is clear from the typical passage above that the negativity of Eckhart's theology is not just something said by means of emphatically negative vocabularies, for it consists in his sense of the failure of language as such, and so of negative language, too. Nonetheless, Eckhart the preacher wants theological language in some way to participate, as one might put it, in the event of its own failure. Negativity, therefore, is not just a stylistic or decoratively metaphoric emphasis of Eckhart's theology; it is a living, organizing feature of the language itself and is intrinsic to its compositional style as theological writing. Here we come to what Oliver Davies has called Eckhart's "poeticization" of metaphysics. It is as if Eckhart were trying to get the paradoxical nature of his theology (it is at once a language, a communication by means of sensuous sign, and, as Michael Sells has put it in a neat oxymoron, "a language of unsaying")[11] into the materiality of the language itself, so that it both directly says and as directly unsays in the one act of saying. He "foregrounds" the signifier only immediately to disrupt its signification, block it, divert it, postpone it. Thereby the language performs rhetorically what it says technically: the performance utters what the utterance performs. This rhetorical device, as it were, of forcing into the sensuous, material sign the character of its own self-subversion as signifier accounts for that most characteristic feature of Eckhart's language: its rhetorical self-consciousness, its strained and strenuous, hyperactively paradoxical extravagance—its apophasis by excess of speech. The language, naturally, bursts at the seams under the pressure of the excessive forces it is being made to contain; the language *as body* bursts open under the weight of its overload of significance. Such is Eckhart's *poeticization* of his metaphysics: it is theology done as poetry.

Thomas Aquinas and the "Poetic"

The rhetorical contrast between Eckhart's hyperbolic exuberance and the deliberate sobriety of Aquinas's theological discourse could not be more marked. If Thomas can understate the case, he will seize the opportunity to do so. If a thought can be got to speak for itself, he will do as little as necessary to supplement it. Thomas is famous for his lucidity: one could say that the materiality of his theological signifiers disappears entirely into what is signified by them. And there is, in Thomas, an almost ruthless literary self-denial, a refusal of "rhetoric": the language is made to absent itself in any role other than that of signifying. Hence, for the most part, Thomas's theology aims for a language of pure transparency; it has the transparency of the language of physics or of any strictly technical discourse, in which terms as far as possible are made to do no work of any kind except to mean the one thing that is stipulated by the language-game to which they belong. On a continuum with the purely technical, stipulative lucidity of physics at one end and the material densities of poetry at the other, Thomas's theological language is closer to the former, and Eckhart's closer to the rhetorical thicknesses of poetic diction.

Here we come to that vexed question—though I wish it were *more* controversially vexed than it is—of Thomas's supposed depreciation, not to say dismissal, of poetry as a theological medium. Thomas says that poetry, being characterized by its use of metaphor, is "infima inter omnes doctrinas" [the most modest of all teaching methods],[12] and I suppose that even on the most charitable interpretation of what he means, to say that it is the lowest on any scale is not exactly what people want to hear from an advocate of poetry's theological potential. Still, when I first read this passage in the *Summa* and then the equivalent passage in the earlier but much more extended discussion of *Quodlibetal Questions* 7, q. 6— and I admit that I, too, was reading these passages on the conventional assumption that here one found Thomas's dismissal of the theological worth of poetry—I was much puzzled to find that although he says poetry is the most modest of them all, still, he says that it *is* a *doctrina*. And since what Thomas is up to in the first question of the *Summa* is explaining, in terms of all their complexities, what those many elements are which are constitutive of theology as *sacra doctrina*, it seemed that, contrary to expectations, he was saying that metaphor, and hence poetry, *does* have a place and a role, albeit a humble one, in the construction of theology as a *scientia*.

When one looks closely at the context of his famous remark about poetry, whether in the later *Summa* or in the earlier *Quodlibet*, the impression of a negative assessment of it begins to be removed altogether. In both places the context is that of determining on what sort of reading of scripture a properly scientific theology can be based, a theology that can be expected to meet standard criteria of good and bad evidence in scripture and good and bad inference from it; a theology, that is to say, which is *argumentativa*. On this score Thomas is firm, and he follows Augustine's view in his Letter to Vincentius the Donatist that no theological argument may depend for support on a merely allegorical interpretation of scripture; it must depend on its literal sense.[13] But that being so, Thomas is faced with a problem. For very nearly the whole weight of the traditions of formal theory and practice of scriptural exegesis before him, and nearly all of his contemporaries, took it to be a matter of course that scriptural metaphors either are, or else require to be treated as, allegorical forms of the *spiritual* sense of scripture and not part of the literal sense. And on that account all biblical poetry—the Song of Songs, for example, which is pure poetry and wholly metaphorical in character— can have no literal sense at all, but only a spiritual sense. But if that is accepted, and if, as Thomas says, theological argument can rely only on the foundations of the literal sense, then on this account much of scripture and all its poetry are ruled out as the foundation for a properly scientific theology. Of course, the exegetical strategy of allowing no literal sense to biblical metaphors nicely suited the many, perhaps especially those in the monastic traditions of exegetical practice, who had every motive for denying literal sense to the intensely carnal eroticism of the Song's imagery, so openly lewd and bawdy did its literal sense seem.

Thomas, however, will have none of such strategies. For him, metaphor and—in that extended sense in which he speaks of metaphor— poetry in general are *as such* part of the literal sense of scripture.[14] Metaphor is one of the ways of talking truthfully about real events, the *res* of history, according to Thomas. Allegory comes after that, and only on the condition of metaphor. So scriptural poetry does not fail of that literalness of scriptural language which is required as a foundation for theology as *sacra doctrina*. We might therefore fairly gloss his famous remark about poetry's theological worth thus: it is the lowest of the *doctrinae* in the sense that it is the most demotic, the closest to our ordinary ways of groping towards the unutterable and ungraspable mystery of God—but *doctrina* it certainly is. And when we have got this far down the road to rereading Thomas as advocating a positive view of poetry, we might as well remind ourselves that in the same article in the *Summa* he quotes with approval the view of pseudo-Dionysius that expressing ourselves theologically in "low" language is a good strategy, because it is so much the less likely than "high-flown" language to mislead us into supposing we know what we are talking about when talking about God.[15] And finally, in this context it is worthwhile reminding ourselves of another fact, namely, that the poetic vernacular of the *Commedia* is not for the most part that of the "high" courtly style of the lyric poet (as advocated, for example, by Dante in the *De vulgari eloquentia*), but rather is often closer to the plain vernacular of the common speech, however complex syntactically it sometimes is. I simply say that I see no reason why Thomas would have disapproved. At any rate, I see no reason for disapproval in the famous text in which he says that poetry is "infima inter omnes doctrinas" [the most modest of all teaching methods]. For Thomas, poetry is no bad way of expressing oneself theologically. Although he does not do theology poetically himself, scripture, he says, certainly does, and does so when in the literal, and therefore strictly theological, mode.

And so, while of course it is no use denying the differences between Thomas's theological rhetoric and that of an Eckhart or a Dante, I am not, after all, convinced that these differences amount to any serious inconsistency between them on the score of theological strategies. I concede that, at face value, it is easier to think that there is a wide divergence of this kind than to deny it, and there are indeed modern readings of Eckhart—and of Dante—that would set both apart from Thomas in a more radical way on the score of theological method, and especially on the score of poetry's theological worth. Perhaps this is why when some Dante scholars look for convergences between Dante and Thomas, they look at matters of substantive theological doctrine for that commonality, rather than in their conceptions of how to do theology with words. For the reasons outlined above, however, I think this approach is mistaken.

Demotic Theology

Thomas's famous economy and formal lucidity of speech have their roots in a general attitude towards language which is, in itself, distinctly unpoetic—this I concede. But the reason for such an approach to language on Thomas's part, I think, sets him curiously in a closer relation with Dante and Eckhart theologically than one might have expected. Thomas's economy and lucidity accompanies, and probably derives from, a fundamental confidence in the theological worth of ordinary speech, a trust that our ordinary ways of talking about creation are fundamentally in order as ways of talking about God, needing only to be subordinated to a governing apophaticism, expressed as a second-order epistemological principle: that all theological affirmation is both necessary and deficient. We must say of God anything true of what he has created, because that is all there is to hand with which to say anything about God, because there is no special "hyperessential" meaning available to the theologian, and because we know that whatever we say is in any case inadequate. There is, therefore, for Thomas, only ordinary speech to do theology in. One might almost say, in a sense close to Dante's meaning, that for Thomas, theology has available to it only a vernacular: for all his Latinity, his theological language is no *gramatica*.[16] So long as we know that everything we say about God ultimately fails anyway, we can freely indulge the materiality of those metaphors, the carnality of that imagery, and calmly exploit all the possibilities of formal inference and logic, which appear to unnerve the linguistically anxious Eckhart. That is what Thomas says, even if he does say it with unpoetic technical lucidity.

But in the contrasting symptoms of that linguistic anxiety of Eckhart's—he is forever messing theological language about, refusing to let it settle down—some of a postmodern mentality believe they see reflected, by anticipation, their own logophobia. The best known of these, of course, is Jacques Derrida, who claims to see some, or at any rate a partial, connection between Eckhart's apophatic rhetorical strategies and his own strategies of "deconstruction." And there is indeed in common between Eckhart and these postmodernists a temperamental restlessness, an impatience with any desires for or expectations of linguistic stability; and as a result, in both Eckhart and these postmodernists, the rhetoric appears fraught with anxiety, with a fear of the sign, a horror of the "constative." Eckhart seems perpetually afflicted with a theological neurosis lest he get God idolatrously wrong, so he watches his theological language with a vigilance so anxious—violent, even—as to arouse a suspicion that he writes as if striving for that which he also knows to be impossible; as if there were some ideal theological syntax reserved for addressing God correctly, which his rhetoric strains, deficiently, to attain. Or, in Derridian terms, Eckhart's language seems to strain for an impossible hyperessentiality—a hyperessentiality which, for all its impossibility, nonetheless figures as a spurious measure of our apophatic failure. By contrast, slow, leaden-footed Thomas (cf. *Par.* 13.112), knowing that we will never get God finally right anyway, and that that applies to anything we say, seems less anxious. Hence, an unstrained, technical, but demotic ordinariness of speech is all as right, one way or another, as it will ever be, for there is no other, higher, language by which its deficiency can be measured. So we come back to our question: What accounts for this difference in theological temperament and style?

One reason appears to be that Eckhart, as I have said, wants to constrain all the paradoxical tensions of the theological project into each and every theological speech act. Language itself is the bearer of these contrary forces of saying and unsaying, of affirmativeness and negativity, and so his discourse must be made endlessly to destabilize itself. And Eckhart must in this way compel the material rhetorical dimension of his discourse into a constant interplay with its formal significance; he must bend and twist and stretch theological language, because he wants theology as language "poetically" to do what it says, to both speak God and at the same time speak its own failure as speech. Eckhart does not simply preach *about* the unknowability of God. He wants to transact that unknowing in the very discourse with the congregation to whom he preaches. Eckhart wants his act of preaching to draw his listeners into the unknowing he preaches about, into a community in that unknowing. His preaching aims to effect what it signifies.

It would be easy to conclude that in the end, Eckhart differs from Thomas on a point of very fundamental theological principle: that Eckhart cannot trust creatures to proclaim God, and so he mistrusts the ordinariness, the demotic character, of theological speech as Thomas conceives of it. In that linguistic ordinariness, from which there is no escape, and in comparison to which no impossible and distorting alternative is envisaged, we can, for Thomas, speak confidently of God; the reason is because that same theological act by which our carnal speech is shown to be justified as theology also shows that the God thus demonstrated lies, in unutterable otherness, beyond the reach of anything we can say. Hence, for Thomas, unlike Eckhart, there is no need to try especially hard to say it. We have not, and could not have, and should not anxiously seek to have any measure of the deficiency of our speech about God; we could not know and should not try to know how far all our language falls short of God. Eckhart's strategy, on a postmodern account, is closer to that of Dante's Ulysses[17]—to a striving for an arcane and solipsistic, impossible self-transcendence—than to the demotic ordinariness of a Dante or a Thomas. One could well imagine Thomas offering to a postmodernistically construed Eckhart the advice the angel gave to Gerontius in Newman's *Dream*: "it is thy very energy of thought which keeps thee from thy God."[18]

Once one has read Eckhart in those terms of contrast with Thomas, it is also not hard to see why some modern scholars, especially of a postmodern tendency of mind, are tempted to deduce from these differences a picture of Eckhart's theology in thoroughgoing anti-metaphysical and anti-foundationalist terms, and as being engaged in some proto-postmodern project of theological deconstruction—a project which would displace all metaphysics with an apophatic rhetoric of "difference," of postponement, and of the generalized destabilization of language. It is also why they experience no temptation to enlist the support of Thomas Aquinas to that end. And I suspect that Dante sometimes finds himself caught somewhere between the two of them. But my point is that such a reading does no justice either to Eckhart or to Dante. Eckhart would have had little sympathy with the anti-metaphysical implications of such a postmodern reading. Moreover, what Oliver Davies argues about Eckhart applies equally to Dante, namely, that postmodern attempts to skim off Eckhart's rhetorical "apophaticism" from the medieval cosmology and metaphysics on which it is firmly based inevitably results in a failed attempt to repeat, by means of an uprooted rhetoric, that which is possible only on a metaphysical ground. Eckhart's dialectical theology would suffer reduction to a *mere* rhetoric, to a rhetoric, one might say, *as* "mere." As Davies puts it, "if we jettison the medieval cosmology which underlies Eckhart's system of participation, then we appear to want the fruits of a medieval world view without buying into the fourteenth century physics which supported it."[19] Only on an unjustifiably selective account of Eckhart is it possible to be misled about his purposes (as were some of his contemporaries, and not only them) into suspecting him of a certain paradoxical "hypostatization" of the negative, a certain reduction of theology to a rhetoric of postponement; indeed, into suspecting a sort of postmodern spirituality or, worst of all, an anti-metaphysical "mysticism."

The same applies to Dante. It would be just as mistaken in his case as in Eckhart's to read Dante's poeticization of theology as permitting the neglect, as if it were incidental to his theological purposes, of the complex cosmology that he so carefully articulates in the *Commedia*. Nor would it do, in the name of the third of the propositions from which we started, to construe the ethical in terms of a contrast with, and marginalization of, that cosmology. After all, if love "constrains" Dante's will ("nulla vedere e amor mi costrinse"), it is one and the same love that "moves the sun and the other stars" (*Par.* 33.145). It will do no good at all to set either the poetics of Dante or his ethics in relations of opposition theologically to his cosmology or his metaphysics. On the contrary, the power of Dante's poem is in the way in which he articulates the relations between the apophatic, the poetic, the ethical, the cosmological, and the metaphysical. I do not say that Eckhart, Thomas, and Dante articulate these theological components in the same way; but I do say that in all three theologians, these are the components integral to the theologies they construct.

In this respect all three, Dante, Thomas, and Eckhart, converge theologically. Dante, of course, wrote *De vulgari eloquentia*; my argument is that the other two could have written a significant portion of at least the first eight chapters of book 1 of that work, even if neither would have written the rest and neither could have written a *terzina* of the *Commedia*. All three are vulgar theologians in their different ways. After all, if all theology must begin in, be mediated by, and end in the darkness of unknowing, as both Eckhart and Thomas held; and if, that being so, all creation in some way speaks of God as irreducibly "other" than it; then why should not our language, being the natural expression of human rationality in its created materiality, speak of God as unutterably other, not only in what we say in it but also in the manner in which we say it, in its rhetorical forms themselves? That Thomas rarely exploits these rhetorical possibilities is neither here nor there. Eckhart's enthusiastic exploitation of them is perfectly consistent with Thomas's theology. Thomas *says*: all theological language ultimately fails. Eckhart's rhetoric gets theological language itself to fail, so that its *failure* says the same. Thomas *says*: all talk about God breaks down. Eckhart gets the *breakdown of language* to say the same: the rhetoric says what he and Thomas both say in it. The material voice of the rhetoric speaks theologically at one with the formal significance which it utters.

There is, after all, something almost frighteningly "materialistic" about Eckhart's theology, which, when looked at in this way, could with good reason be cause to revise some assumptions about Eckhart's dauntingly high-minded and supposedly elitist "mysticism." Eckhart's theology is in principle a demotic theology, and in his sermons it has taken on the character almost of a drama; it has become an act, for it enacts in its performance what it is about as word. When Eckhart looks for God, he looks for him in what is most "material," even "animal," within our rational nature: the materiality of the "foregrounded signifier." And if in this respect Eckhart's theology has, as Davies says, something of the character of the "poetic," we can also say that it has something of the character of the sacramental: its enactment says what it signifies. It is as true of Eckhart as it is of Thomas that he wants to find God in the created order; he differs from Thomas in that he discovers and "makes" the divine transcendence as much in our created language as in the creation that language describes. But then, it is not in language's theologically expressive ability that he finds God, except insofar as that expressive ability is supremely exercised in its being pushed to the point of its failure, in the sustaining of quasi-poetic tensions between signifier and signified, each in turn subverting and transcending the other. Insofar, then, as God is found in human language, within its characteristic rationality, God is found not, as Nietzsche thought, in the good order of "grammar"[20] but in the disordered collapse of speech into paradox, oxymoron, and the negation of the negation. Within this disordered and theologically contrived dislocation of language, a dislocation that must be endlessly repeated and renewed, our created discourses open up a space towards which they can, as it were, gesture but cannot occupy: through the cracks in the fissured surface of theological language, we can glimpse the "space" of the transcendent. For Eckhart, therefore, reason, language, "at the end of its tether," has the same shape as it has for Thomas—the form of an openness to an unknowable otherness. Eckhart's rhetoric says for itself that which cannot be said in it.

The *De vulgari eloquentia* and the *Commedia*

And so we return to Dante, and to those four propositions with which I began. I do not know what Dante scholars will say about so high-handed and aprioristic a reading of the *Commedia*'s theological strategies as I am proposing, as if the *Commedia* had been deduced straight out of some of the propositions of the first eight chapters of *De vulgari eloquentia*.[21] And of course I do know that just because those philosophical and theological propositions fit with much that seems to be going on in the *Commedia*, that proves nothing about the *Commedia*'s having been written to fit the agenda of *De vulgari eloquentia*. One cannot suppose without detailed textual support that because certain theoretical propositions, even Dante's own, entail a particular reading of the *Commedia*'s theology, therefore the *Commedia* is correctly read in those terms. That would be to commit the logical error which Dante himself would have known as the "fallacy of the consequent." All I can do is invite readers to consider just how closely the theory and the poetry fit, and to reflect on some of the theological implications that this might have.

What would you expect to find in the *Commedia* if you supposed it were written based on the theoretical propositions of the early chapters of *De vulgari eloquentia*? Bearing in mind what Dante says in the earlier work about the mutualities with which the sensuous and the rational play off one another within the sign, you would at least expect to find in the poem some sensitivity to the ways in which bodies signify, some awareness of the materialities of human discourse, and some awareness of the body *as* language and of language *as* body. And find it you do, and not only in key episodes of smiles, withholdings of smiles, and other such gestures on which swings, as on turning points, the narrative structure;[22] you find in every canto that the language of persons is the language of their bodies.

As to those smiles: would you not suspect a peculiarly twentieth-century anxiety about the verbal—alien to Dante—to be present in any proposal to trade off those smiles against words dichotomously on the score of immediacy? I should, at any rate, if I were taking seriously what Dante implies in the *De vulgari eloquentia*, namely, that it is only in speaking animals that the rictus of the lips amounts to a smile.[23] Because cats cannot use their lips to utter words, they cannot use their lips to smile with, either. And in what way are smiles less mediated semiotically than words? In what way are there fewer problems with an apophaticism of the gesture than with an apophaticism of talk? From where in *Dante* would you get such dichotomies?

And if you were to hypothesize that the propositions of *De vulgari eloquentia* which highlight language as the intrinsically human form of communication have found their way into the *Commedia*, you might expect to find there that sense that the quality of language both shapes and is shaped by the quality of the human communities whose language they are. Again, key episodes, illuminating the structure of the *Commedia* as a whole, foreground the intimacy with which language, community, and the body intertwine inseparably—such as, negatively, Dante's encounter with Ugolino, thrust deep into the frozen wastes of non-speech, incapable of response to his children's pleas (*Inf.* 32.124–33.90); and, more positively, Dante's encounter with his ancestor Cacciaguida, with its depiction of an ideal Florence and the proclamation of Dante's poetic mission (*Par.* 15–17). Such episodes are instances of a strategy that dominates the entire structure of the *Commedia*. Everywhere you can find that same complexity of interplay between speech and silence, subtly differentiated between the vastly different communities of *Paradiso* and

Purgatorio, on the one hand, and between both and the anti-community of *Inferno*, on the other.

Given all this, if, having read *De vulgari eloquentia*, you were to wonder how Dante would be expected to articulate in light of it, in his own poetic terms, the interplay between the cataphatic and the apophatic dimensions of theological language, then might you not expect to find him doing so precisely, as suggested by the third of the propositions with which we began, in terms of the "ethical"? For would it not seem to follow that it is in the nature of our language as theological, and thus as expressive of the God of a love that remains ultimately beyond our comprehension, that it should be subject to an endless play of revision and subversion by the interaction of selfhood with the ungraspable otherness of other people? And how surprised should you be, if your expectations of the *Commedia* are governed by the theoretical principles of the prose work, to find that for Dante the apophatic and the cataphatic are features of theological language *just because* they are features of human relatedness? At any rate, that is certainly what you would expect to find in the *Commedia* if you supposed that Dante wrote it in the light of that startling proposition of the *De vulgari eloquentia*, that it is more human for a human being to be perceived than to perceive.

If you were to concede that much, you would be conceding that at the theological center of the *Commedia* is the Incarnation, just as it is also the Incarnation into which the Trinitarian mystery of the godhead is dissolved at the end of the poem (*Par.* 33.106–45). That is not a surprising conclusion—everyone who has read to the end, although too few do, knows that about the *Commedia*. But if that is true and obvious theologically, then perhaps, just as importantly if less obviously, we can see that that same Incarnation is also the key to Dante's theological *poetics*, a poetics for which human speech as such is caught up into the divine communication with human beings. If we humans are animals inserted into language, then we are also thereby inserted, *as* linguistic animals, into the mystery of the Word made flesh; and in that way language especially, in its character as poetry, has the character of the Incarnation. The Word's being made flesh must be the supreme case and archetype of the poetic act itself, of the utterance that transforms, of the carnality that speaks God, "effecting what it signifies." If so, then it is that same Incarnation which, in constituting the *Commedia* as theology, also constitutes it as poetry, the one because of the other.

Notes

1. See also, especially for Aquinas and Eckhart, my *Faith, Reason and the Existence of God*.
2. See Montemaggi, "'Nulla vedere.'"
3. *ST* IIIa.62.1.ad4.
4. O. Davies, *Meister Eckhart*, 180.
5. Austin, *How to Do Things with Words*.
6. Thomas distinguished between an *actus hominis*—an act performed by a human being but without human significance—and an *actus humanus*—an act performed by a human *qua* human (*ST* IaIIae.1.1.corp). Human beings are no different from any other material object if, having jumped off a bridge, they fall to the ground. However, only a human being can commit suicide.
7. I emphasize that this is a stipulation. It is not intended as a definition of the classical conception of rhetoric.
8. Eckhart, *Sermon* 83, *Renovamini Spiritu*, in Eckhart, *The Essential Sermons*, 208.
9. Pseudo-Dionysius, *Mystical Theology* 5, 1048B.
10. Aristotle, *Peri Hermeneias* 6, 17a33–35; see also *ST* Ia.58.4.ad2.
11. Sells, *Mystical Languages of Unsaying*.
12. "Procedere . . . per similitudines varias et repraesentationes est proprium poeticae, quae est infima inter omnes doctrinas" (*ST* Ia.1.9.obj1) [to carry on with various similitudes and images is proper to poetry, the most modest of all teaching methods].
13. Augustine, *Ad Vincentium*, 334.
14. See *ST* Ia.1.9.corp and ad1; *ST* Ia.1.10.corp and ad3.
15. *ST* Ia.1.9.ad3. The reference is to *De coelestia hierarchia* 2.
16. See *Dve* 1.1.3.
17. See *Inf.* 26.85–142.
18. Newman, *The Dream of Gerontius*, sect. 3 (p. 21).
19. O. Davies, "Revelation and the Politics of Culture," 121.
20. Nietzsche, *Twilight of the Idols*, 3.5.
21. There also are, of course, crucial differences between the first eight chapters of the *De vulgari eloquentia* and the *Commedia* (Dante's change of opinion concerning the language spoken by Jesus being one of the most important). Moreover, the rest of the treatise is in the form of a search for the ideal poetic vernacular, which Dante hypothesizes he would find in the "high" style of a pan-Italian court, were any such court to exist; whereas the *Commedia*, as we have already recalled, is in fact written in a "lower" poetic style than that advocated in the *De vulgari eloquentia*.
22. See, for example, *Par.* 21.61–63 and 23.1–75.
23. Alongside the texts already referred to, see *Dve* 2.1.6.

AFTERWORDS

Dante, Conversation, and Homecoming

JOHN TOOK

> *The greatest poetic expression of the Existentialist point of view in the Middle Ages is Dante's* Divina Commedia. *It remains, like the religious psychology of the monastics, within the framework of scholastic ontology. But within these limits it enters the deepest places of human destruction and despair as well as the highest places of courage and salvation, and gives in poetic symbols an all-embracing existential doctrine of man.*
> —Paul Tillich

There is, I think, much to be said for seeing the *Commedia* as an essay in re-theologization—that is, for seeing it, following a tendency in the *Convivio* towards the de-theologization of human experience under the conditions of time and space, as a bringing back of that experience into closer communion with its specifically theological *rationes*. The idea needs careful statement, for de-theologization as a feature of the *Convivio* does not mean an elimination of its theological perspective (we need only think of the "E però che naturalissimo è in Dio volere essere" [since, furthermore, what is most natural to God is the will to be] clause of 3.2.7 or the "essa anima massimamente desidera di tornare a quello" [the soul desires first and foremost to return to Him] clause of 4.12.14), but rather means a periodization of human experience such that each successive phase of that experience has about it its own finality and sufficiency. This pattern of thought is everywhere discernible in the text. It is discernible in book 2 of the *Convivio*, where ethics, considered as architectonic in respect of every other form of philosophical concern, prevails over metaphysics as the most consummate of the human sciences,[1] and in book 3 of the *Convivio*, where Dante, surprisingly, restricts human desiring here and now to what in fact can be known in this life, this marking the far limit of man's curiosity.[2] Each of these emphases testifies to a permanent feature of Dante's moral and intellectual temperament, namely, to a tendency to interrupt the long perspective in favor of proximate concern, in favor of areas of moral and intellectual activity each conducive to its own kind of properly human happiness and each subject to its own particular authority, be it philosophical, papal, or imperial. This, then, is what it means to speak of the process of de-theologization at work in the *Convivio*—not the abolition *tout court* of theological perspective in the book, but its foreshortening in favor of the *perseitas* or in-and-for-itselfness of proximate concern, and this under the aspect both of substance and of jurisdiction.[3]

In the *Commedia*, however, there is a different emphasis, for here it is a question, not of identifying areas of proximate concern and of particular jurisdiction in and for themselves, but of the transparency of each and every inflection of the spirit to its depth-dimensionality, to the properly speaking theological substance of the moral and intellectual life in its moment-by-moment unfolding. More exactly, it is a question of the accountability of each and every specifically cultural initiative to the act of existence, as that whereby the individual may be said to participate in the being of God himself. Here, clearly, there is no room—at least in any absolute sense—for an interpretation of human experience in terms of its discrete moments. On the contrary, the discrete moment is subsumed by a single and, in its singularity, unspeakably urgent order of concern, by a *telos* or finality tending at every stage to confirm its deep consistency and purposefulness. The result of this is a theological statement of, I would say, astonishing sophistication, as precise cosmologically—in terms, that is to say, of the propositional substance of the religious life—as it is powerful ontologically, in respect of its laying open the truth of being (by which we mean this or that instance of properly human being) in its positive implementation. Cosmologically, it is a question of Dante's commitment to the notion of a God known to himself in and through a love-energy or kinesis apt at every point to sustain the universe in its struggle for an orderly and intelligible act of existence. First, then, comes the Godhead itself, all-circumscribing but uncircumscribed,[4] present to itself in the perichoretic energy of its threefoldness,[5] and forever opening out in what amounts to a process of affective self-extrinsication.[6] Humanity, for its part, having lived through the catastrophe of Eden precipitated by its own willfulness,[7] knows itself in the re-empowerment of human nature as accomplished through the infinite merits of the cross and as preserved by the sacramental presence of the Church as the continuing life of Christ here and hereafter.[8]

Theologically, Christologically, and ecclesiologically, therefore, everything is present and correct; Dante's *Commedia* is in this sense a faithful—but by no means passive—restatement of the Christian profession as he himself sees and understands it. Everywhere indebted, and self-consciously so, to those of his *auctores* whom he most loves and admires (Augustine, the Pseudo-Dionyius, Albert, Thomas, and Bonaventure), he nonetheless fashions a discourse in all these areas of concern as acquiescent as it is courageous, as recognizant as it is resolute in its rethinking of the matter to hand. But—and this now is the point—within the economy of the whole the cosmological component of his thought is taken up in its ontological component, in the nature and function of the poem, not simply as a restatement of the contents of credal or catechismal consciousness, of the "faith" as somehow subsisting in its reification over against the individual, but as a species of *Dasein* analytic tending by way of a special combination of the prophetic and the dramatic to engage every individual man or woman as concerned on the plane of being-as-existence, as alert to the tension within self between those forces making for being and those making for nonbeing. The Heideggerian emphasis is apposite, for Dante's too is a sense of humanity as present to itself by way of elementary projectedness, of a primordial interpretation of self in terms of—as far as the *Commedia* is concerned—the kind of trans-humanity to which we are called from beforehand.[9] And it is at this point that the substance of his discourse, by turns triumphant and tragic, and of this as an object of properly theological attention comes clearly into view; for to the degree to which the soul lays hold of its own tremendous calling, it knows itself both in the possession and in the overflowing of its proper humanity, in the *pax* and *gaudium* constituting between them the static and the ecstatic moods, respectively, of specifically human being in its authenticity. To the degree, by contrast, to which the individual stands over against the prior and subsistent exigencies of his being-in-the-world as a creature in potential to the most radical kind of self-transcendence, he knows himself only in the precariousness and near-nothingness of that being-in-the-world, in the imminence of his ceasing-to-be in any recognizably human sense of the term at all. More exactly, he knows himself in the fear, disorientation, self-inexplicability, anger, restlessness, and—as the boundary condition of properly human being in its alienation—despair of self as lost to self, as made over, in full consciousness of the tragedy of it all, to the alternative or surrogate project.[10] Nothing less than this will do as an account of what fundamentally is going on in the *Commedia*. Dante's poem is a laying open of being in the truth of that being, an act of disclosure in respect of the "what is" of this or that discrete instance of specifically human existence, as known to the subject himself by way of its complex phenomenology.

The implications of all this for a conference on Dante and theology can, I think, be summed up under the headings of conversation and of homecoming. By "conversation" I mean the invitation implicit in Dante's *Commedia* to enter into a dialogue on the basis of common intentionality, of what Hans-Georg Gadamer used to describe as a fusion of horizons.[11] Dante at every point is in conversation with those of his *auctores* whom he most loved and admired. He speaks with the Pseudo-Dionysius about the hierarchical structure of the universe and about the means of theological predication, and with Richard of St. Victor about the exquisite psychology of ecstasis. He speaks with Albert the Great about the possibility of integrating a Neoplatonic and a Neoperipatetic world view; with Bonaventure about the form and substance of the soul's journey into God; and with Thomas about the finality of human experience under the conditions of time and eternity, about the precise relationship within that experience of seeing and willing, and about the desiderata of stable philosophical and theological discourse. In none of these cases is it a question of systematic alignment, of Dante's entering into conversation for the purposes of confirming a specific emphasis or set of emphases in philosophy and theology. Rather, he enters into conversation with his authorities in the manner of a pilgrim spirit, of souls, such as those on the road to Emmaus, who are engaged in a matter of common concern.[12] But—and this now is the point—the range and depth of Dante's conversation with those of his peers and predecessors whom he most loved and admired is, I would say, transcended by the substance and urgency of his conversation with those "who will call this time ancient"[13]—with our own generation, that is to say, as similarly caught up in the struggle to be, and as likewise implicated in the affirmation of being over nonbeing as properties of historical selfhood. In this sense, Dante reaches out beyond the structures of Scholastic consciousness to engage all those who in more recent times have sought, by way either of philosophy or of psychology or of theology, to address the problems of specifically human being in its moment-by-moment implementation. Among the philosophers, he reaches out to engage Martin Heidegger and Karl Jaspers in respect of a henceforth shared meditation upon the projectedness of being under the conditions of time and space, on the status of the mood as an ontological indicator, and on the mechanisms of self-preservation in the state of estrangement. Among the psychologists, depth-psychologists, and psychopathologists, he reaches out to engage such pioneering figures as Karen Horney and Erich Fromm in respect of the self-destructive function of the leading preference and of the structure and directionality of authentic loving. Among the theologians he reaches out to engage Søren Kierkegaard in respect of the distraught symptomatology of being in its lostnesss, Nikolai Berdyaev in respect of freedom as a property of being *ex parte subiecti*, and Paul Tillich in respect of the structure of the existential situation generally, of the kairotic and eschatological significance of the historical instant, and of courage as the response to existential destitution. At no point here is it a question of scholarly velleity, of an at best slightly eccentric and at worst positively ill-conceived anxiety to redeem Dante from the mists of medieval antiquity, for it is Dante himself who summons the reader of his text to a state of ontological attention, to a fresh account of the by turns tragic and triumphant structure of his existence. This, then, is what it means to speak of conversation with Dante, and this too is what it means to speak of his homecoming. It is in fact high time that Dante was brought home to us — in a manner sensitive, perhaps, to the Gadamerian notion of the absolute present of the text, of its status as a *tota simul*, an unending now, of historical consciousness[14] — as a party to our continuing discussion. It is high time that we saw in him an ordinary, as distinct from an extraordinary or unwanted, guest in our midst. As Tillich rightly opined, few in our tradition have seen with equal perspicacity the height and depth of our existence, the highest places of courage and the darkest places of despair. Our conference and this volume have been, let us hope, but the first in a series of indispensable initiatives in this respect.

Notes

Translations of the *Commedia* are from Dante, *Divine Comedy*, tr. Mandelbaum (slightly amended).

1. "Lo Cielo cristallino, che per Primo Mobile dinanzi è contato, ha comparazione assai manifesta alla Morale Filosofia; ché [la] Morale Filosofia, secondo che dice Tommaso sopra lo secondo de l'Etica, ordina noi a l'altre scienze. Ché, sì come dice lo Filosofo nel quinto de l'Etica, 'la giustizia legale ordina le scienze ad apprendere, e comanda, perché non siano abbandonate, quelle essere apprese e amaestrate'" (*Conv.* 2.14.14–15) [The Crystalline Heaven, described as the First Moving Body in the account given above, is quite clearly similar to Moral Philosophy, because, as Thomas says in his commentary on the second book of the *Ethics*, Moral Philosophy directs us towards the other sciences. For, as the Philosopher states in the fifth book of the Ethics, "civic justice directs that the sciences be learned in due order, and, to ensure that they never be abandoned, commands that they be both learned and taught"]. See especially Gilson, *Dante and Philosophy*, 121 ff., where the notion is explored in terms of the intimate or "lived" character of ethics, as distinct from metaphysics, in human experience ("At the risk of slightly stretching Dante's thought, but with the object of bringing out what seems to me the idea which a great number of passages suggest, I am going to say, in definitely stating that the formula is not his, that metaphysics as conceived by Dante remains *in itself* the loftiest and most perfect of the sciences, but that it is not so *as far as we are concerned*" [122, Gilson's emphases]).

2. "Veramente può qui alcuno forte dubitare come ciò sia, che la sapienza possa fare l'uomo beato, non potendo a lui perfettamente certe cose mostrare; con ciò sia cosa che 'l naturale desiderio sia [nel]l'uomo di sapere, e sanza compiere lo desiderio beato essere non possa. A ciò si può chiaramente rispondere che lo desiderio naturale in ciascuna cosa è misurato secondo la possibilitade della cosa desiderante: altrimenti anderebbe in contrario di se medesimo, che impossibile è; e la Natura l'avrebbe fatto indarno, che è anche impossibile" (*Conv.* 3.15.7–8) [However, at this point a person may seriously wonder how it can be that wisdom can make man happy, if it cannot perfectly show certain things to him, since the natural desire of man is to know, and he cannot be happy unless that desire is satisfied. To this the clear answer can be given that the natural desire in everything is in accordance with the capacity of the thing which desires; otherwise the thing would strive in a fashion contrary to its own being, which is impossible; and Nature would have made it in vain, which is also impossible].

3. Similarly notable, as far as the *Convivio* is concerned, is Dante's discussion of the "successional" character of properly human understanding in 4.13, his sense of intellection as a movement of the mind from one perfection to the

next. As far as the *Monarchia* is concerned, note his separating out of the moral-philosophical and of the theological in point of substance and finality for the purposes of resolving a specifically publicistic issue (3.16.7 ff.); in the event, the distinction in respect of the moral and intellectual life in its totality precipitates a movement of misgiving (the "non sic stricte recipienda est" [should not be taken so literally] clause of 3.16.17). On the foreshortening of the theological perspective in the *Convivio* (in the *Monarchia* the issue is set up in terms of parallel rather than of proximate possibility), see Kenelm Foster in the first of his two essays entitled "The Two Dantes": "all through the *Convivio* we find a certain indifference to theological considerations; one of its more striking differences from the *Comedy*. Certainly the writer is a Catholic Christian, but he is evidently far more concerned to draw out certain cherished philosophical insights than to anticipate possible objections from the side of the theologians.... Thus we see Dante in the *Convivio* coming out with ideas about the perfectibility of man in this life, and of the soul in the next, without its apparently crossing his mind that he was begging the question (from the standpoint of orthodox Christianity) as to whether man *could* reach perfection, here or hereafter, unassisted by divine grace. In the *Convivio* the Christian doctrine of grace—and so of man's *de facto* inherent sinfulness and natural incapacity to bring himself, by his own effort, to union with God—is virtually ignored" (Foster, *The Two Dantes*, 159). Whether or not Dante's leading preoccupation in the *Convivio*—namely, to define a species of happiness proper to those bowed down here and now by the burden of domestic and civic care—necessarily involves him in a discussion of grace as a response to sinfulness, I am not sure. Probably not. However, insofar as, in a moment of enthusiasm (*en theos mania*), he associates philosophy as the end of all properly human yearning with God himself (the "È adunque la divina filosofia de la divina essenzia, però che in esso non può essere cosa alla sua essenzia aggiunta" [Divine Philosophy, then, pertains to the divine essence, since in God nothing can be added to His essence] of 3.12.13), the question does indeed arise; the general drift of Foster's remarks are in this sense unexceptionable.

4. "O Padre nostro, che ne' cieli stai, / non circunscritto, ma per più amore / ch'ai primi effetti di là sù tu hai" (*Purg.* 11.1–3) [Our Father, You who dwell within the heavens— / but are not circumscribed by them—out of / Your greater love for Your first works above]; "Quell' uno e due e tre che sempre vive / e regna sempre in tre e 'n due e 'n uno, / non circunscritto, e tutto circunscrive" (*Par.* 14.28–30) [That One and Two and Three who ever lives / and ever reigns in Three and Two and One, / not circumscribed and circumscribing all]. See also, for example, Thomas, *Summa contra Gentiles* 3.68; *ST* Ia.8.2 and Ia.8.4.

5. See, in addition to the "Quell' uno e due e tre che sempre vive / e regna sempre in tre e 'n due e 'n uno" component of the *Par.* 14 passage of the previous note, the "O luce etterna che sola in te sidi, / sola t'intendi, e da te intelletta / e intendente te ami e arridi!" [Eternal Light, You only dwell within / Yourself, and only You know You; Self-knowing, / Self-known, You love and smile upon

Yourself!] of *Par.* 33.124–26, Dante's finest meditation on the notion—as well as on the literature—of circumincession.

6. "La divina bontà, che da sé sperne / ogne livore, ardendo in sé, sfavilla / sì che dispiega le bellezze etterne" (*Par.* 7.64–66) [The Godly Goodness that has banished every / envy from Its own Self, burns in Itself; / and sparkling so, It shows eternal beauties], and, especially, the exquisite "s'aperse in nuovi amor l'etterno amore" [Eternal Love opened into new loves] of *Par.* 29.18. Thomas has "ad productionem creaturarum nihil aliud movet Deum nisi sua bonitas, quam rebus aliis communicare voluit secundum modum assimilationis ad ipsum" (*Summa contra Gentiles* 2.46.6) [the only thing which moves God to produce creatures is his goodness, which he wished to communicate to other things by likening them to Himself]; and the Pseudo-Dionysius, "Ex amore enim bonitatis suae processit quod bonitatem suam voluit diffundere et communicare aliis, secundum quod fuit possibile, scilicet per modum similitudinis" (*De divinis nominibus* 4.9) [For out of the love of his own goodness it happens that he wills to diffuse and communicate his own goodness to others, in so far as is possible, namely, through the mode of similitude].

7. *Par.* 7.25–27 ("Per non soffrire a la virtù che vole / freno a suo prode, quell' uom che non nacque, / dannando sé, dannò tutta sua prole" [Since he could not endure the helpful curb / on his willpower, the man who was not born, / damning himself, damned all his progeny]); *Purg.* 29.22–30; *Par.* 32.121–23.

8. Decisive in respect of the notion of re-empowerment as God's principal work in Christ is the "ché più largo fu Dio a dar sé stesso / per far l'uom sufficiente a rilevarsi" [for God showed greater generosity / in giving His own self that man might be / empowered to rise] moment of *Par.* 7.115–16, God's love-recreative initiative in the Cross thus involving, for Dante, making man equal to the historical and eschatological exigencies of his proper nature—*re*-substantiation, we might say, rather than *trans*-substantiation as God's way of dealing with man. The question of Dante's ecclesiology, involving as it does questions both of grace in and for itself and of the transmission of grace, ultimately must be considered in relation to his theology of culture generally, of—in effect—the sacramental status of every significant encounter in human experience. Prominent among the many passages bearing on Dante's general ecclesiology are *Mon.* 3.10.7; *Mon.* 3.15.3 (Christ as the foundation of the Church and as the form of its continuing existence); *Conv.* 2.5.5 (the Church as the bride of Christ); *Inf.* 19.90–117 (the poverty and evangelical simplicity of the Church); *Mon.* 3.1.5; *Mon.* 3.16.10 (the pope as shepherd and *claviger regni celorum*); *Mon.* 3.3.7; *Mon.* 3.6.2–6; *Purg.* 9.115–29; *Par.* 23.136–39; *Par.* 27.49–51 (the Petrine Commission, the power of the keys, and papal jurisdiction).

9. For the terminology, see *Par.* 1.70–71 ("Trasumanar significar *per verba* / non si poria" [Passing beyond the human cannot be / worded]), while for the antecedent or coextensive character of the call, *Par.* 2.19–21 ("La concreata e perpetüa sete / del deïforme regno cen portava / veloci quasi come 'l ciel vedete"

[The thirst that is innate and everlasting— / thirst for the godly realm—bore us away / as swiftly as the heavens that you see]) and 7.142–44 ("ma vostra vita sanza mezzo spira / la somma beninanza, e la innamora / di sé sì che poi sempre la disira" [but your life is breathed forth immediately / by the Chief Good, who so enamors it / of His own Self that it desires Him always]). See too, on the inkling of an ultimate good, *Purg.* 17.127–29 (with reference to Thomas, *ST* Ia.2.1.ad 1).

10. On fear, see *Inf.* 1.4–6 and 13–15 ("Ahi quanto a dir qual era è cosa dura / esta selva selvaggia e aspra e forte / che nel pensier rinova la paura! ... Ma poi ch'i' fui al piè d'un colle giunto, / là dove terminava quella valle / che m'avea di paura il cor compunto" [Ah, it is hard to speak of what it was, / that savage forest, dense and difficult, / which even in recall renews my fear ... But when I'd reached the bottom of a hill— / it rose along the boundary of the valley / that had harassed my heart with so much fear]); on disorientation, *Inf.* 1.1–3 ("Nel mezzo del cammin di nostra vita / mi ritrovai per una selva oscura, / ché la diritta via era smarrita" [When I had journeyed half of our life's way, / I found myself within a shadowed forest, / for I had lost the path that does not stray]); on inexplicability, *Inf.* 1.10–12 ("Io non so ben ridir com' i' v'intrai, / tant' era pien di sonno a quel punto / che la verace via abbandonai" [I cannot clearly say how I had entered / the wood; I was so full of sleep just at / the point where I abandoned the true path]); on anger, *Inf.* 3.103–5 ("Bestemmiavano Dio e lor parenti, / l'umana spezie e 'l loco e 'l tempo e 'l seme / di lor semenza e di lor nascimenti" [they execrated God and their own parents / and humankind, and then the place and time / of their conception's seed and of their birth]); and on restlessness, *Inf.* 3.52–57 ("E io, che riguardai, vidi una 'nsegna / che girando correva tanto ratta, / che d'ogne posa mi parea indegna; / e dietro le venìa sì lunga tratta / di gente, ch'i' non averei creduto / che morte tanta n'avesse disfatta" [And I, looking more closely, saw a banner / that, as it wheeled about, raced on—so quick / that any respite seemed unsuited to it. / Behind that banner trailed so long a file / of people—I should never have believed / that death could have unmade so many souls]). See Took, *Dante's Phenomenology*, 102–78.

11. "When our historical consciousness transposes itself into historical horizons, this does not entail passing into alien worlds unconnected in any way with our own; instead, they together constitute the one great horizon that moves from within and that, beyond the frontiers of the present, embraces the historical depths of our self-consciousness. Everything contained in historical consciousness is in fact embraced by a single historical horizon. Our own past and that other past towards which our historical consciousness is directed help to shape this moving horizon out of which human life always lives and which determines it as heritage and tradition" (Gadamer, *Truth and Method*, 304).

12. Dante on companionship and the road to Emmaus, *Purg.* 21.7–15 ("Ed ecco, sì come ne scrive Luca / che Cristo apparve a' due ch'erano in via, / già surto fuor de la sepulcral buca, / ci apparve un'ombra, e dietro a noi venìa, / dal piè guardando la turba che giace; / né ci addemmo di lei, sì parlò pria, / dicendo:

'O frati miei, Dio vi dea pace.' / Noi ci volgemmo sùbiti, e Virgilio / rendéli 'l cenno ch'a ciò si conface" [and here—even as Luke records for us / that Christ, new-risen from his burial cave, / appeared to two along his way—a shade / appeared; and he advanced behind our backs / while we were careful not to trample on / the outstretched crowd. We did not notice him / until he had addressed us with: "God give / you, o my brothers, peace!" We turned at once; / then, after offering suitable response, Virgil began . . .]).

13. The "che questo tempo chiameranno antico" [those who will call this present, ancient times] of *Par.* 17.120.

14. "In comparison with all other linguistic and nonlinguistic tradition, the work of art is the absolute present for each particular present, and at the same time holds its word in readiness for every future. The intimacy with which the work of art touches us is at the same time, in enigmatic fashion, a shattering and a demolition of the familiar. It is not only the 'This art thou!' disclosed in a joyous and frightening shock; it also says to us 'Thou must alter thy life!'" (Gadamer, "Aesthetics and Hermeneutics," 104).

Dante as Inspiration for Twenty-First-Century Theology

DAVID F. FORD

My participation in the conference from which this volume sprang was an inspiration for me as a theologian. In my academic work I concentrate mainly on thinking through Christian theology in the contemporary context with a view to the future. Particular concerns include the interpretation of scripture today, the character of theology as a discipline, the ways in which Christians and others have responded to the massive challenges of Western modernity, and the relations between Christianity and the other Abrahamic faiths, Judaism and Islam. Reading over the transcript of what I said in the final session of the conference, after a weekend of immersion in the papers and discussion, has transported me back into my main response at the time: a sense both of amazement and delight at the multifaceted richness of Dante's poetry, and of inadequacy in the face of the challenge of responding to this today as a theologian.[1]

The experience of the conference demonstrated convincingly that the study of Dante is an extraordinarily rich way into historical theology and some of the fundamental issues of the Christian tradition. That came out in one paper after another, and it is even more fully shown in the completed contributions to this volume. It is a paradox of contemporary theology (though it is perhaps true of many other fields) that the most fruitful moves may be the apparent detours where one engages intensively, and with great precision, with one small part of the past, and then finds that it opens up all sorts of contemporary issues with relevance for the future. I know that I will never be a Dante scholar, and will never have the ability to work with that precision on Dante's text in the *Commedia*, but what a privilege, and how worthwhile it was, to sit at the feet of those who have spent years and even decades studying it. Robin Kirkpatrick's essay alone could stimulate several chapters of contemporary theological response. That, and the other essays have set me a theological agenda, centered on the question: What, on the basis of the present volume, might twenty-first-century theology learn from Dante?

My attempted answer will consist of seven basic thoughts. These concern genre (covering commentary, argument, liturgy, narrative, and wisdom); the "moods" of faith (especially the optative); the relation of Christian theology to non-Christian sources (including the sensitive matter of Mohammed's teachings); the primacy of a "middle distance" narrative perspective; the immersion of theology in the contingencies of history, yet with an eschatological orientation; the relation of scripture to philosophy; and the desirability of twenty-first-century theologians relating deeply to twenty-first-century poets.

Genre

The idea of "theology as poetry" clearly raises the question of genre, and several of the contributions to this volume deal with it. At stake is not only the genre of the *Commedia* in relation to the genres in which theology is written, but also the genre of responses to the issue. Robin Kirkpatrick courageously tackles the academic's temptation to comment in safe second-order discourse. Yet he is not against commentary; rather, he sets sail on what he calls "those dangerous waters of first-order discourse, where the heady confession of ignorance is as likely to be revealing as our learned footnotes." He proposes "that both poetry and theology are better realized in a detailed engagement with texts and historical situations than in any pursuit of vision or theoretical system. On this view, close reading, or practical criticism, seems a very Dantean way to truth."

I find this a deeply congenial view of theology, resulting in commentary, especially on scripture, being "first theology." To see, with Kirkpatrick, "Aquinas as a literary critic" does not then seem too remarkable — Aquinas was simply basing his theology, in line with both the ancient monastic and the newer medieval university practice, on attention to *sacra pagina*. Accompanying that, he provided, of course, argumentative, dialectically rational discourse about disputed points (especially disputed points of scripture). But the performance for which theology was a preparation was that of living before God, articulated above all in liturgical practice—as Matthew Treherne convincingly shows.

Treherne traces Dante's ways of combining liturgy and narrative in poetry that is not only steeped in biblical and liturgical language (and shows Dante's awareness of the traditions of commentary on both scripture and liturgy) but also re-creates the experience of liturgical performance. Robin Kirkpatrick, Peter Hawkins, Vittorio Montemaggi, Denys Turner, and others enrich still further this appreciation of the complexity of the *Commedia*'s relation to various genres that are also theological—commentary, narrative, proclamation, argument, and liturgical poetry and prose. The simultaneity of several genres, none of which can claim to be the master, characterizes the *Commedia*, and it is of great significance that this is also the case with the Bible and with any Christian theology that stays true to it. Reading the *Commedia* as theology might help to inspire theologians today to work in many genres and to resist hegemonic or homogenizing tendencies. And it seems to me that the key discipline in successful resistance is accurately identified by Kirkpatrick as "detailed engagement with texts and historical situations."

Yet there does seem to me to be something like a meta-genre in scripture, in Christian tradition, and in Dante: wisdom. Wisdom is not really a genre. Of course, biblical scholars say there is Wisdom literature in scripture, and they differ about how to define that as a genre. Yet wisdom is pervasively important in the Bible, whether in the shaping of narratives or laws or in prophetic proclamation or the worship of the Psalms. "Wisdom" is also arguably the most adequate single term for what theology is seeking in relation to God—and this seems, in line with Augustine, Aquinas, and many others, to have been Dante's understanding, too. As the essays of this book repeatedly suggest, Dante's whole seeking, his core desire, is for a wisdom of love, received from God and directed to God. To see the *Commedia* as a performance of that wisdom in relation to the whole cosmos and the particularities of human existence is to identify its primary lesson for theology today or at any other time. It holds together in relation to the Trinity all the different leaves of the universe. In this ultimate "ecology" are combined the intellectual, the ethical, and the aesthetic; the apophatic and cataphatic; and judgment and transformation in relation to individuals, societies, and the Church. As Christian Moevs said to me in conversation at the conference: "There is no reductionism in Dante, you're always led into all the rest. You get in there and you can't just say 'I've got it there.' You inevitably have to make all these rich connections." It seems to me that is what wisdom is about: holding all those together simultaneously; making the deep connections; making the practical connections. And part of what Dante should be about for theologians is daring to improvise on this wisdom (as Dante improvised on the wisdom he received) for the sake of God and God's purposes in the twenty-first century.

One of my favorite biblical commentaries is that by Ellen Davis on Proverbs, Ecclesiastes, and the Song of Songs.[2] Her discourse is strongly and vulnerably first-order, in Kirkpatrick's terms, and she offers a contemporary wisdom through performing her commentary on the three biblical books. Again and again she insists that these texts are mostly poetry, just as most of the book of Job is poetry. This affects deeply how their wisdom is to be understood and what the appropriate ways are to argue from it and to carry on this tradition today. Intelligence, imagination, and discernment come together in teaching that is continually distilling wisdom from diverse sources, past and present, relying heavily on poetic forms. What if twenty-first-century theology were to take this seriously? And what if some twenty-first-century poet, well-educated in such theology, were to take up the challenge as daringly and wisely as did Dante in his time?

The Moods of Faith

The second thought is about what I call the "moods" of faith and the need simultaneously to have different moods. Mostly, when one thinks of faith one probably has in mind the indicative mood ("This is what is believed") or the imperative mood ("Do this")—faith and ethics, belief and practice. But, being fascinated by the importance of moods, I have noticed how often essays in this collection refer to other moods as being significant for Dante and his theology. I will note three.

First is the interrogative mood, that sense of Dante being deeply and persistently interrogative, exploring and disturbing faith as well as feeding it. He had interiorized the critical role of the *quaestio* in medieval theology, and of wonder in philosophy more generally, and the interrogative tone pervades the *Commedia*.

There is also the subjunctive mood of "maybe" and "might be," the experimental mood of "perhaps" and "possibly." The audacity of Dante's imagination is frequently noted, with its inevitably fictional dimension. One might say that the whole *Commedia* is a "maybe"—what Hell, Purgatory, and Heaven may be like. The faith shown in the poem is extraordinarily rich and complex as regards the relation of history and fiction to theological truth. Its meditation on the ways in which "finding" and "fashioning," "discovery" and "invention," come together and play off each other in the attempt to do justice to the inexpressible truth of God and God's creation leads far beyond any faith dominated by indicatives or imperatives. Today, in the face of great dangers coming from those of diverse religions, especially Judaism, Christianity, and Islam, who aggressively champion their faiths using neat indicative/imperative packages (and are often countered by equally impoverished secularist packages), it is especially important to cultivate the sort of wise, civilized, vigorously inquiring, and imaginative faith represented by Dante.

Finally, there is the most embracing of all Dante's moods. In Greek it is called the optative, the mood of longing and desire, of "if only . . . !" Many of the essays explore some aspect of Dante as a poet of desire. It may be that in our culture, so concerned with the arousal and manipulation of desire, Dante's greatest contribution could be to inspire a faith that is animated by the education, transformation, and fulfillment of desire for God and what pleases God. It really matters to Christian faith which its dominant mood is. Not only the indicative and imperative hold dangers when they become the overarching framework of faith. Too dominantly interrogative a faith undermines the integrity of all the other moods. Too subjunctive and experimental a faith can fail to achieve adequate definiteness, practicality, or future orientation. Domination is hardly the right term for the role of desire in faith—the language of hegemony is not appropriate here. Rather, faith is best pervaded, shaped, and led by desire for God and what pleases God. It matters greatly to religious traditions, communities, and individuals whether the embracing mood is the optative rather than one or more of the others. Dante is for me the supreme poetic example in the Christian tradition of the realization of this embrace. In its cognitive dimension it is above all the desire for wisdom—in line with what Theresa Federici says of the Psalms (those unsurpassed classics of desire-led faith in all five moods) as a compendium of all wisdom. And this wisdom is above all oriented towards love of God and neighbor, love of both Beatrice and the Trinity.

It is worth adding a final emphasis on the pedagogical dimension of desire-led faith. This is concerned with the maturing of whole persons over time in all their faculties and relationships, involving continual learning and transformation. There can be decisive moments of faith, but faith is not simply a matter of having or not having faith, or of being in or out of a community. It depends on complex transformative processes of learning, with all its difficulties, delights, and moods. The education of desire in wisdom and love stretches all human capacities by receiving God and God's gifts in the mode of grace, culminating in the ultimate transformation of the *Paradiso*'s final canto.

Non-Christian Sources for Christian Theology

The third thought is about drawing on non-Christian sources in Christian thought. I am a classicist by training, and thus came to Dante via Virgil. I have been increasingly impressed by the way in which Dante models one of the most fundamentally important things in Christian theology: its relation to the non-Christian. Dante's hermeneutic of generosity in relation to Virgil is exemplary in many ways, and it reaches far beyond Virgil. Dante is a theologically sensitive model for the discriminating appropriation of pagan sources, combining affirmation, judgment, and transformative adoption. He follows no simplistic rule of thumb or religious ideology but considers each case on its merits, aiming at wise discernment. Many of his particular judgments are of course questionable seven hundred years later, but at a time when, on the one hand, some secularist ideologies want to bracket out, neutralize, or eliminate the religious dimensions of civilization, and, on the other hand, there are within religious traditions strong advocates of exclusivism and confrontation with the secular and with other religions, Dante offers an approach that has great potential to help the flourishing of the twenty-first-century world.

Dante's principles of hermeneutical generosity, as demonstrated in his engagement with Greek and Roman civilization, also open ways of retrospectively correcting some of his own judgments. For example, his treatment of Mohammed is deeply offensive and even blasphemous to many Muslims today, and there have been campaigns to remove Dante from the syllabus of Italian schools. What might be the result of exercising on Mohammed the sort of hermeneutic Dante applies to the classical world? What if Mohammed were not to end up in the place in the *Inferno* to which Dante consigns him? What if it were rather a learning relationship, and Mohammed were to be a non-Christian companion in doing our theology today? This would be a case of doing the sort of thing Dante does, rather than simply repeating what he says. Just as Dante shows the fruitfulness of the pagan "other" in Christian theology, so we need his hermeneutic of generosity (together with retrieval, judgment, and transformation) in order to engage with different "others" today, including some towards whom he was not so generous.

Middle Distance Perspective

The fourth thought is about the primary perspective of the *Commedia*. I remember years ago serendipitously picking up J. P. Stern's marvelous book on realism just when I needed one of its central concepts to make sense of the primary perspective of the Gospel narratives.[3] Stern proposed the idea of the "middle distance perspective" with special reference to realistic novels, and it is also applicable to Dante's narrative. The primary perspective is not the cosmology, the big system. Neither is it that of interiority, that is, what goes on inside Dante or his characters, their stream of consciousness. Rather, the primary perspective is the face-to-face, as expressed in some of the comments on smiles in this volume. This is the perspective of people and events in interaction over time, within which character is developed as meaning and value are shaped and embodied in communication, desire, action, and suffering. No attempted overview of such interactions from a cosmic perspective can do justice to the face-to-face engagements and exchanges—these require the particularity of human life, which in literary terms is best rendered in realistic narrative or dramatic form.

Part of the secret of the capacity of the *Commedia* to grip readers generation after generation may lie, like that of the Gospels, in this "ordinary life" perspective, conveying much of its meaning in the vivid narrative that portrays people and their relationships as it unfolds its plot. This narrative perspective is deeply appropriate to a faith with an incarnation at its heart. Just as in the Gospels it does not matter much what Jesus' conception of cosmology was, so the *Commedia*'s elaborate understanding of the universe might be inaccurate in many respects without falsifying the narrated, "middle distance" truth of the poem. Its challenge to theology is also connected with this perspective, and that leads into my fifth thought.

Contingencies with Eschatology and Joy

This fifth thought is sparked off by Kirkpatrick's comments on Aquinas and Cacciaguida in the central cantos of the *Paradiso*: "The whole thrust of Aquinas's speech is thus to displace any speculative appetite for intellectual system and to concentrate attention on the *ways* in which we think and conduct ourselves within a world of 'brevi contingenze' (13.63) [brief contingencies], of time and decay, of growth and change.... These cantos at the central point of the *Paradiso*—which at first demonstrate a surprising emphasis upon temporal rather than eternal existence—directly translate the implications of Solomon's wisdom into a consideration of the forms of activity—ethical, civic, linguistic, and poetic—that for Dante seem to stand as the truest expression of Christian theology."

This is theological wisdom immersed in the contingencies of life, yet with the expansiveness and hope of eschatological orientation to the love and joy of God. Holding together what Dietrich Bonhoeffer called the penultimate and ultimate is one of the most difficult tasks of living. One is involved in sufferings and evil and all the things that our world is about, but with an eschatological orientation. On the one hand, it can seem scandalous that there is such evil and contingency in a world created by a good God; on the other hand (and I sometimes think that in our time this is the greater problem for many people), there is the scandal of a God of love and joy, the virtual impossibility of imagining utter delight, blessedness, goodness, peace, joy, and love. Dante's achievement in articulating a "baptised imagination," so that such dynamic perfection is not only conceivable but even interesting and gripping, could be prophetic for our century. It seems to me unlikely that anything less than the most radical vision of delight in God and God's creation is sufficient to motivate the sorts of healthy renewal and transformation in the "ethical, civic, linguistic, and poetic" spheres for which the twenty-first century is crying out.

Philosophy and Scripture

The sixth thought is about philosophy and scripture. One essay after another gives rise to fruitful reflections on this relationship, but I will choose just one, Piero Boitani's tour de force on Dante and creation. His description of *Paradiso* canto 29 suggests the extraordinary intensity and complexity of scripture and philosophy in relation to each other and to the rest of the poem:

> a canto which is absolute, which speaks with one voice alone, that of Beatrice, sweeping down from before the beginning to the earthly world of the fourteenth century and back again to the fullness of the heavens. Canto 29 predicates being in its primeval forms, and moves through time and space to hover over out-of-time and outside-space; it moves constantly from the instant to eternity, from the "point" to the celestial waters and on to the final "eccelso" [height] and "larghezza" [breadth]. It also boldly re-scripts Scripture, rewriting the Hebrew-Christian Genesis and the prologue of John's Gospel in the Greek-Latin-Scholastic language of the Platonists and the Aristotelians, and roundly dismissing any anthropomorphism from the Beginning in favor of metaphysics and the categories of thought. The canto is divided into three clear parts (lines 1–81; 82–126; 127–45), proceeding like an inverted parabola, the third part returning to the subject and heights of the first.

As Boitani shows, Dante's profound, imaginative engagement with scripture is inseparable from being a truly "metaphysical" poet, alert to the rigors, riches, and intricacies of Platonic and Aristotelian thought. This double attentiveness is a constant source of theological insight, and theology needs continually to relearn how to sustain it fruitfully.

In recent years I have learnt most in this respect from a group of Jewish philosophers and text scholars, called "Textual Reasoning." What they discovered was that the text scholars did not pay much attention to philosophy, and that the philosophers stuck to their modern philosophy and did not (at least as philosophers) pay attention to Talmud or scripture—and they never talked much to each other. They formed the Textual Reasoning group (the title simply represents their two main interests), and some of us Christian academics used to sit on the edge of it when it gathered at the annual meeting of the American Academy of Religion. Out of that grew a group of Christians and Jews called "Scriptural Reasoning"; and later (about ten years ago), Muslims joined too, so that now we study Tanakh, Bible, and Qur'an together. The fruitfulness of Scriptural Reasoning in scriptural interpretation, philosophical reflection, theology, ethics, politics, and interfaith friendships has convinced me that the marriage of intensive scriptural study with wise reasoning is essential to healthy twenty-first-century theology, not only within and between faith communities but also in the simultaneously interfaith and secular environment of the contemporary university. Dante performs the coinherence of scripture and philosophy in his very different setting in a way that is nevertheless exemplary of this.

Poet and Theologian as Friends

The final thought is about twenty-first-century poets and theologians getting together. One of the most fundamental things for me as a theologian has been having as one of my best friends, a poet, Micheal O'Siadhail.[4] For nearly forty years, since before he was a poet and before I was a theologian, we have engaged intensively with each other; and I suspect that our friendship is part of the reason why I have become a theologian and he a poet. It has been a privilege to see a poet's vocation up close (and rather frightening at times, as when in early middle age he risked giving up his professorship to be a poet full-time).

All that time he has been a close reader of Dante. I have been intrigued by the Dantean resonances in his poetry, which are rarely explicit. His three most recent books have perhaps echoed Dante most. He immersed himself in Holocaust literature for more than four years in order to write *The Gossamer Wall: Poems in Witness to the Holocaust*, an exercise comparable to facing the reality of Hell. In *Love Life* he witnessed to more than thirty-five years of marriage, a very different relationship to that of Dante with Beatrice, yet with fascinating cross-lights. The most recent work, *Globe*, describes and probes the character of our twenty-first century and what has shaped it. It seems a world away from Dante's

Europe, but Kirkpatrick's "detailed engagement with texts and historical situations" is recognizable, as are the "brief contingencies." The primacy of the "middle distance" perspective is realized above all, as in Dante, through the vivid portrayal of particular people, both well and less known, who have tied some of the knots in the weave of modern history—Gregor Mendel, Emmanuel Lévinas, Patrick Kavanagh, William Shakespeare, Jean Vanier, Sigrid Undset, Nelson Mandela, Mahatma Gandhi, Bartolomé de Las Casas, Máirtín Ó Cadhain.

I too have been a reader of Dante during that time. Having alongside me a contemporary poet attempting work with some similarities has not only illuminated the work of both but has also been a constant inspiration in doing theology. So much so, indeed, that if there is one thing I would add to my wish for all theologians to befriend Dante, it is that they might also befriend at least one of those who are at present apprenticed in a kindred spirit to the same craft.

Notes

1. In this written response I follow fairly closely what was said at the time of the conference, but also improvise upon it in places.
2. E. Davis, *Proverbs, Ecclesiastes and the Song of Songs*.
3. Stern, *On Realism*.
4. On O'Siadhail's poetry, see Caball and Ford, *Musics of Belonging*.

BIBLIOGRAPHY

Primary Texts

Works By Dante

Commedia. Edited and with commentary by Anna Maria Chiavacci Leonardi. 3 vols. Milan: Mondadori, 1991–97.
La Commedia secondo l'antica vulgata. Edited by Giorgio Petrocchi. 2nd ed. 4 vols. Florence: Le Lettere, 1994.
Convivio. Edited by Franca Brambilla Ageno. 3 vols. Florence: Le Lettere, 1995.
Convivio. Edited by Cesare Vasoli. In Dante Alighieri, *Opere minori*, vol. 1, part 2. Milan and Naples: Ricciardi, 1988.
[Convivio]. The Banquet. Translated by Christopher Ryan. Saratoga, Calif.: ANMA Libri, 1989.
Dantis Alagherii Epistolae: The Letters of Dante. Emended text, with introduction, translation, notes, et al., by Paget Toynbee. 2nd ed. Oxford: Clarendon Press, 1966.
De vulgari eloquentia. Edited by Pier Vincenzo Mengaldo. In Dante Alighieri, *Opere minori*, vol. 2, 3–237. Milan and Naples: Ricciardi, 1979.
De vulgari eloquentia. Edited and translated by Stephen Botterill. Cambridge: Cambridge University Press, 1996.
La Divina Commedia. Edited and with commentary by Natalino Sapegno. 3 vols. Scandicci (Florence): La Nuova Italia, 1997.
La Divina Commedia, Paradiso. Edited by Umberto Bosco and Giovanni Reggio. Florence: Le Monnier, 1985.
The Divine Comedy. Translated by Robin Kirkpatrick. 3 vols. London and New York: Penguin, 2006–7.
The Divine Comedy. Translated by Allen Mandelbaum. 3 vols. Toronto and London: Bantam, 1980.
The Divine Comedy. Translated by Mark Musa. 3 vols. New York: Penguin, 1971–84.
The Divine Comedy. Translated by John D. Sinclair. 3 vols. New York and Oxford: Oxford University Press, 1961.
The Divine Comedy. Translated by C. H. Sisson. Oxford and New York: Oxford University Press, 1993.
Epistola a Cangrande. Edited by Enzo Cecchini. Florence: Giunti, 1995.

Monarchia. Edited and translated by Prue Shaw. Cambridge: Cambridge University Press, 1995.
Purgatorio. Edited and translated by Robert M. Durling. Introduction and notes by Robert Durling and Ronald L. Martinez. Oxford: Oxford University Press, 2003.
Vita nuova. Edited by Domenico De Robertis. In Dante Alighieri, *Opere minori*, vol. 1, part 1, 3–247. Milan and Naples: Ricciardi, 1984.

Bible

Biblia Sacra iuxta vulgatam versionem. 4th rev. ed. Edited by B. Fischer, R. Weber, R. Gryson, et al. Stuttgart: Deutsche Bibelgesellschaft, 1994.
The Holy Bible translated from the Latin Vulgate, Douay Rheims version. Revised by Richard Challoner. 1899. Rockford, Ill.: TAN Books and Publishers, 1989.

Other Primary Works

Ambrose, Saint. *Commentarius in Cantica Canticorum e Scriptis Sancti Ambrosii a Guillelmo Abbate Sancti Theodorici Collectus.* Edited by Gabriele Banterle. Milan and Rome: Biblioteca Ambrosiana-Città Nuova, 1993.
Analecta hymnica medii aevi. Edited by Guido Maria Dreves and Clemens Blume. 55 vols. Leipzig: Reisland, 1886–1922.
Anonimo Fiorentino. *Commento alla Divina Commedia d'Anonimo Fiorentino del secolo XIV.* Edited by Pietro Fanfani. 2 vols. Bologna: G. Romagnoli, 1868.
Aquinas, Saint Thomas. *In Duodecim Libros Metaphysicorum Aristotelis Expositio.* Turin-Rome: Marietti, 1964.
———. *Summa contra gentiles.* Edited by A. Gautier. Besançon: Lethielleux, 1961.
———. *Summa Theologiae.* Edited and translated by the English Dominicans. Reprinted edition. Cambridge: Cambridge University Press, 2006.
Aristotle. *Aristotle's De anima, in the Version of William of Moerbeke and the Commentary of St. Thomas Aquinas.* Translated by Kenelm Foster and Silvester Humphries. New Haven: Yale University Press, 1951.
———. *Aristotle's Metaphysics: A Revised Text with Introduction and Commentary.* Edited by W. D. Ross. 1924. 2 vols. Oxford: Oxford University Press, Clarendon, 1948.
———. *The Complete Works of Aristotle.* Rev. Oxford translation. Edited by Jonathan Barnes. 2 vols. Princeton: Princeton University Press, 1984.
———. *On the Parts of the Animals.* Translated by James G. Lennox. Oxford: Clarendon, 2001.
Augustine, Saint. *The City of God against the Pagans.* Translated and edited by R. W. Dyson. Cambridge: Cambridge University Press, 1998.
———. *Confessions.* Translated by Henry Chadwick. World's Classics. Oxford: Oxford University Press, 1992.

———. *Confessionum libri XIII*. Edited by Lucas Verheijen. *CCSL* 27. Turnhout: Brepols, 1981.
———. *De baptismo contra donatistas*. *CSEL* 51. Vienna: F. Tempsky, 1866.
———. *De civitate Dei*. Edited by Bernardus Dombart and Alphonsus Kalb. 1928–29. *CCSL* 47–48. Turnhout: Brepols, 1970.
———. *De Genesi ad litteram libri duodecim*. Edited by Joseph Zycha. *CSEL* 28. Vindobonae: F. Tempsky, 1894.
———. *De Genesi contra Manichaeos*. *PL* 34. Edited by J.-P. Migne. Paris, 1841–64.
———. *De poenitentibus*. *PL* 39. Edited by J.-P. Migne. Paris, 1841–64.
———. *De vera religione*. Edited by Klaus D. Daur. *CCSL* 32. Turnhout: Brepols, 1962.
———. *Enarrationes in Psalmos*. Edited by Eligius Dekkers and Johannes Fraipont. *CCSL* 38–40. Turnhout: Brepols, 1956.
———. *Epistola 93, Ad Vincentium*. *PL* 33. Edited by J.-P. Migne. Paris, 1841–64.
———. *Expositions of the Psalms*. Translated by Maria Boulding. 6 vols. New York: New City Press, 2000.
———. *In epistolam Iohannis ad Parthos tractatus X*. *PL* 35. Edited by J.-P. Migne. Paris, 1841–64.
———. *In Iohannis Evangelium tractatus*. Edited by Radbod Willems. *CCSL* 36. Turnhout: Brepols, 1954.
———. *The Literal Meaning of Genesis*. Translated by John Hammond Taylor. Ancient Christian Writers 41–42. New York and Mahwah: Paulist Press, 1982.
———. *Of True Religion*. Translated by J. H. S. Burleigh. Chicago: Regnery, 1959.
———. *Sermons*. Translated by Edmund Hill. 17 vols. New York: New City Press, 1995.
Beckett, Samuel. *The Lost Ones*. New York: Grove Press, 1972.
Bede. *In cantica canticorum allegorica expositio*. Edited by David Hurst. *CCSL* 119. Turnhout: Brepols, 1960.
———. *Hexameron*. *PL* 91. Edited by J.-P. Migne. Paris, 1841–64.
Bernard of Clairvaux, Saint. *Five Books on Consideration* [*De consideratione*]. Translated by John D. Andrews and Elizabeth T. Kennan. Kalamazoo, Mich.: Cistercian Publications, 1976.
———. *De diligendo Deo*. Edited by J. Leclercq, C. H. Talbot, and H. M. Rochais. Rome: Editiones Cistercienses, 1963.
———. *On Loving God*. Translated by Robert Walton. In *Treatises II*, vol. 5 of *The Works of Bernard of Clairvaux*. Cistercian Fathers 13. Washington, D.C.: Cistercian Publications, Consortium Press, 1974.
———. *Sermones super Cantica Canticorum*. Edited by J. Leclercq, C. H. Talbot, and H. M. Rochais. 2 vols. Rome: Editiones Cistercienses, 1957.
Boccaccio, Giovanni. *Trattatello in laude di Dante*. Edited by Mario Marti. Milan: Rizzoli, 1965.
———. *The Life of Dante*. Edited by Vincenzo Zin Bollettino. New York and London: Garland Publishing, 1990.

———. *Life of Dante*. Translated by John G. Nichols. London: Hesperus Press, 2002.

Boethius. *The Consolation of Philosophy*. With an English translation by S. J. Tester. Cambridge, Mass.: Harvard University Press, 1973.

Bonaventure, Saint. *Commentarius in Evangelium Lucae. Opera Omnia*, vol. 7.

———. *Itinerarium mentis in Deum. Opera omnia*, vol. 5, 295–313.

———. *Legenda maior S. Francisci Assisiensis*. Ad Claras Aquas (Quaracchi): Collegii S. Bonaventurae, 1941.

———. *Opera omnia*. 10 vols. Ad Claras Aquas (Quaracchi): Collegii S. Bonaventurae, 1882–1902.

———. *Sententiarum*. Ad Claras Aquas (Quaracchi): Collegii S. Bonaventurae, 1885.

Buti, Francesco da. *Commento di Francesco da Buti Sopra la "Divina Commedia" di Dante Alighieri*. 1858–62. Edited by Crescentino Giannini. 3 vols. Pisa: N. Lischi, 1989.

Cassiodorus. *Explanation of the Psalms*. Translated by P. G. Walsh. Ancient Christian Writers 51–53. New York and Mahwah, N.J.: Paulist Press, 1990–91.

———. *Expositio Psalmorum*. Edited by Marcus Adriaen. *CCSL* 97–98. Turnhout: Brepols, 1958.

Cicero. *De re publica; De legibus*. Translated by Cllinton Walker Keyes. 1928. Loeb Classical Library 213. Cambridge: Harvard University Press, 1994.

Coleridge, Samuel Taylor. "Lecture on Dante." In *Dante: The Critical Heritage*, edited by Michael Caesar, 439–47. London: Routledge, 1989.

———. *Marginalia. II Camden to Hutton*. Edited by George Whalley. London and Princeton: Routledge and Princeton University Press, 1984.

[Pseudo-]Dionysius [the Areopagite]. *De divinis nominibus*. In *Corpus Dionysiacum*, vol. 1. Edited by Beate Regina Suchla, Günter Heil, and Adolf Martin Ritter. Berlin: de Gruyter, 1990.

———. *The Complete Works*. Translated by Colm Luibheid. Edited by Paul Rorem. New York: Paulist Press, 1987.

Durand, William. *Rationale divinorum officiorum*. Edited by Anselme Davril and Timothy M. Thibodeau. *CCCM* 140–40B. 3 vols. Turnhout: Brepols, 1995.

Eckhart, Meister. *The Essential Sermons, Commentaries, Treatises, and Defense*. Translated by Edmund Colledge and Bernard McGinn. New York: Paulist Press, 1981.

———. *Meister Eckhart. A Modern Translation*. Edited and translated by Raymond Bernard Blakeny. New York: Harper, 1941.

Glossa Ordinaria. PL 113. Edited by J.-P. Migne. Paris, 1841–64.

Gregory the Great. *Commentaire sur le Cantique des Cantique*. Edited by Rodrigue Bélanger. Sources Chrétiennes 314. Paris: CERF, 1984.

———. *Expositio in Canticum Canticorum*. Edited by Patrick Verbraken. *CCSL* 144. Turnhout: Brepols, 1963.

———. *Homeliae in evangelia*. Edited by Raymond Étaix. CCSL 141. Turnhout: Brepols, 1999.
———. *Moralia in Job*. Edited by Marci Adriaen. CCSL 143–43A-B. Turnhout: Brepols, 1979–85.
Heaney, Seamus. *Seeing Things*. London: Faber, 1991.
Hegel, Georg Wilhelm Friedrich. *Lectures on The Philosophy of Religion*. Vol. 1, *Introduction and the Concept of Religion*. Edited by Peter C. Hodgson. Translated by R. F. Brown, P. C. Hodgson, and J. M. Stewart, with the assistance of H. S. Harris. Oxford: Clarendon Press, 2007.
Heidegger, M. *Sein und Zeit*. Tübingen: Max Niemeyer Verlag, 1979.
Hopkins, Gerard Manley. "As Kingfishers Catch Fire." In *God's Grandeur and Other Poems*, 36.
———. "God's Grandeur." In *God's Grandeur and Other Poems*, 15.
———. *God's Grandeur and Other Poems*. New York: Dover Publications, 1996.
———. "The Wreck of the Deutschland." In *God's Grandeur and Other Poems*, 3–12.
Horace. *Satires, Epistles and Ars poetica*. With an English translation by H. Rushton Fairclough. Cambridge, Mass.: Harvard University Press, 1991 [1929].
Jerome, Saint. *Commentariorum in Epistulam ad Titum*. PL 26. Edited by J.-P. Migne. Paris, 1841–64.
———. *Commentariorum in Evangelium Matthaei*. PL 26. Edited by J.-P. Migne. Paris, 1841–64.
Jurgens, William A., ed. and trans. *The Faith of the Early Fathers*. 3 vols. Collegeville, Minn.: The Liturgical Press, 1970–79.
Landino, Cristoforo. *Comento sopra la Commedia*. 1481. Edited by Paolo Procaccciali. 4 vols. Rome: Salerno, 2001.
Latini, Brunetto. *Li livres dou trésor de Brunetto Latini*. Edited by Francis J. Carmody. Berkeley: University of California Press, 1948.
Leo, the Great, Saint. "Incipit de Ascensione Domini (I. VI. 444)." Sermon 73 in *Sancti Leonis Magni Romani Pontificis Tractatus Septem et Nonaginta*. Edited by Antoine Chavasse. CCSL 138–38A. Turnhout: Brepols, 1973. Translation from Jurgens, *The Faith of the Early Fathers*, 3:279.
Lucretius Carus, Titus. *De rerum natura*. Edited and translated by W. H. D. Rouse. Cambridge, Mass.: Harvard University Press, 1975.
Merleau-Ponty, Maurice. *The Visible and the Invisible*. Evanston, Ill.: Northwestern University Press, 1968.
Merrill, James. *The Changing Light at Sandover: A Poem*. New York: Alfred A. Knopf, 1993.
Milton, John. *The Areopagitica*. New York: Columbia University Press, 1930.
———. *Paradise Lost*. Edited by Alastair Fowler. 2nd ed. Harlow: Longman, 1998.
Newman, John Henry. *The Dream of Gerontius*. London: Mowbray, 1986.
Nietzsche, Friedrich. "Skirmishes of an Un-ruly Man." In *Twilight of the Idols; or, How to Philosophise with the Hammer. The Anti-Christ; Notes to Zarathustra;*

and Eternal Recurrence, translated by Anthony M. Ludovici, 1–120. Edinburgh: Foulis, 1911.

———. *Twilight of the Idols*. Translated by Duncan Large. Oxford: Oxford University Press, 1998.

Origen. *Commentarius in Canticum canticorum*. Die griechischen christlichen Schriftsteller der ersten drei Jahrhunderte 33. Edited by W. A. Baehrens. Leipzig: J. C. Hinrichs, 1925.

———. *Commentarius in Iohannis euangelium*. Edited by Cècil Blanc. Sources Chrétiennes 120, 157, 222, 290, 385. Paris: CERF, 1966–92.

———. *Commentarius in Matthaei euangelium*. Die griechischen christlichen Schriftsteller der ersten drei Jahrhunderte 38. Edited by Erich Klostermann and Ernst Benz. 2nd ed., revised by Ursula Treu. Berlin: Akademie-Verlag, 1976.

———. *Homélies sur la Genèse*. Translated by Louis Doutreleau. Sources Chrétiennes 7. Paris: CERF, 1985.

———. *Omelie sul Cantico dei Cantici*. Edited by Manilo Simonetti. Milan: Valla-Mondadori, 1998.

Ottimo Commento. The Dartmouth Dante Project. http://dartmouth.dante.edu.

Ovid. *Fasti*. 2nd rev. ed. Translated by James G. Frazer. Revised by George P. Goold. Cambridge, Mass.: Harvard University Press, 1989.

Peter Lombard. *Commentarium in Psalmos*. PL 191. Edited by J.-P. Migne. Paris, 1841–64.

———. *Four Books of Sentences*. English translation at http://www.franciscan-archive.org/lombardus/opera/. (Accessed September 2008.)

———. *Sententiae in IV Libris Distinctae*. 3rd ed. 4 vols. Grottaferrata: Editiones Collegii S. Bonaventurae ad Claras Aquas, 1971.

Plato. *The Collected Dialogues of Plato, Including the Letters*. Edited by Edith Hamilton and Huntington Cairns. Princeton: Princeton University Press, 1961.

Plotinus. *Enneads*. With an English translation by A. H. Armstrong. 7 vols. Cambridge, Mass.: Harvard University Press, 1966–88.

Richard of Saint Victor. *Richard of St. Victor: The Twelve Patriarchs, the Mystical Ark, Book Three of the Trinity*. Translated by Grover A. Zinn. Classics of Western Spirituality. New York: Paulist Press, 1979.

Rilke, Rainer Maria. *Duino Elegies and the Sonnets to Orpheus*. With a translation by A. Poulin, Jr. Boston: Houghton Mifflin, 1977.

Schelling, Friedrich Wilhelm Joseph. "On Dante in Relation to Philosophy" [Über Dante in philosophischer Beziehung]. Translated by Elizabeth Rubenstein. In *German Aesthetic and Literary Criticism: Kant Fichte, Schelling, Schopenhauer, Hegel*, edited by David Simpson, 140–48. Cambridge: Cambridge University Press, 1984.

Scriptores Historiae Augustae (The). With an English Translation by David Magie. 3 vols. Cambridge, Mass.: Harvard University Press, 1967–68.

Stevens, Wallace. *Collected Poems.* New York: Vintage, 1954.
———. *The Necessary Angel: Essays on Reality and Imagination.* London and Boston: Faber 1960.
"Texts and Translations for Chants Mentioned by Dante." Collected by Paul Walker. http://www.worldofdante.org/docs/chanttexts_translations.pdf. (Accessed 22 September 2008.)
Virgil. *Eclogues, Georgics, Aeneid 1–6.* Translated by H. Rushton Fairclough. Revised by George P. Goold. Cambridge, Mass., and London: Harvard University Press, 1999.
Voragine, Jacobus de. *The Golden Legend: Readings on the Saints.* Translated by William Granger Ryan. 2 vols. Princeton: Princeton University Press, 1993.
William of Saint-Thierry. *Expositio super Cantica Canticorum.* Edited by Paul Verdeyen. *CCCM* 77. Turnhout: Brepols, 1997.
———. *Exposition on the Song of Songs.* Translated by Mother Columba Hart. *The Works of William of St. Thierry,* vol. 2. Cistercian Fathers 6. Shannon: Irish University Press, 1970.

Secondary Works

Agliano, Sebastiano. "Gloria." In *ED* 3:240–42.
Ardissino, Erminia. "I canti liturgici nel Purgatorio dantesco." *Dante Studies* 108 (1990): 39–65.
Armour, Peter. *Dante's Griffin and the History of the World: A Study of the Eartly Paradise (Purgatorio, cantos XXIX–XXXIII).* Oxford: Clarendon Press, 1989.
———. *The Door of Purgatory: A Study of Multiple Symbolism in Dante's "Purgatorio."* Oxford: Clarendon Press 1983.
Ascoli, Albert. *Dante and the Making of a Modern Author.* Cambridge: Cambridge University Press, 2008.
———. "Palinode and History in the Oeuvre of Dante." In *Dante: Contemporary Perspectives,* edited by Amilcare Iannucci, 23–50.
Astell, Ann W. *The Song of Songs in the Middle Ages.* Ithaca, N.Y., and London: Cornell University Press, 1990.
Auerbach, Erich. "Figura." In *Scenes from the Drama of European Literature: Six Essays,* 11–76.
———. "Francesco d'Assisi nella *Commedia.*" In *Studi su Dante,* 221–35.
———. "Il canto XI del *Paradiso.*" In *Letture dantesche. Paradiso,* 217–35.
———. "Sacrae Scripturae sermo humilis." In *Studi su Dante,* 165–73.
———. *Scenes from the Drama of European Literature: Six Essays.* New York: Meridian Books, 1944.
———. "St Francis in Dante's *Commedia.*" In *Scenes from the Drama of European Literature: Six Essays,* 79–98.
———. *Studi su Dante.* Milan: Feltrinelli, 1991.

Austin, J. L. *How to Do Things with Words.* Oxford: Oxford University Press, 1962.
Azzetta, Luca. "La tradizione del *Convivio* negli antichi commenti alla *Commedia*: Andrea Lancia, l'*Ottimo Commento*, e Pietro Alighieri." *Rivista di studi danteschi* 5 (2005): 3–34.
Bader, Günter. "Geist und Buchstabe—Buchstabe und Geist, ausgehend von Schleiermachers Reden 'Über die Religion.'" *Internationales Jahrbuch für Hermeneutik* 5 (2006): 95–140.
Baldelli, Ignazio. "Il Canto XI del *Paradiso.*" In *Nuove letture dantesche* 6:93–105.
Barański, Zygmunt. *Dante e i segni: Saggi per una storia intellettuale di Dante Alighieri.* Naples: Liguori, 2000.
———. "Dante's Biblical Linguistics." *Lectura Dantis* 5 (1989): 105–43.
———. "Dante's Signs: An Introduction to Medieval Semiotics and Dante." In *Dante and the Middle Ages: Literary and Historical Essays*, edited by John C. Barnes and Cormac Ó Cuilleanáin, 139–80. Dublin: Irish Academic Press, 1995.
———. "La lezione esegetica di *Inferno* I: Allegoria, storia e letteratura nella *Commedia.*" In *Dante e le forme dell'allegoresi*, edited by Michelangelo Picone, 79–97.
———. "L'iter ideologico di Dante." In *Dante e i segni*, 9–39.
———. "The 'New Life' of 'Comedy': The *Commedia* and the *Vita Nuova.*" *Dante Studies* 113 (1995): 1–30.
———. "Poetics of meter." In *Dante Now*, edited by Theodore J. Cachey, Jr., 3–41.
———. "*Sole nuovo, luce nuova*": *Saggi sul rinnovamento culturale in Dante.* Turin: Scriptorium, 1996.
Barbi, Michele. *Problemi fondamentali per un nuovo commento della "Divina Commedia."* Florence: Sansoni, 1956.
Barblan, Giovanni, ed. *Dante e la Bibbia.* Florence: Olschki, 1988.
Barnes, John C. "Vestiges of the Liturgy in Dante's *Comedy.*" In *Dante and the Middle Ages: Literary and Historical Essays*, edited by John C. Barnes and Cormac Ó Cuilleanáin, 231–70.
Barnes, John C., and Cormac Ó Cuilleanáin, eds. *Dante and the Middle Ages: Literary and Historical Essays.* Dublin: Irish Academic Press, 1995.
Barnes, John C., and Jennifer Petrie, eds. *Dante and the Human Body: Eight Essays.* Dublin: Four Courts Press, 2007.
———, eds. *Word and Drama in Dante.* Dublin: Irish Academic Press, 1993.
Barolini, Teodolinda. *Dante's Poets: Textuality and Truth in the Comedy.* Princeton: Princeton University Press, 1984.
———. *The Undivine Comedy: Detheologizing Dante.* Princeton: Princeton University Press, 1992.
Barolini, Teodolinda, and H. Wayne Storey, eds. *Dante for the New Millennium.* New York: Fordham University Press, 2003.
Barth, Bernhard. *Schellings Philosophie der Kunst: Göttliche Imagination und ästhetische Einbildungskraft.* Freiburg and Munich: Verlag Karl Alber, 1991.

Basile, Bruno. "Il viaggio come archetipo: Note sul tema della 'peregrinatio' in Dante." In *Letture Classensi* 15:9–26. Ravenna: Longo, 1986.
Battaglia Ricci, Lucia. *Dante e la tradizione letteraria medievale: Una proposta per la "Commedia."* Pisa: Giardini Editori, 1983.
———. "Figure di contraddizion: Lettura dell'XI canto del *Paradiso*." In *Le varie fila: Studi di letteratura italiana in onore di Emilio Bigi*, 34–50. Milan: Principato, 1997.
———. "Scrittura e riscrittura: Dante e Boccaccio 'agiografi.' " In *Scrivere di santi. Atti del II convegno di studio dell'Associazione italiana per lo studio della santità, dei culti e dell'agiografia, Napoli, 22–25 ottobre 1997*, edited by Gennaro Luongo, 147–75. Rome: Viella, 1999.
Beal, R. S. "Psalms." In *The Dante Encyclopedia*, edited by Richard Lansing, 218–19.
Beierwaltes, Werner. *Platonismus und Idealismus*. Frankfurt am Main: Klostermann, 1972.
———. *Proklos: Grundzüge seiner Metaphysik*. 2nd ed. Frankfurt am Main: Klostermann, 1979.
Benfell, V. Stanley. "David." In *The Dante Encyclopedia*, edited by Richard Lansing, 289–90.
Berger, Charles, and David Lehman, eds. *James Merrill: Essays in Criticism*. Ithaca, N.Y.: Cornell University Press, 1983.
Beyer, Gerald J. "The Love of God and Neighbour According to Aquinas: An Interpretation." *New Blackfriars* 84 (2003): 116–32.
Biller, Peter. "Confession in the Middle Ages: Introduction." In *Handling Sin: Confession in the Middle Ages*, edited by Peter Biller and Alistair J. Minnis, 1–33.
Biller, Peter, and Alistair J. Minnis, eds. *Handling Sin: Confession in the Middle Ages*. York: York Medieval Press, 1998.
Binski, Paul. "The Angel Choir at Lincoln and the Poetics of the Gothic Smile." *Art History* 20 (1997): 350–74.
Blasucci, Antonio. "La costituzione gerarchica della Chiesa in S. Bonaventura." *Miscellanea francescana* 68 (1968): 81–101.
Boitani, Piero. "Creazione e cadute di *Paradiso* XXIX." *L'Alighieri* 19 (2002): 87–103.
———. *Dante's Poetry of the Donati. The Barlow Lectures on Dante Delivered at University College London, 17–18 March 2005*. Occasional Papers 7. Edited by John Lindon. Leeds: Maney Publishing for the Society of Italian Studies, 2007.
———. "Dante's Sublime: Ancient, Medieval and Modern." *Poetica* 47 (1997): 1–32.
———. "The Poetry and Poetics of the Creation." In *The Cambridge Companion to Dante*, 2nd ed., edited by Rachel Jacoff, 218–35.
———. *The Tragic and the Sublime in Medieval Literature*. Cambridge: Cambridge University Press, 1989.
Bosco, Umberto. "Canto XI." In *Lectura Dantis Scaligera. Paradiso*, 387–418. Florence: Le Lettere, 1990.
———. *Dante vicino*. Rome: Sciascia, 1966.

———. "Domesticità del *Paradiso* (Lettura del xiv canto)." In *Studi in onore di Alberto Chiari*, vol. 2, 217–34. Brescia: Paideia, 1973.

———. "San Francesco." In *Dante vicino*, 316–41.

Botterill, Steven. "Canto XII." In *Dante's "Divine Comedy": Introductory Readings*, vol. 3, *Paradiso*, edited by Tibor Wlassics, 172–85.

———. *Dante and the Mystical Tradition: Bernard of Clairvaux in the "Commedia."* Cambridge: Cambridge University Press, 1994.

———. "Mysticism and Meaning in Dante's *Paradiso*." In *Dante for the New Millennium*, edited by Teodolinda Barolini and H. Wayne Storey, 143–51.

———. "'Not of This World': Spiritual and Temporal Powers in Dante and Bernard of Clairvaux." *Lectura Dantis* 10 (Spring 1992): 8–21.

Boyde, Patrick. *Dante Philomythes and Philosopher: Man in the Cosmos*. Cambridge: Cambridge University Press, 1981.

———. *Perception and Passion in Dante's "Comedy."* Cambridge: Cambridge University Press, 1993.

Boyle, Nicholas. "The Idea of Christian Poetry." In *Who Are We Now? Christian Humanism and the Global Market from Hegel to Heaney*, 283–311.

———. *Sacred and Secular Scriptures: A Catholic Approach to Literature*. London: Darton, Longman and Todd, 2004.

———. *Who Are We Now? Christian Humanism and the Global Market from Hegel to Heaney*. Edinburgh: T & T Clark, 1998.

Braet, Herman. "What about Medieval Humour?" In *Risus Mediaevalis: Laughter in Medieval Literature and Art*, edited by Braet et al., 1–9. Leuven: Leuven University Press, 2003.

Braida, Antonella. *Dante and the Romantics*. London: Palgrave Macmillan, 2005.

Branca, Vittore, and Giorgio Padoan, eds. *Dante e la Cultura Veneta*. Florence: Leo S. Olschki Editore, 1966.

Brandeis, Irma. *The Ladder of Vision: A Study of Dante's "Comedy."* London: Chatto & Windus, 1960.

Brezzi, Paolo. "Chiesa." In *ED* 1:960–68.

———. "Dante e la Chiesa del suo tempo." In *Dante e Roma. Atti del Convegno di Studi*, 97–114.

Brown, David. *Discipleship and Imagination: Christian Tradition and Truth*. Oxford: Oxford University Press, 2002.

Brownlee, Kevin. "Why the Angels Speak Italian: Dante as Vernacular 'Poeta' in 'Paradiso' 25." *Poetics Today* 5, no. 3 (1984): 597–610.

Burrell, David. *Faith and Freedom: An Interfaith Perspective*. Malden, Mass.: Blackwell, 2004.

———. *Knowing the Unknowable God: Ibn-Sina, Maimonides, Aquinas*. Notre Dame, Ind.: University of Notre Dame Press, 1986.

Bundy, Murray Wright. *The Theory of the Imagination in Classical and Western Thought*. University of Illinois Studies in Language and Literature 12. Urbana: University of Illinois Press, 1927.

Burrows, John A. *Gestures and Looks in Medieval Narrative.* Cambridge: Cambridge University Press, 1992.
Busnelli, Giovanni. *Cosmogonia e antropogenesi secondo Dante Alighieri e le sue fonti.* Rome: Civiltà Cattolica, 1922.
———. *L'origine dell'anima razionale secondo Dante e Alberto Magno.* 2nd ed. Rome: Civiltà Cattolica, 1929.
Caball, Marc, and David F. Ford, eds. *Musics of Belonging: The Poetry of Michael O'Siadhail.* Dublin: Carysfort Press, 2007.
Cacciari, Massimo. *L'angelo necessario.* 5th ed. Milan: Adelphi, 1998.
Cachey, Theodore J., Jr., ed. *Dante Now.* Notre Dame, Ind.: University of Notre Dame Press, 1995.
Calvo, Franceso. "Le api dell'invisibile." In *Il solco della parola: Origine della poesia.* Naples: Edizioni Scientifiche Italiane, 1994.
Cameron, Michael. "Augustine's Use of the Song of Songs against the Donatists." In *Augustine Biblical Exegete*, edited by Frederick Van Fleteren and Joseph C. Schnaubelt, 99–127. New York: Peter Lang, 2001.
Campagnola, Stanislao da. "Francesco di Assisi." In *ED* 3:17–23.
———. "Le prime biografie del Santo." In *Francesco d'Assisi: Storia e Arte*, edited by Francisco Porzio, 36–48.
Carugati, Giuliana. *Dalla menzogna al silenzio: La scrittura mistica della "Commedia."* Bologna: Il Mulino, 1991.
———. "Dante 'mistico'?" *Quaderni d'italianistica* 10, nos. 1–2 (1989): 237–50.
Castellani, Victor. "Heliocentricity in the Structure of Dante's *Paradiso.*" *Studies in Philology* 78, no. 3 (Summer 1981): 211–23.
The Catholic Encyclopaedia. 15 vols. New York: Encyclopaedia Press, 1913–14.
Cestaro, Gary P. "Canto X." In *Dante's "Divine Comedy": Introductory Readings*, vol. 3, *Paradiso*, edited by Tibor Wlassics, 146–55.
———. *Dante and the Grammar of the Nursing Body.* Notre Dame, Ind.: University of Notre Dame Press, 2003.
Chandler, S. Bernard, and J. A. Molinaro, eds. *The World of Dante: Six Studies in Language and Thought.* Toronto: University of Toronto Press, 1966.
Charity, Alan C. *Events and Their Afterlife: The Dialectics of Christian Typology in the Bible and Dante.* Cambridge: Cambridge University Press, 1966.
Chenu, Marie-Dominique. *La théologie au douzième siècle.* Paris: Vrin, 1957.
Chiarenza, Marguerite. "Dante's Lady Poverty." *Dante Studies* 111 (1993): 153–75.
Chiari, Alberto. "San Francesco cantato da Dante." *Esperienze letterarie* 9 (1984): 3–23.
Chiavacci Leonardi, Anna Maria. "Il Paradiso di Dante: L'Ardore del desiderio." In *Letture Classensi* 27:101–12. Ravenna: Longo, 1998.
Chydenius, Johan. *The Typological Problem in Dante.* Helsinki: Societas Scientiarum Fennica, 1960.
Coakley, Sarah, ed. *Religion and the Body.* Cambridge: Cambridge University Press, 1997.

Cogan, Marc. *The Design in the Wax: The Structure of the "Divine Comedy" and Its Meaning.* Notre Dame, Ind.: University of Notre Dame Press, 1999.
Coglievina, Leonella, and Domenico De Robertis, eds. *Sotto il segno di Dante: Scritti in onore di Francesco Mazzoni.* Florence: Le Lettere, 1998.
Colombo, Manuela. *Dai mistici a Dante: Il linguaggio dell'ineffabilità.* Florence: La Nuova Italia, 1987.
Comollo, Adriano. *Il dissenso religioso in Dante.* Florence: Olschki, 1990.
Congar, Yves. "L'ecclésiologie de S. Bernard." In *Saint Bernard Théologien, Actes du Congrès de Dijon 15–19, 1953,* 136–90. Rome: Editiones Cistercienses, 1953.
Contini, Gianfranco. "*Paradiso* XXVIII." In *Lectura Dantis Scaligera,* 1001–26. Florence: Le Monnier, 1968.
———. *Un'idea di Dante.* Turin: Einaudi, 1976.
Cornish, Alison. *Reading Dante's Stars.* New Haven and London: Yale University Press, 2000.
Cornish, Alison, and Dana E. Stewart, eds. *Sparks and Seeds: Medieval Literature and Its Afterlife. Essays in Honor of John Freccero.* Turnhout: Brepols, 2000.
Cosmo, Umberto. *Con Madonna Povertà. Studi francescani.* Bari: Laterza, 1940.
———. "Il primo libro francescano." In *Con Madonna Povertà,* 3–58.
———. "I ministri dell'ordine nell'universo." In *L'ultima ascesa: Introduzione alla lettura del "Paradiso,"* 355–71. Bari: Laterza, 1936.
———. "Le mistiche nozze di Frate Francesco con Madonna Povertà." *Giornale dantesco* 6 (1898): 49–82 and 97–117.
Cousins, Ewert H. "'*Intravi in intima mea*': Augustine and Neoplatonism." *Archivio di filosofia* 51:1–3 (1983): 281–92.
Croce, Benedetto. *La poesia di Dante.* Bari: Laterza, 1921.
Curtius, Ernst Robert. *European Literature and the Latin Middle Ages.* Translated by W. R. Trask. Princeton: Princeton University Press, 1953.
D'Alfonso, Rossella. *Il dialogo con Dio nella "Divina Commedia."* Bologna: Cooperativa Libraria Universitaria Editrice Bologna, 1988.
Dante e Roma. Atti del Convegno di Studi. Florence: Le Monnier, 1965.
Davies, Brian, ed. *Language, Meaning and God: Essays in Honour of Herbert McCabe OP.* London: Geoffrey Chapman, 1987.
Davies, Oliver. *The Creativity of God: World, Eucharist, Reason.* Cambridge: Cambridge University Press, 2004.
———. *Meister Eckhart, Mystical Theologian,* London: SPCK, 1991.
———. "Revelation and the Politics of Culture." In *Radical Orthodoxy? A Catholic Enquiry,* edited by Laurence Paul Hemming. Aldershot: Ashgate, 2000.
———. "The Sign Redeemed: A Study in Christian Fundamental Semiotics." *Modern Theology* 19 (2003): 219–41.
———. *A Theology of Compassion: Metaphysics of Difference and the Renewal of Tradition.* London: SCM, 2001.

———. "World and Body: A Study in Dante's Cosmological Hermeneutics." In *Dante and the Human Body: Eight Essays*, edited by John C. Barnes and Jennifer Petrie, 195–213.
Davies, Oliver, Paul D. Janz, and Clemens Sedmak, eds. *Transformation Theology: Church in the World*. London: T&T Clark, 2007.
Davies, Oliver, and Denys Turner, eds. *Silence and the Word: Negative Theology and the Incarnation*. Cambridge: Cambridge University Press, 2002.
Davis, Charles T. "Dante and Ecclesiastical Property." In *Law in Mediaeval Life and Thought*, edited by Edward B. King and Susan J. Ridyard, 244–57. Sewanee, Tenn.: The Press of the University of the South, 1990.
———. "Dante and the Empire." In *The Cambridge Companion to Dante*, 1st ed., edited by Rachel Jacoff, 67–79.
———. *Dante and the Idea of Rome*. Oxford: Oxford University Press, 1957.
———. "Poverty and Eschatology in the *Commedia*." *Yearbook of Italian Studies* 4 (1980): 59–86.
———. "Roma e Babilonia in Dante." In *Studi Americani su Dante*, edited by Gian Carlo Alessio and Robert Hollander, 267–95. Milan: F. Angeli, 1989.
Davis, Ellen F. *Proverbs, Ecclesiastes and the Song of Songs*. Louisville, Ky.: Westminster John Knox Press, 2000.
de Vogel, Cornelia. "*Amor quo caelum regitur*." *Vivarium* 1 (1963): 1–34.
Delcorno, Carlo. "Cadenze e figure della predicazione nel viaggio dantesco." In *Letture Classensi* 15:42–60. Ravenna: Longo, 1986.
D'Entrèves, Alessandro Passerin. *Dante as a Political Thinker*. Oxford: Oxford University Press, 1952.
Dictionnaire de théologie catholique. Edited by Alfred Vacant et al. 15 vols. Paris: Letouzey et Ané, 1909–50.
Dronke, Peter. *Dante and Medieval Latin Traditions*. Cambridge: Cambridge University Press, 1986.
———. *Dante's Second Love: The Originality and the Contexts of the "Convivio."* Leeds: The Society for Italian Studies, 1997.
———. "'L'amor che move il sole e l'altre stelle.'" In *The Medieval Poet and His World*, 439–75.
———. *The Medieval Poet and His World*. Rome: Edizioni di Storia e Letteratura, 1984.
Ducros, Franc. "L'esigenza poetica dinanzi all'esperienza del divino (L'ultimo canto della *Divina Commedia*)." In *Poesia e Mistica*, edited by Paule Plouvier, translated by M. R. Del Genio. Città del Vaticano: Libreria Editrice Vaticana, 2002.
Dufournet, Jean, ed. *"Le chevalier au lion": Approches d'un chef-d'oeuvre*. Paris: Champion, 1988.
Durling, Robert M., and Ronald L. Martinez. *Time and the Crystal: Studies in Dante's "Rime petrose."* Berkeley: University of California Press, 1990.
Eagleton, Terry. "'Decentring' God." *New Blackfriars* 57 (1976): 148–51.

Eco, Umberto. *The Name of the Rose.* Translated by William Weaver. London: Picador, 1983.
Enciclopedia Dantesca. Edited by Umberto Bosco. 1970–78. 2nd ed. 5 vols. plus appendix. Rome: Istituto dell'Enciclopedia Italiana, 1984.
Enciclopedia dell'Arte Medievale. 12 vols. Rome: Istituto dell'Enciclopedia Italiana, 1991–2002.
Esposito, Enzo, ed. *Memoria biblica nell'opera di Dante.* Rome: Bulzoni Editore, 1996.
Evans, Gillian R. *The Language and Logic of the Bible: The Earlier Middle Ages.* New York: Cambridge University Press, 1984.
———. *Law and Theology in the Middle Ages.* London and New York: Routledge, 2002.
———. *Philosophy and Theology in the Middle Ages.* New York and London: Routledge, 1993.
"Exinanition." In *Oxford English Dictionary.* http://www.oed.com. (Accessed 19 September 2008.)
Fallani, Giovanni. *Dante, poeta, teologo.* Milan: Marzorati Editore, 1965.
———. "Il canto XIV del Paradiso." In *Nuove letture dantesche* 6:147–62.
———. "Le gerarchie angeliche." In *Dante, poeta, teologo,* 288–301.
Fehlner, Peter D. *The Role of Charity in the Ecclesiology of St. Bonaventure.* Rome: Editrice Miscellanea francescana, 1965.
Ferrante, Joan M. *The Political Vision of the "Divine Commedia."* Princeton: Princeton University Press, 1984.
Finan, Thomas. "Dante and the Religious Imagination." In *Religious Imagination,* edited by James P. Mackey, 65–86.
Fleming, John V. *An Introduction to Franciscan Literature.* Chicago: Franciscan Herald Press, 1977.
Ford, David F. *Christian Wisdom: Desiring God and Learning in Love.* Cambridge: Cambridge University Press, 2007.
———. *Self and Salvation: Being Transformed.* Cambridge: Cambridge University Press, 1999.
Foster, Kenelm. "The Canto of the Damned Popes: *Inferno* XIX." *Dante Studies* 87 (1969): 47–68.
———. "The Celebration of Order: *Paradiso* X." In *The Two Dantes,* 120–36.
———. "Dante and St Thomas." In *The Two Dantes,* 56–65.
———. "Dante as a Christian Poet." In *God's Tree,* 1–14.
———. "Gli elogi danteschi di S. Francesco e di S. Domenico." In *Dante e il francescanesimo,* 231–49. Cava dei Tirreni: Avagliano, 1987.
———. *God's Tree: Essays on Dante and Other Matters.* London: Blackfriars Publications, 1957.
———. "The Mind in Love." In *Dante: A Collection of Critical Essays,* edited by John Freccero, 43–60.

———. "Teologia." In *ED* 5:564–568.
———. "The Theology of the *Inferno*." In *God's Tree*, 50–66.
———. "Tommaso d'Aquino." In *ED* 5:626–49.
———. *The Two Dantes, and Other Studies*. Berkeley: University of California Press, 1977.
Franke, William. *Dante's Interpretive Journey*. Chicago: University of Chicago Press, 1996.
Franz, Michael. *Schellings Tübinger Platon-Studien*. Göttingen: Vandenhoeck & Ruprecht, 1996.
Frattini, Alberto. "Il canto XXVII del *Paradiso*." In *Lectura Dantis Romana*, 5–35. Turin: Società Editrice Internazionale, 1960.
Freccero, John. "Casella's Song (*Purg*. II. 112)." In *Dante: The Poetics of Conversion*, 186–94.
———. *Dante: The Poetics of Conversion*, edited by Rachel Jacoff. Cambridge, Mass., and London: Harvard University Press, 1996.
———. "Paradiso X: The Dance of the Stars." *Dante Studies* 86 (1968): 85–111.
———, ed. *Dante: A Collection of Critical Essays*. Englewood Cliffs, N.J.: Prentice Hall, 1965.
Friedman, Joan Isobel. "La processione mistica di Dante: Allegoria e iconografia nel canto XXIX del *Purgatorio*." In *Dante e le forme dell'allegoresi*, edited by Michelangelo Picone, 125–48. Ravenna: Longo, 1987.
Frye, Northrop. *The Great Code: The Bible and Literature*. New York and London: Harcourt, 1987.
Gadamer, Hans-Georg. "Aesthetics and Hermeneutics." In *Philosophical Hermeneutics*, translated by David E. Linge, 95–104.
———. *Philosophical Hermeneutics*. Translated by David E. Linge. Berkeley, Los Angeles, and London: University of California Press, 1976.
———. *Truth and Method*, translated by Joel Weinsheimer and Donald G. Marshall. 1960. London: Sheed and Ward, 1989.
Gaehtgens, Thomas, ed. *Künstlerischer Austausch/Artistic Exchange*. 2 vols. Berlin: Akademie, 1993.
Gage, John. *Colour and Culture: Practice and Meaning from Antiquity to Abstraction*. London: Thames, 1993.
Gatti, Andrew, and Paola Zanardi, eds. *Filosofia, scienza, storia: Il dialogo tra Italia e Gran Bretagna*. Ferrara: Il Poligrafo, 2005.
Gilson, Etienne. *Dante and Philosophy*. Translated by D. Moore, 1939. New York, Evanston, Ill., and London: Harper and Row, 1963.
———. *Dante et Béatrice: Études Dantesques*. Paris: Vrin, 1974.
Gilson, Simon. *Dante and Renaissance Florence*. Cambridge: Cambridge University Press, 2005.
———. *Medieval Optics and Theories of Light in the Works of Dante*. Lewiston, N.Y.: E. Mellen Press, 2000.

———. "'Rimaneggiamenti danteschi' di Aristotele: *Gravitas* e *levitas* nella *Commedia.*" In *Le culture di Dante: Studi in onore di Robert Hollander. Atti del quarto Seminario dantesco internazionale, University of Notre Dame (Ind.), USA, 25–27 settembre 2003,* edited by Michelangelo Picone, Theodore J. Cachey, Jr., and Margherita Mesirca, 151–77.

Girardi, E. Noè. "La struttura del *Paradiso* e i Canti del Sole (Par. x–xiv, 81)." In *Studi in onore di Alberto Chiari,* vol. 1, 629–52. Brescia: Paideia, 1973.

Gombrich, Ernst Hans. *Symbolic Images.* London: Phaidon, 1972.

Gragnolati, Manuele. *Experiencing the Afterlife: Soul and Body in Dante and Medieval Culture.* Notre Dame, Ind.: University of Notre Dame Press, 2005.

Grant, Edward. *Planets, Stars and Orbs: The Medieval Cosmos, 1200–1687.* Cambridge: Cambridge University Press, 1996.

Harper, John. *The Forms and Orders of Western Liturgy from the Tenth to the Eighteenth Century.* Oxford: Clarendon Press, 1991.

Hart, Kevin. *The Trespass of the Sign: Deconstruction, Theology and Philosophy.* Cambridge: Cambridge University Press, 1989.

Hartman, Geoffrey H. *Easy Pieces.* New York: Columbia University Press, 1985.

Hauerwas, Stanley. *A Community of Character: Toward a Constructive Christian Social Ethic.* Notre Dame, Ind., and London: University of Notre Dame Press, 1981.

Havely, Nick. *Dante and the Franciscans: Poverty and the Papacy in the "Commedia."* Cambridge: Cambridge University Press, 2004.

———. "Poverty in Purgatory: From *Commercium* to *Commedia.*" *Dante Studies* 114 (1996): 229–43.

———, ed. *Dante's Modern Afterlife: Reception and Response from Blake to Heaney.* New York: St. Martin's, 1999.

Hawkins, Peter S. "All Smiles: Poetry and Theology in Dante." *PMLA* 121, no. 2 (2006): 371–87.

———. "Dante and the Bible." In *The Cambridge Companion to Dante,* 1st ed., edited by Rachel Jacoff, 120–35.

———. *Dante's Testaments: Essays in Scriptural Imagination.* Stanford, Calif.: Stanford University Press, 1999.

Hawkins, Peter S., and Rachel Jacoff, eds. *The Poets' Dante: Twentieth-Century Reflections.* New York: Farrar, Straus and Giroux, 2001.

Hedley, Douglas. "Dante's Romantic Imagination: A Neoplatonic Fantasy?" In *Filosofia, scienza, storia: Il dialogo tra Italia e Gran Bretagna,* edited by Andrea Gatti and Paola Zanardi, 113–34.

———. *Living Forms of the Imagination.* London: T & T Clark, 2008.

Hendrix, Scott H. *"Ecclesia in Via": Ecclesiological Developments in the Medieval Psalms Exegesis and the Dictata Super Psalterium (1513–1515) of Martin Luther.* Leiden: Brill, 1974.

Henry, H. T. "Miserere." In *The Catholic Encyclopaedia,* vol. 10.

Henry, Nathalie. "The Lily and the Thorns: Augustine's Refutation of the Donatist Exegesis of the Song of Songs." *Revue des Études Augustiniennes* 42 (1996): 255–66.

Herrin, Judith. *The Formation of Christendom*. Princeton: Princeton University Press, 1987.

Higgins, David H. *Dante and the Bible: An Introduction*. Bristol: University of Bristol Press, 1992.

Holladay, William L. *The Psalms through Three Thousand Years*. Minneapolis: Fortress Press, 1996.

Hollander, Robert. *Allegory in Dante's "Commedia."* Princeton: Princeton University Press, 1969.

———. "Babytalk in Dante's *Commedia*." In *Studies in Dante*, 115–29.

———. "Dante as Uzzah? (*Purg.* X 57, and *Ep.* XI 9–12)." In *Sotto il segno di Dante: scritti in onore di Francesco Mazzoni*, edited by Leonella Coglievina and Domenico De Robertis, 143–51.

———. "Dante's Use of the Fiftieth Psalm (A Note on *Purg.* XXX, 84)." In *Studies in Dante*, 107–13.

———. "Dante *Theologus-Poeta*." In *Studies in Dante*, 38–89.

———. *Studies in Dante*. Ravenna: Longo Editore, 1979.

Honess, Claire. "Communication and Participation in Dante's *Commedia*." In *In amicizia: Essays in Honour of Giulio Lepschy*, edited by Zygmunt G. Barański and Lino Pertile. Special Supplement to *The Italianist* 17 (1997).

———. "Expressing the Inexpressible: The Theme of Communication in the Heaven of Mars." *Lectura Dantis* 14–15 (1994): 42–60.

Iannucci, Amilcare A. "Theology." In *The Dante Encyclopedia*, edited by Richard Lansing, 811–15.

———, ed. *Dante: Contemporary Perspectives*. Toronto: University of Toronto Press, 1997.

Jacobelli, Maria Caterina. *Il risus paschalis e il fondamento teologico del piacere sessuale*. Brescia: Queriniana, 1990.

Jacoff, Rachel. "Merrill and Dante." In *James Merrill: Essays in Criticism*, edited by Charles Berger and David Lehman, 145–58.

———. "Our Bodies, Our Selves: The Body in the *Commedia*." In *Sparks and Seeds: Medieval Literature and Its Afterlife: Essays in Honor of John Freccero*, edited by Alison Cornish and Dana E. Stewart, 119–37.

———. "The Post-Palinodic Smile: *Paradiso* VIII and IX." *Dante Studies* 98 (1980): 111–22.

———, ed. *The Cambridge Companion to Dante*. 1st ed. Cambridge: Cambridge University Press, 1993.

———, ed. *The Cambridge Companion to Dante*. 2nd ed. Cambridge: Cambridge University Press, 2007.

Jacomuzzi, Angelo. "Il *topos* dell'ineffabile nel *Paradiso*." In *L'Imago al Cerchio e altri studi sulla "Divina Commedia,"* 78–113.

——. *L'Imago al Cerchio e altri studi sulla "Divina Commedia."* Milan: Franco Angeli, 1995.
Jungmann, Joseph. *The Mass of the Roman Rite: Its Origins and Development.* Translated by Francis A. Brunner. New York: Benziger, 1950.
Kantorowicz, Ernst H. "Dante's Two Suns." In *Selected Studies*, 325–38.
——. *The King's Two Bodies: A Study in Mediaeval Political Theology.* Princeton: Princeton University Press, 1957.
——. *Selected Studies.* Locust Valley, New York: Augustin, 1965.
Kaske, Robert E. "Dante's *Purgatorio* XXXII and XXXIII: A Survey of Christian History." *University of Toronto Quarterly* 43 (1974): 193–214.
Kay, Richard. "The Pope's Wife: Allegory as Allegation in *Inferno* 19, 106–11." *Studies in Medieval Culture* 12 (1978): 105–11.
Keck, David. *Angels and Angelology in the Middle Ages.* New York: Oxford University Press, 1998.
Kerr, Fergus. "Charity as Friendship." In *Language, Meaning and God: Essays in Honour of Herbert McCabe OP*, edited by Brian Davies, 1–23.
——. "Derrida's Wake." *New Blackfriars* 55 (1974): 449–60.
——. *Immortal Longings: Versions of Transcending Humanity.* London: SPCK, 1997.
Kerr, John. "Proserpinan Memory in Dante and Chaucer." Ph.D. dissertation. University of Notre Dame, 2000.
Kirkpatrick, Robin. *Dante's "Inferno": Difficulty and Dead Poetry.* Cambridge: Cambridge University Press, 1987.
——. *Dante's "Paradiso" and the Limitations of Modern Criticism.* Cambridge: Cambridge University Press, 1978.
Klauser, Theodor. *A Short History of the Western Liturgy: An Account and Some Reflections.* Translated by John Halliburton. Oxford: Oxford University Press, 1969.
Kleinhenz, Christopher. "Dante and the Bible: Biblical Citation in the Divine Comedy." In *Dante: Contemporary Perspectives*, edited by Amilcare A. Iannucci, 74–93.
Knowlson, James. *Damned to Fame: The Life of Samuel Beckett.* London: Bloomsbury, 1999.
Kretzmann, Norman. "Philosophy of Mind." In *The Cambridge Companion to Aquinas*, edited by Norman Kretzmann and Eleonore Stump, 128–59. Cambridge: Cambridge University Press, 1993.
Kuczynski, Michael P. *Prophetic Song: The Psalms as Moral Discourse in Late Medieval England.* Philadelphia: University of Pennsylvania Press, 1995.
Kugel, James L. "David the Prophet." In *Poetry and Prophecy: The Beginnings of a Literary Tradition*, edited by James Kugel, 45–55.
——, ed. *Poetry and Prophecy: The Beginnings of a Literary Tradition*, edited by James Kugel. Ithaca, N.Y., and London: Cornell University Press, 1990.

Lacoste, Jean-Yves. *Expérience et Absolu: Questions disputées sur l'humanité de l'homme*. Paris: Presses Universitaires de France, 1994.

La Favia, Louis M. "'Ché quivi per canti' (*Purg.*, XII. 113): Dante's Programmatic Use of Psalms and Hymns in the *Purgatorio*." *Studies in Iconography* 9 (1984–86): 53–65.

Lansing, Richard. "Narrative Design in Dante's Earthly Paradise." *Dante Studies* 112 (1994): 101–13.

———, ed. *Dante: The Critical Complex*. Vol. 4, *Dante and Theology: The Biblical Tradition and Christian Allegory*. New York and London: Routledge, 2003.

———, ed. *The Dante Encyclopedia*. New York: Garland, 2000.

Lash, Nicholas. "Anselm Seeking." In *The Beginning and the End of 'Religion,'* 150–63.

———. *The Beginning and the End of 'Religion.'* Cambridge: Cambridge University Press, 1996.

———. "Creation, Courtesy and Contemplation." In *The Beginning and the End of 'Religion,'* 164–82.

———. *Holiness, Speech and Silence: Reflections on the Question of God*. Aldershot: Ashgate, 2004.

———. "When Did the Theologians Lose Interest in Theology?" In *The Beginning and the End of 'Religion,'* 132–49.

Lauand, Luiz Jean. "*Ludus* in the Fundamentals of Aquinas's World-View." Translated by Alfredo H. Alves. *International Studies on Law and Education* 2 (1999). http://www.hottopos.com/harvard2/ludus.htm. (Accessed 12 August 2008.)

Leclercq, Jean. *L'amour des lettres et le desir de Dieu: Initiation aux auteurs monastiques du Moyen Age*. Paris: Editions du Cerf, 1957.

———. *Monks and Love in Twelfth-Century France*. Oxford: Clarendon Press, 1979.

LeGoff, Jacques. "Laughter in the Middle Ages." In *A Cultural History of Humour*, edited by Jan Bremmer and Herman Roodenburg, 40–53. Cambridge: Polity, 1997.

Lentzen, Manfred. *Studien zur Dante-Exegese Christoforo Landinos*. Cologne: Böhlau, 1971.

Letture dantesche. Paradiso. Edited by Giovanni Getto. Florence: Sansoni, 1961.

Lloyd, A. C. "*Nosce Teipsum* and *Conscientia*." *Archiv für Geschichte der Philosophie* 46 (1964): 188–200.

Lombardi, Elena. *The Syntax of Desire: Language and Love in Augustine, the Modistae and Dante*. Toronto: University of Toronto Press, 2007.

Lubac, Henri de. *Exégèse médiévale*. 4 vols. Paris: Aubier, 1959–64.

———. *Medieval Exegesis*. Translated by Mark Sebanc. 4 vols. Grand Rapids, Mich.: Wm B. Eerdmans, 1998.

MacIntyre, Alasdair. *Three Rival Versions of Moral Enquiry: Encyclopeida, Genalogy and Tradition; being Gifford Lectures delivered in the University of Edinburgh in 1988*. London: Duckworth, 1990.

Mackey, James P., ed. *Religious Imagination*. Edinburgh: Edinburgh University Press, 1986.

Magli, Ida. *Gli uomini della penitenza*. Bologna: Cappelli Editori, 1967.

Mahnke, Dietrich. *Unendliche Sphäre und Allmittelpunkt: Beiträge zur Genealogie der mathematischen Mystik*. Halle: Niemeyer, 1937.

Malato, Enrico. "'Sì come cieco va dietro a sua guida / per non smarrirsi': Lettura del Canto XVI del *Purgatorio*." *Rivista di Studi Danteschi* 2, no. 2 (2002): 225–61.

Mandelstam, Osip. "Conversation about Dante." In *The Collected Critical Prose and Letters*, edited by Jane Gary Harris, translated by Jane Gary Harris and Constance Link, 397–451. London: Collins Harvill, 1991.

Manselli, Raoul. "Il canto XII del *Paradiso*." In *Nuove letture dantesche* 6:107–28.

———. "Dante e l'*ecclesia spiritualis*." In *Dante e Roma. Atti del Convegno di Studi*, 115–35.

———. "San Francesco e San Domenico nei canti del *Paradiso*." In *Da Gioacchino da Fiore a Cristoforo Colombo: Studi sul francescanesimo spirituale, sull'ecclesiologia e sull'escatologismo bassomedievali*, 201–11. Rome: Istituto Storico per il Medioevo, 1997.

Marietti, Marina. "Au Ciel du Soleil. (*Paradis*, X–XIV)." *Chroniques italiennes* 57 (1999): 29–48.

Martinez, Ronald L. "The Pilgrim's Answer to Bonagiunta and the Poetics of the Spirit." *Stanford Italian Review* 3 (1983): 37–63.

———. "The Poetics of Advent Liturgies: Dante's *Vita Nuova* and *Purgatorio*." In *Le culture di Dante: Studi in onore di Robert Hollander*, edited by Michelangelo Picone, Theodore J. Cachey, Jr., and Margherita Mesirca, 271–304.

Marzot, Giulio. *Il linguaggio biblico nella Divina Commedia*. Pisa: Nistri-Liselli Editori, 1956.

Mastrobuono, Antonio C. *Dante's Journey of Sanctification*. Washington, D.C.: Regnery Gateway, 1990.

Matter, E. Ann. *The Voice of My Beloved*. Philadelphia: University of Pennsylvania Press, 1990.

Mazzeo, Joseph Anthony. *Medieval Cultural Tradition in Dante's "Comedy."* Ithaca, N.Y.: Cornell University Press, 1960.

———. *Structure and Thought in the "Paradiso."* Ithaca, N.Y.: Cornell University Press, 1958.

Mazzotta, Giuseppe. *Dante, Poet of the Desert: History and Allegory in the "Divine Comedy."* Princeton: Princeton University Press, 1979.

———. *Dante's Vision and the Circle of Knowledge*. Princeton: Princeton University Press, 1993.

———. "The Heaven of the Sun: Dante between Aquinas and Bonaventure." In *Dante for the New Millennium*, edited by Teodolinda Barolini and H. Wayne Storey, 152–68.

McCabe, Herbert. *God Matters*. London: Geoffrey Chapman, 1987.

———. "Sacramental Language." In *God Matters*, 165–79.
McCracken, Andrew. "*In Omnibus Viis Tuis*: Compline in the Valley of the Rulers (*Purg.* VII–VIII)." *Dante Studies* 111 (1993): 119–29.
McDougal, Stuart Y., ed. *Dante among the Moderns*. Chapel Hill: University of North Carolina Press, 1985.
McIntosh, Mark Allen. *Mystical Theology: The Integrity of Spirituality and Theology*. Malden, Mass.: Blackwell, 1998.
Meekins, Angela G. "Reflecting on the Divine: Notes on Dante's Heaven of the Sun." *The Italianist* 18 (1998): 28–70.
———. "The Study of Dante, Bonaventure and Mysticism: Notes on Some Problems of Method." In *In amicizia: Essays in Honour of Giulio Lepschy*, edited by Zygmunt G. Barański and Lino Pertile, 83–99. Special Supplement to *The Italianist* 17 (1997).
Meersseman, Gilles G. "Penitenza e Penitenti nella vita e nelle opere di Dante." In *Dante e la Cultura Veneta*, edited by Vittore Branca and Giorgio Padoan, 229–46.
Mellone, Attilio. "Gerarchia angelica." In *ED* 3:122–24.
———. "Gli angeli in Dante." In *ED* 1:268–71.
———, ed. *I primi undici canti della "Commedia."* Lectura Dantis Metelliana 2. Rome: Bulzoni, 1992.
Ménard, Philippe. *Le rire et le sourire dans le roman courtois en France au moyen âge (1150–1250)*. Geneva: Droz, 1969.
———. "Rires et sourires dans le roman du *Chevalier au lion*." In *"Le chevalier au lion": Approches d'un chef-d'oeuvre*, edited by Jean Dufournet, 1–9.
Metzger, Bruce M., and Michael David Coogan, eds. *The Oxford Companion to the Bible*. Oxford: Oxford University Press, 1993.
Mineo, Niccolò. "Il canto XI del *Paradiso*." In *I primi undici canti della "Commedia,"* edited by Attilio Mellone, 221–320.
———. *Profetismo e Apocalittica in Dante*. Catania: Università di Catania, 1968.
Milbank, John. "The Name of Jesus." In *The Word Made Strange*, 145–68.
———. *Theology and Social Theory: Beyond Secular Reason*. 2nd ed. Malden, Mass.: Blackwell, 2006.
———. *The Word Made Strange: Theology, Language, Culture*. Oxford: Blackwell, 1997.
Minnis, Alistair J. *Medieval Theory of Authorship*. London: Scholars' Press, 1988.
Montemaggi, Vittorio. "'La rosa in che il verbo divino carne si fece': Human Bodies and Truth in the Poetic Narrative of the *Commedia*." In *Dante and the Human Body*, edited by John C. Barnes and Jennifer Petrie, 159–94.
———. "'Nulla vedere e amor mi costrinse': On Reading Dante's *Commedia* as a Theological Poem." Ph.D. dissertation. University of Cambridge, 2006.
———. "'Padre mio ché non m'aiuti?': Ugolino and the Poetics of the *Commedia*." In *Dante and the Ethical Uses of Poetry*, edited by Claire Honess. Supplement to *The Italianist*, forthcoming.

Moevs, Christian. *The Metaphysics of Dante's "Comedy."* New York: Oxford University Press, 2005.

Murray, Alexander. "Counselling in Medieval Confession." In *Handling Sin: Confession in the Middle Ages*, edited by Peter Biller and Alistair J. Minnis, 63–77.

Nardi, Bruno. "L'arco della vita (nota illustrative al *Convivio*)." In *Saggi di filosofia dantesca*, 110–38.

———. "Il canto di s. Francesco." In *'Lecturae' e altri studi danteschi*, 173–84.

———. *Dante e la cultura medievale*. Edited by Paolo Mazzantini. 2nd ed. Rome: Editori Laterza, 1950.

———. "Dante profeta." In *Dante e la cultura medievale*, 265–326.

———. *'Lecturae' e altri studi danteschi*. Florence: Le Lettere, 1990.

———. "L'immortalità dell'anima." In *Dante e la cultura medievale*, 225–43.

———. "Lo discorrer di Dio sovra quest'acque." In *Nel mondo di Dante*, 307–13.

———. "L'origine dell'anima umana secondo Dante." In *Studi di filosofia medievale*, 9–68.

———. *Nel mondo di Dante*. Rome: Edizioni di Storia e Letteratura, 1944.

———. *Saggi di filosofia dantesca*. 2nd ed. Florence: La Nuova Italia, 1967.

———. *Studi di filosofia medievale*. Rome: Edizioni di Storia e Letteratura, 1960.

———. "Sull'origine dell'anima umana." In *Dante e la cultura medievale*, 207–24.

Nasti, Paola. *Favole d'amore e "saver profondo": La tradizione salomonica in Dante*. Ravenna: Longo, 2007.

———. "La memoria del *Canticum* e la *Vita Nuova*: Una nota preliminare." *The Italianist* 18 (1998): 14–27.

———. "Of This World and the Other: Dante's Ecclesiology in *Paradiso*." *The Italianist* 27, no. 2 (2007): 206–32.

———. "The Wise Poet: Solomon in Dante's Heaven of the Sun." In *Dante: Current Trends in Dante Studies* (journal issue title), *Reading Medieval Studies* 27 (2001): 103–38.

Nuove letture dantesche. 8 vols. Florence: Le Monnier, 1966–78.

O'Connell, Daragh, and Jennifer Petrie, eds. *Art and Nature in Dante*. Dublin: Four Courts Press, forthcoming.

Ohly, Friedrich. *Hohelied-Studien: Grundzüge einer Geschichte der Hoheliedauslegung des Abendlandes bis um 1200*. Wiesbaden: Steiner Verlag, 1958.

O'Siadhail, Micheal. *Globe*. Tarset: Bloodaxe Books, 2007.

———. *The Gossamer Wall: Poems in Witness to the Holocaust*. Tarset: Bloodaxe Books, 2002.

———. *Love Life*. Tarset: Bloodaxe Books, 2005.

Padoan, Giorgio. "Apollo." In *ED* 1:318.

———. "Il canto XXVIII del *Paradiso*." In *Nuove letture dantesche* 7:175–227.

Paolini, Shirley J. *Confessions of Sin and Love in the Middle Ages: Dante's "Commedia" and St. Augustine's "Confessions."* Washington, D.C.: University Press of America, 1982.

Parker, Deborah. *Commentary and Ideology: Dante in the Renaissance.* Durham, N.C., and London: Duke University Press, 1993.
Pasquazi, Silvio. "San Francesco." In *D'Egitto in Ierusalemme: Studi danteschi,* 181–217. Rome: Bulzoni, 1985.
Pattison, George. *The End of Theology—And the Task of Thinking about God.* London: SCM, 1998.
———. *Kierkegaard and the Crisis of Faith.* London: SPCK, 1997.
Penna, Angelo. "Salmo." In *ED* 4:1078.
Pépin, Jean. *Théologie Cosmique et Théologie Chrétienne.* Paris: Presses Universitaires de France, 1964.
Pertile, Lino. "*Cantica* nella tradizione medievale e in Dante." *Rivista di Storia e Letteratura Religiosa* 27 (1991): 389–412.
———. "'Canto'—'Cantica'—'Comedìa' e l'*Epistola a Cangrande*." *Lectura Dantis* 9 (1991): 105–23.
———. "'Così si fa la pelle bianca nera': L'enigma di *Par.* XXVIII 136–138." *Lettere italiane* 43 (1991): 3–26.
———. "Dante's *Comedy* beyond the *Stilnuovo.*" *Lectura Dantis* 13 (1993): 47–77.
———. "A Desire of Paradise and a Paradise of Desire: Dante and Mysticism." In *Dante: Contemporary Perspectives,* edited by Amilcare A. Iannucci, 148–66.
———. "Il nodo di Bonagiunta, le penne di Dante e il Dolce Stil Novo." *Lettere italiane* 46 (1994): 52–61.
———. "La *Commedia* tra il dire e il fare." In *Sotto il segno di Dante: Scritti in onore di Francesco Mazzoni,* edited by Leonella Coglievina and Domenico De Robertis, 233–47.
———. "'La punta del disio': storia di una metafora dantesca." *Lectura Dantis* 7 (1981): 3–28.
———. *La puttana e il gigante. Dal Cantico dei cantici al Paradiso Terrestre di Dante.* Ravenna: Longo, 1998.
———. "Lettera aperta a Bob Hollander." http://www.princeton.edu/~dante/ebdsa/lino.htm. (Accessed 2 April 2008.)
———. "*Paradiso*: A Drama of Desire." In *Word and Drama in Dante,* edited by John C. Barnes and Jennifer Petrie, 143–80. Dublin: Irish Academic Press, 1993.
Petrocchi, Giorgio. *L'ultima dea.* Rome: Bonacci, 1977.
Pickstock, Catherine. *After Writing: On the Liturgical Consummation of Philosophy.* Oxford: Blackwell, 1998.
Picone, Michelangelo, ed. *Dante e le forme dell'allegoresi.* Ravenna: Longo, 1987.
Picone, Michelangelo, Theodore J. Cachey, Jr., and Margherita Mesirca, eds. *Le culture di Dante: Studi in onore di Robert Hollander. Atti del quarto Seminario dantesco internazionale, University of Notre Dame (Ind.), USA, 25–27 settembre 2003.* Florence: Cesati, 2004.
Pite, Ralph. *The Circle of Our Vision: Dante's Presence in English Romantic Poetry.* Oxford: Clarendon Press, 1994.

Plouvier, Paul. *Poesia e Mistica.* Translated by M. R. Del Genio. Città del Vaticano: Libreria Editrice Vaticana, 2002.
Pope, Marvin H. *Song of Songs: A New Translation and Commentary.* New York: Anchor Bible, 1977.
Porena, Manfredi. "Noterelle Dantesche." *Studj romanzi* 20 (1930): 201–15.
Porzio, Francesco, ed. *Francesco d'Assisi: Storia e Arte.* Milan: Electa, 1982.
Poulet, Georges. *Metamorphoses of the Circle.* Translated by Carely Dawson and Elliott Coleman. Baltimore: Johns Hopkins University Press, 1966.
Priest, Paul. "Dante and the *Song of Songs*." *Studi danteschi* 49 (1972): 79–113.
Psaki, Regina. "*Paradiso* XXVIII." In *Dante's "Divine Comedy": Introductory Readings,* vol. 3, *Paradiso,* edited by Tibor Wlassics, 424–34.
Quash, Ben. *Theology and the Drama of History.* Cambridge: Cambridge University Press, 2005.
Raffa, Guy P. *Divine Dialectic: Dante's Incarnational Poetry.* Toronto: University of Toronto Press, 2000.
Raffi, Alessandro. *La gloria del volgare: Ontologia e semiotica in Dante dal "Convivio" al "De vulgari eloquentia."* Soveria Mannelli: Rubbettino Editore, 2004.
Randles, W. G. L. *The Unmaking of the Medieval Christian Cosmos, 1500–1760.* Aldershot: Ashgate, 1999.
Ravasi, Gianfranco. *Il Cantico dei cantici: Commento e attualizzazione.* Bologna: Edizioni Dehoniane, 1992.
Righetti, Mario. *Manuale di storia liturgica.* 4 vols. Milan: Ancora, 1950–59.
Rigo, Paola. *Memoria Classica e Memoria Biblica in Dante.* Florence: Leo S. Olschki Editore, 1994.
Robb, Nesca A. *Neoplatonism of the Italian Renaissance.* London: Allen & Unwin, 1935.
Rorem, Paul. *Pseudo-Dionysius: A Commentary on the Texts and an Introduction to Their Influence.* New York: Oxford University Press, 1993.
Ryan, Christopher. "The Theology of Dante." In *The Cambridge Companion to Dante,* 1st ed., edited by Rachel Jacoff, 136–52.
Sarolli, Gian Roberto. "Salomone." In *ED* 4:1079–83.
Sauerländer, Willibald. *Cathedrals and Sculpture.* 2 vols. London: Pindar, 2000.
Scott, John A. "Dante's Allegory." *Romance Philology* 26, no. 3 (1973): 558–91.
———. "The Rock of Peter and *Inferno* XIX." *Romance Philology* 23 (1970): 462–79.
———. *Understanding Dante.* Notre Dame, Ind.: University of Notre Dame Press, 2004.
———. "The Unfinished *Convivio* as a Pathway to the *Commedia*." *Dante Studies* 113 (1995): 31–56.
Scrivano, Riccardo. "Intelligenza del cosmo." In *Dante, "Commedia," le forme dell'oltretomba,* 107–9. Rome: Nuova Cultura, 1997.
Sells, Michael A. *Mystical Languages of Unsaying.* Chicago and London: University of Chicago Press, 1994.

Singleton, Charles. *Dante's "Commedia": Elements of Structure.* Baltimore: Johns Hopkins University Press, 1977.
———. *Journey to Beatrice.* Baltimore: Johns Hopkins University Press, 1958.
Smalley, Beryl. *The Study of the Bible in the Middle Ages.* 3rd ed. Oxford: Blackwell, 1983.
Smoroński, Kasimierz. "Et Spiritus Dei ferebatur super aquas: Inquisitio Historico-Exegetica in Interpretationem Textus Gen. 1. 2c." *Biblica* 6 (1925): 140–56, 275–93, 361–95.
Southern, Richard W. *Western Society and the Church in the Middle Ages.* New York: Penguin Books, 1970.
Soskice, J. Martin. *The Kindness of God: Metaphor, Gender and Religious Language.* Oxford: Oxford University Press, 2007.
———. *Metaphor and Religious Language.* Oxford: Clarendon Press, 1985.
———. "Monica's Tears: Augustine on Words and Speech." *New Blackfriars* 83 (2002): 448–58.
Spera, Francesco. "La poesia degli angeli: Lettura del canto XXVIII del *Paradiso*." *Lettere italiane* 92 (1990): 537–53.
Steiner, George. *Grammars of Creation.* New Haven: Yale University Press, 2001.
Stern, J. P. *On Realism.* London and Boston: Routledge and Kegan Paul, 1973.
Svanberg, Jan. "The Gothic Smile." In *Künstlerischer Austausch/Artistic Exchange*, edited by Thomas Gaehtgens, vol. 2, 357–70.
Taddeo, Edoardo. "Il canto XXVIII del *Paradiso*." *Giornale storico della letteratura italiana* 153 (1961): 161–85.
Tambling, Jeremy. *Dante and Difference: Writing in the "Commedia."* Cambridge: Cambridge University Press, 1988.
Tellenbach, Gerd. *The Church in Western Europe from the Tenth to the Early Twelfth Century.* New York: Cambridge University Press, 1992.
Tentler, Thomas N. *Sin and Confession on the Eve of the Reformation.* Princeton: Princeton University Press, 1977.
Thomson, John A. F. *The Western Church in the Middle Ages.* London and New York: Arnold Publishers, 1998.
Took, John. "Canto XIII." In *Dante's "Divine Comedy": Introductory Readings*, vol. 3, *Paradiso*, edited by Tibor Wlassics, 186–97.
———. "Dante's Incarnationalism: An Essay in Theological Wisdom." *Italian Studies* 61, no. 1 (2006): 3–17.
———. *Dante's Phenomenology of Being.* Glasgow: Glasgow University Press, 2000.
———. *L'Etterno Piacer: Aesthetic Ideas in Dante.* Oxford: Clarendon Press, 1984.
Toynbee, Paget. *Dante in English Literature from Chaucer to Gary (c. 1380–1844).* 2 vols. London: Methuen, 1909.
Treherne, Matthew. "Art and Nature Put to Scorn: On the Sacramental in *Purgatorio*." In *Art and Nature in Dante*, edited by Daragh O'Connell and Jennifer Petrie. Dublin: Four Courts Press, forthcoming.

———. "Ekphrasis and Eucharist: The Poetics of Seeing God's Art in *Purgatorio* X." *The Italianist* 26, no. 2 (2006): 177–96.

———. "Liturgical Imaginations: Ritual, Narrative and Time in the Religious Poetry of Dante and Tasso." Ph.D. dissertation. University of Cambridge, 2007.

Trouillard, Jean. *La purification plotinienne*. Paris: Presses Universitaires de France, 1955.

Trovato, Mario. "Canto XI." In *Dante's "Divine Comedy": Introductory Readings*, vol. 3, *Paradiso*, edited by Tibor Wlassics, 156–71.

———. "Due elementi di filosofia psicologica dantesca: L'anima e l'intelligenza." *Forum Italicum* 4, no. 1 (March 1970): 185–202.

Truijen, Vincent. "David." In *ED* 2:322.

———. "Sacramento." In *ED* 5:1065–66.

Trumble, Angus. *A Brief History of the Smile*. New York: Basic-Perseus, 2004.

Turner, Denys. *The Darkness of God: Negativity in Christian Mysticism*. Cambridge: Cambridge University Press, 1995.

———. *Eros and Allegory: Medieval Interpretations of the Song of Songs*. Kalamazoo: Cistercian Publications, 1995.

———. *Faith, Reason and the Existence of God*. Cambridge: Cambridge University Press, 2004.

Ulivi, Ferruccio. "Il 'magnanimo' S. Francesco di Dante." In *Dante e il francescanesimo*, 77–94. Cava dei Tirreni: Avagliano, 1987.

———. "San Francesco e Dante." *Letture Classensi* 11:9–24. Ravenna: Longo, 1982.

Van Wolde, Ellen J. *Stories of the Beginning: Genesis 1–11 and Other Creation Stories*. Translated by John Bowden. London: SCM Press, 1996.

Vandelli, Giuseppe. "Il canto XIII del *Paradiso*." In *Letture dantesche. Paradiso*, 255–78.

———. "Il canto XXVIII del *Paradiso*." In *Letture dantesche. Paradiso*.

Vasoli, Cesare. "La Bibbia nel *Convivio* e nella *Monarchia*." In *Dante e la Bibbia*, edited by Giovanni Barblan, 19–39.

Venard, Olivier-Thomas. *Thomas d'Aquin Poète Théologien*. Vol. 1, *Littérature et Théologie: Une saison en enfer*. Geneva: Ad Solem, 2002.

———. *Thomas d'Aquin Poète Théologien*. Vol. 2, *La langue de l'ineffable*. Geneva: Ad Solem, 2004.

Von Richthofen, Erich. "The Twins of Latona, and Other Symmetrical Symbols for Justice in Dante." In *The World of Dante: Six Studies in Language and Thought*, edited by S. Bernard Chandler and J. A. Molinaro, 117–27.

Ward, Graham. *Theology and Contemporary Critical Theory*. 2nd ed. Basingstoke: Macmillan, 2000.

Wendland, Volker. *Ostermärchen und Ostergelächter*. Frankfurt: Lang, 1980.

Williams, A. N. *The Divine Sense: The Intellect in Patristic Theology*. Cambridge: Cambridge University Press, 2007.

———. "The Theology of the *Comedy*." In *The Cambridge Companion to Dante*, 2nd ed., edited by Rachel Jacoff, 201–17.
Williams, Rowan. *Grace and Necessity: Reflections on Art and Love*. London: Continuum, 2005.
———. *On Christian Theology*. Oxford: Blackwell, 2000.
———. "Poetic and Religious Imagination." *Theology* 80 (1977): 178–87.
———. "Theological Integrity." In *On Christian Theology*, 3–15.
Wlassics, Tibor, ed. *Dante's "Divine Comedy": Introductory Readings*, vol. 3, *Paradiso*. Special issue of *Lectura Dantis Virginiana* 16–17 (1995).
Yourcenar, Marguerite. *Mémoires d'Hadrien*. Paris: Gallimard, 1974.
Zino, Agostino. "Liturgia e musica francescana nei secoli XIII–XIV." In *Francesco d'Assisi: Storia e Arte*, edited by Francesco Porzio, 127–54.

NOTES ON CONTRIBUTORS

PIERO BOITANI is Professor of Comparative Literature at the University of Rome, "La Sapienza." His many publications include *The Tragic and the Sublime in Medieval Literature* (1989), *The Shadow of Ulysses: Figures of a Myth* (1994), and *The Bible and Its Rewritings* (1999).

OLIVER DAVIES is Professor of Christian Doctrine at King's College, University of London. He is the author of *Meister Eckhart: Mystical Theologian* (1991), *A Theology of Compassion: Metaphysics of Difference and the Renewal of Tradition* (2001), and *The Creativity of God: World, Eucharist, Reason* (2004).

THERESA FEDERICI carried out post-graduate research at the University of Reading, and teaches in the School of Modern Languages and Cultures at the University of Durham.

DAVID F. FORD is Regius Professor of Divinity and Fellow of Selwyn College at the University of Cambridge. His publications include *Self and Salvation: Being Transformed* (1999), *Shaping Theology: Engagements in a Religious and Secular World* (2007), and *Christian Wisdom: Desiring God and Learning in Love* (2007).

PETER S. HAWKINS is Professor of Religion and Literature at Yale University. His publications include *Dante's Testaments: Essays in Scriptural Imagination* (1999), *The Poets' Dante: Twentieth-Century Reflections* (co-edited with Rachel Jacoff, 2001), and *Dante: A Brief History* (2006).

DOUGLAS HEDLEY is Reader in Hermeneutics and Metaphysics and Fellow of Clare College at the University of Cambridge. His publications include *Coleridge, Philosophy and Religion: Aids to Reflection and the Mirror of the Spirit* (2000), *Living Forms of the Imagination* (2008), and *Platonism at the Origins of Modernity: Studies on Platonism and Early Modern Philosophy* (co-edited with Sarah Hutton, 2008).

Notes on Contributors   357

ROBIN KIRKPATRICK is Professor of Italian and English Literatures and Fellow of Robinson College at the University of Cambridge. His publications include *Dante's "Paradiso" and the Limitations of Modern Criticism* (1978), *Dante's "Inferno": Difficulty and Dead Poetry* (1987), and a verse translation of the *Commedia* (2006–7).

CHRISTIAN MOEVS is Associate Professor in the Department of Romance Languages and Literatures at the University of Notre Dame, where he is a Fellow of the Medieval Institute. His publications include *The Metaphysics of Dante's "Comedy"* (2005).

VITTORIO MONTEMAGGI is Assistant Professor of Religion and Literature in the Department of Romance Languages and Literatures at the University of Notre Dame, where he is also Concurrent Assistant Professor in the Department of Theology and Fellow of the Nanovic Institute for European Studies. His publications include essays on the theology of the *Commedia*.

PAOLA NASTI is Lecturer in Italian at the University of Reading. Her publications include *Favole d'amore e "saver profondo": La tradizione salomonica in Dante* (2007).

JOHN TOOK is Professor of Dante Studies at University College London. His publications include *L'Etterno Piacer: Aesthetic Ideas in Dante* (1984), *Dante's Phenomenology of Being* (2000), and *Il Fiore: Introduction, Text, Translation and Commentary* (2004).

MATTHEW TREHERNE is Senior Lecturer in Italian at the University of Leeds and Co-Director of the Leeds Centre for Dante Studies. His publications include articles on Dante and on Renaissance culture, and *Forms of Faith: Religious Culture in Sixteenth-Century Italy* (co-edited with Abigail Brundin, 2009).

DENYS TURNER is Horace Tracy Pitkin Professor of Historical Theology at Yale University. He is the author of *Eros and Allegory: Medieval Exegesis of the Song of Songs* (1995), *The Darkness of God: Negativity in Christian Mysticism* (1995), and *Faith, Reason and the Existence of God* (2004).

INDEX OF NAMES AND SUBJECTS

Adam
  creation of, 102, 128n.21, 273
  Fall of, 99, 193, 207n.27, 310, 315n.7
  first word of, 28, 142–44, 155, 159n.20
Adonis, 251
adultery, 191–92, 207n.27
Albert the Great
  De causis, 128n.22
  De natura et origine animae, 104
  influence on Dante, 310, 311
  on "lumen gloriae," 160n.30
  as teacher, 288
Alexander of Hales, 105
allegory
  in the Bible, 3, 7, 216, 226–27, 295–96
  Coleridge on Dante and allegory, 248–49
  vs. literal truth, 3, 295–96
  in poetry, 3, 7
Ambrose, St.: on the Church, 227
analogy, 7, 262
angels
  Aquinas on angelic hierarchy, 39, 40, 55n.9
  Aquinas on creation of, 123, 169–70
  Augustine on creation of, 143–44, 277
  Beatrice on affections of, 123–24
  Beatrice on angelic hierarchy, 38–43, 55n.5, 110, 111, 119, 258, 276
  Beatrice on creation of, 121–22, 123, 153, 277
  Bernard on angelic hierarchy, 39, 56n.11
  Bonaventure on angelic hierarchy, 39, 55n.9
  communication between, 164–65, 169–70, 291
  creation of, 63–64, 110, 113, 119–21, 123, 129n.54, 143–44, 152–53, 169–70, 273, 277
  Dionysius on angelic hierarchy, 39–41, 43, 55nn.8, 9, 110, 258
  as fallen/Lucifer, 120–21, 129n.54, 136, 277
  Gregory the Great on angelic hierarchy, 39–43, 54, 55nn.7, 9, 56n.11, 110, 119, 258
  vs. human beings, 64, 67, 121, 164–65, 169–70, 273, 277, 291
  "Index of Angels," 55n.6
  intellect of, 64, 117, 119, 129n.54, 273, 277, 282n.6, 284n.17
  and liturgy, 138, 139, 196, 197–98
  Lombard on angelic hierarchy, 39, 56n.11
  memory of, 121–22, 123, 129n.54
  number of, 123
  Paul on, 38, 40–41, 43, 55n.9, 56n.10, 258
  and praise of God, 143–44, 152–53, 154, 169
  will of, 121, 129n.54
Anonimo Fiorentino, 196
Aquinas, Thomas
  on *actus hominis* vs. *actus humanus*, 305n.6
  on angelic hierarchy, 39, 40, 55n.9

on the Ascension, 175, 176
on beatitude, 152
on contrition and repentance, 185–86
on creation of angels, 123, 169–70
on creation of substances, 123, 129n.51
vs. Dante, 286, 287, 297, 300–301, 320
on Dionysius the Areopagite, 39, 40
vs. Eckhart, 11, 286, 287, 288, 289, 294, 297–302
on eclipse during Christ's Passion, 123
on *excessus* of soul from body, 173
Exp. Eth. 10, lect. 10, 2092, 128n.22
on glory, 151, 152
on God as Creator, 116, 315n.6
on God's goodness, 315n.6
on Hesiod and love, 96
on humility, 203
on humor, 44
In Duodecim Libros Metaphysicorum Aristotelis 1.4, 984b29, lect. 5, 102, 127n.1
influence on Dante, 2, 16, 124, 162, 165, 297, 310, 311
on light, 160n.30
on love for God, 135
on memory of angels, 123
on metaphor, 295–96
on Moses, 173
in *Paradiso*, 16, 22, 25–26, 40, 43, 50, 117–18, 123, 124, 136, 153, 156, 222, 325
on participation in divine being, 7
on St. Paul, 173, 178n.9
on play (*ludus*), 58n.19
on poetry, 288, 294–97, 305n.12
on power of the priest's absolution, 186
on prophets, 194

on Purgatory, 132
Quodlibetal Questions 7, q. 6, 295
on resurrection of the body, 170
on sacraments, 287
on salvation, 176
and scripture, 318–19
on the soul, 98, 132
on speech of angels, 169
on theological language, 6, 11, 294–97, 298–99, 301
Aquinas, Thomas, *Summa contra Gentiles*
2.46.6, 315n.6
3.68, 314n.4
Aquinas, Thomas, *Summa Theologiae*
Ia.1.9.ad3, 305n.15
Ia.1.9.corp and ad1, 305n.14
Ia.1.9.obj1, 305n.12
Ia.1.10.corp and ad3, 305n.14
Ia.6.1, 130n.59
Ia.8.2, 314n.4
Ia.8.4, 314n.4
Ia.12.2, 92n.4
Ia.39.8, 127n.2
Ia.45.7, 92n.15
Ia.46.3.resp, 129n.51
Ia.57, 165, 170
Ia.58.4.ad2, 305n.10
Ia.60.1.ad3, 159n.15
Ia.60.5.ad4, 159n.15
Ia.61.3 and resp, 129n.52
Ia.65.2.ad1, 152
Ia.66.1.ad2, 129n.41
Ia.79.2, 127n.4
Ia.107, 165, 178n.7
Ia.108.6.ad, 55n.9
Ia.108.6.resp4, 55n.9
IaIIae.1.1.corp, 305n.6
IaIIae.2.3, 152
IaIIae.2.3.ad2, 152
IaIIae.3.1–8, 55n.5
IIaIIae.83.11.ad3, 159n.7

Aquinas, Thomas, *Summa Theologiae* (*cont.*)
  IaIIae.132.1, 151
  IaIIae.175.3.ad1, 178n.8
  IIIa44.2, 129n.53
  IIIa57.4–5, 179n.13
  IIIa57.6, 179n.16
  IIIa.62.1.ad4, 305n.3
  Supplement 92, ad1–3, 55n.5
Ardissino, Erminia, 158n.5
Aristotle
  on contemplation, 256, 268, 270
  De anima, 34n.5, 127n.4, 258, 281n.4
  De generatione animalium, 104, 127n.20
  on divine thought, 268, 281n.3
  on happiness, 98
  on human intellect, 127n.20, 258, 272
  influence on Dante, 2, 96, 104–5, 107, 110, 116–17, 122, 123, 125, 126, 248, 262, 264n.3, 326
  on language and the world, 257
  on laughter, 53, 59n.32
  on logic, 293
  on matter, 116–17, 126
  Metaphysics, 41, 96, 105, 124, 128n.22, 130nn.57, 59, 268, 281nn.3, 4
  on moral philosophy, 313n.1
  On the Parts 3.10, 672b, 59n.32
  Peri Hermeneias, 305n.10
  on potency, 117, 126
  on self-awareness, 268, 281n.3
  on the soul, 98, 104–5, 258
  on substance, 107, 126
  on Unmoved Mover, 96, 130n.59, 255, 268, 281n.3
  on vice as habit, 135
Armour, Peter, 158n.6
Auerbach, Erich, 2

Augustine, St., 25, 238, 251, 253, 320
  Ad Vincentium/Letter to Vincentius, 295
  on the *boni fedeles*, 214–15, 216
  on charity, 215, 216–17, 219, 237
  on confession, 187
  on contemplation of self, 270, 282n.8
  conversion of, 278–79
  on creation of angels, 143–44, 277
  on King David, 187–88, 191, 207n.27
  De baptismo, 239nn.14, 16
  De civitate Dei, 239n.14
  De doctrina Christiana, 239n.14
  De Genesi ad litteram, 143–44, 152, 282n.8
  De Genesi contra Manichaeos 1.7.12, 129n.41
  De poenitentibus, 187
  De vera religione, 282n.8
  and Donatists, 213–14, 239nn.15, 19, 295
  ecclesiology of, 213–17, 219, 223, 229–30, 237, 239n.14
  Ennarrationes in Psalmos, 134, 147–48, 149, 192, 194, 207n.27, 239n.14, 243nn.60, 63, 282n.8
  on God as Creator, 116
  In epistolam Iohannis, 239nn.17, 18
  influence of Neoplatonism on, 270
  influence on Dante, 3, 310
  on memory of angels, 123
  on original sin, 207n.27
  on penitence, 187–88
  on Psalm 50, 147–48, 149, 184, 192, 194, 207n.27
  on Psalm 118, 134
  on sacraments, 287
  on theological language, 6
  on theology and biblical interpretation, 295

Augustine, St., *Confessions*
 7.10.16, 282n.8
 7.17, 282n.8
 8.12, 278–79
 9.10, 282n.8
 10.27.38, 282n.8
Austin, J. L.: on performative
 utterance, 289–90
authority of the *Commedia*, 4, 23, 37,
 53, 125
 regarding angelic hierarchy, 38–43
 regarding creation, 119, 122–23
 and King David, 10, 182, 199,
 200–206
 and Eagle sequence, 107, 109
Averroes, 130n.60, 272
 on the human intellect, 104
Avicenna, 130n.60
Azzetta, Luca, 159n.19

Bader, Günter, 178n.1
Bamberg Cathedral
 Lachengel at, 45
 Last Judgment scene at, 45
 St. Stephen at, 45
Barański, Zygmunt, 57n.12, 159n.20,
 201
Barnes, John
 on liturgy, 149–50, 158n.5
 on penitence, 186
Barolini, Teodolinda
 on Dante and David, 200–201,
 205, 206n.4
 on Dante's humility, 204, 205
 Dante's Poets, 206n.4
 The Undivine Comedy, 32, 159nn.11,
 19, 206n.1
Basile, Bruno, 159n.19
Beatrice
 on angelic hierarchy, 38–43, 55n.5,
 110, 111, 119, 258, 276
 on angels' affections, 123–24

on angels' contemplation of God,
 121
on Apollo and Diana/balance, 274,
 275–78
and ascent of the soul to God, 254
and Christ, 72
on creation, 110–24, 145, 153, 277
on creation of angels, 121–22, 123,
 153, 277
on Dante's hope, 200
and Dante's penitence, 196–98,
 204
on Dante's sin, 190–91, 250
eyes of, 170–72, 179n.15, 268
on fallen angels/Lucifer, 36, 153
on flesh and spirit, 39
on freedom of the will, 31
on God as Creator, 157
on God as point (*punto*), 268–69,
 274–79, 281n.5, 282n.6
on God's glory, 153, 154
on God's grace, 121
on God's immanence vs.
 transcendence, 38
humility of, 28–29
on the Incarnation, 36
in *Inferno*, 170, 195
on St. Jerome and angels, 43–44
and love, 254–55
on moon spots, 36, 42
vs. Nathan, 196, 197–98
in *Paradiso*, 21, 24, 31, 36–37,
 38–44, 49–51, 62, 110–24, 136,
 145, 153, 170–72, 174, 196,
 209n.45, 235, 254, 256, 259–60,
 261, 262, 268–69, 275–76,
 281n.5, 282nn.6, 7, 326
praise of, 28–29
in *Purgatorio*, 49, 89, 160n.31,
 190–91, 196–97, 204, 250–51,
 252
on sense perception, 262

Beatrice (*cont.*)
   smiles of, 46, 47, 49, 50–51, 156, 171–72
   on space, 268–69, 274, 275–76
   on time, 269, 274, 275–76
   on the universe, 260
   on vision of God, 121
   in *Vita nuova*, 18, 28–29, 46, 50, 72, 174, 273
Beckett, Samuel: *The Lost Ones*, 48
Bede, St., 223, 238
Benedict, St.
   and humor, 44, 58n.18
   Rule of, 44, 58n.18
Berdyaev, Nikolai, 312
Bergson, Henri, 252
Bernard of Clairvaux, St., 241n.42
   on angelic hierarchy, 39, 56n.11
   on Church as Bride of God, 224–25, 238
   on Church Militant and Triumphant, 230
   De diligendo Deo, 243n.66
   ecclesiology of, 224–25, 230, 232, 233, 237
   Five Books on Consideration, 56n.11
   influence on Dante, 218–19, 232, 233, 237
   on love for God, 225
   in *Paradiso*, 51, 98, 241n.42
   on resurrection of the body, 232, 233
   Sermones super Cantica Canticorum, 99–100, 218–19, 223–24, 240n.33, 241n.41, 242nn.44, 46, 243n.61
   on theological language, 6
   on union with God, 156, 160n.32
   on wisdom, 218–19
Bible, the
   allegorical interpretations, 3, 7, 216, 226–27, 295–96
   anagogical interpretations, 226–30
   angels in, 38–39, 295–96
   creation in, 108, 110, 113–16, 119
   exile in, 252
   figurative language in, 210, 238
   relationship to ecclesiology, 10, 212–13, 214–17, 221–26
   relationship to philosophy, 319, 326–27
   tropological/moral interpretations, 226–27, 237
   See also David, King; Psalms; *Song of Songs*
Binski, Paul, 46, 54, 57n.16
   on smiling vs. laughter, 58n.23
Boccaccio, Giovanni
   on Dante's epitaph, 210
   on Dante's lust, 191
   on theology and poetry, 211
   Vita de Dante, 191
Boethius, 251
   Consolation of Philosophy, 117, 254, 255
Bonaventure, St.
   on angelic hierarchy, 39, 55n.9
   on charity, 216, 220, 221, 225, 228, 237, 240nn.32, 37, 242n.56, 244n.72
   Commentarius in Evangelium Lucae, 241n.38
   on contemplation, 270
   ecclesiology of, 216, 220–21, 225, 226, 228, 233, 234, 237, 240n.32
   on St. Francis and poverty, 243n.71
   on God's grace, 225, 228, 244n.72
   on God's love, 235, 240n.37, 244n.72
   on human soul, 311
   influence on Dante, 220, 220–21, 225, 233, 234, 237, 242n.56, 310, 311
   Itinerarium mentis in Deum 5.4, 92n.4
   Legenda maior, 243n.71
   in *Paradiso*, 43, 220, 222–23

on resurrection of the body, 233–34
Sententiarum, 240n.37, 241n.38
on theological language, 6
on the Trinity, 220, 221, 225, 229, 234, 240n.37, 242n.56
on wisdom, 218
Bonfrate, Giuseppe, 129n.50
Bonhoeffer, Dietrich, 325
Boniface VIII, 33, 225
Bosco, Umberto, 55n.5
Botterill, Steven, 178nn.3, 10
Boyde, Patrick, 55n.6
 Dante Philomythes and Philosopher, 284nn.17, 22
 on metaphor in the *Paradiso*, 124, 125
Boyle, Nicholas: on the *Commedia*, 32
Braet, Herman, 57n.16
Brandeis, Irma, 259
Brownlee, Kevin, 202–3
Buddhism, 44, 57n.16
Bundy, Murray: on dream visions in *Purgatorio*, 262–63
Burrell, David: on poetry and theology, 7
Burrows, John A.: *Gestures and Looks*, 57n.15
Busnelli, Giovanni, 284n.17

Cacciari, Massimo, 120
Calvin, John: on body of Jesus, 175
Carlyle, Thomas, 252
Cary, Francis, 248, 265n.9
Cassiodorus
 on praise of God, 229
 on Psalm 50, 184
Cavalcanti, Guido, 130n.58, 151
Cavallini, Pietro, 99
charity (*caritas*)
 Augustine on, 215, 216–17, 219, 237
 Bonaventure on, 216, 220, 221, 225, 228, 237, 240nn.32, 37, 242n.56, 244n.72

 and the Church, 10, 215, 216–17, 219–21, 223–38
 vs. faith, 215, 216, 230
 vs. hope, 230
 and Platonic *eros*, 264n.1
 relationship to wisdom, 218–19
 and the Trinity, 219–21, 225, 226, 233–34, 240n.37
 See also God, as love; love
Chiavacci Leonardi, Anna Maria, 128nn.32, 34
Chrétien de Troyes: *Perceval*, 45
Church, the
 Augustine on, 213–17, 219, 223, 229–30, 237, 239n.14
 Bernard on, 224–25, 230, 232, 233, 237
 Bonaventure on, 216, 220–21, 225, 226, 228, 233, 234, 237, 240n.32
 as Bride of God, 10, 213, 214–17, 221–38, 315n.8
 and charity, 10, 215, 216–17, 219–21, 223–38
 Church Militant, 213, 217, 221–22, 226, 227–31, 234–38
 Church Triumphant, 213, 214, 217, 227, 229–31, 232–34
 as mystical body, 212, 213, 223
 papacy, 212, 315n.8
 relationship to Christ, 213, 215, 216, 222–23, 224–25, 226, 227, 230
 relationship to the Bible, 10, 212–13, 214–17, 221–26
 relationship to the Trinity, 220–21, 225, 228, 229, 233–34
 as true Body of Christian Truth, 25
 See also Dominicans; ecclesiology of Dante; Franciscans
Church Fathers, 123, 180, 183
Cicero, Marcus Tullius
 De senectute 15.53, 105, 128n.24
 on the knot of everything, 274
Cistercians, 233

close reading, 8, 15–16, 319, 327–28
Cogan, Marc: *Design in the Wax*, 159n.11
Coleridge, Samuel Taylor
　and Cary, 248, 265n.9
　on Dante, 246, 247, 248–49, 255–56, 261–62
communion of saints, 221
community
　breakdown of, 167–68
　and pursuit of virtue and knowledge, 80, 82
　relationship to poetry, 70, 76, 77–78, 303–4
　relationship to truth, 75, 78, 80, 82
　of Resurrection, 25, 26
　See also Church, the; ecclesiology of Dante
confession, 148, 182, 185–86, 187–88, 195, 197, 198, 204, 251
Congar, Yves, 213
contemplation, 228–29, 256, 262, 269–71, 282n.8
Contini, Gianfranco: *Un'idea di Dante*, 128n.31
Convivio
　allegory of poets vs. theologians in, 3
　angels in, 41–42
　vs. *Commedia*, 19, 41–42, 46–47, 51, 57n.12, 82, 151, 159n.19, 217–18, 250, 267, 284n.17, 308–9, 313n.3
　desire for glory in, 151
　desire for God in, 139–40
　desire for material goods in, 139–40
　de-theologization in, 308–9
　ethics in, 309, 313n.1
　God in, 308, 313n.3
　happiness in, 309, 313n.3
　human desire in, 139–40, 151, 308, 309, 313n.2
　human soul in, 99, 102, 313n.3
　vs. *Monarchia*, 313n.3
　the point (*punto*) in, 267, 275
　smiles in, 46–47, 59n.27
　ultimate truth in, 82
　views on scriptural and nonscriptural allegory in, 3, 7
　views on vernacular Italian in, 18, 31
　views on wisdom in, 217–18
　Wisdom/Philosophy in, 46, 59n.27
Cornish, Alison, 275, 277, 284nn.22, 23
cosmos: as icon of its source, 245–46, 249, 251
creation
　of Adam, 102, 128n.21
　of angels, 121–22, 123, 143–44, 153, 169–70, 277
　of Hell, 96–97, 101
　of human soul, 9, 68–69, 73, 82, 97–100, 101–2, 103–6, 139–40, 272–73, 284n.17
　See also God, as Creator
Croce, Benedetto: on *poesia* and *non-poesia* in the *Commedia*, 2, 36, 124, 245
Curtius, Ernst Robert, 57n.17
Cyprian, St., 216

Da Buti, Francesco, 209n.43
Daniello, Bernardino, 127n.3
David, King
　as archetypal/model penitent, 10, 20, 181, 182, 184–85, 186, 187–88, 189–99, 203–6
　as author of Psalms, 10, 107, 108–9, 125, 180–82, 183–84, 189–90, 192, 194, 199–206, 206n.1, 209n.46
　and Christ, 180, 193–94
　as Dante's literary forerunner, 181–82
　and Holy Spirit, 108, 182, 199
　humility of, 203–6
　in *Inferno*, 181, 182

Minnis on, 182, 193
as model for poets, 199–201
as moral prophet, 192–99, 203–4, 205
in *Paradiso*, 10, 107, 181–82, 187, 188, 199–203
in *Purgatorio*, 181, 182, 204, 205
Davies, Oliver: on Eckhart, 289, 293, 300, 301
Davis, Ellen: *Proverbs, Ecclesiastes and the Song of Songs*, 321
death, 83–86, 90
Derrida, Jacques, 166, 178n.6, 298
de Vogel, Cornelia, 255, 259, 265n.24
De vulgari eloquentia
vs. *Commedia*, 19, 142–43, 155, 301, 302–4, 305n.21
courtly style advocated in, 296, 305n.21
humanity and being perceived in, 165, 287, 304
humanity and speech in, 163–66, 291
and materiality of signs, 165–66
primiloquium in, 28, 142–43, 155
and smiles, 303
Dionysius the Areopagite, 130n.59
on angelic hierarchy, 39–41, 43, 55nn.8, 9, 110, 258
Celestial Hierarchy, 39–41, 55n.8, 56n.11
on contemplation, 270
De divinis nominibus, 130n.59, 315n.6
on God as Creator, 315n.6
on God's goodness, 130n.59, 315n.6
influence on Dante, 310, 311
Neoplatonism of, 113
and St. Paul, 39, 40–41, 55n.9, 56n.10
on the soul, 270
on theological language, 6, 293, 296

Dominic, St., 220, 222–23, 234–35
Dominicans, 2, 38, 43, 44, 288
Donatists, 213–14, 239nn.15, 19
Donne, John: on exinanition, 256
Dostoevsky, Fyodor: on Hell, 97
Durand, William
Rationale divinorum officiorum 4.34.1, 150
on the Sanctus, 150
Durling, Robert, 158n.5, 274–75, 284n.23

Easter: laughter at, 45, 58n.22
ecclesiology of Dante, 17, 216–21, 315n.8
and charity, 10, 215, 216–17, 219–21, 223–38, 240n.32
Church as Bride of God, 10, 213, 214–17, 221–38
relationship to medieval ecclesiology, 211, 212–13
Eckhart, Meister
vs. Aquinas, 11, 286, 287, 288, 289, 294, 297–302
vs. Dante, 11, 286, 287, 288, 289, 293, 299, 300–301
Davies on, 289, 293, 300, 301
on God's eye, 255
on the human soul, 246, 270
Latin treatises, 289
and postmodernists, 298, 299–300
Sermons, 288, 289
theological rhetoric of, 10, 288–89, 292–94, 297–302
on the Trinity, 52
Eco, Umberto: Jorge de Burgos in *The Name of the Rose*, 58n.19
Eliot, T. S., 245
Ariel Poems/Animula, 99, 127n.7
vs. Dante, 20–21, 99, 126, 127n.5, 130n.62
Four Quartets/"The Dry Salvages," 126, 130n.62

Enlightenment, the, 14–15
Enoch, 252
epiphanies, 17–21, 22
Eriugena, John Scotus, 39, 246
eschatology and contingencies of life, 319, 325–36
Eucharist, the, 106, 145–49, 175, 177
Evans, Gillian: on medieval penitence, 184–85
evil, 96–97
exile of Dante, 27–28, 33, 209n.46, 252
Ezekiel, 37, 251

faith
  vs. charity, 215, 216, 230
  Dante's examination regarding, 31–32
  moods of, 319, 321–23
  and self-awareness, 271
Fall, the, 99, 193, 207n.27, 310, 315n.7
Fallani, Giovanni, 55n.6
Federici, Theresa: on the Psalms, 323
Fehlner, Peter D.: on Bonaventure, 244n.72
Ficino, Marsilio, 58n.25, 264n.1
Florence, 20
  and Cacciaguida, 26–27
  economic expansion, 26–27
form vs. content, 61, 73
Foster, Kenelm, 2, 90, 128n.26, 313n.3
Fourth Lateran Council, 185
Francis, St., 220, 222
  and charity, 243n.71
  on joy, 45
  in *Paradiso*, 224, 234–37
  and penitence, 186
  and poverty, 243n.71
Franciscans, 2, 38, 43, 44, 58n.21, 207n.20, 224, 239n.9, 241n.42
Frege, Gottlob, 166

Freud, Sigmund: on the pleasure principle, 98
Fromm, Erich, 312

Gadamer, Hans-Georg
  on absolute present of the text, 312, 317n.14
  on fusion of horizons, 311, 316n.11
Gandhi, Mahatma, 328
Garden of Eden, 132, 142–43, 155, 157, 310
genre and the *Commedia*, 319–21
gestures, 290, 291, 303
  See also smiles
Gilson, Étienne, 2
  Dante and Philosophy, 313n.1
Gilson, Simon, 285n.27
Giovanni del Virgilio, 210
glory
  of God, 150–58
  and light, 152, 153, 154, 156, 158, 160n.31
  and pride, 151–52, 153–54
Glossa Ordinaria, 208n.39
God
  beatific vision of, 21, 38, 46, 47, 49, 50, 51–53, 54, 88–89, 121, 152, 157, 160n.24, 173, 233, 256–57, 260, 263, 270–71, 279–80
  Being of, 7, 113, 271
  as circumscribing but uncircumscribed, 259, 310, 314n.4
  as Creator, 5–6, 7, 9, 28, 31, 43–44, 53, 59n.34, 62, 63–64, 69, 73, 87, 90, 95–98, 100, 101–5, 106, 107–8, 110–24, 132, 135–37, 139–40, 142–44, 146, 149, 150, 151, 152–53, 154, 156, 157–58, 172–73, 225, 230, 271, 272–73, 276, 277, 278, 279, 280, 284n.15, 297, 315n.6, 325
  as Empyrean, 62, 267–70, 271, 276, 281nn.2, 5

as eternal, 112–13, 114, 267
glory of, 150–58
Goodness of, 113, 115, 117, 120–21, 152, 283n.13, 315nn.6, 9, 325
grace of, 121, 179n.20, 199, 200, 205, 223–24, 225, 226, 235, 237, 313n.3, 315n.8, 323
as ground of existence, 5–6, 7, 61–62, 63–65, 72, 74, 87, 90, 136, 139, 141, 148, 157, 267–71, 273, 276, 277, 279, 309–10
human beings as image of, 5–6, 53, 98, 100, 101
joy of, 52–53, 59n.34, 69, 98, 281n.2, 325
justice of, 97, 107, 110, 185
knowledge about, 9, 62–63, 64–66, 67, 72, 74, 75–76, 78, 82, 86, 87, 100, 112, 152–53, 229, 240n.32, 269–72, 287
as light, 42, 152, 153, 154, 156, 158, 172, 174–75, 260–61, 267–68, 276, 279–80, 281n.2, 283n.13
as love, 38, 61–62, 63–67, 69, 71–74, 76, 78, 89, 95–97, 113–14, 115, 127n.1, 136, 155, 159n.16, 172, 235, 254, 255, 257, 260, 268–69, 270, 276, 281n.2, 282n.6, 283n.13, 300, 304, 309–10, 314n.5, 315nn.6, 8, 320, 325
love for, 46, 64, 71, 72, 91, 105, 135, 143–44, 216, 225, 229, 233–34, 235–38, 244n.73, 292, 320, 323
mercy of, 183, 185, 197, 244n.73
Otherness of, 25
as point (*punto*), 111–12, 267–69, 270–72, 278, 280, 281n.5, 282n.6, 283n.14
praise of, 24, 28, 72, 132, 137–58, 168, 169, 198, 206n.4, 208n.39, 229

as pure intellect, 267–69, 281nn.2, 3
self-awareness of, 268–72, 273, 276, 280, 281n.3, 310, 314n.5
smile of, 51–53, 54, 156, 157, 174–75, 176, 314n.5
as source of motion, 33, 63, 65, 69, 71, 74, 95, 96, 98, 152, 172, 254, 257, 282n.6, 300
transcendence vs. immanence of, 38
union with, 5, 10–11, 63, 65–66, 72, 73, 74, 87, 89, 91, 144, 155–57, 160n.24, 223, 227, 231, 233, 246, 256–57, 260, 270–72, 273, 280, 308, 309, 313n.3
unity and simplicity of, 7, 267, 271, 283n.13, 292
unknowability of, 62, 64–65, 66, 67, 75–76, 82, 86, 87, 286, 287, 289, 292–94, 296, 297–99, 301, 304
will of, 64, 65–67, 71, 76, 78–79, 157, 225
See also Jesus Christ; liturgy; theological language; Trinity, the
Goethe's *Faust*, 113
Gombrich, Ernst: on Platonism, 257
Gothic smile, 45–46, 58n.23
Gragnolati, Manuele: on Purgatory, 159n.11
Greek gods, 248–49
Gregory the Great
on angelic hierarchy, 39–43, 54, 55nn.7, 9, 56n.11, 110, 119, 258
on charity, 244n.73
Expositio in Canticum Canticorum, 127n.8, 238, 244n.73
Homiliae in evangelia, 55n.7, 56n.11
Moralia in Job, 39, 41, 42, 55n.7
on theological language, 6
Guillaume de Saint Thierry's *Commentary*, 99–100
Guinizelli, Guido, 151

Hadewijch of Brabant, 289
Hadrian: on the soul, 99
Hartman, Geoffrey H., 166
Hawkins, Peter
  "Dante and the Bible," 252
  on Dante's exile, 209n.46
  Dante's Testaments, 128n.30,
    178n.10, 202, 203, 206n.1,
    209nn.45, 46
  on Psalm 9 and Dante's authority,
    203
Heaney, Seamus, 18
Hegel, G. W. F., 251
  on theology, 255
Heidegger, Martin, 131, 253, 312
  on *Dasein*, 310
  on *Vorhandenheit* vs. *Zuhandenheit*,
    178n.4
Hesiod, 96
Hinduism, 57n.16
Historia Augusta, 99
history and Christianity, 32–33
Hollander, Robert, 196
  on David and Dante, 181, 194,
    205, 206n.4
Holy Spirit, 52, 96, 119
  and David, 108, 182, 199
  and Jerome, 101
  Origen on, 101
  relationship to poetry, 73–74
  See also Trinity, the
Homer, 126, 130n.61
hope
  vs. charity, 230
  Dante's examination regarding,
    199–200, 201–2, 209n.45
Hopkins, Gerard Manley
  "As kingfishers catch fire . . . ," 20
  and Christ, 20, 22
  vs. Dante, 17, 20, 21, 22
  "God's Grandeur," 17
  "Harry Ploughman," 21
  "The Windhover," 20
  "The Wreck of the Deutschland,"
    20, 290
Horace: *Ars poetica*, 99
Horney, Karen, 312
Hugh of St. Victor, 287, 311
human beings
  vs. angels, 64, 67, 121, 164–65,
    169–70, 273, 277, 291
  as embodied beings, 4, 9, 67–69, 70,
    72, 82, 163, 164–65, 169–70,
    173–74, 232–34, 284n.17, 291, 303
  freedom of the will, 31
  as horizons between eternity and
    time, 272, 277–78
  as image of God, 5–6, 53, 98, 100,
    101
  imagination in, 245–46, 262–63
  See also human intellect; human
    language; human soul; human
    will; personhood; smiles
human intellect
  Aristotle on, 127n.20, 258, 272
  and knowledge of God, 61–63,
    68–69, 74–75, 113, 122, 269
  and love, 64
  as rational soul, 103–6, 272–73,
    274, 283n.14
  relationship to language, 163–65,
    291
  self-awareness of, 269–72, 273,
    276, 277, 280, 310
  See also contemplation
human language
  infant speech, 68–69, 82–89, 91,
    163, 272
  as performative, 287, 289–91, 299,
    301–2, 304
  primiloquium, 28, 142–43, 155,
    159n.20
  relationship to God, 8–9, 60–61,
    62–63, 69, 71–74, 82

Index of Names and Subjects   369

relationship to human intellect,
   163–65, 291
relationship to personhood, 60,
   68–74, 89
See also De vulgari eloquentia;
   poetry; theological language
human soul
   as ascending to God, 245–47,
      251–54
   as circular, 258–59
   creation of, 9, 68–69, 73, 82,
      97–100, 101–2, 103–6, 139–40,
      272–73, 284n.17
   as form of the body, 67–69
   likeness to divinity, 245–47,
      270–72, 276
   Origen on, 99–101
   rational soul, 103–6, 272–73, 274,
      283n.14
   sensitive soul, 68–69, 104, 272, 273
   vegetative soul, 68–69, 104, 273
   as young child, 99–102
   See also human intellect
human will, 64, 65–67, 71, 79, 89,
   274, 283n.14
humility
   of Beatrice, 28–29
   of Dante, 29–30, 203–6
   of King David, 203–6
   vs. humor, 44
   of penitence, 23, 184
   relationship to poetry, 203–6
Husserl, Edmund: *Logical
   Investigations*, 166

Inferno
   Averroes in, 130n.60
   Avicenna in, 130n.60
   Cerberus, 167
   circular movement in Hell, 259
   King David in, 181, 182
   Farinata in, 23–24

Francesca in, 21–24, 47, 278, 279,
   280, 283n.14
gates of City of Dis, 167
humor in, 37
language of the damned in,
   166–68
Limbo, 130n.60
Mohammed in, 324
vs. *Paradiso*, 23–24, 36–37, 59n.34,
   110, 182, 304
vs. *Purgatorio*, 167–68, 182, 304
Satan's body, 280
three beasts in, 252
Ugolino in, 9, 63, 76, 83–86,
   89–90, 93n.25, 291, 303
Ulysses in, 9, 23–24, 30–31, 63,
   76–79, 80, 81, 251, 278, 299
upper Hell vs. lower Hell, 249–50
Vanni Fucci in, 23
Virgil in, 36, 47, 167, 170, 181,
   195, 200, 202, 208n.37, 252
intention and sin, 249–50
Islam, 5, 318, 319, 322, 324, 327
Italian language, 18, 31, 202–3

Jacobus de Voragine: *The Golden
   Legend*, 56n.10
Jacoff, Rachel, 42
Jaspers, Karl, 312
Jean de la Rochelle, 105
Jerome, St.
   on angels, 43–44, 129n.54
   on creation, 119, 123, 129n.54
   on Holy Spirit, 101
   In ad Titum, 129n.52
Jesus Christ
   and angels, 41–42
   Ascension, 9, 175–78, 179n.20
   Atonement, 186
   on being the true wine, 106
   body of, 173–74, 175–78
   as bread of Heaven, 146

Jesus Christ (*cont.*)
  on children and kingdom of
    heaven, 100–101
  and the Church Militant, 213, 215,
    216, 222–23, 224–25, 226, 227,
    230
  and the Church Triumphant, 230
  and creation, 144, 160n.22
  Crucifixion, 21–23, 27–28, 44, 63,
    67, 69, 72, 75–76, 82, 86, 87,
    123, 142, 144, 147–48, 149, 157,
    159n.11, 222, 224–25, 226, 231,
    272, 278, 279, 280, 283n.14, 310,
    315n.8
  cry on the Cross, 63, 66–67, 86,
    87, 92n.6, 142, 143, 148, 155
  exinanition of, 256
  on the Father as husbandman, 106
  and Hopkins, 20
  and humor, 44, 45
  Incarnation, 4, 36, 75, 82, 87, 113,
    126, 146, 147, 174, 230, 271, 273,
    276, 278, 280, 283n.14, 304,
    315n.8, 325
  and Judas, 290
  love of, 67, 69, 74, 86, 230
  mercy of, 138
  as model, 62
  poverty of, 243n.71
  and praise of God, 142, 143,
    144–45, 149, 150, 157
  as Redeemer, 67, 138, 149, 193,
    231
  relationship to David, 180, 193–94
  relationship to the point (*punto*),
    271, 283n.14
  Resurrection, 4, 9, 23, 91, 170, 174,
    175–78, 230, 232–34, 277, 311,
    316n.12
  Transfiguration, 4, 173–74
  and unknowability of God, 67
  weeping of, 44, 52, 53, 57n.16
  will of, 67, 79
  as the Word/Logos, 106, 108, 113,
    125–26, 128n.33, 271, 304
  See also Trinity, the
Joachim, 43, 239n.9
John, St., 125, 251, 255
John of Salisbury, 39
John the Divine, 37
Josephus, Flavius: *De bello judaico*,
  148–49
Judaism, 5, 318, 322, 326–27

Kavanagh, Patrick, 328
Keck, David: on angelic ranking,
  55nn.6, 9
Kierkegaard, Søren, 162, 178n.1, 253,
  312
knowledge
  about God, 9, 62–63, 64–66, 67,
    72, 74, 75–76, 78, 82, 86, 87,
    100, 112, 152–53, 229, 240n.32,
    269–72, 287
  relationship to virtue, 77–78, 79,
    80, 81–82
  See also truth
Kretzmann, Norman, 284n.17
Kuczynski, Michael: *Prophetic Song*,
  192, 205, 206n.1, 208n.39
Kugel, James
  on David as literary model, 202
  on prophets, 193, 202

Lacoste, Jean-Yves: on liturgy,
  131–32
La Favia, Louis M., 158n.5
Landino, Cristoforo, 116, 253, 264n.1
Las Casas, Bartolomé de, 328
Latini, Brunetto: *Trésor*, 99
Lauand, Luiz Jean: on Aquinas and
  play (*ludus*), 58n.19
LeGoff, Jacques: "Laughter in the
  Middle Ages," 57nn.16, 17,
  58nn.18, 21
Leo the Great: on the Ascension, 176

Letter to Can Grande, 261
Lévinas, Emmanuel, 328
Liber de causis, 115, 128n.22, 130n.59
light, 64–65, 247
   Aquinas on, 160n.30
   and glory, 152, 153, 154, 156, 158, 160n.31
   God as, 42, 152, 153, 154, 156, 158, 172, 174–75, 260–61, 267–68, 276, 279–80, 281n.2, 283n.13
   in Neoplatonism, 258–59, 260–61
   triadic spheres of, 258–61, 266n.39
Lincoln Cathedral: Angel choir at, 45
literary criticism, 8, 24
liturgy, 3, 30, 33, 320
   Agnus Dei, 133, 134
   and angels, 138, 139, 196, 197–98
   Barnes on, 149–50, 158n.5
   Compline service, 133
   daily office, 133
   "Dio Laudamo," 150
   Gloria in excelsis Deo, 137–39, 150, 154–55
   and glory of God, 150–57
   Greater Doxology, 138–39
   Hosanna, 150
   Labia mea, Domine, 134, 137, 141, 146–47, 188
   Lacoste on, 131–32
   Miserere, 181, 183, 184, 186, 187–88, 189–90
   in *Paradiso*, 137, 149–58
   Pater Noster, 133, 134, 137
   Pickstock on, 131, 138, 158n.2
   and praise of God, 28, 132, 137–45
   in *Purgatorio*, 132–49, 150, 151–52, 154–55, 156–57, 158n.5, 159n.17, 168, 188, 196, 197–98
   relationship to moral change, 134, 135
   relationship to personhood, 9, 131–58
   and repetition, 133, 135

Salve Regina, 133
Sanctus, 150
Summae Deus clementiae, 133, 134–35
Te Deum laudamus, 137, 150
Te lucis ante, 133, 156
types of utterances in, 131, 138
Lombard, Peter
   on angelic hierarchy, 39, 56n.11
   and angels' creation, 129n.54
   Commentarium in Psalmos, 208n.39
   on contrition and repentance, 185
   on creation, 116, 123, 129n.54
   vs. Dante, 123, 129n.54
   on God as Creator, 116
   Sententiae, 56n.11, 129nn.41, 54
Louis, St., 44
love
   of contingent, secondary goods, 135–36, 139–41, 142, 145–46, 148, 149, 153, 154, 155, 157, 159n.17
   for God, 46, 64, 71, 72, 91, 105, 135, 143–44, 216, 225, 229, 233–34, 235–38, 244n.73, 292, 320, 323
   human capacity to love, 64
   as metaphor, 221, 241n.39
   of others, 62–63, 72, 75–76, 86, 87, 89–90, 91, 323
   relationship to personhood, 90
   relationship to theological language, 9, 63, 70–74, 89–90, 91
   of self, 135–36
   See also charity (*caritas*); God, as love
Lucifer, 120–21, 129n.54, 136, 277
Lucretius
   vs. Dante, 22, 34n.5, 126, 263
   De rerum natura 2.14–19, 34n.5
Luther, Martin: on the Ascension, 175, 176, 177

Magdeburg Cathedral, 45
Magli, Ida, 186, 207n.20
Mandela, Nelson, 328
Mandelstam, Osip, 33
Martinez, Ronald, 158n.5, 274–75, 284n.23
Mary, Blessed Virgin, 75, 178n.9
  Annunciation, 26, 41, 45
  human perfection of, 90
  smiles of, 51, 54
  at wedding of Cana, 148, 149
Mary of Jerusalem, 148–49
materiality, 9, 178n.2, 274
  vs. meaning of signs, 165–68
  of signifiers, 294, 301
McCracken, Andrew, 158n.5
Mechtild of Magdeburg, 289
Mellone, Atilo, 55n.6
Ménard, Philippe: *Le rire et le sourire dans le roman courtois en France au moyen âge*, 44–45, 58n.23
Mendel, Gregor, 328
Merleau-Ponty, Maurice: *The Visible and the Invisible*, 166, 178n.5
Merrill, James: on Dante in *The Changing Light at Sandover*, 42, 57n.13
metaphors, 7, 9, 14, 30, 35n.12, 210, 211
  Aquinas on, 295–96
  Boyde on metaphors in *Paradiso*, 124, 125
  of Eckhart, 292, 293
  flower images, 231–33, 243n.65
  of light, 64–65
  Mineo on love as metaphor in *Paradiso*, 221, 241n.39
  See also similes
middle distance perspective, 319, 324–25, 328

Milton, John
  on creation, 114, 128n.36
  on fall of angels, 120
  Paradise Lost 1.19–22, 114
  Paradise Lost 7.218–42, 114–15
  on Spenser, 36
Mineo, Niccolò
  on Dante and Virgil, 195
  on the Heaven of the Sun, 221, 241n.39
Minnis, Alistair: on David, 182, 193
Modernism, 14–15
Monarchia
  the Church in, 315n.8
  vs. *Commedia*, 25
  vs. *Convivio*, 313n.3
Montemaggi, Vittorio, 286
  on love and perception of God, 287
Murray, Alexander: on confession, 186

Nardi, Bruno, 2, 105, 284n.17
Naumberg Cathedral, 45
Neo-Darwinians, 263
Neoplatonism
  contemplation in, 256, 270
  divine immanence in, 10
  Ficino, 58n.25, 264n.1
  human intellect in, 258–59
  human language in, 257
  indwelling divine spirit in, 245–47
  influence on Augustine, 270
  influence on Dante, 2, 10, 106, 113, 136, 245–47, 248, 250–51, 253, 255–56, 258–61, 263–64, 264n.3, 270, 274, 311
  influence on Milton, 128n.36
  light in, 258–59, 260–61
  the One/Absolute in, 247, 258–59, 274
Proclus, 255, 266n.39

during Renaissance, 246, 264n.1
during Romantic period, 245, 246, 264n.1
symbols in, 262
triadic spheres of light in, 258–61, 266n.39
world soul in, 274
Newman, John Henry: *The Dream of Gerontius*, 299
Nietzsche, Friedrich, 263, 302
on Dante, 36
non-Christian sources for Christian theology, 319, 323–24
Novello, Guido, 210

Ó Cadhain, Máirtín, 328
Origen
  Commentary and *Homilies* on the Song of Songs, 99–100, 127n.10, 216, 223
  Commentary on Matthew, 100–101
  on the Holy Spirit, 101
  on the soul, 99–101
original sin, 99, 193, 207n.27, 310, 315n.7
O'Siadhail, Micheal, 327–28
Osiris, 251
Ottimo Commento, 198
Ovid
  exile of, 252
  Fasti 2.285–86, 115, 129n.38

papacy, 315n.8
  and Empire, 212
Paradiso
  act and potency in, 116, 117–19, 126
  angelic hierarchy in, 38–43
  Apollo-Diana/sun-moon balance in, 274, 275–78, 279, 284n.23
  Aquinas in, 16, 22, 25–26, 40, 43, 50, 117–18, 123, 124, 136, 153, 156, 222, 325

Beatrice in, 21, 24, 31, 36–37, 38–44, 49–51, 62, 110–24, 136, 145, 153, 170–72, 174, 196, 209n.45, 254, 256, 259–60, 261, 262, 268–69, 275–76, 281n.5, 282nn.6, 7, 326
Bernard in, 51, 98
Bonaventure in, 43, 220, 222–23
brief contingencies in, 26, 136
Cacciaguida in, 22, 26–28, 32, 33, 50, 107, 127n.17, 256, 303, 325
candida rosa in, 51
creation of universe in, 9, 106–24
Cunizza in, 42–43
dancing theologians in, 168–69
Dante's examination regarding faith, hope, and charity, 25, 31–32, 199–200, 201–3, 209n.45
King David in, 10, 107, 181–82, 187, 188, 199–203
St. Dominic in, 222–23
Eagle sequence, 106–10, 150
eclipse in, 279
Empyrean, 37–38, 50–51, 53, 62, 70, 121, 156, 178n.9, 187, 267–71, 273, 276, 279, 280, 281nn.2, 3
flower images in, 231–33, 243n.65
Folchetto da Marsiglia, 127n.17
Folco of Marseilles, 43
Folquet in, 225
form and matter in, 116–19, 126
Gratian in, 50
Heaven of Justice, 199
Heaven of Mars, 22, 256
Heaven of Saturn, 50
Heaven of the Fixed Stars, 155, 199–200
Heaven of the Sun, 3, 43, 102–3, 153, 212, 213, 217–38
Heaven of Venus, 42
humor in, 37

Paradiso (cont.)
- vs. *Inferno*, 23–24, 36–37, 59n.34, 110, 182, 304
- St. James, 199–200, 201–2
- St. John, 178n.9
- Justinian in, 50
- liturgy in, 137, 149–58
- Marsyas, 252, 255–56, 265nn.19, 29
- moon spots, 36, 42
- Orosius in, 50
- the papacy in, 315n.8
- canto 29, 110, 326
- Peter Damian in, 64, 160n.30
- Piccarda in, 49–50, 65–66, 67, 71, 73, 76, 89
- praise of God in, 24, 137, 149–58
- *Primo Mobile*, 37–38, 41, 42, 110, 115, 267–68, 269–70, 272, 273–75, 276, 277, 279, 281nn.2, 3
- vs. *Purgatorio*, 106, 132, 137, 149, 150, 151, 154–55, 156–58, 168–69, 182, 303–4
- Ruth in, 188
- Siger of Brabant in, 43
- smiles in, 21, 37, 40, 42–43, 46, 47, 49–54, 155–56, 157, 171–72
- King Solomon in, 16, 22, 26, 218, 233, 325
- theological language in, 9, 63–66, 73–74, 90–91
- and truth, 39–44
- wisdom in, 212, 217–18

Pascal, Blaise, 253
Passio Petri et Marcellini, 99
Pattison, George: *Kierkegaard and the Crisis of Faith*, 178n.1
Paul, St.
- on angels, 38, 40–41, 43, 55n.9, 56n.10, 258
- on the Ascension, 177, 179n.20
- on Christ's exinanition, 256
- and Dionysius, 39, 40–41, 43, 55n.9, 56n.10
- on the Psalms, 183
- on *symphonia* between husband and wife, 100
- in third heaven, 39, 40, 178n.9, 204, 251–52, 258
- on those loving God, 46
- vision on road to Damascus, 175–76, 179n.15, 253

penitence
- contrition, 188, 189–90, 197, 198, 204, 208n.39
- deathbed penance, 187–88
- and humility, 23, 184
- medieval notions of, 182–86
- pilgrim Dante vs. David as penitents, 10, 181, 182, 188, 189–99, 203–6, 206n.4, 207n.23, 208n.39
- and Psalm 50, 183, 184, 186, 187–88, 194–95, 207n.23
- in *Purgatorio*, 132, 136–37, 138, 149, 157, 168, 186, 188
- relationship to praise of God, 157

performative language, 289–91, 299
- vs. sacraments, 287, 289, 301–2, 304

personhood
- and the Cross, 75–76
- and poetry, 15
- relationship to human language, 60, 68–74, 89
- relationship to liturgy, 9, 131–58
- relationship to love, 90
- relationship to praise, 28–29
- relationship to theological propositions, 21–26, 28, 30
- Trinity as paradigm of, 24
- *See also* human beings

Pertile, Lino, 57n.12, 159n.19, 160n.24, 226, 227
Peter, St., 31–32
philosophy
- phenomenology, 166
- and scripture, 319, 326–27

Pickstock, Catherine: on liturgy, 131, 138, 158n.2
Pillars of Hercules, 77, 78
Plato
  on contemplation, 256
  on *eros*, 255, 264n.1
  influence on Dante, 107, 110, 116–17, 122, 123, 174, 252, 256, 258, 326
  influence on Milton, 128n.36
  on matter, 116, 117
  Phaedrus, 252, 261
  on the soul, 258
  Symposium, 261
  Timaeus, 117, 258
  See also Neoplatonism
Plotinus
  on artists and spiritual realities, 261
  on contemplation, 256
  on the One, 258–59
  on the soul, 258–59
  on triadic spheres of light, 258–59, 266n.39
poetry
  allegory in, 3, 7
  Aquinas on, 288, 294–97, 305n.12
  epic narrative vs. lyric poetry, 18–19
  priests vs. poets, 17–18, 20
  relationship to community, 70, 76, 77–78, 303–4
  relationship to Holy Spirit, 73–74
  relationship to humility, 203–6
  relationship to inward sentiment, 249
  relationship to love, 70–71, 72–74
  relationship to prophecy, 252
  relationship to truth, 3, 15–16, 71, 72, 73, 74, 76, 77, 83–88, 89, 119, 123, 172–73, 248–49, 250, 263–64
  as rhetorical, 291

theology-poetry relationship, 1–3, 4–5, 6–10, 11, 14, 15, 16–17, 60–63, 70–74, 106, 161–63, 210–11, 238, 261–62, 286, 287, 288–89, 292–97, 300, 302–4, 310–12, 318–28
Porena, Manfredi, 284n.22
Porete, Marguerite, 289
Postmodernists, 263, 298, 299–300
praise
  of Beatrice, 28–29
  of God, 24, 28, 72, 132, 137–58, 168, 169, 198, 206n.4, 208n.39, 229
  polemics of, 15, 28–33
  of the Trinity, 24, 34n.6, 150, 154–55, 156
prayer, 228
pride
  Dante-pilgrim as guilty of, 190–92
  of David, 191–92, 207n.23
  and glory, 151–52, 153–54
  as root of sin, 191–92, 203, 204
priesthood
  priests vs. poets, 17–18, 20
  and the sacramental, 17–18
Proclus, 255, 266n.39
Psalms
  and Church calendar, 183, 208n.40, 209n.43
  David as author of, 108–9, 125, 180–82, 183–84, 189–90, 192, 194, 199–206, 206n.1
  division in three sections, 208n.39
  and medieval notions of penitence, 182–86
  Psalm 50, 134, 139, 141, 142, 146–47, 149, 181, 182, 183, 184, 186, 187–88, 189–90, 192, 194–95, 196, 197–98, 203, 207nn.23, 27, 208n.37, 209n.43
  and wisdom, 320, 323

Pseudo-Dionysius. *See* Dionysius the Areopagite
punto (point)
  and Argo simile, 279–80
  and Augustine's conversion, 278–29
  as body-soul nexus, 272–73
  as center of earth, 280, 285n.27
  of creation, 279
  and Eliot's *Four Quartets*/"The Dry Salvages," 130n.62
  and Francesca, 278, 279, 280, 283n.14
  God as, 111–12, 267–69, 270–72, 278, 280, 281n.5, 282n.6, 283n.14
  as human-divine nexus, 10–11, 270–72, 274, 277
  relationship to Christ, 271, 283n.14
  and Satan's body, 280
  of sleep, 280
Purgatorio
  Ante-Purgatory, 132–33, 187
  Beatrice in, 49, 89, 160n.31, 190–91, 196–97, 204, 250–51, 252
  Belacqua in, 48
  Bonagiunta in, 70–71, 145
  Casella in, 42, 47, 81–82
  Cato in, 78–79
  creation of human soul in, 9, 97–98, 103–6
  King David in, 181, 182, 204, 205
  dream visions in, 262–63
  Earthly Paradise, 89, 92n.14, 132, 143, 181, 187, 190–91, 196, 198, 204, 250, 252
  Forese Donati in, 66–67, 68, 69, 73, 79, 140–42, 148, 156
  gluttons in, 66–67, 140–42, 146–47, 155
  Guido del Duca in, 127n.17
  humility in, 204
  vs. *Inferno*, 167–68, 182, 304
  liturgy in, 132–49, 150, 151–52, 154–55, 156–57, 158n.5, 159n.17, 168, 188, 196, 197–98
  Manfredi in, 47, 113
  Marco Lombardo in, 140
  Matelda in, 48–49
  and moral change, 133, 134, 135, 142
  Oderisi in, 87–88, 151
  papacy in, 315n.8
  penitence in, 132, 136–37, 138, 149, 157, 168, 186, 188
  and praise of God, 132, 137–49, 150, 151–52, 154–55, 156–57, 168
  and psychological change, 132, 133, 159n.11
  road to Emmaus in, 311, 316n.12
  and the sacraments, 132
  smiles in, 47–49, 54, 81–82
  Sordello in, 250
  spiral motion in, 259
  Statius in, 48–49, 68–69, 104–5, 202, 272, 284n.17
  terraces in, 132, 133–36, 139, 146–49, 153, 155, 159n.17, 188, 250
  theological language in, 9, 63, 66–74, 90–91
  Valley of the Negligent Princes, 133
  vices being purged, 132, 133–35, 139–42, 145, 146–49, 159n.17, 188
  Virgil in, 48–49, 68, 74–75, 78, 79–80, 89, 93n.17, 133, 135, 136, 200, 202, 250
  waters of Lethe, 197, 199

readers' relationship to the *Commedia*, 10–11, 30–31, 87, 106, 125, 161–63, 172, 279, 280, 312
  See also authority of the *Commedia*
Reformation, the, 175, 177
Regensburg Cathedral, 45

Reggio, Giovanni, 55n.5
Reims Cathedral
　angel of the Annunciation at, 45
　Le sourire de Reims, 45
Renaissance, the, 14–15, 264n.1
Ricci, Battaglia, 243n.71
Richard of St. Victor: on
　contemplation, 270
Rilke, Rainer Maria, 126
　on creation, 120
　Duineser Elegien, 120
Romanticism, 10, 15, 162, 245, 246,
　247–51, 264n.1
Ryan, Christopher, 247

sacraments, 9, 20, 132, 158n.6, 216, 310
　confession, 148, 182, 185–86,
　　187–88, 195, 197, 198, 204, 251
　Eucharist, 106, 145–49, 175, 177
　vs. performative language, 287,
　　289, 301–2, 304
　and priesthood, 17–18
Salvani, Provenzano, 151
Santa Maria dell'Ammiraglio
　(Palermo): *Dormition of the
　Virgin* in, 99
Santa Maria in Trastevere: Cavallini
　mosaics in, 99
Sayers, Dorothy, 245
Schelling, Friedrich Wilhelm Joseph
　on Dante, 246, 247–48
　*Vorlesungen zur Philosophie der
　Kunst*, 248
Scholastics, 39, 122, 123, 135, 162
Schopenhauer, Arthur, 263
Scott, John A., 159n.19
Scriptural Reasoning group, 327
self-awareness
　Aristotle on, 268, 281n.3
　of God, 268–72, 273, 276, 280,
　　281n.3, 310, 314n.5
　of human intellect, 269–72, 273,
　　276, 277, 280, 310

Sells, Michael, 293
Shakespeare, William, 328
Siger of Brabant, 43
similes
　Apollo-Diana/sun-moon, 274–78,
　　279, 284n.23
　Argo simile, 279–80
　Church as Bride of God, 10, 213,
　　214–17, 221–38, 315n.8
　in the *Commedia*, 8, 59n.33,
　　220–21, 224, 226, 273–80
　See also metaphors
Singleton, Charles, 2
Sistine Chapel: God in, 113
smiles
　of Beatrice, 46, 47, 49, 50–51, 156,
　　171–72
　in *Convivio*, 46–47, 59n.27
　and *De vulgari eloquentia*, 303
　God's smile, 51–53, 54, 156, 157,
　　174–75, 176, 314n.5
　and middle distance perspective,
　　324
　in *Paradiso*, 21, 37, 40, 42–43, 46,
　　47, 49–54, 155–56, 157, 171–72
　in *Purgatorio*, 47–49, 54, 81–82
　of Virgin Mary, 51, 54
Solomon, King
　and Church Triumphant, 233
　in *Paradiso*, 16, 22, 26, 218, 233, 325
Song of Songs
　image of the Bride in, 10, 213,
　　214–17, 221–38
　as poetry, 295, 296
Spenser, Edmund: Milton on, 36
Spinoza, Benedict de, 263
Stephen, St., 45
Stern, J. P.: *On Realism*, 324
Stevens, Wallace, 120

Taylor, Jeremy, 256
Tentler, Thomas: on penitence and
　confession, 185, 186

Textual Reasoning group, 326–27
theological language, 5–8, 15
  apophatic mode of discourse, 9,
    62–63, 82, 87, 91, 286–87,
    292–94, 297–302, 303, 304
  Aquinas on, 6, 11, 294–97,
    298–99, 301
  cataphatic/affirmative mode
    of discourse, 9, 62–63, 91,
    286–87, 304
  and coincidence between facts
    and words, 83–86
  vs. infant speech, 82–89, 91
  in *Paradiso*, 9, 63–66, 73–74,
    90–91
  in *Purgatorio*, 9, 63, 66–74,
    90–91
  relationship to love, 9, 63,
    70–74, 89–90, 91
  theological propositions and
    personhood, 21–26, 28
  theological rhetoric, 287, 288–89,
    292–94
  Rowan Williams on, 24, 30
  See also human language
theory of the four senses, 252
Tillich, Paul: on Dante, 308, 312
time
  Beatrice on, 269, 274, 275–76
  and poets, 17–19, 33
  and priests, 17–18
  and Purgatory, 133
Toledo Cathedral: *Virgen Blanca* at,
  45
Tommaso of Celano: *Vita Prima*,
  243n.71
Took, John, 158n.6
Trilling, Lionel: on Shakespeare and
  Dante, 245
Trinity, the, 23, 70, 273, 314n.4, 320,
  323
  Bonaventure on, 220, 221, 225, 229,
    234, 240n.37, 242n.56

  Father, 52, 73–74, 96, 101, 108,
    128n.33, 136, 159n.16, 176,
    218–20
  Holy Spirit, 52, 73–74, 96, 101,
    108, 119, 182, 199
  order of charity in, 219–21, 225,
    226, 233–34, 240n.37
  as paradigm of personhood, 24
  perichoresis in, 52, 59n.31, 310
  praise of, 24, 34n.6, 150, 154–55,
    156
  and the *punto* (point), 274
  relationship to the Church,
    220–21, 225, 228, 229, 233–34
  Son, 51–53, 73, 96, 101, 108,
    128n.33, 136, 138, 144, 159n.16,
    174, 176, 219, 229
Trouillard, Jean: on Platonism, 255
Truijen, Vincent, 158n.6
Trumble, Angus, 57n.16
truth
  and *Paradiso*, 39–44
  relationship to beauty, 247
  relationship to community, 75, 78,
    80, 82
  relationship to poetry, 3, 15–16,
    71, 72, 73, 74, 76, 77, 83–88, 89,
    119, 123, 172–73, 248–49, 250,
    263–64
  See also knowledge

Undset, Sigrid, 328
University of Paris, 44
University of Tübingen, 264n.1
Urs von Balthasar, Hans, 24
uttering performances, 289–91

Vanier, Jean, 328
vernal equinox, 279
Victorines, 39
Virgil
  Aeneid 1.147, 115, 204
  Aeneid book 6, 20

in *Inferno*, 36, 47, 167, 170, 181, 195, 200, 202, 208n.37, 252
influence on Dante, 18, 20, 323
vs. Nathan, 195, 196, 200, 208n.37
in *Purgatorio*, 48–49, 68, 74–75, 78, 79–80, 89, 93n.17, 133, 135, 136, 200, 202, 250
smile of, 47
virtue: relationship to knowledge, 77–78, 79, 80, 81–82
Vita nuova
Beatrice in, 18, 28–29, 46, 50, 72, 174, 273
Beatrice's birth, 273
Beatrice's smile in, 46, 50
and Cavalcanti, 130n.58
vs. *Commedia*, 46–47, 50, 70–72, 145, 173–74, 253

"Donne ch'avete intelletto d'amore," 70, 72, 145
transfiguration in, 173–74
Von Richthofen, Reich, 284n.23

Walpole, Horace: on Dante, 36
William of Saint-Thierry: on Church as Bride of God, 228
Williams, Charles, 59n.31
Williams, Rowan: on theology, 24, 30
Williamson, Oliver, 7
wisdom, 320–21, 323, 325
Wisdom literature, 254, 320
Wittgenstein, Ludwig, 290
wonder, 253–54

Zwingli, Huldrych: on body of Jesus, 175

INDEX OF PASSAGES FROM DANTE'S WORKS

Commedia
Inferno
  1.1, 253
  1.1–3, 316n.10
  1.3, 31
  1.4–6, 316n.10
  1.10, 195
  1.10–12, 316n.10
  1.11–12, 280
  1.13–15, 316n.10
  1.13–18, 250
  1.28–60, 252
  1.38–40, 95–96, 279
  1.64, 187
  1.64–65, 188
  1.65, 181
  1.82–129, 252
  1.122, 31
  2.28–36, 252
  2.32, 204
  3.1–9, 96, 110
  3.5–8, 146
  3.12, 146
  3.22, 166
  3.25–30, 166–67
  3.52–57, 316n.10
  3.103–5, 316n.10
  4.42, 200
  4.98–99, 47
  4.131, 130n.49
  5.92, 279
  5.99, 279
  5.120, 279
  5.132, 278, 283n.14
  5.133, 47
  5.138, 278
  6.19, 167
  7.125, 167
  8.52–60, 36
  9.14, 167
  9.61–63, 261
  10.35, 23
  10.64, 280
  11.99–105, 173
  19.90–117, 315n.8
  21.139, 36
  23.142–44, 36
  24.65–66, 167
  25.1–3, 23
  26.85–142, 305n.17
  26.90–142, 77
  26.98–99, 77
  26.120, 77
  26.136, 79
  26.141, 78
  32.1–12, 83–87
  32.9, 86
  32.124–33.90, 303
  33.37–75, 84–86
  33.64, 291
  33.69, 86
  34.110–11, 289
Purgatorio
  1.20, 47
  1.28–108, 78
  1.118–20, 253
  1.121–29, 78–79
  1.130–36, 79
  1.132, 93n.20
  2.1–6, 279
  2.52–133, 93n.21
  2.61–66, 79–80, 93n.17
  2.67–87, 80–81
  2.80–81, 82

380

Index of Passages from Dante's Works 381

2.83, 47
3.1–105, 93n.21
3.16–27, 74–75
3.28–29, 90
3.28–39, 72, 74–76, 93n.17
3.112, 47
3.134, 113
4.122, 48
5.24, 187
7.82, 133
8.13, 133
8.14–15, 156
8.19–21, 261
9.70–72, 263
9.115–29, 315n.8
9.126, 145
9.140, 137
10.66, 205
10.94, 146
10.95, 204
10.124–26, 153–54
11.1–3, 259, 314n.4
11.1–24, 137
11.7–9, 133
11.10–12, 151
11.18, 134
11.19, 134
11.37, 94n.28
11.91, 151
11.94–99, 94n.28
11.98, 151
11.103–7, 87–88
11.133, 151
12.109–14, 168
12.136, 48
13.50–51, 134
13.136–38, 190
14.93, 127n.17
16.17–19, 134
16.19, 133
16.19–21, 134
16.24, 145
16.64–105, 140

16.75, 250
16.85–93, 97–98, 101–2, 105, 113
16.89, 59n.34
16.90, 127n.17
17.13–18, 263
17.85–139, 135
17.115–16, 136
17.118–19, 136
17.121–22, 136
17.127–29, 315n.9
17.133–37, 135–36
18.19–21, 127n.5
18.46–75, 250
19.73, 134
20.133–41, 137–39
20.136–41, 139
20.140, 138
21.7–15, 316n.12
21.58–60, 138
21.114, 48
21.121–23, 48
22.64–73, 93n.17
22.142–44, 148, 149
23.1–3, 139, 140
23.10–12, 137, 187, 188
23.11, 134, 149
23.11–12, 147
23.12, 156
23.15, 145
23.28–30, 148–49
23.61–75, 141, 149
23.70–75, 66–67, 79, 86, 141–42, 144
23.72, 156
23.74, 69, 92n.5
23.84, 133
23.101–2, 140
24.49–54, 70–71, 72
24.51, 145
24.52–54, 145
24.53, 73
24.55–56, 145
24.58–60, 145

24.115–17, 143
25.37–60, 272
25.61–65, 283n.14
25.61–75, 68–69
25.61–78, 103–6
25.70, 71
25.71, 73
25.75, 273
25.121, 134
25.136–37, 133
27.44–45, 48
28.67, 48
28.76, 48
28.96, 48, 80
28.145–47, 48–49
29.22–30, 315n.7
29.105, 37
30.22–31.90, 89
30.40–57, 89
30.55–57, 89
30.82–84, 187, 196
30.124–25, 250
30.127–32, 190–91
31.5–6, 197
31.34–35, 136
31.34–36, 197
31.37–39, 197
31.43–45, 197
31.45, 191
31.53, 191
31.59–60, 191
31.64–66, 204
31.82–90, 251
31.85–89, 197
31.91–102, 209n.43
31.98, 187, 197
31.133–45, 49
31.139–45, 49
32.5–6, 49
33.91–92, 49
33.115, 160n.31
33.130–31, 89

Paradiso
1.1–2, 152
1.1–12, 253–54
1.4–6, 252
1.13–21, 252, 265n.19
1.13–33, 284n.23
1.37–45, 279
1.64–69, 170–71
1.70, 246, 256
1.70–71, 315n.9
1.73–75, 252
1.95, 49
1.136–41, 246
2.1–18, 30–31
2.7, 128n.25
2.8–9, 284n.23
2.10, 32
2.10–11, 106
2.13–15, 106
2.16–17, 128n.26
2.18, 128n.26
2.19–20, 249
2.19–21, 315n.9
2.37–42, 252
2.52, 49
2.136–38, 283n.13
3.24, 49
3.25, 49
3.42, 49
3.67, 50
3.70–87, 65–66
4.37–45, 35n.12
4.37–48, 113
4.40–48, 262
5.97, 47
5.126, 50
6.32, 54
7.1, 150
7.17, 50
7.25–27, 315n.7
7.33, 113
7.43–45, 250

Index of Passages from Dante's Works 383

7.53, 145
7.64–66, 117, 118, 315n.6
7.70, 116
7.73–81, 153
7.115–16, 315n.8
7.132, 117, 118
7.135, 117, 118
7.142–44, 315n.9
9.35, 43
9.76, 127n.17
9.103–5, 43
9.106–7, 127n.18
9.139–42, 225
10.1–2, 52
10.1–6, 219
10.7–12, 102–3
10.10–12, 241n.39
10.22–24, 103
10.25–27, 103
10.27, 204
10.49–51, 219–20
10.55–59, 241n.39
10.61, 50
10.62, 50
10.64–66, 242n.56
10.73–77, 242n.56
10.82–85, 241n.39
10.88–90, 241n.39
10.9, 94n.28
10.91–93, 231
10.103, 50
10.103–4, 156
10.109–14, 218
10.114, 16
10.116–17, 40
10.118, 50
10.139–48, 222, 226–31, 235
10.145, 153, 154
11.10–12, 153
11.17, 50
11.28–36, 222, 223–25, 226, 235
11.58–63, 236–37

11.76–81, 241n.42
11.118–20, 220
12.1–6, 168–69
12.6–9, 242n.56
12.19–20, 231
12.22–25, 242n.56
12.22–27, 169
12.40–45, 222–23, 225, 226, 227, 235
12.118–20, 220–21
13.25, 284n.23
13.52–54, 136
13.52–66, 117–18
13.54, 128n.33
13.55–60, 283n.13
13.59, 153
13.63, 26, 136, 325
13.63–72, 173, 273
13.73, 273
13.73–75, 283n.14
13.75, 273
13.112, 298
13.112–30, 16
14.13–15, 232
14.28–30, 314nn.4, 5
14.28–33, 24, 34n.6, 242n.56
14.36, 26
14.61–66, 91, 234
14.86, 47, 156
14.88–124, 26
14.89, 30
14.103–8, 76, 87, 90, 91
14.103–17, 21–23
14.118–26, 150
14.124, 150
15.34, 50, 156
15.61–63, 256
15.97–99, 26–27
15.118–26, 34n.9
15.121–23, 127n.17
17.36, 50
17.52–66, 34n.10

17.112–14, 171
17.120, 317n.13
17.129, 27
18.19, 50
18.19–21, 171
18.82–87, 109
18.109–11, 107
19.7–8, 109–10
19.34–39, 150
19.40–45, 107–8
20.13, 47
20.38, 107, 108, 182
20.40, 199
20.117, 80
21.4–12, 50
21.61–63, 305n.22
21.83–87, 160n.30
21.83–90, 92n.4
21.83–102, 64–65
22.135, 37
23.1–75, 305n.22
23.29, 284n.23
23.46, 261
23.46–48, 50
23.55–66, 19
23.59, 50
23.64–66, 29
23.70–72, 171
23.79–84, 284n.23
23.136–39, 315n.8
24.85, 31–32
24.86–87, 31–32
24.113, 150
25.1, 181–82
25.1–2, 125, 200
25.2, 181
25.5, 15
25.24, 150
25.52–53, 200
25.54, 284n.23
25.61–66, 272
25.62, 272
25.67–69, 200

25.70–72, 200
25.71, 272
25.71–72, 108
25.72, 108, 182
25.73, 108
25.73–74, 202
25.73–75, 200
25.75, 273
25.76–78, 201–2
25.98, 202
25.113, 149
25.118–29, 178n.9
26.10–12, 179n.15
26.16–18, 230–31
26.25–26, 125
26.37–39, 130n.59
26.38–39, 125
26.40, 125
26.42, 125
26.43–45, 125
26.53, 125
26.55–60, 231
26.64–66, 155
26.69, 150
26.76–78, 172, 179n.15
26.82–84, 102
26.124–38, 92n.6, 143
27.1–2, 150
27.1–9, 154–57
27.3, 156
27.4–5, 47
27.5, 156
27.49–51, 315n.8
27.100–30.54, 273
27.104, 50
27.106–14, 259–60, 281n.2
28.16, 111
28.41–42, 260, 268
28.42, 112
28.43–45, 282n.6
28.52–54, 281n.2
28.64–78, 281n.2
28.74, 269

Index of Passages from Dante's Works

28.76, 38
28.79–87, 282n.7
28.83–84, 47
28.87, 39, 269–70
28.94, 150
28.95–96, 111–12
28.106–14, 55n.5
28.109–11, 55n.5
28.118, 150
28.130–39, 40, 258
28.135, 110
29.1–9, 111–12, 130n.62
29.1–12, 273–79, 284n.15
29.1–81, 110, 326
29.5–6, 94n.28
29.9, 283n.14
29.10–12, 112
29.12, 157
29.13, 112, 153
29.13–18, 63, 93n.19, 283n.13
29.14–15, 153, 154
29.15, 92n.5
29.16–17, 112
29.17, 50, 112
29.18, 113, 315n.6
29.19–21, 113–16
29.23, 119
29.24, 118
29.25–30, 118–19
29.26–27, 119
29.27, 116
29.29–30, 116
29.31, 119
29.32, 119
29.37–68, 44
29.40, 119
29.41, 119
29.46–47, 119
29.51, 120
29.55–57, 136, 153
29.58–59, 136, 153
29.58–60, 153
29.61–62, 153

29.64–66, 121
29.67, 121
29.70, 121
29.71, 121
29.74, 121–22
29.79–81, 121
29.82, 122
29.82–126, 110, 326
29.83, 122
29.84, 122
29.85, 122
29.85–86, 123
29.93, 122
29.95, 122
29.111, 122
29.127–45, 110, 326
29.130–35, 123
29.136–38, 123
29.140–41, 124
29.142–45, 113, 283n.13
29.145, 123
30.11, 283n.14
30.11–12, 278, 282n.6
30.15, 62, 287
30.26–27, 50
30.38–42, 281n.2
31.1, 51
31.28–29, 261
31.49–50, 51
31.49–51, 21, 172
31.82–84, 254
31.91–93, 50–51
32.10–12, 188
32.61–66, 98–99
32.121–23, 315n.7
32.135, 150
33.5–6, 90
33.40–42, 51
33.49–50, 51
33.52–66, 256–57
33.58–66, 59n.33
33.94–96, 280
33.106–14, 88–89

33.106–20, 260–61
33.106–45, 304
33.115, 89
33.124–26, 52, 156
33.127–33, 174
33.131, 52
33.142–45, 121, 257
33.145, 172, 254, 300

Convivio
1.3.8–9, 284n.17
1.8, 31
1.13.12, 34n.3
2.4.18, 284n.17
2.5.2, 41–42
2.5.5, 42, 315n.8
2.13.26–27, 275
2.13.27, 267
2.14.14–15, 313n.1
3/Canzone seconda 55–56, 47
3/Canzone seconda 57–58, 46
3.2.4–7, 130n.59
3.2.7, 308
3.2.14, 284n.17
3.2.17–19, 284n.17
3.6.4–6, 284n.17
3.6.11–12, 284n.17
3.7.3, 115–16
3.8, 46–47
3.12.7, 250, 276
3.12.13, 313n.3
3.15.6–10, 82
3.15.7–8, 313n.2
3.15.16, 128n.29
4.2.18, 128n.22
4.4.3, 151
4.12, 99, 100
4.12.14, 139–40, 308
4.12.15, 140
4.12.16, 140–41

4.13, 313n.3
4.21, 104
4.21.4–10, 284n.17
4.21.10, 273
4.23.6, 284n.17
4.25.6, 284n.23

De vulgari eloquentia
1.1.3, 163, 305n.16
1.2, 291
1.3, 163–64, 178n.3, 291
1.4, 28
1.4.4, 142–43
1.5.1, 165, 287
1.5.2, 143
2.1.6, 305n.23
2.3, 68
2.4, 20
2.7, 34n4
2.7.3–4, 94n.32

Epistola a Cangrande 15, 261

Monarchia
1.3, 284n.17
1.11, 284n.17
3.1.5, 315n.8
3.3.7, 315n.8
3.4, 284n.23
3.10.7, 315n.8
3.15.3, 34n.8, 315n.8
3.16, 92n.9
3.16.3, 272
3.16.3–4, 277
3.16.7, 55n.5, 313n.3
3.16.10, 315n.8

Vita nuovo
18–19, 72
19.4, vv. 1–4, 28–29

INDEX OF SCRIPTURAL PASSAGES

Acts
  9:3–19, 175
  9:6, 253
  22:6–16, 175
  26:12–18, 175
Colossians 1:16, 38
1 Corinthians
  2:9, 46
  3:1–2, 101
  7:5, 100
  8:6, 160n.22
  13:11, 101
2 Corinthians
  12:1–6, 204
  12:2–3, 39, 40, 178n.9
Daniel 7:10, 123
Ephesians
  1:21, 38
  4:7–10, 177, 179n.20
Exodus
  3:14, 113
  33:19, 130n.58
Genesis
  1:1, 129n.45
  1:1–3, 114–16
  1:3, 96
  1:4–5, 114
  1:6, 96
  1:6–7, 114
  1:14, 96
  1:26–27, 100
  2:7, 100, 128n.21
Hebrews
  1:2, 160n.22
  13:15, 144–45
Isaiah 64:6, 46

1 John
  4:8, 127n.1
  4:12, 62
John, Gospel of
  1:3, 160n.22
  2:1–12, 106
  6:61, 146
  11:35, 44
  15:1, 106
  20:24–29, 179n.12
  21:4–14, 179n.12
Jude 1:9, 38
Luke
  2:8–14, 138
  15:8–10, 55n.7
  18:17, 100–101
  23:47–48, 82, 93n.22
Mark
  15:34, 92n.7
  15:39, 93n.22
Matthew
  6:9–13, 133
  18:1–4, 101
  18:5, 101
  19:14, 100
  25:1–13, 45
  27:46, 67, 142
  27:54, 82, 93n.22
Philippians 2:8, 256
Proverbs
  8:27–29, 128n.29
  8:30, 99
  8:30–31, 52
Psalms
  Ps 9, 10, 200, 202–3, 209n.46
  Ps 21:2, 92n.7

Psalms (*cont.*)
  Ps 30, 196–97, 208n.40
  Ps 50, 10, 134, 139, 141, 142,
    146–47, 149, 181, 182, 183, 184,
    186, 187–88, 189–90, 192,
    194–95, 196, 197–98, 203,
    207nn.23, 27, 208n.37, 209n.43
  Ps 55, 183
  Ps 56, 183
  Ps 109, 175
  Ps 118, 134
Romans 13:13–14, 279
2 Samuel
  11:2–4, 189
  11:15, 189
  11:17, 189
  12:5, 189
  12:7, 189
  12:13, 187, 189
  24:10, 207n.23
Sirach 18:1, 129n.45
Song of Songs
  1:3, 223–24, 227
  2:10, 227
  2:14, 214
  4:12, 214
  5:2, 214
  5:2–6, 236–37
  6:9, 214
1 Thessalonians 4:16, 38

www.ingramcontent.com/pod-product-compliance
Lightning Source LLC
Chambersburg PA
CBHW051249300426
44114CB00011B/949